A History of the Criticism of
the Acts of the Apostles

by

W. WARD GASQUE

William B. Eerdmans Publishing Company
Grand Rapids

1273600   9/27/79AP

This American edition is by special arrangement with J. C. B. Mohr (Paul Siebeck), Tübingen, Germany. The book appears as No. 17 in the series *Beiträge zur Geschichte der biblischen Exegese*, edited by Oscar Cullmann, Nils A. Dahl, Ernst Käsemann, Hans-Joachim Kraus, Heiko A. Oberman, Harald Riesenfeld, and Karl Hermann Schelkle.

Library of Congress Cataloging in Publication Data

Gasque, W   Ward.
A history of the criticism of the Acts of the
Apostles.

1.   Bible. N. T. Acts — Criticism, interpreta-
tion, etc. — History. I. Title.
BS2625.2.G37   226'.6'0609   75-9654
ISBN 0-8028-3461-2

TO LAUREL

TABLE OF CONTENTS

LIST OF PRINCIPAL ABBREVIATIONS

AbThANT	Abhandlungen zur Theologie des Alten und Neuen Testaments
AJT	American Journal of Theology
AnLov	Analecta Lovaniensia Biblica et Orientalia
ATR	Anglican Theological Review
Bauer-Arndt-Gingrich	A Greek-English Lexicon
BC	The Beginnings of Christianity, ed. by F. J. Foakes-Jackson and K. Lake, 5 vols.
BJRL	Bulletin of the John Rylands Library
Blass-Deberunner-Funk	A Greek Grammar of the New Testament
ChQR	Church Quarterly Review
CIG	Corpus Inscriptionum Graecarum
CIL	Corpus Inscriptionum Latinarum
CN	Coniectanea Neotestamentica
DNB	Dictionary of National Biography
EB	The Encyclopaedia Britannica
EGT	The Expositor's Greek Testament
EncBib	Encyclopaedia Biblica
EvTh	Evangelische Theologie
Expos.	The Expositor
ExpT	The Expository Times
HDB	Hasting's Dictionary of the Bible, 5 vols.
HDCG	Hasting's Dictionary of Christ and the Gospels
HNT	Handbuch zum Neuen Testament
HTR	Harvard Theological Review
IDB	The Interpreter's Dictionary of the Bible
Interp.	Interpretation
JAOS	Journal of the American Oriental Society
JBL	Journal of Biblical Literature
JHS	Journal of Hellenic Studies
JJS	Journal of Jewish Studies
JNES	Journal of Near Eastern Studies
JPT	Jahrbücher für Protestantische Theologie
JR	Journal of Religion
JRS	Journal of Roman Studies
JTC	Journal for Theology and the Church

JTS	Journal of Theological Studies
KEK	Kritisch-exegetischer Kommentar über das Neue Testament, founded by H. A. W. Meyer
NewCathEnc	The New Catholic Encyclopaedia
NIC/NLC	The New International Commentary = The New London Commentary
NKZ	Neue kirchliche Zeitschrift
NovTest	Novum Testamentum
NTD	Das Neue Testament Deutsch
NTS	New Testament Studies
ODCC	Oxford Dictionary of the Christian Church
P-W	Pauly-Wissowa (eds.), Real-Encyclopädie der classischen Altertumswissenschaft
RAC	Reallexicon für die Antike und Christentum
RB	Revue Biblique
RE2 or 3	Realencyclopädie für protestantische Theologie und Kirche, 2nd ed., or 3rd ed.
RGG3	Die Religion in Geschichte und Gegenwart, 3rd ed.
SJT	Scottish Journal of Theology
ST	Studia Theologica
ThJ	Theologische Jahrbücher
TZ	Theologische Zeitschrift
TLZ	Theologische Literaturzeitung
TR	Theologische Rundschau
TSK	Theologische Studien und Kritiken
TU	Texte und Untersuchungen zur Geschichte der altchristlichen Literatur
TZTh	Tübinger Zeitschrift für Theologie
VC	Vigiliae Christianae
ZNW	Zeitschrift für die neutestamentliche Wissenschaft
ZTK	Zeitschrift für Theologie und Kirche
ZWT	Zeitschrift für wissenschaftliche Theologie

FOREWORD

The present monograph began as a thesis for the degree of Doctor of Philosophy at The University of Manchester and was accepted by the University, on the recommendation of the examiners, in May 1969. Since that time I have lived with the subject, read and re-read the manuscript, reflected further, and made a considerable number of revisions and corrections. Although parts of the work have been re-written, I have resisted the temptation to expand an already lengthy manuscript and have thus been content with relatively few additions. If I have failed to notice all of the publications on Luke-Acts which have come out of scholarly circles in the past few years, it has not been because I have been unaware of these but rather due to a concern to keep the subject in perspective.

Appreciation is due first of all to Professor F. F. Bruce, under whose capable supervision my thesis was originally written; his careful scholarship has set a high standard for me in my own research, though I am painfully aware that I have fallen far short of the pattern of his example. Professors Bo Reicke and Oscar Cullmann were also of considerable help and encouragement to me during my time in Basel, of which I will always cherish pleasant memories. Special thanks are offered to Professor Cullmann and also to Professor Nils A. Dahl for their recommendation of my manuscript for the present monograph series.

Others who have helped in various ways include Professor R. P. C. Hanson, Dr. F. W. Ratcliffe, Professor A. J. Mattill, Jr., Mrs. Donald Tinder, Dr. Colin Hemer, Dr. Peter O'Brien, Dr. Norman Young, Mrs. Mervyn Brockett, and Mr. Charles Wanamaker. Without their help my study would have contained many more errors and weaknesses than it actually does.

Vancouver, B. C., Canada
October 1974

Ward Gasque

PREFACE

In the introduction to his important commentary on the Book of Acts, Ernst Haenchen[1] deplores the lack of a critical history of *Actaforschung* comparable to Albert Schweitzer's histories of Gospel criticism and Pauline research. It is true that there have been a few brief surveys of research, such as the influential essay by A. C. McGiffert[2], which was contributed to the second volume of *The Beginnings of Christianity*, and the more recent attempts of W. Bieder[3] and Haenchen[4]; but there has been no full scale history of critical research.

The recent resurgence of Lucan studies has, however, produced a number of partial surveys. The monograph by J. Dupont[5] gives the student of Acts an adequate account of the history of the source criticism of Acts and is a model of historical research. The study of the problem of the historical value of Acts and the way this has been met by scholars since 1840 by the American scholar, A. J. Mattill, Jr.[6], is the closet to a comprehensive study of the subject. F. Bovon[7] has written a valuable study of the interpretation of Acts 10.1–11.8 in the first six centuries, which contains brief introductions to the writings of Ephraim, Didymus the Blind, Chrysostom, Ammonius, Arator, and Cassiodorus and opens up the relatively unexplored area of pre-critical exegesis of Acts. M. Wilcox[8] has written a brief survey

---

[1] *Die Apostelgeschichte*, KEK, 13th ed. (Göttingen, 1961), p. 13n.

[2] "The Historical Criticism of Acts in Germany", *BC* 2 (1922), pp. 263–95. Cf. also M. Goguel, *Introduction au Nouveau Testament III. Le Livre des Actes* (Paris, 1922), pp. 37–72; and E. Jacquier, *Les Actes des Apôtres* (Paris, 1926), pp. XV–LV.

[3] *Die Apostelgeschichte in der Historie* (Zürich, 1960).

[4] *Die Apostelgeschichte*, pp. 13–47; an appendix (670–89) carries the survey up to 1961.

[5] *Les Sources du Livre des Actes* (Bruges, 1960); E. T. *The Sources of Acts: The Present Position* (London, 1964).

[6] *Luke as a Historian in Criticism since 1840* (unpublished dissertation, Vanderbilt University, 1959).

[7] *De Vocatione Gentium: Histoire de l'interprétation d'Act. 10,1–11,18 dans les six premiers siècles, Beiträge zur Geschichte der Biblischen Exegese 8* (Tübingen, 1967).

[8] *The Semitisms of Acts* (Oxford, 1965), pp. 1–19.

of the investigations into the language of Acts as an introduction to his excellent monograph on the semitisms of Acts. C. K. Barrett[9] and W. C. van Unnik[10] have traced some of the main lines of the recent discussion, while D. Guthrie[11] has filled in some of the bibliographical details — but still there has been no comprehensive history.

Although I recognize my personal limitations — I am certainly no Albert Schweitzer! — I offer the present work, the product of three and a half years of research (primarily at the Universities of Manchester and Basel) and a further two years of continued reflection, as a modest attempt to fill the present void. I have learned a great deal from my study. My hope is that others will benefit also from this account of the results of my investigations.

My task would have been much easier had I been content to depend, at least to some degree, on secondary sources of information; this, however, I have not done. My method has always been to go to the original sources — to read, and to ponder what I have read. This approach has been extremely time-consuming, as one can imagine; and it has been discouraging to work through several hundred pages of German, time and again, only to discover that nothing new has been said, and then to summarize one's efforts in a sentence or a footnote, or to leave the book unmentioned! Nevertheless, it has seemed to me that this has been the necessary manner in which to conduct the present investigation.

In short, I have attempted a fresh, independent study of the history of the criticism of the book of Acts. This has led me to emphasize the work of some scholars whose writings have been largely neglected by some of the subsequent schools of critical thought and to attempt to correct many mistaken assumptions concerning the history of criticism. Obviously, I have had to be selective in the material I have included in my study. A work of history is not the same as a chronicle, and a history of critical research is not a bibliographical essay. I have deliberately avoided cluttering the pages of the present study by listing every work which has made a contribution to research (though the footnotes have been numerous enough as it is); instead, I have sought to discuss only the most iuportant books and essays, giving a detailed account of a limited number of

---

[9] *Luke the Historian in Recent Study* (London, 1961).

[10] "Luke-Acts, A Storm Center in Contemporary Scholarship", in *Studies in Luke-Acts*, ed. by L. E. Keck and J. L. Martyn (New York and Nashville, 1966), pp. 15–32.

[11] "Recent Literature on the Acts of the Apostles", *Vox Evangelica II*, ed. by R. P. Martin (London, 1963), pp. 33–49. See also below pp. 252n.–253n.

key writings, instead of listing the names of a much larger number[12]. Moreover, although it is almost universally recognized today that Luke-Acts is a two-volumed work by the same author and, therefore, that the two volumes should be treated together, I have concentrated on Acts. Since the problems related to the study of the Third Gospel are so closely bound to those related to the Gospels of Matthew and Mark, and since the Book of Acts has often been treated entirely (or almost entirely) independently of the Gospel according to Luke, it has seemed justified, if only for the sake of simplicity, to limit myself, for the most part, to the second volume of Luke's "History of Christian Origins".

I have centered the discussion around the major issues of New Testament introduction, around the central problems of criticism and interpretation, rather than the exegesis of individual verses and sections of Acts. Because Dupont has done his job so very well, it has been unnecessary to stress the source criticism of Acts. It has also seemed best to omit discussion of matters of textual criticism in all but a few cases, since (a) this is relatively independent of the other problems of introduction and (b) I do not have the technical expertise to deal with the subject adequately.

The fundamental assumption of my work is that New Testament criticism is an international and interconfessional enterprise. Ever since the work of Schweitzer, who confesses in the preface of his *Geschichte der paulinischen Forschung* (1911) that he has failed to include English or American authors in his survey of research, "since the works in question were not in all cases accessible to me, and an insufficient acquaintance with the language raised a barrier"[13], there has been a tendency among the writers of historical surveys to regard the work of New Testament criticism as the exclusive prerogative of a small band of German Protestant scholars. Even inside Germany, the valuable contributions of more theologically conservative scholars have often been mentioned only to be dismissed; the writings of Roman Catholic scholars of all nationali-

---

[12] Since the publication of A. J. Mattill, Jr., and M. B. Mattill, *A Classified Bibliography of Literature on the Acts of the Apostles* (Leiden, 1966), such a bibliographical approach is even less justified.

[13] E. T. *Paul and His Interpreters: A Critical History* (New York, 1912), p. xi. This was after he had been engaged in academic research nearly fifteen years. It is highly probable that Schweitzer simply did not think that there was anything written in English which made it worthwhile for him to take the trouble to learn the language. Cf. the opening paragraph of his *Von Reimarus zu Wrede* (1906); E. T. *The Quest of the Historical Jesus* (London, 1910). Although Schweitzer was neither the first nor the last to express such adulation of radical German criticism, there have been others who do not share this view.

ties have rarely been mentioned, except by other Roman Catholics; and the course of criticism outside of Germany has been largely ignored[14]. However this may have been justified a generation or two ago, there is no justification for such a provincial approach to criticism today.

An attempt to present a well rounded, rather than one-sided, history of critical discussion has led me to regard the attempt to divide the history of research into neatly defined periods (e. g., the periods of *Tendenzkritik*, *Quellenkritik*, *Formgeschichte*, and *Redaktionsgeschichte*) as an oversimplification which is more misleading than it is helpful. For one thing, the discussion of "purpose" did not start and end with the Tübingen critics, nor was Harnack the last to be concerned with the question of the sources of Acts; there is a general variety of interests and points of view at any given time, and justice must be done to all of these. In addition, the outlines which are usually suggested (as, for example, by Haenchen) give no recognition to the fact of the contribution of British and American scholars[15]; they also fail to indicate the importance of many of the most important students of Acts even on the Continent[16]. Therefore, in attempting to do full justice to the work of New Testament scholarship as a whole — to the work of German, British, and American scholar, conservative and radical, Protestant and Catholic — I have abandoned the usual schematization of the history of *Actaforschung*[17].

In addition, the attempt to write a history of *the* criticism of the Book of Acts, rather than a history of *a particular school of* criticism, has compelled me to draw attention to the diversity of critical opinion. In 1923, Eduard Meyer wrote these words:

Über den Wert dieses Werkes (*sc.* Luke-Acts), seinen Verfasser und die Zeit seiner Entstehung, über die Frage, ob es in seiner ursprünglichen Gestalt oder in vielleicht sogar mehrfacher Überarbeitung auf uns gekommen ist, über seine Quellen, die Berechtigung der Auffassung, von der es

---

[14] An exception to this rule is S. Neill, *The Interpretation of the New Testament, 1861–1961* (Oxford, 1963). A number of reviews have accused the author of giving undue emphasis to the work of British scholarship, but a glance at the index will demonstrate that this is not true. What he has done is simply redress the balance by giving *equal* place to the work of British New Testament critics and by taking notice of a few of the most important American contributions. (I write as a "neutral" American!)

[15] See especially chapters 6, 7 (on Ramsay), 8 and 9.

[16] See especially chapters 3, 7 and 9.

[17] I am conscious of the inadequacy of my treatment of the work of Roman Catholic critics. This is due to my own lack of familiarity with the writings of all but a few of the most important scholars.

beherrscht ist, und seine Zuverlässigkeit überhaupt, gehn freilich die Ansichten auf das stärkste auseinander, und nach einer nun bereits nahezu über ein Jahrhundert sich erstreckenden Diskussion ist man von einer Einigung auch nur über die Hauptfragen entfernter als je[18].

Although nearly fifty years have passed since Meyer wrote these words and new trends and schools of criticism have come and gone, the situation is very much the same, as anyone who has read very much of the current literature must be aware. It would, in fact, be a very easy task to line up scholars with formidable academic reputations, past or present, on opposing sides of almost every important issue of critical debate. Yet many scholars persist in giving the misleading impression that critical scholars are agreed among themselves on the important issues. Such an impression is made possible only by an almost total neglect of reference to the work of critics outside of one's own group. In the present study I have carefully and deliberately attempted to avoid this pitfall. It is to be hoped that I have not erred in overemphasizing the divergence of opinion among scholars.

One of the problems concerning which there has been and still is a great deal of disagreement among students of Acts is the question of the historical value of the book. On this, as also on a number of other issues, I have taken sides in the debate. My study of the history of criticism, as well as the narrative of the Book of Acts and the historical problems involved, has strengthened my conviction that those critics who rate the author as a reliable historian of early Christianity are essentially correct in their conclusions. Contrary to the impression given by some recent writers, this is not a minority opinion among scholars. One of the purposes of my study is to indicate precisely *why* a large number of scholars take this positive view toward the history in Acts, in spite of the arguments to the contrary. The individual critic has the right to his personal point of view, but it is uncritical to dismiss the conclusions of other serious scholars without giving them a fair hearing. My own impression is that the defenders of "Luke the historian" have seldom been given a fair hearing by those who take the contrary position.

A word should be said concerning my method of citation. Where this has been possible, I have used the first or the significant edition of the book or essay under discussion *in the language in which it was written*. To reduce the number of footnotes, the page numbers have often been given in the body of the text (in parentheses). This has only been done in the case of books which have featured in the

---

[18] *Ursprung und Anfänge des Christentums* 3 (Stuttgart and Berlin, 1923), p. 4.

discussion; secondary references have been confined to the footnotes. Since complete bibliographical data for nearly all work on Acts prior to 1961 have been made readily available by Dr. and Mrs. Mattill's *Bibliography* (n. 12 above), I have felt free to abbreviate the footnotes to some extent.

In order to conserve on space, the Index of Authors and Books has been made to serve as a bibliography.

Standard American spellings have been used throughout (except in quotations).

In the American edition, for the convenience of readers who may not be familiar enough with French or German to read it fluently, the quotations from these languages in the text have been translated into English and appear as an appendix at the end of the book. The guide numbers in the outside margin of the body of the text and footnotes refer to the numbered, translated passages in the appendix.

W.W.G.

Chapter I

PRE-CRITICAL STUDY OF THE BOOK OF ACTS

Very little information has come down to us concerning the study of the Book of Acts during the fifteen centuries prior to the Reformation. A total of nineteen books or fragments are all that remain from this period of the Church's history[1]. Some have inferred from a frequently quoted statement of John Chrysostom, in which he says that some people were not even aware of the book's existence[2], that the study of the Acts of the Apostles was greatly neglected in the early Church; however, it seems clear that his remark is merely a

---

[1] Homilies or commentaries — many of which exist only in a very fragmentary form — are attributed to nineteen different authors.

From the third century: (1) Origen and (2) Pamphilus of Caesarea in Palestine.

Fourth century: (3) Ephraem the Syrian, (4) Didymus the Blind, the last leader of the famous catechetical school at Alexandria, (5) Eusebius, the Semi-Arian bishop of Emesa (Homs) in Syria, and (6) Euthalius the Deacon.

Fifth century: (7) John Chrysostom, (8) Cyril of Alexandria, (9) the Alexandrian presbyter by the name of Ammonius, (10) Hesychius, the presbyter of Jerusalem, and (11) the poet Arator.

Sixth century: (12) Cassiodorus, the Roman senator and consul.

Seventh century: (13) Andrew of Caesarea in Cappadocia.

Eighth century: (14) the Venerable Bede.

Ninth century: (15) Isho'dad, the Nestorian bishop of Merv.

Tenth Century: (16) Leo Magister and (17) Oecumenius, bishop of Tricca in Thessaly (often confused with the author of a sixth century commentary on the Book of Revelation).

Eleventh century: (18) Theophylactus, archbishop of Achrida in Bulgaria.

Twelfth century: (19) Dionysius bar Salibi, the Syrian Monophysite.

Cf. W. Bieder, *Die Apostelgeschichte in der Historie* (Zürich, 1960), pp. 4—10; and A. J. and M. B. Mattill, *A Classified Bibliography of Literature on the Acts of the Apostles* (Leiden, 1966). Bieder lists twelve; Mattill, an additional seven.

[2] Πολλοῖς τοῦτο τὸ βιβλίον οὐδ' ὅτι ἐστὶ γνώριμόν ἐστιν οὔτε ὁ γράψας αὐτὸ καὶ συνθείς (the introductory statement to his *Homilies on the Acts of the Apostles*). Cf. the similar statement contained in the introductory paragraph to his *Homilies on Romans*. I do not think anyone has taken this latter statement to mean that the epistles of Paul were little known in Chrysostom's day.

homiletical device and refers only to the lack of knowledge of the contents of the book by some of the preacher's contemporaries.

The situation is rather different when one comes to the three centuries lying between the Reformation and the rise of historical criticism. As is very well known, the events associated with the Protestant Reformation marked the beginning of a revival of biblical study and preaching from the Bible. The Book of Acts, along with the rest of the New Testament, became the object of numerous detailed commentaries by both Protestant and Roman Catholic divines[3]. The recently published bibliography of the literature on the Acts of the Apostles lists works by nearly two hundred different authors during this period[4]. A few of the most important of these are worthy of special mention as an introduction to the main period of research dealt with in this study.

John Calvin (1509—64) may be remembered by most people as being primarily a theologian[5], but New Testament scholars will always think of him as an exegete[6]. Indeed, the bulk of his legacy to the Church consists in commentaries on the books of the Old and New Testaments, commentaries which tower far above all the others of his epoch and which are still of real value after more than four centuries[7]. Although Luther's commentaries on the Epistles of Paul to the Romans and Galatians may be singled out as possibly more influential, Calvin's commentaries are marked by a quality of timelessness and common-sense exegesis that not even Luther displays.

In the preface to his commentary on Romans, Calvin gives us his

---

[3] Erasmus's work on Acts in his *Paraphrases in Novum Testamentum* (Basel, 1516) seems to have been the first of this series. An interesting discussion of the major biblical commentaries of this period is provided by B. Hall in *The Cambridge History of the Bible: The West from the Reformation to the Present Day* (Cambridge, 1963), pp. 76—93.

[4] Mattill, *Bibliography*. 187 by my count.

[5] Cf. the large number of studies on Calvin which are entitled *The Doctrine of ... in the Theology of John Calvin* or the like.

[6] On Calvin as a biblical interpreter, cf. A. Jülicher, "Calvin als Schriftausleger", *Die Christliche Welt* 23 (1909), pp. 655—57; K. Fullerton, "Calvin, the Exegete and Theologian", in his *Prophecy and Authority* (New York, 1919), pp. 139—64; H. Clavier, "Calvin commentateur biblique", in his *Etudes sur le calvinisme* (Paris, 1936), pp. 99—140; P. T. Fuhrmann, "Calvin, the Expositor of Scripture", *Interpretation* 6 (1952), pp. 188—209; J. Haroutunian, "Calvin as a Biblical Commentator", in *The Library of Christian Classics: Vol. 23. Calvin: Commentaries* (London, 1958), pp. 15—50; T. H. L. Parker, "Calvin the Biblical Scholar", *Courtney Studies in Reformation Theology: I. John Calvin*, G. E. Duffield (ed.) (Abingdon, Berks., 1966), pp. 176—86; and T. H. L. Parker, *Calvin's New Testament Commentaries* (London, 1971).

[7] An evidence of this is that new translations and editions are currently being published in English, French and German.

conception of the duty of an expositor of Scripture. The primary aim of the interpreter is, he says, "lucid brevity"[8]. And although his commentaries originally were public lectures given in church, he lived up to this aim to a remarkable degree. The degree of his success is especially noteworthy when placed alongside other commentaries which had a public lecture origin, and, more especially, other commentaries of the Reformation and post-Reformation generations. As F. W. Farrar observed in his Bampton Lectures for 1885, Calvin "never drags his weary reader through a bewildering mass of opinions, of which some are absurd, the majority impossible, and of which all but one must be wrong"[9]. His goal was always to determine what the author really meant by his choice of words, and then to let him say what he says — without attributing to him what the commentator thinks he *ought* to say[10]. He may not have achieved his goal in every instance — what commentator, ancient or modern, has? — but it seems safe to say that he was more successful in this than any of the others of his age.

Calvin's two-volumed commentary on the Acts of the Apostles[11] illustrates his abiding value as a New Testament commentator. Although it is by no means "critical" in the modern sense of the word, it is marked by an essentially grammatical-historical interpretation of the text which is truly remarkable for his day. And as is true of his other commentaries, it is characterized by a deeply spiritual insight and freedom from polemic which are even more remarkable.

Calvin does not discuss the general problems of date, authorship, and historical background — items which would be more of interest to the modern commentator than to the reformer and theologian of Geneva. He begins his work, however, with a discussion of purpose, which he entitles "the theme of Acts" (I, 17—20). Acts, according to Calvin, belongs to the genre of sacred histories which

show that God has cared for His Church from the beginning, that always He stood by, a just vindicator, for those who turned to Him for

---

[8] "Dedication to Simon Grynaeus", prefaced to *The Epistles of Paul the Apostle to the Romans and to the Thessalonians*, trans. by R. MacKenzie (Edinburgh and London, 1961), p. 1.

[9] *History of Interpretation* (London and New York, 1886), p. 344.

[10] Could this be the reason why students of Calvin sometimes find it difficult to harmonize the theology of the *Institutes* with the theology of the commentaries?

[11] First editions in Latin and French were published in Geneva in 1552 (vol. 1) and 1554 (vol. 2). The best English edition is found in the new translation of Calvin's commentaries edited by D. W. and T. F. Torrance, *The Acts of the Apostles*, 2 vols., trans. by J. W. Fraser and W. J. G. McDonald (Edinburgh and London, 1965—66). The references which follow are to this edition

support and protection, and that he was gracious to miserable sinners (I, 17).

The emphasis of the author of Acts is, first of all, on the work of the Holy Spirit, who was sent to confirm the promise of Christ, to make his presence known to his people, and to be the one through the power of the Gospel as it was proclaimed in the world and the corresponding opposition of Satan which was raised wherever it was proclaimed; thus the experiences of the early Christians themselves are given as lessons in boldness and endurance. Calvin makes the further observation that the apostles' speeches make up an important part of the book and are included for didactic purposes, but he does not develop fully his thoughts concerning their place in the aim of the author. The lasting significance of Acts is that it helps the Church of each age to understand its beginnings: how the preaching of the Gospel first took place, what successes and obstacles faced this preaching, and how the earliest Christians triumphed over all the opposition of the world through the help of God. He concludes his introductory remarks by observing the stark contrast between the narrative of the canonical Acts and the fanciful reconstructions of both the apocryphal Acts and the so-called *Clementine Homilies*.

Although his primary concern is with the practical and devotional application of the message of the book to the Church of his own day, Calvin does not hesitate to go into details of geography and history as the occasion demands[12]. He seeks to interpret the Book of Acts against its historical background in first century Palestine, Asia Minor, Greece, and Italy — rather than sixteenth century Europe — although he has no doubts concerning its applicability to both ages. In addition to a careful examination of the Greek text, which he compares with both Erasmus's Latin translation and the Vulgate, he makes frequent reference to Hebrew, especially in the discussion of Old Testament quotations and allusions[13]. He observes places where Luke departs from the Hebrew text of the Old Testament and attempts to explain why the change was made[14]. He is perfectly well aware that an Old Testament passage may be used by the author or one of the speakers in a quite different sense from the meaning intended by its original author; this he defends by saying that the author only "applied" the Scripture to his own situation, rather than meant for the event to be understood as a direct fulfillment of prophecy; or by arguing for the legitimacy of the

---

[12] Cf. his comments on 5.36—37, 7.2—4, 8.27, 12.1, 13.6, 17.18, 17.36, 23.2, 23.25, 24.24 (Calvin 24.25), and 28.11.

[13] On 1.20, 1.26, 2.25—27, 7.44, 8.33, 13.34—35, 23.7.

[14] For example, on 15.16.

typological use of the Old Testament[15]. His belief in the divine
inspiration of the Bible, a doctrine which is just as clearly expressed
in his commentaries as in his *Institutes*[16], does not cause him to
overlook the human aspects of the book. Thus he often draws attention to the author's special purpose in including one event in his
narrative and neglecting to mention others[17]. Where he observes
historical problems in the text, he makes an attempt to solve them,
if possible. When he is unable to find a satisfactory solution, he confesses his ignorance. An example of this is his attempted solution of
the problem of the disagreement between Josephus and the narrative of Acts (5.36—37) concerning the order of the uprisings under
Theudas and Judas the Galilean. He suggests that Luke (or Gamaliel) is not indicating a chronological order, but rather a logical one
(I, 153—54). His approach to Stephen's speech in chapter 7 is a
further example of his willingness to take historical problems seriously. The difficulty of harmonizing some of Stephen's statements
about Jewish history with the Old Testament is recognized. The
problem of harmonizing Acts 7.2 with the narrative of Genesis, for
example, is solved by supposing that Abraham received two calls
from God, one in Mesopotamia and another at Haran (I, 173).
However, in reference to Acts 7.16, where Stephen says that the
bones of all the patriarchs were carried to the land of Canaan and
buried (the Old Testament mentions only Joseph), he suggests that
Luke is in error.

Either there is a synecdoche here [i. e., Joseph stands for the patriarchs
as a group], or Luke has reported this not so much from Moses as from
ancient tradition *(fama)*, as the Jews long ago used to have many things
handed down, as it were, from the fathers (I, 182).

This last statement, incidentally, is a good illustration of the manner in which Calvin refers to the speeches of Acts, which he regards
as brief outlines of what was said on certain occasions, rather than
as verbatim reports, and as the work of both the speaker and the

---

[15] On 1.20—21, 2.17—21, 2.25—28, 3.25, 13.33, 15.16—17, and 18.26.

[16] In his comments on Acts 1.16, Calvin speaks of David and all the prophets
as speaking "solely under the direction of the Spirit, so that they themselves
were not the source of the prophecies but rather the Spirit who used their
tongues as an instrument". He adds this further comment: "Since therefore our
dullness is such that we ascribe far less authority to Scripture than we ought,
we should take careful note of expressions of this kind [i. e., "which the Holy
Spirit foretold"] and make ourselves familiar with them, that our faith may be
confirmed by constantly remembering the authority of God." With this, cf. his
comments on 2.39, 7.38, 20.37—38, and above all his exegesis of 2 Timothy 3.16
and 2 Peter 1.20—21 in the respective commentaries.

[17] Cf. his comments concerning the theme of Acts and, further, on 13.6.

author[18]. In his comment on Acts 22.2, Calvin suggests that Luke is probably mistaken in saying that Paul spoke Hebrew in Acts 22.2, rather than "Syrian" (i. e. Aramaic)[19].

The name Hugo Grotius (1583–1645) is one of the significant names in both the history of law and of theology. The Dutch jurist is often referred to as "the father of international law" because of his great work, *De Jure Belli ac Pacis*[20], through which he achieved the separation of law from theology by arguing that the principle of justice is grounded in the unalterable Law of Nature, which has its source in man as a social being, rather than being a part of God's special revelation. His most important theological work was *De Veritate Religionis Christianae*[21], a handbook for missionaries in which he sought to uphold the evidences of natural theology and to establish the superiority of Christianity to all other faiths. His significance in the area of biblical criticism is due to his multi-volumed commentary on the Old and New Testaments, which began to be published in Paris in 1641 and was only completed in 1650, five years after his death.

His commentary on the Acts of the Apostles[22] has, in many ways, the appearance of a modern (though abbreviated) critical commentary. It is not at all devotional or homilitical in its purpose, not even ostensibly theological, but is strictly linguistic and historical. His method is to cite the Greek text and give a literal Latin translation. This is followed by brief observations concerning the precise meaning of the words, with references to the Old Testament, classical literature, patristic commentators, textual variations in the manuscripts, and related New Testament passages as they may apply to the passage at hand. One is impressed by both the breadth of his learning and the judicious character of his comments. In addition to a mastery of Greek and Latin literature, which he had gained in his youth through the tutoring of Joseph Scaliger, the greatest philologist of the sixteenth century, his commentary displays a profound knowledge of the Hebrew and Greek Old Testaments. His comments are brief, and he does not pause long enough to go into

---

[18] On 1.18, 2.40, 3.26, 5.36, 13.28–29, 17.22, 22.9, and 24.19–22.

[19] Calvin did not allow possible discrepancies like this disturb his high view of the Bible. As he points out in his comments on the apparent discrepancy between Numbers 25.9 and 1 Corinthians 10.8, the writers of Scripture were not especially interested in numerical minutiae, but in spiritual realities (on 1 Cor. 10.8).

[20] (Paris, 1625). [21] (Paris, 1622).

[22] "Annotationes in Acta Apostolorum", in his *Annotationes in Novum Testamentum*, tom. 2 (Paris, 1646) = *Operum Theologicorum*, tom. 2, vol. 1 (Amsterdam, 1679), pp. 579–668. The latter edition was used in this survey.

the problems of general introduction[23]. Yet his work is a model of careful exegesis and is the prototype of the best critical commentaries which appeared in the following centuries.

The commentaries of a French Protestant reformer who wrote in Geneva and a Dutch jurist who wrote in Paris have been singled out as the first two commentaries of special significance in the history of the exegesis of the Book of Acts since the Reformation. The next bright light shone in England.

John Lightfoot (1602—1675) was a parish minister in Staffordshire from 1630 to 1642 and afterwards master of Catherine Hall, Cambridge, for thirty-four years. He devoted his scholarly life to the application of Hebrew and Talmudic studies to the New Testament. In 1629 he published the first of a series of works in this area, a book entitled *Erubhim: or Miscellanies, Christian and Judaical*[24]. This was followed by a commentary on Genesis[25] and many other learned studies over the course of the years.

Lightfoot's first work of special significance for the Lucan scholar is a commentary on Acts 1—12[26], which was published in 1645. It consists of a detailed commentary interwoven with historical details concerning Jewish and Roman history which he had gathered from a study of Josephus and the Roman historians. In the preface he states that he was compelled to publish his work partly for the satisfaction of his readers and partly for his own satisfaction, but chiefly so that both readers and author together may observe the hand of God,

good and gracious in the preservation and propagation of his Church, and just and avengefull in his indignation and judgements upon those two Nations that persecuted the Church . . . . For as there were two Theeves that were crucified with our Savior, the one on the right hand, and the other on the left; so were there two worse by far that crucified him, the Jew and the Roman: The former of ignorance, and so shall obtain mercy; the latter even against the confession of his innocency, and so shall perish forever (no page number).

Lightfoot evidently had access to many New Testament manuscripts, possibly through his friendship with Brian Walton and others with whom he collaborated in the production of the *Polyglot Bible*,

---

[23] He does observe, however, that the proper subject of the book is not "the Apostles" in general, which might be implied from the title, but Peter and Paul in particular. He makes this further observation: "Nam caeterorum ferme obiter tantum fit mentio, et postquam Paulum sectatus est Lucas, de eo solo pergit loqui. De caeterorum Apostolorum actibus vix ad nos fama manavit" (579).

[24] (London, 1629).   [25] (London, 1642).

[26] *A Commentary upon the Acts of the Apostles* (London, 1645).

[*1*]

which appeared in six folio volumes in 1655—57 under Walton's name. He frequently refers to differing textual readings, generally displaying quite remarkable judgment in deciding the best text, even though he lived in what we may call the primal history of textual citicism. He makes frequent use of the Syriac and Arabic versions, as well as the Latin and modern European translations. His knowledge of Greek is not limited to the classical authors, as has been the case too often among New Testament exegetes — especially prior to the twentieth century; it is especially noteworthy that he refers to the Septuagint much more often than to secular authors in attempting to bring out the precise meaning of a Greek word or phrase[27]. Both in his commentary on the early chapters of Acts and in his later *Horae Hebraicae et Talmudicae in Acta Apostolorum*[28] he brings a profound knowledge of Hebrew to bear on the text in his discussion of the etymologies of names, Old Testament quotations and allusions, and the like; and he often quotes from the Talmud or Rabbinic writings to illustrate a point of the text. He seldom quotes from the works of other commentators. Rather, he carefully applies his knowledge of Greek and Semitic languages, as well as secular history, to the text of Acts in an attempt to achieve his aim of a grammatical-historical interpretation of the book.

In his introductory notes to the first chapter of Acts, Lightfoot

[27] Cf., for example, his note on the phrase, ἐπὶ τὸ αὐτό (51).

[28] There is some uncertainty about the date of the first edition of this work. According to *DNB* 33 (1893), p. 230, it was first published posthumously in 1678 in London, being prepared for the press by Richard Kidder; however, I have only been able to verify its existence as an appendix to an edition of his *Horae Hebraicae et Talmudicae in Quatuor Evangelistas*, published in Leipzig by Johann Benedict Carpzov in 1679 (repr. 1684). Matill's entry (*Bibliography*, nr. 2918), indicating an English edition of 1645 is based on a listing in J. A. Fabricius, *Salutaris Lux Evangelii* (Hamburg, 1731), p. 79, who probably mistakenly identified this work with Lightfoot's earlier commentary on Acts 1—12. J. E. Walch, *Bibliotheca theologica selecta* 4 (Jena, 1765), p. 360, contains the same error and is possibly dependant on Fabricius. An English translation is contained in vol. 8 of his *Works*, edited by J. R. Pitman (London, 1823), pp. 353—501, and in subsequent editions of his *Works*.

According to the Library of Congress *Catalogue of Printed Cards* 88 (1963), p. 174, the work was "originally written in Latin ... It is not known by whom the translation was made." S. Neill, *The Interpretation of the New Testament, 1861—1961* (London, 1964), p. 293, n. 1, says that the whole of Lightfoot's *Horae* was written originally in English, though I can find no evidence to suggest that this statement is true.

In passing, it is striking to note how similar in format and plan Lightfoot's *Horae Hebraicae et Talmudicae* is to the later *Kommentar zum Neuen Testament aus Talmud und Midrasch* by H. L. Strack and P. Billerbeck (4 vols.; München, 1922—28). The Leipzig edition by Carpzov must rank among the most beautifully printed books of the seventeenth century.

observes the close connection between the Gospel according to Luke
and the Acts of the Apostles. In the third Gospel the evangelist narrates the life and teaching of Jesus, that is, "all that Jesus began to
do"; he now continues the story by telling of the work as carried on
by his disciples (1—2)[29].

Lightfoot divides the book into two parts: "From the beginning
of the Book to the end of the twelfth Chapter, he [i. e., the author]
discourseth the state of the Church and the Gospel among the Jews;
and from thence forward to the end of the Book he doth the like,
of the same among the Gentiles" (2). Although the traditional title
of the book is "the Acts of the Apostles", it is really the story of
only two apostles, Peter and Paul, the chief minister to "the circumcision" and the chief minister to "the uncircumcision". The chief
actor of part one is Peter; of part two, Paul (2).

Lightfoot, as Calvin, stands out high above the other men of his
age. Although his work is marked by the age in which he lived — as
all works of merit necessarily are — his commentaries represent a
further development in the direction of the modern critical commentary. This is especially true in his observation of the various
possible interpretations of a given point of grammar and in his insight into many of the problems of the text. In spite of the antique
print and rather archaic style of writing, one sometimes has the impression when reading Lightfoot that one is reading a fairly recently
written commentary.

Two other significant works on the Book of Acts were published
in England during the course of the seventeenth century and should
be mentioned in passing. The first was by Henry Hammond (1605
to 1660), whose *Paraphrase and Annotations upon all the Books of
the New Testament*[30] was very influential throughout the English
church. The second was a series of lectures on Acts which appeared
in 1688. The author was John Pearson[31] (1613—86), Lady Mar-
garet Professor of Divinity at Cambridge. Pearson's work was the
more scholarly of the two, but Hammond's was probably the more
widely read. Neither of them quite measured up to the standard of
excellence and originality set for them by Lightfoot.

Johann Albrecht Bengel (1687—1752), the Pietist scholar whose
text and critical apparatus of the Greek New Testament, which he
published in 1734 and thereby launched the modern science of New
Testament textual criticism, was also the author of one of the most

---

[29] Cf. his comments on Acts 1.1 in the *Horae*.

[30] (London, 1653). His commentary on Acts comprises pp. 330—436.

[31] *Lectiones in Acta Apostolorum* ... (London, 1688) = *Bishop Pearson's
Five Lectures on the Acts of the Apostles* (Cambridge and London, 1851).

influential commentaries on the New Testament ever written. The reference is, of course, to his *Gnomon Novi Testamenti*, published in 1734[32].

Bengel's work ranks with Calvin's in both its influence and in the manner in which it stands out above both its contemporaries and predecessors, and with Grotius' and Lightfoot's in critical acumen. In many ways his exposition is superior to Calvin's. In addition to his sympathy with the biblical writers and his ability to enter into their very thought, Bengel has the gift of careful and exact expression which Calvin never had. He uses words sparingly — an all too rare characteristic of theologians — choosing each expression carefully, until every sentence is a model of terse and polished expression. He avoids debate with other commentators. In the influential *Praefatio* to his commentary, where he explains his conception of the task of the New Testament exegete, he observes that it is quite useless to take time and space to refute all the views from which one differs. His aim is, rather, a careful and concise exposition of the thought of the biblical writers, coupled with an application of their spiritual teaching to the life of the Church[33].

In his notes on the Book of Acts, Bengel emphasizes the importance of the Holy Spirit in the mind of the author. As the Gospels speak of Christ, the Head of the Church, so the Acts of the Apostles shows that the same deeds are being carried out by the Church, his body, "which is quickened and animated by His Spirit, is harassed by the world, and is defended and exalted by God" (II, 510). Luke's second volume "describes, not so much the Acts of the Apostles, as the Acts of the Holy Spirit; even as the former treatise contains the Acts of Jesus Christ" (II, 510)[34].

Bengel makes the further observation that Luke's emphasis is on "the victory of the Gospel" as it spreads from a single room in Jerusalem, being preached everywhere and to an infinite variety of men and women, until it finally reaches Rome (II, 511). He calls special attention to the significance of ἀκωλύτως ("without hin-

---

[32] The full title is *Gnomon Novi Testamenti in quo ex nativa verborum vi simplicitas, profunditas, concinnitas, salubritas sensuum coelestium indicatur* (Tübingen, 1742). English translation by A. R. Fausset, many editions; the quotations in the text are from the 5th ed., 1863.

[33] On Bengel as an exegete, cf. E. Nestle, *Bengel als Gelehrter* (Tübingen, 1893); E. Ludwig, *Schriftsverständnis und Schriftauslegung bei Johann Albrecht Bengel* (Stuttgart, 1952); and C. T. Fritsch, "Bengel, the Student of Scripture", *Interp.* 5 (1951), pp. 203—15.

[34] "In eo prior Lucae liber desinit, alter incipit, non tam apostolorum, quam Spiritus sancti Acta describens, sicut prior liber Acta Jesu Christi habet." (comment on 1.1).

drance"), the final word of the Book of Acts, which underlines "the victory of the Word of God": "Paul at Rome forms the crowning point of the Gospel preaching, and the End of Acts" (II, 732).

These two observations of Bengel — i. e., that the Book of Acts is an account of the Acts of the Risen Lord indwelling his Church through the Holy Spirit and that it places special emphasis on the triumph of the Gospel in the Roman Empire until it reaches Rome itself — may seem to be self-evident to the student of Acts who lives more than two centuries after Bengel's time. But they do not seem to have been made before; at least, they do not seem to have been singled out as important themes of the book as a whole. These observations will be made again and again in the course of the history of New Testament criticism, and many scholars will apparently think that they have made them for the first time.

William Paley (1743—1805), sometime Cambridge tutor and parish priest, was the author of very popular and influential textbooks on moral philosophy[35], Christian apologetics[36], and natural theology[37]. His *Evidences of Christianity* was the standard textbook on the subject at Cambridge for nearly a century. However, it is his small book entitled *Horae Paulinae*[38] which connects his name with the history of the criticism of the Book of Acts.

The significance of Paley's work lies not in his apologetic motive — at least not insofar as New Testament criticism is concerned — but rather in his careful examination of one of the most important and oft-discussed problems of New Testament research: the problem of the Paul of the Acts and the Paul of the epistles. He does not phrase the question in the same manner as more recent scholars, but he is concerned with essentially the same problem. Indeed, Paley is the first to examine the problem in detail; and, although his argument is rather dated and would have to be corrected in many respects in the light of the two centuries of criticism which have passed since his day, the points he raises are still foundational for any discussion of the problem[39].

Paley's method is to approach both the Book of Acts and the letters of Paul as though they were ancient documents which were only recently discovered in the recesses of some library. For the

---

[35] *Principles of Moral and Political Philosophy* (London, 1785).

[36] *A View of the Evidences of Christianity* (London, 1794).

[37] *Natural Theology* (London, 1802).

[38] *Horae Paulinae: or the Truth of the Scripture History of St. Paul evinced by a Comparison of the Epistles which bear his name with the Acts of the Apostles and with one another* (London, 1790). Repr. many times.

[39] Cf. the evaluation of the significance of Paley's work by H. J. Cadbury, *The Book of Acts in History* (London, 1955), pp. 123—127.

sake of argument, he assumes neither the genuineness of the letters nor the historical reliability of the narrative of Acts; rather, he attempts a careful comparison of the two documents in order to ascertain whether the letters are truly genuine and whether the historical events referred to in both documents are, in fact, likely to have occurred. The real test is not whether they agree in regard to central matters — this could be the case if the letters were forged on the basis of the history of Acts, or if the history were written on the basis of a knowledge obtained from reading the letters. The real question is whether they agree in matters of incidental detail.

In other words, in examining the agreement between two ancient documents the mark of truth and originality is "undesignedness". There must be agreements; but these agreements must be of the type that could not be the result of special design on the part of one of the writers. If the narrative of Acts, for example, can be demonstrated to be truly independent of a knowledge of the content of the Pauline epistles — a view which is almost universally acknowledged today[40] — and yet the two documents can be shown to contain scores of "undesigned coincidences" of agreement, then this points to the *substantial*[41] historicity of the narrative of Acts and the genuineness of the epistles. This agreement in matters of incidental details could not be the result of mere chance, but must be due to the fact that they both have their foundation in the same historical realities. Thus if we see the repetition in Acts of names[42], incidents of Paul's private life which are of no central significance, and other details known from his letters, these arguments give us strong reason to suppose the general truth of the narrative. The argument is briefly this:

St. Paul's Epistles are connected with the history by their particularity, and by the numerous circumstances which are found in them. When we descend to an examination and comparison of these circumstances, we not only observe the history and the epistles to be independent documents unknown to, or at least unconsulted by, each other, but we find the substance, and oftentimes very minute articles, of the history, recognized in the epistles, by allusions and references, which can neither be imputed to

[40] An exception is M. S. Enslin, " 'Luke' and Paul", *JAOS* 58 (1938), pp. 81 ff. John Knox argues that the author knew, or knew of, the epistles of Paul, but deliberately refrained from using them because of their use by pre-Marcionite or Marcionite schismatics whom he is writing to correct. Cf. his article, "Acts and the Pauline Letter Corpus", *Studies in Luke-Acts*, pp. 279—87.

[41] Paley italicizes that word in his text. He is not arguing for the inerrancy of the narrative of Acts in every detail, but only for its *essential* reliability.

[42] "I think it is fair to say that three-quarters of the persons associated with Paul in Acts reappear in the epistles, or at least persons of the same names" (Cadbury, *Book of Acts*, p. 125).

design, nor, without a foundation in truth, be accounted for by accident: by hints and expressions, and single words dropping as it were fortuitously from the pen of the writer, or drawn forth, each by some occasion proper to the place in which it occurs, but widely removed from any view to consistency or agreement (ch. 16, para. 15).

Paley's method is to go systematically through the whole of the Pauline corpus seeking to find allusions to the narrative of Acts. He finds "undesigned coincidences" in such things as, for example, Paul's reference to the collection he was organizing and the allusions to the same in Acts, the circumstances at the time of the writing of the Epistle to the Romans, the incidental statement in Romans and Acts of Paul's plan to go to Rome after his trip to Jerusalem, Paul's sense of the danger which awaited him in Jerusalem[43], and the similarity of the argument of Romans with the character of his work as portrayed in Acts in seeking to gain an equality in the Church between Jewish and Gentile converts.

Many of Paley's "proofs" would have to be modified in the light of more recent criticism, for we have different views concerning the historical background of some of the letters and cannot be as certain as was Paley about the Pauline authorship of others. Yet one is still impressed with the substantial number of incidental allusions which Paul makes in his letters to events and details which are also mentioned in the Book of Acts. To put it in another way would be to say that details of the narrative of Acts are confirmed again and again by comments made in passing by the hero of Acts in his letters. These may not be quite so numerous as Paley believed[44], and he may have minimized the important divergencies; yet the agreements are still numerous enough to be quite impressive, if they are indeed agreements between independently written documents.

In conclusion, we may point out a few features which appear in the above, very sketchy survey which are of significance for more recent research.

At least as early as Calvin — and he was probably not the first to make this observation — the importance of the Holy Spirit in the thought of the author of Acts was discerned. Although some modern scholars seem to think that all students of Acts up to the

---

[43] Cf. Romans 15.30–31 with Acts 20.22–23. The Acts passage is often assumed to refer to Paul's death *ex eventu*; in reality it says no more than Romans 15.31.

[44] However, Cadbury adds the coincidence of Paul's own name. "It is Acts alone (which) gives us his Jewish name, Saul. It is only in Paul's letters (Romans and Philippians) that we learn that he was of the tribe of Benjamin, and no doubt named for King Saul, the most famous previous member of that tribe, whom indeed Acts elsewhere so describes (13.21)" (*Book of Acts*, p. 125).

nineteenth century regarded the speeches of Acts as verbatim reports of what was said on each particular occasion, we have observed that this was not the case. Calvin, and probably anyone else who has thought very deeply on the matter, recognized the dual role of the author and the speaker (or source) in forming the material, and that at most they were intended by the author to represent summaries of what was said on the occasion represented.

Both Grotius and Lightfoot observed the almost self-evident fact that the book does not live up to what is implied by its traditional title; it is primarily the Acts of Peter and Paul, rather than the Acts of the Apostles. Lightfoot pointed out in addition its intimate connection with the Gospel of Luke in telling the story of how work which Jesus began was carried on by his disciples (cf. Acts 1.1)[45].

Bengel may have been the first to designate the book as "the Acts of the Holy Spirit". Whether or not this is so, he did underline an important theme of Acts which will appear in numerous commentaries and essays in the future, that is, the activity of the Risen Lord in his Church through the Holy Spirit which came to his disciples in fulfillment of his promise. In addition, he stressed the note of victory on which the book ends, and in this too he was not the last.

The contribution of Paley can be considered independently of any apologetic purpose which he may have had, as indeed it must be. He points out the problem of the agreements and divergencies of the Book of Acts and the epistles of Paul. In Paley's mind the divergencies pointed to the fact of the independency of the two; and the agreements, to the substantial reliability of the Book of Acts. This line of argument has impressed many scholars in the two centuries which have followed. However, another line of argument is possible. Paley emphasized the agreements; others, only a few years later, were to emphasize the divergencies. And the debate continues until the present day.

---

[45] It is debated by scholars whether ἤρξατο should be regarded as emphatic (so Bruce *et al.*) or merely as a Semitizing auxiliary (so Haenchen *et al.*). Whether or not Luke intended to imply this here, it is certainly probable that he intended the parallel between the Gospel (what Jesus *began* to do and teach) and Acts (what he *continued* to do and teach through the Holy Spirit in his Church).

Chapter II

TENDENZKRITIK: F. C. BAUR AND THE TÜBINGEN SCHOOL

What is the purpose of Acts? Can one, by an examination of the contents of the book, discern the underlying aim of the author which has guided him in his selection and organization of his materials? This important question has been asked time and time again by New Testament scholars over the past two centuries. It was, in fact, the question with which the modern critical study of the Book of Acts began[1].

Admittedly, this question regarding the purpose of Acts had been asked by the writers surveyed in the first chapter of this study. But there it was only one among a number of questions; and it did not receive the detailed treatment and special interest it was to receive in the nineteenth century. Nor did it have the same significance for early writers[2].

As early as 1721, C. A. Heumann[3] (1681—1764) had argued that Luke's two volumed "history of Christ and the apostles" was written "as an apology for the Christian religion" for the benefit

---

[1] The rise of historical criticism as it applies to the study of the Bible lies outside the immediate scope of this study. In his Bampton Lectures for 1962, Alan Richardson has provided an excellent discussion of the subject (*History Sacred and Profane* [London, 1964], pp. 17—124). His study is all the more excellent because of his treatment of the subject in the context of the general history of ideas. Cf. also W. G. Kümmel, *Das Neue Testament: Geschichte der Erforschung seiner Probleme* (Freiburg and München, 1958), pp. 41—143; K. Barth, *Die protestantische Theologie im 19. Jahrhundert* (Zollikon and Zürich, 1947), pp. 60—152; E. Hirsch, *Geschichte der neuern evangelischen Theologie* (Gütersloh, 1949—54), especially vol. 5 (1954), pp. 1—70. G. Hornig, *Die Anfänge der historisch-kritischen Theologie: Johann Salomo Semlers Schriftverständnis und seine Stellung zu Luther* (Göttingen, 1961) has provided a careful study of one of the most important figures in the process; see especially pp. 56—83, 176—210.

[2] Cf. McGiffert, *BC* 2 (1922), pp. 363—95. The surveys of this period by E. Haenchen, *Die Apostelgeschichte*, pp. 13—17, and W. Bieder, *Die Apostelgeschichte in der Historie*, pp. 24—31, are dependent on McGiffert.

[3] "Dissertation de Theophilo, cui Lucas Historiam Sacram Inscripsit", *Bibliotheca Historico-Philogico-Theologica*, Class. 4 (1721), pp. 483—505.

of a pagan magistrate by the name of Theophilus, who was probably a Roman or Italian. Thus Luke comes to the fore as the first —
and in Heumann's opinion "the best" — of the early Christian apologists.

More detailed attention was given to the problem of the purpose
of Acts by J. D. Michaelis (1717—91), professor of Oriental languages and theology at Göttingen, in his *Introduction to the New
Testament*, which first appeared in 1750[4]. The Book of Acts is, in
his view, a continuation of the Third Gospel and written by the
same author (1298). The author of both books is Luke, a Gentile
and a physician, the travelling companion of the Apostle Paul (1163
—1171). Michaelis thinks he can detect the fact that the author is
a medical doctor by his literary style (1168—69). He rejects the
identification of Luke (Λουκᾶς) with Lucius (Λούκιος), the prophet
of Antioch (Acts 13.1) and/or companion of Paul (Rom. 16.21),
as had been suggested by Heumann, Lardner, and Wettstein (1171
—1175)[5]. The book was probably written at Rome about A.D. 63,
that is, at the end of the story narrated by the author.

[2]   Es ist aber auch nicht glaublich, dass er sie später geschrieben habe, sonst
würde er seine Geschichte weiter fortgesetzet, und zum wenigsten den Ausgang des ersten Römischen Gefängnisses Pauli, auf den sein Leser begierig
seyn muss, gemeldet haben (1299).

Luke did not wish merely to narrate the history of the Church
during the first thirty years after the ascension of Christ. If this had
been his main aim, he would have gone into more detail and selected
his material differently. If it had been his purpose to give a history
of the Church, then he would have undoubtedly devoted more space
to the Palestinian Church, which he leaves to the one side after
telling of the conversion of Paul, as well as to the activity of the
other eleven apostles in addition to Peter. And he also omits mention of many other important events in the history of the early
Church, such as the spread of the Gospel eastward into the region
of the Euphrates and the Tigris, the foundation of the church in
Rome, and even many things from the life of Paul about which we
have knowledge from his letters. The author never once quotes
from Paul's letters, nor does he mention the many persecutions and

---

[4] *Einleitung in die göttlichen Schriften des Neuen Bundes*, 2. Theil (Göttingen, 1750; 2nd ed., 1766; 3rd ed., 1777). The second edition is quoted in the
text.

[5] The idea is at least as old as Origen and Ephraem Syrus; it has been
advocated in the twentieth century by A. Deissmann, *Light from the Ancient
East* (E. T. 1927; repr. Grand Rapids, 1965), pp. 435—38, and B. Reicke, *The
Gospel of Luke* (Richmond, 1964), pp. 12—16.

shipwrecks which Paul enumerates in 2 Corinthians 11. Many of these events probably took place when Luke was not with Paul and, therefore, had no knowledge of them; yet he omits enough of those concerning which he would have had thorough knowledge to demonstrate that he is not concerned to write a history of Paul's life (1300—04).

When one gives attention to the content of the author's narrative, writes Michaelis, one observes a double purpose.

1. Die erste Ausgiessung des heiligen Geistes nebst denen ersten Wunderwerken glaubwürdig aufzuzeichnen, durch welche die Wahrheit der christlichen Religion bestätiget wird. Es war eine glaubwürdige Nachricht hievon unentbehrlich nöthig, da Christus seinen Jüngern den heiligen Geist so oft verheissen hatte. Und wenn ein Heide dem Evangelio Glauben beymessen sollte, so muste er zuförderst diese Frage aufwerfen: wie das Evangelium zuerst zu Jerusalem bekannt geworden und beglaubiget sey. [3]

2. Diejenigen Nachrichten mitzutheilen, welche das Unrecht der Heiden an der Kirche Christi erweisen, welches von den Juden sonderlich um die Zeit angefochten ward, als Lucas seine Geschichte der Apostel schrieb. Selbst Paulus, dessen Gefährte Lucas zu seyn pflegte, sass damahls zu Rom gefangen, weil er von den Juden verklaget war, die ihn darüber anfeindeten, dass er die Heiden in die Kirche aufnahm (1304—05).

It is for this reason that Luke mentions the conversion of the Samaritans in chapter 8 and the story of Peter's preaching to and then baptizing Cornelius in chapter 11, even though he was uncircumcised, as a result of a direct command of God. This too is the reason why the Jerusalem Council and the conversion and commissioning of Paul by the Lord to preach to the Gentiles receive such strong emphasis in Acts (1305—06).

In response to Michaelis' suggestion, we find the same attention given to the question of purpose in the standard New Testament Introductions and commentaries during the next seventy-five years. In various ways Acts was viewed as a defense of Paul, a testimony of God's help in the spread of Christianity, a history of Christian missions, or an attempt to persuade Jews to become Christians[6]. Although the various scholars differed slightly in their definitions of the purpose of the author of Acts, they all agreed that the story presented — for whatever purpose — was basically historically reliable.

---

[6] Cf. McGiffert, BC 2, pp. 364—66. It should be observed that the way some of these scholars define the purpose of Acts differs little from the observations of Calvin and Bengel which have already been noted. Cf. especially the views of Eckermann, Hänlein, Eichhorn, and Mayerhoff.

This assumption of the essential trustworthiness of Acts as a historical document was first challenged by Wilhelm Martin Leberecht de Wette[7] (1780—1849).

De Wette's name would most certainly appear on anyone's list of the dozen most influential biblical critics or theologians of the nineteenth century. In fact, there is hardly an area of the whole theological curriculum in which he was not in some way influential and to which he did not dedicate a major work. He was a student of J. J. Griesbach and H. E. G. Paulus in Jena and later professor at Heidelberg (1807—10) and then in Berlin (1810—19), where he joined J. A. W. Neander and F. D. E. Schleiermacher in the newly organized faculty of theology. He was deprived of his chair at Berlin in 1819 and exiled from the city as a result of writing a letter of sympathy to the mother of a young Swiss theological student who was executed for the assassination of the writer, August von Kotzebue. In 1822 he was called to be professor of theology at Basel, where he was the mainstay of the faculty of theology for a quarter of a century. There he devoted the remainder of his days to writing new books, issuing new editions of his old books, and (one would suppose) teaching.

At the age of twenty-five de Wette had laid the foundations of modern Pentateuchal criticism by his *Contributions to the Introduction of the Old Testament*[8]. This was followed by a complete *Introduction to the Old Testament* some eleven years later[9], in which he developed the ideas of his earlier study. His *Introduction to the New Testament*, first published in 1826[10], is rightly considered to be the first of a long series of modern, "critical" New Testament Introductions published in the German language[11]. He also pro-

---

[7] On de Wette, cf. R. Smend, *W. M. L. de Wettes Arbeit am Alten und Neuen Testament* (Basel, 1958); P. Handschin, *W. M. L. de Wette als Prediger und Schriftsteller* (Basel, 1958); E. Staehelin, *Dewettiana: Forschungen und Texte zu W. M. L. de Wettes Leben und Werk* (Basel, 1956). De Wette is properly spelled with a small "d", unless it appears at the beginning of a sentence (*Ibid.*, p. 10), and should be alphabetized under "W"; however, it is sometimes found spelled DeWette or even Dewette and listed accordingly.

[8] *Beiträge zur Einleitung in das Alte Testament*, 2 vols. (Halle, 1806—7).

[9] *Lehrbuch der historisch-kritischen Einleitung in die Bibel Alten und Neuen Testaments. Erster Teil: Die Einleitung in das Alte Testament enthaltend* (Berlin, 1817).

[10] *Lehrbuch der historisch-kritischen Einleitung in die Bibel Alten und Neuen Testaments. Zweyter Teil: Die Einleitung in das Neue Testament enthaltend* (Berlin, 1826; 5th ed., 1847). The first edition is referred to in the text.

[11] W. G. Kümmel appropriately quotes from the foreword to de Wette's first edition in introducing his revision of P. Feine—J. Behm, *Einleitung in das Neue Testament*, 12th ed. (Heidelberg, 1963), p. v.

duced a translation of the whole Bible which remains one of the best German translations ever produced[12].

In his *Introduction to the New Testament* de Wette follows the suggestion of Heumann in regarding Acts as the second part of a "Geschichte des Urchristenthums" which the author wrote for the benefit of some one by the name of Theophilus, probably a distinguished Roman or Italian, who was either a Christian or at least sympathetic to the Christian faith (182, 202). The book consists of two parts: chapters 1—12, which are more of a general nature, and chapters 13—28, in which Paul is the active person. There is no evidence, according to de Wette, that the work was developed according to a comprehensive plan and definite purpose. The general purpose of the book is to follow the growth of the young Church; it is an attempt at a Christian church history dedicated to a friend in which there are many uncompleted and defective details. The special purposes suggested by Michaelis, Paulus, Eckermann, and others are at most unintentional and in no way represent the entire purpose of the writer (202—03).

According to the traditional and natural interpretation of the so-called "we"-sections (16.10—17, 20.5—15, 21.1—17, 27.1—28.19), the author was a companion of the Apostle Paul and an eyewitness of part of the history. Against this view, however, de Wette suggests the following: (1) In his foreword (Luke 1.1—4) the author makes the distinction between himself and the eyewitnesses of the events about which he is writing. (2) The information concerning Paul is partly miraculous, partly false[13], and partly incomplete. The main cause of doubt, however, is found in the observation that (3) the author knows only the miraculous side of certain facts and includes uncertain sayings. A companion of Paul would have been in the position to write a better account of these things. It remains possible, however, that the author is dependent on the work of another in the passages where he speaks as though he were a participant in the narrative (203—04).

De Wette finds evidence of possible sources in the Jewish color of the narrative and speeches of the first part of Acts, in the other long speeches of the book, and in the differences existing between various parts of the book. He regards the account of the two jour-

---

[12] Translated first with J. C. W. Augusti. The Old Testament appeared in 1809—10; Apocrypha, 1811; and New Testament, 1813. He re-worked the whole and published it under his own name in 1831—32.

[13] The only datum he includes in this connection is a note inviting comparison of Acts 9.26 and 12.17 (*sic*) with Gal. 1.17—18, and Acts 11.30 with Gal. 2.1.

neys of Paul to Jerusalem in chapters 11 and 15 as in reality doublets of one visit. Wherever the author has used sources, he has
freely re-worked them and molded them into a unified work (204
—207).

Although the obvious interpretation of the ending of Acts would
be that it was written at the end of Paul's two years' imprisonment
in Rome, various references in the Gospel of Luke (21.7, 12, 24
—27)[14] demand a date after the destruction of Jerusalem in A.D.
70 (182, 107). Why then did the author end the story with Paul's
two years' imprisonment ending in A.D. 61 or 62? In an attempt
to answer this perplexing question de Wette hypothesizes that the
author purposed to carry the story farther, but he either lacked the
information to do so, or had neither the time nor leisure required
(207)[15].

Following de Wette, the next significant name in the unfolding
history of Acts-criticism belongs to the most influential figure in
nineteenth century New Testament criticism in Germany. As far as
his influence on the study of the Book of Acts and the epistles of
Paul is concerned, he would probably be considered the most influential German critic of all time. The name is, of course, Ferdinand Christian Baur[16] (1792—1860).

Baur was professor of theology at Tübingen from 1826 until his
death in 1860 and founder of the so-called Tübingen School *(Tübinger Schule)* of New Testament criticism, which was the source of
such widespread debate and influence during the middle decades of
the nineteenth century. His most famous students were David Friedrich Strauss and Albrecht Ritschl, both of whom broke with their
mentor in later years. His ideas concerning the New Testament were
further developed by his son-in-law, Eduard Zeller, and Albert
Schwegler, to mention only the most important disciples, and came
to have a dominating influence on German New Testament research

---

[14] Luke 21 is the only evidence he lists in support of a post-A. D. 70 date.

[15] Essentially the same ideas are expressed in de Wette's brief commentary
on Acts, which he published twelve years later as vol. 3, part 4 of his *Kurz-
gefasstes exegetisches Handbuch zum Neuen Testament: Kurze Erklärung der
Apostelgeschichte* (Leipzig, 1838).

[16] Two thorough studies of Baur as a theologian have recently been published: P. C. Hodgson, *The Formation of Historical Theology: A Study of F.
C. Baur* (New York, 1966) and W. Geiger, *Spekulation und Kritik: Die Ge-
schichtstheologie F. C. Baurs* (München, 1964). Hodgson's study is the more
thorough of the two, but his work is somewhat marred by his urge to defend
Baur almost *in toto.* See K. Penzel, "Will the Real Ferdinand Christian Baur
Please Stand Up", *JR* 48 (1968), pp. 310—23, for a helpful comparison of the
two books. Hodgson, pp. 291—94, contains a select list of the numerous studies
which have been devoted to Baur over the years.

until nearly the end of the century. Indeed, as we shall have occasion to observe later, the influence of his interpretation of the nature of early Christianity continues in some circles until the present, although it exists in a somewhat modified form.

F. C. Baur was not primarily an exegete or New Testament critic, but rather a theologian — specifically a student of the history of dogma. Yet he published five books[17] and a similar number of significant essays[18] in the area of New Testament research. His basic thesis concerning the nature of the early Christianity which forms the environment of the books of the New Testament and other non-canonical books, a view which remains essentially the same throughout his writings[19], was first put forward in 1831 in an essay devoted to the problem of the so-called Christ-party of Paul's letters to the Corinthian church[20].

His thesis is basically this. In spite of the impression which one gains from a superficial reading of the New Testament documents, viz. that the early Church was essentially uniform in its doctrine and practice, a closer examination of the literature demonstrates that this was not the real situation. Rather than being united in its confession of faith, early Christianity was marked by a severe conflict between two groups representing two very different conceptions of Christianity: a Jewish (Petrine) Christian party and a Gentile (Pauline) Christian party. A large part of the early Christian documents can be understood in the light of this basic division of thought and action.

In his essay on the Christ-party in the Corinthian church, Baur uses the method which later came to be known as *Tendenzkritik* — "tendency criticism", the study of a New Testament writing in terms of its special theological point of view within the context of the history of primitive Christianity. His point of departure is 1 Corinthians 1.11, which mentions four factions in the Corinthian church,

---

[17] On the Pastoral Epistles (1835), Paul (1845), the four Gospels (1847), the Gospel of Mark (1851), and the theology of the New Testament (posthumous, 1864). Cf. Hodgson, *Op. cit.*, pp. 285—6 and Geiger, *Op. cit.*, pp. 248—9, for complete bibliographical data.

[18] Notably on the Christ-party in the Corinthian church (1831), Apollonius of Tyana and Christ (1832), the purpose and occasion of the Epistle to the Romans (1836), the origin of the episcopacy in the Christian church (1838), and the composition and character of the Gospel of John (1844). Cf. Hodgson, *Op. cit.*, p. 288 and Geiger, *Op. cit.*, pp. 248—9 for complete bibliographical data.

[19] Cf. Hodgson, *Op. cit.*, pp. 22, 196.

[20] "Die Christuspartei in der korinthischen Gemeinde, der Gegensatz des petrinischen und paulinischen Christenthums in der ältesten Kirche, der Apostel Petrus in Rom," *TZTh* 5 (1831), 4. Heft, pp. 61—206.

identifying them respectively with Paul, Apollos, Cephas (Peter), and Christ[21]. These four represent actually only two parties: the basically Gentile party of the Church (represented by Paul and Apollos) and the Jewish Christians who remained faithful to Judaism and the Law (represented by Peter and James). Concerning the Jewish Christian party, Baur comments:

[4]   Sie nannte sich τοὺς κηφᾶ, weil Petrus unter den Judenaposteln den Primate hatte, τοὺς Χριστοῦ aber, weil sie die unmittelbare Verbindung mit Christus als Hauptmerkmal des ächten apostolischen Ansehens aufstellte, und eben daher den erst später und auf eine ganz eigenthümliche Weise als Apostel aufgetretenen Paulus nicht als ächten und ebenbürtigen Apostel anerkennen wollte, ihn zum wenigsten den übrigen Aposteln weit nachsetzen zu müssen glaubte (84).

These Jewish Christians, the Cephas-Christ party, were the opponents of Paul in Corinth, before whom he defends himself, especially in 2 Corinthians[22]. This same group is to be identified with the opponents of Paul referred to in the Philippian and Galatian letters.

In addition to the New Testament data which Baur adduces in support of his theory, he finds evidence for this basic division of thought in the primitive Church in an Ebionite tradition concerning Paul (115) and in the so-called Clementine Homilies (116 ff.)[23]. In the former tradition Paul is said to have been a Gentile who became a proselyte because he wanted to marry the daughter of the Jewish High Priest; this being refused, he left Jerusalem in anger and began preaching against the Sabbath, circumcision, and the Law. In the Clementine Homilies he thought he found evidence for a polemic against Paul, veiled as an imaginary debate between Peter and Simon Magus[24]. Baur argues that both these imaginary and tendentious stories provide evidence for his view that a strong and signi-

---

[21] It is questionable whether this is the *real* point of departure for Baur. My impression is that his view is derived primarily from his interpretation of the pseudo-Clementine literature and *then* applied to the study of the New Testament, although he treats them in reverse order in his essay. Cf. however Hodgson, *Op. cit.*, pp. 4, 22, 196—212.

[22] In this connection it is interesting to note Baur's interpretation of the much-debated phrase, "to know Christ κατὰ σάρκα" (2 Cor. 5.16), which he interprets as meaning "to recognize Jesus as the Jewish Messiah," a direct reference to the doctrine of the Petrine-party (cf. pp. 90—101 of his essay).

[23] On the pseudo-Clementine literature, see B. Rehm, "Clemens Romanus III, *RAC* 3 (1957), pp. 198—206, with bibliography; and A. C. Headlam, "The Clementine Literature", *JTS* 3 (1902), pp. 41—58.

[24] The suggestion had been made earlier by D. von Cölln, "Clementina", in *Allgemeine Encyclopedia der Wissenschaften und Künste*, ed. by J. E. Ersch and J. G. Gruber (Leipzig, 1828), 18, pp. 36—44.

ficant party of the early Church, a Petrine-party, rejected the work and teaching of the Apostle Paul.

Bei dem genauen Zusammenhange, in welchem die Clementinen mit der Lehre der Ebioniten stehen, und bei dem bekannten Hasse, mit welchem diese Secte gegen den Apostel Paulus erfüllt war, lässt sich nichts anders annehmen, als dass die Lehre der Clementinen insbesondere auch den Grundsätzen entgegengesetzt werden sollte, welche Paulus über das Verhältniss des Mosaischen Gesetzes zum Christenthum aufgestellt hatte (127).

In the final section of the essay (136 ff.) Baur rejects the historicity of the tradition concerning Peter's ministry and martyrdom in Rome — and, incidentally, that of a second imprisonment of Paul following a trip to Spain. The connection of Peter with Rome was, in his opinion, invented by the Judaizing party[25] in the church at Rome to correspond to the experiences of Paul and, therefore, to establish a connection between Peter, the apostle whose authority they recognized (in contradistinction to Paul), and the early days of their own church. Further evidence for this Jewish-Christian opposition to the authority and teaching of Paul is found in the Epistle of James, which he interprets as having been written expressly to contradict Pauline doctrine, and the two epistles of Peter, which were written in an attempt to parallel Peter's ministry and experience with Paul's and, therefore, to establish his claim to authority over against the claims of the Pauline-party, which gave Paul the place of prominence (205—06 n.)[26].

Baur does not discuss the Book of Acts in this early essay, but the conception of the nature of early Christianity as consisting of two opposing parties, centering around the figures of Peter and Paul, in constant conflict because of their very different attitudes toward the Jewish Law and, consequently, the doctrine of salvation, is the foundation of his approach to Acts and, indeed, to the whole New Testament[27]. His views concerning various points of criticism

[25] Baur uses the various terms of "Jewish Christians" *(Judenchristen)*, "the Jewish-Christian party" *(die judenchristliche Partei)*, and "Judaizing party" *(die judaisirende Partei)* as synonyms.

[26] He later argued that the Apocalypse was a narrow, Jewish-Christian work and that passages like Rev. 2.9 and 3.9 were directed toward the followers of Paul. The Gospel according to Matthew (the first written Gospel and upon which Mark and Luke were dependent!) was taken to represent the Jewish-Christian position also. Matt. 7.23, for example, was written to protest against the Pauline doctrine of freedom from the Law. Luke and Acts belonged to the conciliatory period, as did the deutero-Pauline epistles *(sc.* all besides 1 and 2 Cor., Rom., and Gal.). The Gospel of John was written even later, when the reconciliation of the opposing parties was an accomplished fact.

[27] Hodgson, *Op. cit.,* pp. 22, 196—201, argues that it is a misconception to

are developed and modified slightly in the years which follow; but, as has been pointed out above, his conception of the nature of primitive Christianity remains essentially the same as that expressed in this early essay.

In 1836 Baur applied the method of *Tendenzkritik* to the Epistle to the Romans[28] and concluded that it was a polemical tract against the Jewish-Christian party in the church at Rome, in which Paul defends his views concerning the universalism of the Christian faith and justification by faith alone, against Judaistic particularism and belief in salvation through the Law. In support of this thesis Baur brings forward the hypothesis that Acts was written by a "Paulinist" to defend the mission of Paul to the Gentiles against the criticisms of the Jewish-Christian party. The author of Acts argues his point by portraying Paul as everywhere preaching to Jews and only turning to the Gentiles when the Jews had rejected his message, a view very similar to the argument of the Apostle in Romans 9—11. The idea is only mentioned in passing and is not developed at this point, since his only concern is to illustrate his interpretation of the purpose and occasion of Romans. Two years later he developed the idea slightly in a few brief comments in an essay on the origin of the episcopacy[29].

[6]   Ja selbst die Apostelgeschichte ist, ihrer Grundidee und innersten Anlage nach, wie es auch im Übrigen mit ihrer historischen Glaubwürdigkeit stehen mag, der apologetische Versuch eines Pauliners, die gegenseitige Annäherung und Vereinigung der beiden einander gegenüberstehenden Parteien dadurch einzuleiten und herbeizuführen, dass Paulus so viel wie möglich petrinisch, und dagegen Petrus so viel wie möglich paulinisch er-

think of Baur's interpretation of early Christianity as being dependent on the philosophical dialectic of Hegel (thesis-antithesis-synthesis) — a common accusation of the critics of Baur — since this essay was (according to Hodgson) written before he knew of Hegel. Although it is hard to imagine Baur's having studied and taught theology and philosophy in Germany for more than twenty years at a time when Hegel's books and ideas were the center of widespread discussion and never having heard of Hegel, it must be conceded that it is an oversimplification to think of his conception of early Christianity as being *simply* the result of the application of the Hegelian dialectic. However, it remains true that his conception of primitive Christianity as consisting of two dialectically opposed parties — whether dependent on Hegel or exegetically derived — becomes the sieve through which Baur pours the New Testament data in his critical study.

[28] "Über Zweck und Veranlassung des Römerbriefs und die damit zusammenhängenden Verhältnisse der römischen Gemeinde", *TZTh* 9 (1836), 3. Heft, pp. 59—178.

[29] "Über der Ursprung des Episcopats in der christlichen Kirche. Prüfung der neuesten von Hrn. Dr. Rothe hierüber aufgestellten Ansicht", *TZTh* 11 (1838), 3. Heft, pp. 1—185.

scheint, dass über Differenzen, welche nach der eigenen unzweideutigen Erklärung des Apostels Paulus im Galaterbrief ohne allen Zweifel zwischen den beiden Aposteln wirklich stattgefunden haben, so viel möglich ein versöhnender Schleier geworfen, und der das Verhältniss der beiden Parteien störende Hass der Heidenchristen gegen das Judenthum und der Judenchristen gegen das Heidenthum über dem gemeinsamen Hass beider gegen die ungläubigen Juden, die den Apostel Paulus zum steten Gegenstand ihres unversöhnlichen Hasses gemacht haben, in Vergessenheit gebracht wird. Wie die die Apostelgeschichte betreffenden historischen und kritischen Fragen nur dann befriedigend gelöst werden können, wenn sie aus dem Gesichtspunkt einer Parallelisierung der beiden Apostel für den eben bemerkten Zweck betrachtet wird, so erhalten wir dadurch zugleich aus ihr ein neues Moment für die Geschichte der kirchlichen Verhältnisse, und wir sehen an einem neuen Beispiele, wie sehr diese Verhältnisse jene Zeit bewegten und beschäftigten, und wie leicht daher auch das in beiden Parteien zum Bewusstseyn kommende Bedürfniss der Vereinigung Schriften, wie die genannten sind, hervorrufen konnte (1427).

In the same year Karl Schrader published the final volume of a five volumed work on the Apostle Paul[30]. In this he included a brief commentary on Acts (V, 508—74), in which he put forward the view that Acts is a second century work written to defend the doctrines and practices of the Church as it existed in that day. Although it may contain bits and pieces of historical information concerning the actual situation of the Church of the middle decades of the first Christian century, the work is almost wholly unreliable. The situation reflected by the narrative and the theology is that of the middle of the second century, rather than the first.

Schrader interprets different parts of Acts as reflecting different apologetic and polemical interests. Sometimes it is an attack on Gnosticism: sometimes, a defense of Judaistic-hierarchical views against the more loosely constituted Gentile Christian communities. More often, Schrader speaks in general terms of the "apologetischen Zweck des Verfassers" and assumes that this bias led the author to create the purported historical events *ex nihilo*. He also calls attention to the alleged parallelism between Peter and Paul which Baur had observed and lays great stress on what he considers to be the unreconcilable discrepancies between the Paul of the Acts and the Paul of the Epistles. The main discrepancy is, in his view, the

---

[30] *Der Apostel Paulus* (Leipzig, 1830—36). Vol. 1 deals with the problems of chronology; vol. 2, the life of Paul; vol. 3, the teaching of Paul; vol. 4, a translation and interpretation of 1 and 2 Cor. and Rom.; vol. 5, the rest of the Pauline epistles and Acts. It is a very uneven piece of work, a conglomerate of different, and sometimes conflicting, opinions and would not be worthy of special mention if it had not been referred to so often by some of the writers of the period under discussion.

way Acts makes Paul dependent on and inferior to the earliest Jerusalem apostles, which is explicitly denied by Paul himself in Galatians 1 and 2.

Matthias Schneckenburger[31] (1804—48), who had been a student of Baur at Tübingen and of Hegel and Schleiermacher in Berlin and was professor of theology at Bern for fifteen years (1834—48), took the observations of Baur and Schrader as the starting point of his thorough study on the purpose of Acts, which was published in 1841[32]. He agreed with Baur and Schrader that Acts is the work of a Paulinist who writes in defense of his hero. He works out the parallelism between Peter and Paul, to which Baur and Schrader had only alluded, in careful detail. But there is a decisive difference between the two views. Whereas Baur and Schrader had regarded the book as basically unreliable as a work of history, Schneckenburger argues that the author's portrait of Paul, although apologetic and one-sided, is an essentially accurate one.

Schneckenburger argues that the basic purpose of Acts is not to give a history of early Christianity, or even of the spread of the Gospel from Jerusalem to Rome. The view that the primary purpose of the Book of Acts is historical is the result of viewing Luke 1.1—4 as the preface to both the Gospel according to Luke and the Book of Acts, rather than as the preface to Luke alone. This judgment Schneckenburger regards to be incorrect (7—17).

Although both works have a common author, it does not follow that they have the same purpose in view, or that the preface to the first work should be regarded as the preface to the second. Two factors argue against the commonly accepted view.

First, the ending of the Gospel seems to have no direct connection with the beginning of Acts. Luke clearly intends the Gospel to be a complete work in and of itself; there is no real need for what follows, as indeed there is no hint that the story is to be con-

---

[31] On Schneckenburger, cf. E. F. Gelpke, *Gedächtnisrede auf den Doktor und Professor der Theologie Matthias Schneckenburger* (Bern, 1848); and C. B. Hundeshagen in *RE*² 13 (1884), pp. 603—08. Although Schneckenburger is often mentioned in connection with the rise of *Tendenzkritik*, very few scholars seem to have recognized his significance or to have treated his views in any detail. An exception is A. J. Mattill, Jr., who has pointed out that Schneckenburger was the first to devote a full treatise to a careful consideration of the purpose of Acts and that his work remains a powerful argument for the view that although Acts may be a *Tendenzschrift* this fact does not mean that it is therefore unhistorical [*Luke as a Historian in Criticism since 1840* (Diss. Vanderbilt, 1959), pp. 20—46]; cf. also his essay, "The Purpose of Acts", in *Apostolic History and the Gospel*, ed. W. W. Gasque and R. P. Martin (Exeter, 1970), pp. 108—22.

[32] *Über den Zweck der Apostelgeschichte* (Bern, 1841).

tinued beyond the end of chapter 24. Also, when one reads the beginning of Acts, he sees that it is not a direct continuation of the Gospel, "sondern eine neue amplificirte Redaction von Luc. 24,50 bis 53" (10). Also, the differences between the accounts of the ascension of Jesus at the end of the Gospel and the beginning of Acts point to the separateness of the two works. Chapter 1 of Acts is eine ganz neue Einleitung zu dem Folgenden, gleichsam ein an die Schlussbegebenheit des Evangeliums anknüpfender neuer Prolog zu einem ganz andern Werke, dessen Inhalt darin nach seinen Hauptzügen eben so angedeutet ist, wie der Inhalt des Evangeliums im dortigen Prolog (13).

[7]

[8]

Second, the plain meaning of Luke 1.1—4 cannot refer to the contents of Acts. The πεπληροφορημένα ἐν ἡμῖν πράγματα and the λόγοι, περὶ ὧν κατηχήθης certainly cannot refer to such things as Paul's shipwreck on Malta or his sermon on the Areopagus. And the life of the primitive Church, the deeds and fortunes of the early apostles, and the like will not have comprised the παράδοσις by αὐτόπται and ὑπηρέται τοῦ λόγου. Furthermore, the expression πεπληροφορημένα can only be interpreted as meaning the life and teaching of the Messiah in fulfilment of eternal councils and ancient promises and is in no way appropriate of the early history of the Church[33]. Again, in his preface to the Gospel, Luke distinguishes between himself and the αὐτόπται and ὑπηρέται τοῦ λόγου, as de Wette had pointed out; this would not be true of at least parts of Acts, according to the most natural understanding of the "we"-passages[34].

Schneckenburger therefore conducts a careful examination of the Book of Acts — certainly the most careful and critical study which had been published up to this time — in order to ascertain its special purpose. He accepts de Wette's division of the book into two parts, chapters 1—12 and 13—28. He begins with a consideration of the second part, which he regards as the logical place to begin a study of this nature.

Hat nämlich ein Pauliner und paulinischer Begleiter das Buch geschrieben, so muss der besondere Gedanke des Verfassers, die eigenthümliche Tendenz der Abfassung in demjenigen wohl am deutlichsten hervortreten, was er, ohne durch schon fixierte Quellen oder eine stabil gewordene Tradition gebunden zu sein, aus dem Selbsterlebten oder unmittelbar Erkundeten mittheilt, und was den Mann zum Gegenstande hat, zu welchem er im

[9]

---

[33] Here Schneckenburger refers to Luke 24.44, where the Risen Lord speaks: Οὗτοι οἱ λόγοι μου οὓς ἐλάλησα πρὸς ὑμᾶς ἔτι ὢν σὺν ὑμῖν, ὅτι δεῖ πληρωθῆναι πάντα τὰ γεγραμμένα ἐν τῷ νόμῳ Μωϋσέως καὶ τοῖς προφήταις καὶ ψαλμοῖς περὶ ἐμοῦ.

[34] Schneckenburger gives careful consideration to the suggestion made by Schleiermacher and others that the "we"-sections of Acts represent the source used by the author — i. e. Timothy's diary — rather than the author's own presence with Paul, but rejects it as inadequate (20—25).

Verhältniss eines verehrenden Schülers stand. Diess scheint bisher nicht gehörig beachtet worden zu sein. Die früheren Versuche, den Zweck des Buches zu bestimmen, benützten hauptsächlich den reicheren und bunteren ersten Theil. Man ging mehr von den Evangelien aus auf die Apostelgeschichte, und dachte sich die paulinische Geschichte als nacktes Referat eines Augenzeugen, aus dem nicht viel abzunehmen wäre. Aber schon die Verlegenheit, in welche man dabei mit den paulinischen Briefen kommt, sollte eine andere Ansicht aufdringen. Wirklich haben auch die neueren Gelehrten, welche hauptsächlich von dem paulinischen Briefen aus auf die Apostelgeschichte geriethen, Schrader und Baur, dem zweiten Theile grössere kritische Aufmerksamkeit gewidmet (49—50).

[*10*] Schneckenburger agrees with Schrader and Baur that one of the most striking features of Acts is the parallelism between the activity of Peter and Paul — especially in connection with healings (52—55). "Es bleibt nämlich ... kein Grad gesteigerter Wunderwirkung, der von Petrus erzählt wird, ohne entsprechende Analogie von Paulus" (52). For example, Paul's healing of the cripple at Lystra (14. 8—10) has its counterpart in Peter's healing of the cripple at the Beautiful Gate of the Temple (3.1—10). It is noteworthy that the same descriptive phrase is used of each: χωλὸς ἐκ κοιλίας μητρὸς αὐτοῦ (3.2; 14.8), emphasizing the seriousness of his condition; and the reality of the miracle is attested by the sudden and complete cure: immediately the cripple springs up and walks (3.8, 14.10). Peter's healing of a paralytic by the name of Aeneas at Lydda (9.32—34) has as its parallel the healing of the father of Publius, who was sick with fever, by Paul at Malta (28.8). The miraculous effect of Peter's shadow on the sick (5.15) corresponds to the extraordinary miracles effected through the handkerchiefs and aprons which had had contact with Paul's body (19.12). Peter's victory over Simon the magician at Samaria (8.18—24) is more than matched by Paul's power over Elymas at Paphos (13.6—12), the spirit of divination at Philippi (16.16—18), and the sons of Sceva at Ephesus (19.13—20). The miraculous punishment of Ananias and his wife through the word of Peter (5.1—11) is paralleled by the infliction of blindness upon Elymas through the word of Paul (13.6 —12). Both Peter and Paul are credited with a resurrection from the dead (i. e., Tabitha in 9.36—41 and Eutychus in 20.9—12). The reverential fear shown by the crowd toward Peter so that they were afraid to come near to him (5.13 *sic*!), and the attempt of Cornelius to worship him (10.25) are matched by Paul's impression on the people of Malta, who said he was a god (28.6) and the attempt of the people of Lystra to sacrifice to Paul and Silas (14.11—13)[35].

---

[35] Compare Peter's protest in 10.26 (καὶ ἐγὼ αὐτὸς ἄνθρωπός εἰμι) with that of Paul and Silas in 14.15 (καὶ ἡμεῖς ὅμοι παθεῖς ἐσμεν ὑμῖν ἄνθρωποι).

Another striking feature of Acts is the portrayal of Paul as one who fulfilled the requirements of the Law in all his actions, rather than one who had turned away from the Law (63—71). Thus Paul makes a vow, at the suggestion of James, to demonstrate to the believing Jews who were ζηλωταὶ τοῦ νόμου that the report they had heard concerning him — ὅτι ἀποστοσίαν διδάσκεις ἀπὸ Μωϋσέως τοὺς κατὰ τὰ ἔθνη πάντας Ἰουδαίους, λέγων μὴ περιτέμνειν αὐτοὺς τὰ τέκνα μηδὲ τοῖς ἔθεσιν περιπατεῖν — was not true (21.20—26). Thus also the author mentioned Paul's friendship with Aquila, a Jew, with whom he lived as a houseguest for a year and a half (18.2—3,11). Similarly, when the Jews of Ephesus ask Paul to stay with them longer, he declines, saying, δεῖ με πάντως τὴν ἑορτὴν τὴν ἐρχομένην ποιῆσαι εἰς Ἱεροσόλυμα³⁶ (18.20—21).

In similar fashion the author portrays Paul as showing due respect to the earliest Jerusalem apostles, who are in basic agreement with him regarding the Gospel and his mission to Gentiles as well as Jews, and to the Jewish people (71—92). Here one thinks of the so-called Apostolic Council and Decree of chapter 15³⁷, Paul's close connection with Jerusalem from the days of his earliest missionary activity (9.28, 22.17—21, 26.20), his constant practice of preaching the Gospel first to the Jews and only after their rejection of the message turning to the Gentiles, and his discussion with the Jewish elders in Rome, with which the book ends (28.17—28).

Schneckenburger makes the further observation that the speeches attributed to Paul contain little that is specifically Pauline in doctrine (127—51). He regards them as intended by the author as a sample of Paul's preaching, rather than actual reports of what was said on particular occasions. But the significant fact about the speeches of Acts is the similarity of doctrine between those of the first part of Acts with the second. For example, Paul's sermon before the synagogue in Pisidian Antioch has the following features in common with the speeches of the earlier part. It begins with an exaltation of the ancestors of the Jews (13.17—22 cf. 7.2 ff.) and contains a reference to the Messiah as David's Son and the testi-

---

³⁶ This statement is found only in the so-called "Western" and "Byzantine" texts.

³⁷ Note Schneckenburger's important comment concerning the nature of the "decree": "Das Dekret war für die Heiden-Christen der Freibrief gegen die Zumuthungen der Judaisirenden, nicht eine neue Auflage auf sie; denn gewiss hatten sie sich bisher in der Regel mehr als bloss in jenen vier Punkten nach den Juden bequemt, und auch nach paulinischen Grundsätzen mussten sie sich nach den schwachen Gewissen richten" (73). As evidence for the last statement he points to Rom. 14.13 and 1 Cor. 10.3 ff. Cf. his "Beiträge" (see below, n.39), pp. 554, 557.

[11]

mony of John (13.23—26 cf. 3.13 ff.). The unknowing rejection of the Messiah by the Jewish leaders in Jerusalem was in fulfillment of the divine plan (13.27 ff. cf. 3.14 ff.). Those who lived with him are the witnesses to his resurrection (13.31 ff. cf. 1.22). The speech contains an Old Testament proof followed by the argument that what is said cannot refer simply to David (13.34—38 cf. 2.25—32). Then too, Schneckenburger observes, there is a similar emphasis in the speeches of both parts on the resurrection of Christ, rather than on the death *and* resurrection, which we find in the letters of Paul.

However, it is the apologetic speeches which occupy such a large portion of the last part of the Book of Acts, which bring the purpose of the author most clearly to the fore. In his speeches before the Jewish mob (22.1—21), the Sanhedrin (23.1, 6), Felix (24.10 —21), and Agrippa (26.1—23), Paul's concern is to defend himself against the charges of having transgressed the Law and having forsaken the customs of his people. His claim is that he has lived as a faithful Jew up to the present. He argues that belief in Jesus as the Messiah and the proclamation of the message of salvation to Gentiles as well as Jews is the fulfillment, rather than a betrayal, of Jewish hopes and piety. The reason the author of Acts allows such a great proportion of his space for these speeches is that his main concern is to demonstrate this fact[38].

Schneckenburger's careful examination of the Book of Acts, approaching it from the point of view of chapters 13—28, leads him to the conclusion that the author, a Paulinist who was an eyewitness to a large part of the events of the last part of the book (whom he regards to be Luke), does not pursue a purely historical purpose, but seeks rather to place the Apostle in the light in which he can appear to be unoffensive to Jewish Christians and certified for them as a true apostle of Christ (152). This in turn is tested and confirmed by a consideration of chapters 1—12 (152—218).

But, one may ask, is this apologetic picture of Paul an accurate one? Is it true to the facts as they were, or does it represent the facts as the author wished, or thought, they were? Is the Paul of Acts a fictitious creation of the author — as Baur and Schrader had supposed — or is it an essentially historically accurate representation of the true Paul?

Schneckenburger argues forcefully that although Acts is one-sided and definitely "tendential", it presents a basically trustworthy pic-

---

[38] A similar reason is given for the triple account of Paul's conversion and commission (62, 168—70).

ture of the Apostle and the early Christian Church[39]. Acts is indeed a *Tendenzschrift*, but not a *Tendenzroman*.

What about the supposed conflict between the Paul of the epistles and the Paul of the Acts? Schneckenburger argues that the difference between the backgrounds of the two led Paul and Luke to emphasize different aspects of Paul's life and work (92). Paul worked out his arguments in his epistles — especially in Galatians — in debate with Judaizers, who argued that it is necessary for Gentiles to keep the Law of Moses in order to be saved. Therefore, he lays great stress on the freedom of the believer from the Law and the right of Gentiles to be admitted to the Church apart from the observance of the Mosaic Law. And, quite naturally, he does not stress his customary practice of Jewish ceremonies. On the other hand, the author of the Book of Acts developed his argument in order to allay the fears of Jewish Christians (not *Judaizers*!) whose consciences were troubled by the report that Paul had taught Jewish Christians to forsake the customs of their ancestors. Therefore, he emphasizes that Paul carried on his missionary work as a devout Jew, always offering the message of salvation to the Jews (many of whom accepted it) and only turning to the Gentiles when the Jews had rejected the message.

Schneckenburger argues further that Baur and Schrader had overlooked another significant fact. Although the accounts given in the epistles and Acts are both lop-sided and neither is intended to give a straight-forward history of events, one can find traces in the epistles that the Lucan picture is an accurate one. The accounts are complementary, rather than contradictory (76).

As far as Paul's observance of Jewish customs is concerned, Schneckenburger argues that there is not one word in the letters of Paul against the practice of the Law *by Jews* (64, 84, *passim*). It is against the Law as the basis for salvation that he argues, not as an act of piety. Paul makes it crystal clear in Romans 14.5—6 that ceremonial practices in and of themselves are not wrong, as long as they stem from a sense of devotion to the Lord and are not thought of as a means of salvation; but they are not essential. Paul was concerned that the Law should not be urged on believing Gentiles, and with this Acts agrees (71—76).

But what about Paul's constant habit, according to Acts, of

---

[39] He does not have a special section in which he discusses this point, but rather argues this throughout the book. See, however, his criticism of the view of Baur and Schrader (220—26). His "Beiträge zur Erklärung und Kritik der Apostelgeschichte", edited by R. Reutschi, *TSK* 28 (1855), pp. 498—570, argue for this view in greater detail.

preaching first to the Jews and then to the Gentiles? Does this not contradict his conception of his own ministry as being strictly to the Gentiles (Gal. 1.16; 2.2, 7–9)? Schneckenburger answers that there is no basis for saying that Paul considered his ministry to be *limited* to the Gentiles (83–86, 222–24). Paul speaks of the Gospel as God's power unto salvation, Ἰουδαίῳ τε πρῶτον καὶ Ἕλληνι (Rom. 1.16); and speaks of his constant and deep concern for the salvation of his kinsmen according to the flesh (Rom. 9.1–3, 10.1). Paul indeed stresses his practice of identification with both Jew and Gentile in order to win them to Christ (1 Cor. 9.19–23) — a practice which is eloquently attested by Acts (222). Schneckenburger was one of the first to point out the close similarity between the argument of Romans 9–11 and the practice of Paul in Acts (85)[40]. And certainly Paul's practice of using the Jewish synagogue as a base for his evangelistic work would have been a sensible missionary strategy, for here he would have a natural opening into the Gentile world through the Gentiles who were already present in the synagogue.

Is Acts correct, then, in picturing Paul as in basic agreement with, and in some sense dependent on, the earliest apostles? Does this not contradict his claim in Galatians that he received his message and commission directly from the Lord himself, and not from men (especially Gal. 1.12, 16–17)? And what about the conflict between Paul and the Jerusalem apostles which Baur had observed?

In the opinion of Schneckenburger the supposed conflict between Paul and the primitive apostles concerning basic doctrine is a figment of imagination. Even though the famous passage in Galatians 2 implies conflict between Peter and Paul at Antioch, the implication of Paul's account is that there was basic agreement between the two and that this was merely disturbed by the Judaizers who came from Jerusalem (108–12, 226). Paul clearly views this as a transgression by Peter of principles which he himself already recognized as valid. Further, Paul states in Galatians that he and the Jerusalem apostles were in full agreement concerning the Gospel and concerning his mission to the Gentiles (2.7–9); and Paul never so much as hints that Peter, James, and John are worthy of the *anathema* he wishes on those who are guilty of preaching a different Gospel. Moreover, in 1 Corinthians 15.1–10 Paul makes himself subject, both in experience of the Risen Lord and in apostleship, to the earlier apostles (249). And the collection which he was organizing in the churches of his missionary labors, upon which he lays

---

[40] Baur had observed the parallel between the two but had failed to grasp the significance.

great stress in his letters, emphasizes his basic unity with the Jerusalem church (248). According to those letters which are recognized as genuinely Pauline[41], as well as Acts, Paul and the *Urapostel* are in basic agreement[42].

What is the reason, then, for the gaps in Luke's narrative? Why, for instance, should a companion of Paul seek to minimize his sufferings? We know from 1 and 2 Corinthians that Paul suffered greatly in connection with his missionary travels. What is the reason for Luke's omission of most of these experiences? Schneckenburger replies that it is once again necessary to consider the author's main purpose. His concern is to present an impressive picture of the Apostle, and he did not consider these experiences relevant to his main purpose (58—61). Omissions are not, however, the same as falsifications.

In addition to defending the basic trustworthiness of Luke's portrayal of earliest Christianity, Schneckenburger argues for a date subsequent to the death of Paul, but prior to the destruction of Jerusalem[43]. He finds no hint of the destruction of the city or the temple in Acts — or in Luke, for that matter. This silence would be quite unlikely if the city had indeed been destroyed before the time of writing (231—35). Contrary to Schrader, Schneckenburger finds no evidence of the presence of a highly developed Christology belonging to the post-apostolic age (235—41). He concurs with Baur's view that Acts was directed toward the Roman church, and in particular toward the Jewish members of that church (241—51), although he has quite a different understanding of the historical situation from Baur.

Baur published a review hailing the significance of Schneckenburger's work almost as soon as it appeared[44]. He expressed enthusiasm and agreement concerning Schneckenburger's main thesis with regard to the apologetic purpose of Acts, but he expressed doubt whether this view was reconcilable with an acceptance of the book as a historically trustworthy account of early Christianity. Much of the material of this review was incorporated into the introductory chapter to his famous work on Paul, which was published four years later[45]. Baur refused to budge from his original opinion.

---

[41] Schneckenburger uses only the four epistles accepted by Baur as genuine (1 and 2 Cor., Rom., Gal.) and (sometimes) Philippians.

[42] Cf. his "Beiträge", p. 558.

[43] Following H. A. W. Meyer, Schneckenburger interprets Acts 8.26, probably wrongly, as requiring a post-A. D. 66 date. Cf. note in *BC* 4, p. 95.

[44] *Jahrbücher für wissenschaftliche Kritik* 15 (1841), cols. 369—75.

[45] *Paulus, der Apostel Jesu Christi* (Stuttgart, 1845), pp. 1—14. The book is divided into three parts: (1) the life and work of Paul (pp. 15—243), (2) the letters

The Book of Acts, according to Baur, stands in the same basic relationship to the epistles of Paul as the Gospel of John stands in relation to the synoptics. As a comparison of the Synoptics with John leads one to the conclusion that the differences are so great that historical truth can be found only on one side, so it is with the two sources available for a study of the life and teachings of Paul. In such a comparison Baur regards it to be an indisputable canon of historical criticism that "diejenige Darstellung den größern Anspruch auf geschichtliche Wahrheit zu machen hat, die als die unbefangenere erscheint, und nirgends das Interesse verräth, ihren geschichtlichen Stoff einem besondern subjectiven Zwecke unterzuordnen" (5). Since Acts is judged to be "keine objective, sondern nur eine durch ein subjectives Interesse alterirte Darstellung", it is of little value as a true, historical account (5). The Paul of the Acts and the Paul of the epistles are irreconcilable. Acts is dated by Baur as "tief in das zweite Jahrhundert" (12).

[12]

One of the factors which made Baur's work so significant was the presence of a number of gifted disciples who stood by his side from the beginning. He himself merely outlined what came to be known as "the Tübingen view concerning the Book of Acts". He was the creative genius of a school of thought which came to be identified with him. In the course of his many writings he did little of what is properly regarded as exegesis; he merely dropped suggestive hints which pointed the way toward a systematic view of the early Christian writings. It was left to his disciples to develop these suggestions into a consistent whole by studying the New Testament and the early Christian writings in the light of the guiding principles the master had laid down. This work of systematizing was done primarily by Albert Schwegler and Eduard Zeller.

Albert Schwegler[46] (1819—57), at that time *Privatdozent* for philosophy and philology at Tübingen, published in 1846 a two-volumed work in which he interpreted the whole of the early Christian literature in terms of Baur's dialectical conception of primitive Christianity[47]. Schwegler's work became the classic exposition of the "Tübingen" position.

Schwegler's work is given not so much to careful exegesis as it is to a thorough and comprehensive application of Baur's views to

---

of Paul (pp. 245—504), and (3) the theology of Paul (pp. 505—670). Only part one is concerned with the Book of Acts.

[46] On Schwegler, cf. "Albert Schwegler, Historiker und Philosoph", *Schwäbische Lebensbilder* 4 (1948), pp. 312—40, with bibliography.

[47] *Das nachapostolische Zeitalter in den Hauptmomenten seiner Entwicklung*, 2 vols. (Tübingen, 1846).

the literature of the first three Christian centuries. His work is brilliant both in its conception and in its execution of its task. Whatever one may think of the conclusions of the author, one cannot help but be impressed with the magnificent way in which he sets out his case.

Schwegler assigns every work of the first three centuries which is within the scope of his discussion to a definite stage in the evolution of early Christianity. The majority of the writings are identified with the development of either Jewish or Gentile Christianity in Rome. No distinction is made between canonical and non-canonical literature; both are treated together.

Schwegler gives his method away by *first* outlining his conclusions concerning the nature of early Christianity (I, 89—196) *and then* proceeding to discuss the literature in terms of the historical setting which he has thus outlined. His title is also significant. The whole of the New Testament is included in the "post-apostolic age" and is regarded as a witness primarily to this age, rather than to the apostolic. Only five New Testament writings are considered to be true witnesses to the apostolic period; the four major letters of Paul (Romans, Galatians, 1 and 2 Corinthians) and the Apocalypse (I, 90). As far as the Book of Acts is concerned, while at first glance it appears to be a historical work concerned with the apostolic period, it "erweist sich bei näherer Untersuchung als eine Tendenzschrift von so freier Composition und von so geringer geschichtlicher Verläßlichkeit, daß wir sie vorerst ganz bei Seite lassen müssen" (I, 90).

[13]

Earliest Christianity *(das Urchristentum)*, according to the view of Schwegler, was simply a sect within Judaism, differing from orthodox Judaism only in the belief that Jesus was the (Jewish) Messiah (I, 99—104). The later Ebionite Christianity, which was condemned by the then dominant Gentile Christianity as a heresy, was really the legitimate continuation of the views of the earliest Christians (I, 104—07). It was Paul who stepped in and changed Christianity into an independent and universal religion; without him it would have remained a Jewish sect and, as such, it would have died out with the passage of time or, possibly, it might have become eventually the dominant view within Judaism (I, 147—48). The activity and teaching of Paul destroyed all chances of the latter course of development taking place.

Baur's understanding of apostolic Christianity in terms of the constant antagonism between the Jewish and Gentile parties — Peter and the *Urapostel* and their followers on one side *versus* Paul and his converts on the other — became the motif of Schwegler's interpretation. Following Baur, he identifies the opponents of Paul who are mentioned in the Galatian epistle as actual emissaries of the primitive apostles and true representatives of the original point of view (I, 156—61; II, 247—49). So also Paul's opponents in the Corinthian epistles only wanted to know Christ κατὰ σάρκα (2. Cor. 5.16), that is, in the Jewish sense; and they boasted κατὰ σάρκα (2. Cor. 11.18), that is, in their Jewish descent and in their connection with the original apostles and the primitive Palestinian churches (I, 161). Again following Baur, Schwegler interprets the Epistle to the Romans as Paul's defense of his Gospel over against the views of the Jewish Christians in Rome, who represented the earlier point of view (I, 166—69).

The largest part of Schwegler's work is devoted to a reconstruction of the history of the church in Rome (I, 285—522; II, 1—244). This too is understood entirely in terms of the supposed conflict between Jewish and Gentile Christianity, between those who claimed Peter as their authority and those who claimed Paul. The Book of Acts is classified — along with the Gospel of Luke, 1 Clement, Romans 15—16, and Philippians — as a Pauline-conciliatory writing, representing the second stage of the development of Pauline Christianity in Rome. The first stage, represented by 1 Peter and the *Kerygma Petrou*, was marked by a denial of the true nature of Petrine Christianity and the attempt to put Pauline doctrine into the mouth of Peter (II, 1—37). The conciliatory writings aimed at a compromise between the two warring factions in which each party gave up a little (II, 37—135). Thus in Acts Paul is made to appear quite Jewish, and Peter speaks like a Paulinist. The result is a combination of two opposing views. The final stage in the developing process is the dogmatization of the compromise position and the development of the sacramental view of the group Schwegler calls "the Pauline-catholicizing writings", i. e. the Pastorals, the Epistle of Polycarp, and the Letters of Ignatius (II, 136—79).

Very little new is added by Schwegler concerning the Book of Acts. The thesis which Baur had set forth in his article on the episcopacy[48] is simply expanded by combining it with the evidence brought forth by Schneckenburger, particularly the alleged parallelism between Peter and Paul (II, 74—81)[49]. Contrary to Schneckenburger, he argues that this parallelism is not to be ascribed to the author's careful selection of material from existing records and

[14] traditions, but to "dem unhistorischen, willkührlichen, und selbst

---

[48] *Supra*, pp. 30—31. Schwegler begins his discussion of Acts with a quotation (without quotation marks!) from Baur's article (II, 73).

[49] *Supra*, pp. 34—35.

Fictionen nicht scheuenden Verfahren des Verfassers der Apostelgeschichte selbst" (II, 77). His harsh judgment of Acts is suggestive
of the works of Bruno Bauer and the Radical Dutch School which
were to follow.

Wir haben in der Apostelgeschichte weder den historischen Paulus, noch [15]
die historischen Urapostel, namentlich nicht den historischen Petrus vor
uns ... Die Apostelgeschichte ist ... in Form einer Geschichte, denn wenn
allerdings ältere Quellen und Berichte jedenfalls im ersten, und wohl auch
im zweiten Theil zu Grund liegen, so bleibt nichts desto weniger ausser-
ordentlich wenig historisch Haltbares übrig, wenn alles Unwahrscheinliche,
Unmögliche, erweislich Unhistorische oder mit Unhistorischem Zusammen-
hängende, wenn namentlich die frei componirten Reden und die zahlreichen Wiederholungen in Abzug gebracht werden. Gegen die durch-
gehende geschichtliche Glaubwürdigkeit der Apostelgeschichte sprechen
schon ihre zahlreichen tendenzmässigen Auslassungen und Verschweigun-
gen. Wer aber wichtige Vorgänge und Thatsachen absichtlich verschweigt,
um die Gegenstände seiner Darstellung in ein anderes Licht zu rücken,
wer aus einem Charakterbild absichtlich charakteristische Züge weglässt, um
ihm ein anderes Aussehen zu geben, wird auch nicht mehr für zu aufrichtig
und gewissenhaft gehalten werden können, um, so bald es in seinem Interesse liegt, sich auch positive Entstellungen der Geschichte, unhistorische
Erdichtungen zu erlauben. Mit Sicherheit kann nun über unsern Verfasser
jedenfalls so viel gesagt werden, dass er in der Benützung, Gestaltung und
Umbildung des ihm von der Überlieferung gebotenen Materials höchst
willkürlich und durchgreifend zu Werke gegangen ist ... (II, 112—14)

Taken as a whole then Acts is of value only as a historical document for the time, circumstances, and situation to which it owed its
origin (II, 115). In Schwegler's view, the time into which Acts fits
best is the second or third decade of the second century, the time
when the decisive rule of Jewish Christianity in the church was first
beginning to be challenged by the growing strength of the Gentile
party (II, 115—23).

If Schwegler's work may be considered to be the classic exposition of the Tübingen theory as applied to the early Christian literature in general, the work of Eduard Zeller[50] (1814—1908) may be
taken as the classic presentation of the theory as applied to the
Book of Acts in particular. Neither Baur nor Schwegler had applied
himself to a careful analysis of the Acts as a whole. Each had been
satisfied with an application of *Tendenzkritik* to select portions of

---

[50] On Zeller, cf. W. Dilthey, "Aus Eduard Zellers Jugendjahren", in his
Gesammelte Schriften 4 (Leipzig and Berlin, 1921), pp. 433—50. Mattill, *Luke
as a Historian*, pp. 49 ff., gives a detailed description of many of Zeller's most
important views.

Acts, underlining the evidence which proved congenial to his theory of the origin of Acts. Up to the time of Zeller, Schneckenburger was the only representative of *Tendenzkritik* who had provided a full-blown discussion of the whole of Acts, and he had arrived at conclusions quite different from those of the others. Eduard Zeller, who had been a student of Baur and was now his son-in-law, stepped in to fill this gap.

Zeller wrote a series of essays on Acts for the *Theologische Jahrbücher* between 1848 and 1851[51]. These were substantially reworked for publication in book form and appeared in 1854[52]. If the traditionalists were troubled by some of Baur's views concerning Acts, they must have been thoroughly shaken by Zeller. Whereas Baur was content to state his views in the form of suggestions here and there throughout his many writings, Zeller carried out his suggestions by means of an almost exhaustive examination of the details of the narrative of Acts in what is the only really thorough study of Acts ever produced by the Tübingen School[53].

The work of Zeller on Acts invites comparison to the work of David Friedrich Strauss on the Gospels. Indeed, it is significant that Zeller makes frequent reference to Strauss's *Leben Jesu*. As Strauss had interpreted the Gospels "mythically", so Zeller takes the same basic point of view with regard to Acts. In fact, he underlines his assumption that the impossibility of the miraculous is an axiom of historical criticism[54]. And since miracles abound on nearly every page of the Book of Acts, this is a primary reason to question the historicity of the entire framework in which these myths and legends are embedded.

Theoretically, Zeller admits that a book should not be judged as wholly untrustworthy merely because an apologetic aim is discerned. The real criterion of judgment must be a careful examination of the content of the book itself in the attempt to ascertain whether a special purpose can be observed, and whether this purpose has

---

[51] "Die älteste Ueberlieferung über die Schriften des Lukas", *ThJ* 7 (1848), pp. 528–73; "Die Apostelgeschichte und ihr Charakter. Mit Rücksicht auf die neuern Bearbeitungen dieses Gegenstands", *ThJ* 8 (1849), pp. 1–84, 371–454, 535–94; 9 (1850), pp. 303–85; 10 (1851), pp. 95–124, 253–90, 329–88, 433–469.

[52] *Die Apostelgeschichte nach ihrem Inhalt und Ursprung kritisch Untersucht* (Stuttgart, 1854). The references which follow are to this book.

[53] This excludes the work of Schneckenburger, who, although he gave Baur and his disciples ammunition with which to defend their views, is too independent to be classified under the same heading.

[54] Cf. his remarks on p. 86, n. 1. He repeats this same basic assertion many times over in the course of his study.

indeed appreciably affected its historical value. This minute examination of the content of Acts is the task Zeller sets before himself.

The results of Zeller's examination are almost wholly negative, at least insofar as the historical value of Acts is concerned. He finds the entire narrative of the book so full of contradictions, impossibilities, and distortions that scarcely a kernal of historical truth remains. For example, the first really historical material which is found in the first seven chapters of Acts is in regard to Stephen, and even here it is in a rather confused form (146—53)[55]. The earlier part of Acts consists entirely of legends, myths, and fictitious creations of the author; these are rejected not only because the miraculous belongs so much to the warp and woof of the narrative, but also because it is so full of inner contradictions as to be incredible (76—145)[56]. That Philip may have been a historical personage, and that a proselyte from Ethiopia and another proselyte *(sic)* named Cornelius may have been baptized in the early days of the Church Zeller admits; but outside of the bare historical fact of their existence, the author seems to have gotten everything else completely muddled (153—56, 174—76, 179—84). The story of Simon Magus is a reading back of later legends into the earlier history of the Church and does not rest on even a shred of historical substance (158—74).

The second part of Acts, dealing with the activity of Paul, fares no better at the hands of Zeller. The accounts concerning the conversion of Paul are totally unhistorical (191—201). They are judged so for three reasons: (1) the story is clearly miraculous; (2) the three accounts reported in Acts are full of contradictions, both within themselves and between one another ; (3) certain elements in the report — e. g., the light, the blindness, falling to the ground, etc. — are clearly symbolic and reveal the theological purpose of the author. The author's narrative concerning the activity of Paul following his conversion is also completely unreliable (201—209). Here Zeller pushes the brief autobiographical remarks of Paul in Galatians 1 and 2 for all they are worth[57]. The Book of Acts states that Paul remained

---

[55] Luke's disregard for the facts is typified by his designation of Stephen's accusers as "false witnesses" (6.13); actually, the words he puts into their mouths are probably true and point to the real reason behind Stephen's judgment!

[56] Zeller is never very complimentary concerning the author's intellectual ability. He does not seem to realize that it would take a man of considerable acumen to create a work of the unity of Acts with the aid of few, if any, previously existing materials and to carry out his purpose with the single-mindedness which the Tübingen view demands.

[57] If Paul were to have included all the information required by Zeller's

for a time (ἡμέρας τινάς) in Damascus after his conversion (Acts 9.19–22); in Galatians, Paul says he went immediately (εὐθέως) after his conversion to Arabia (Gal. 1.16–17). Acts leaves no room for three years in Arabia, but rather portrays Paul as going directly to Jerusalem a short time after his conversion. Further, in his account in Galatians, Paul is insistent upon his independence of the Jerusalem apostles; the narrative of Acts seems to be the creation of the author to emphasize the exact opposite. Again, according to Galatians, Paul went up to Jerusalem, after three years, for the express purpose of seeing Peter; besides Peter, he saw none of the other apostles, with the exception of James, the brother of the Lord (Gal. 1.18–19). Acts clearly contradicts this by having Barnabas introduce him to the apostles as a group (πρὸς τοὺς ἀποστόλους), with whom he spent some time (Acts 9.27).

In the same manner Zeller finds the account of the beginnings of Gentile Christianity in Antioch unhistorical (209–12), as well as the narrative of Paul's first missionary journey (212–16). In connection with the latter, he views the story of Paul and Elymas as modeled after the story of Peter's encounter with Simon Magus — which is also unhistorical (!), and the healing of the lame man by Peter at the Beautiful Gate is the prototype for the later healing of the lame man at Lystra by Paul. There may be a kernal of historical truth in the account of Paul's stoning (Acts 14.19), since Paul elsewhere mentions having been stoned (2 Cor. 11.25); whether or not this took place at Lystra remains most questionable.

Zeller identifies the visit of Paul to Jerusalem in connection with the so-called Jerusalem Council of Acts 15 with the visit recalled by Paul in Galatians 2.1–10[58]. Outside of the bare fact of the visit, the account in Acts is viewed as the free composition of the author and as being in total disagreement with Paul's own account.

[16]   Die officielle Sendung des Paulus durch die antiochenische Gemeinde, die Stellung, welche er in der Apostelgeschichte zu den Uraposteln einnimmt, die Berathung seiner Angelegenheit in förmlicher Gemeindeversammlung, die Reden, welche bei diesem Anlass dem Petrus und Jakobus, dem Paulus und Barnabas in den Mund gelegt werden, die Beschlüsse der Versammlung und ihre Verkündigung durch ein apostolisches Sendschreiben, das Verfahren, welches demgemäss Paulus in der Sache des Timotheus befolgt haben soll, alle diese Züge konnten wir nur für ungeschichtlich erklären (248).

---

comparison of Galatians 1 and 2 with Acts, he would have to have written an epistle at least as long as Romans!

[58] The earlier visit of Acts 11 is regarded by Zeller as totally unhistorical.

Very little historical reality is left to the "second"[59] missionary journey of Paul when Zeller has finished his examination of the narrative. Certainly the author is correct when he places a journey of Paul through the regions of Phrygia and Galatia at this time; however, the author's inadequacy is illustrated by the way in which he passes over this most important aspect of Paul's missionary endeavor with a brief phrase — διελθόντες τὴν Φρυγίαν καὶ Γαλατικὴν χώραν (16.6) (250). The account of Paul and Silas's activity in Philippi contains "eine Kette von Unwahrscheinlichkeiten" (258) [17] and was probably invented by the author on the basis of his knowledge of 1 Thessalonians 2.2[60]. There is no real basis for judging the account of the visit of Paul to Thessalonica and Berea, except that the accusation of the Thessalonian Jews in Acts 17.6 (οἱ τὴν οἰκουμένην ἀναστατώσαντες οὗτοι καὶ ἐνθάδε πάρεισιν) bears the color of a later age (258—59). The story of Paul's visit to Athens may rest on a legend about a member of the Areopagus having been converted by Paul (i. e., Dionysius), as Baur had suggested, or upon some actual historical event; but the story in the main, and, most obviously, the sermon of Paul, seems to be the creation of the author (259—63). And so it is with the other parts of the narrative. There may be a historical fact lying behind this or that particular event, but it lies far in the background; the narrative itself is the author's conscious creation.

Zeller argues that the author of Acts suppressed the real reason for Paul's final visit to Jerusalem (i. e., the collection from the Gentile churches) and substituted in its place a new one (i. e., his desire to celebrate Pentecost in Jerusalem) which suits his special purposes (266—68). The story of Eutychus at Troas is, of course, unhistorical because of its miraculous character (269). The sermon of Paul to the Ephesian elders on the beach at Miletus is, as are all the speeches of Acts, put into the mouth of Paul by the author; neither the speech, nor the occasion, has any basis in historical reality (269—74).

Participation in a Jewish vow in the way the twenty-first chapter of Acts portrays it — in order to demonstrate to the strict Jews that he had not forsaken the Law — would have been unthinkable for Paul; this would have been a denial of everything he had stood for in his ministry. This event too is another invention of the author,

---

[59] Zeller combines what are usually called the "second" and the "third" missionary journeys into one.

[60] Baur had argued the other way around, i. e., that 1 Thess. 2.2 was created on the basis of the account in Acts (*Paulus*, p. 483). This is one of the few items upon which the master and the disciple seem to have disagreed.

with no foundation whatever in history, to serve the purpose of emphasizing Paul's position in relation to the Jewish Law and the early Jerusalem church (275–79). Paul may have been arrested while he was visiting the temple; but, if so, he was visiting it for some other purpose (280). Paul's speech before the Jewish mob in 21.27–22.29, most of the events concerned with Paul's appearance before the Sanhedrin, and the majority of the events attributed to the time of Paul's imprisonment in Caesarea are all free compositions of the author.

The narrative of Paul's trip to Rome belongs unquestionably to the oldest component parts which make up the Book of Acts, but even here there are unhistorical details — most especially the miraculous features. The final event of the book — the arrival of Paul in Rome and his conversations with the Jewish elders — is also an invention of the author in keeping with his steadfast purpose.

Well, we may ask, what is this all-pervading purpose which has led the author to deal so dishonestly with his materials and to present such an unhistorical picture of Paul and the primitive Christian Church? The answer to this question Zeller reserves until a final section of his study (316–87), only touching upon it in his analysis of the text. One receives the impression, however, that this, rather than the more than three hundred pages which have preceded it, marks the real starting point of his consideration of Acts. At any rate, it is indeed the heart of his study.

Here, however, Zeller says little that is new. He simply points to the material put forward by Schneckenburger and adapted by Baur. He emphasizes that Schneckenburger was wrong, however, in supposing that the author had merely selected material from various trustworthy traditions; the author has, rather, created his own traditions and has presented a picture which does grave injustice to the historical facts (316–19). Thus the parallels which Schneckenburger observed between the activity and teaching of Peter and Paul, between primitive Christianity and Gentile Christianity, are the fictitious creations of the author (320–35). What is the purpose, then, behind the author's extreme falsification of the early [18] Christian history *wie es eigentlich gewesen ist*? Simply this: his aim is to justify the existence of a Gentile Christianity, apart from the Law, side by side with Jewish Christianity. In order to conciliate the Jewish party, he compromises the distinctiveness of Paulinism. In Zeller's own words:

[19] Um dieses durchzusetzen, versteht er sich zu allen jenen Zugeständnissen an den Judaismus, die wir bereits kennen, setzt er die Hauptstücke der paulinischen Lehre bei Seite, lässt den Judenchristen Gesetz und Beschnei-

dung, macht den Paulus selbst zum eifrigen Gesetzesdiener, lässt ihn sogar seine eigenthümlichste Thätigkeit, die Heidenmission, nur gezwungen, und nur unter dem Schutz des Petrus, mit der Erlaubniss der Jerusalemiten, eintreten. Das also ist der Hauptzweck des Verfassers, seine Leser von dem Recht des Heidenchristenthums zu überzeugen, und dies setzt hinwiederum voraus, dass diese Leser jenes Recht bestritten, d. h. dass sie einem judaistischen Partikularismus huldigten. Unser Buch erscheint daher nach dieser Seite hin als ein Versuch, die Anerkennung des Heidenchristenthums in seiner Selbständigkeit und seiner Freiheit vom Gesetz durch Zugeständnisse an die judaistische Parthei zu erreichen (357).

And again:

Unsere Schrift ist der Friedensvorschlag eines Pauliners, welcher die Anerkennung des Heidenchristenthums von Seite der Judenchristen durch Zugeständnisse an den Judaismus erkaufen und in diesem Sinn auf beide Partheien wirken will (363). [20]

Once again following Schneckenburger and Baur, Zeller views the Book of Acts as being directed toward the Jewish Christians in Rome (364—75). In this connection he makes an advance beyond the view of his predecessors by adding a secondary purpose of Acts[61]. The author has an underlying political apologetic, an attempt to demonstrate that Christianity is not a politically dangerous movement, but rather a religious movement within Judaism (365 — 369). At Philippi, for example, the accusation against Paul and Silas is this: οὗτοι οἱ ἄνθρωποι ἐκταράσσουσιν ἡμῶν τὴν πόλιν, Ἰουδαῖοι ὑπάρχοντες, καὶ καταγγέλλουσιν ἔθη ἃ οὐκ ἔξεστιν ἡμῖν παραδέχεσθαι οὐδὲ ποιεῖν Ῥωμαίοις οὖσιν (Acts 16.20—21), that is, an accusation of proselytism, against the spread of a *religio illicita et peregrina*. Again, a similar accusation is repeated at Thessalonica: οἱ τὴν οἰκουμένην ἀναστατώσαντες οὗτοι καὶ ἐνθάδε πάρεισιν καὶ οὗτοι πάντες ἀπέναντι τῶν δογμάτων καίσαρος πράσσουσι, βασιλέα ἕτερον λέγοντες εἶναι Ἰησουν (17.6—7). The accusation against Paul is even clearer at Corinth: παρὰ τὸν νόμον ἀναπείθει οὗτος τοὺς ἀνθρώπους σέβεσθαι τὸν θεόν (18.13). Here Gallio returns the judgment that it is a matter of questions περὶ λόγου καὶ ὀνομάτων καὶ νόμου τοῦ καθ᾽ ὑμᾶς (18.15), i. e., a purely religious controversy within Judaism and of no special concern to the civil authorities. Similarly the town clerk answers the cry of the Ephesian mob to the effect that the Christians have been guilty of neither temple robbery nor blasphemy (19.37). When Paul is taken into Roman custody, his innocence is declared by all the Roman officials involved

---

[61] Schneckenburger (*Über den Zweck*, pp. 244 ff.) had made a few suggestive remarks along this line.

— by Lysias (23.29), by Felix (24.22 ff.), and by Festus (25.18—19) — in spite of the accusation of the Jews (24.5). Agrippa also testifies to the innocence of the Apostle (25.31—32). By showing how Paul was uniformly acquitted by Roman officials the author is attempting to urge these Jewish Christians in Rome, who were afraid of the consequences of a mission to the heathen, to expand their horizons so as to include Gentiles as such within the Church. The time of the composition of the work of the unknown Paulinist is, in Zeller's view, between A. D. 110—30, at a time when the government was becoming more and more hostile to Christianity (466—81); the place, Rome (481—88).

This is not the place for a detailed evaluation of the work of the Tübingen School of Criticism. As the history of the criticism of Acts develops, it will become increasingly evident where F. C. Baur and his disciples went astray. Their work was attacked in the years which immediately followed by both conservative (Chapter 3) and more radical critics (Chapter 4), many of the latter being ex-disciples of Baur. The views of Baur and his followers have never had much influence outside of Germany (cf. Chapter 6), and even there it was acknowledged by almost all critics within the next few decades that their reconstruction of the history of early Christianity and most of their critical conclusions were essentially mistaken[62]. However, a few observations may be made at this stage.

A positive contribution to arise from *Tendenzkritik* was the recognition of the importance of the question of the purpose of Acts. The Tübingen critics may not have been successful in providing a satisfactory answer to the question, but they certainly were correct in raising the question. And this has continued as one of the most important questions to be asked — one could almost say *the* most important question to be asked — in the subsequent history of Acts-criticism. And the Tübingen critics were certainly right in stressing the fact that the author's purpose was not merely to write a history of the Christian Church in its earliest years. This may be accepted as demonstrated, although the question as to whether his purpose is in some sense historical is another question.

A second positive contribution of *Tendenzkritik* stems from the recognition of Paul as the main character of the Book of Acts. Not only does the greater part of the work deal with the activity of Paul, but this activity is the true climax to the earlier chapters. He is the

---

[62] Yet, as it will become clear later, many of the basic assumptions of Baur have been accepted, perhaps unconsciously, in some circles of (primarily) German criticism and maintain a powerful influence on Acts-criticism up to the present.

true hero of the author. The Tübingen critics were wrong in their reconstruction of the historical setting of the book, but they were probably right in viewing it, at least in some sense, as a defense of Paul, or as a defense of the message which Paul preached — as many have argued convincingly in subsequent years.

The parallelism between the ministries of Peter and Paul in Acts, which was suggested by Baur and worked out in such careful detail by Schneckenburger may be accepted as a further contribution of this period of criticism. This may have been overdone. For example, the parallels are not exact parallels, and the material has to be re-arranged considerably to show the parallelism[63]. But the idea that the author intends a basic parallelism between the experiences of Peter and Paul seems certain, and the majority of commentators concur with this observation.

Finally, the work of the Tübingen scholars led to the study of the Book of Acts in a more intensive and careful manner than it had ever been studied before. Conservatives found the very founda-tion of their understanding of early Christianity being shaken and rushed to the study of Acts in an attempt to defend the fortress, or to ascertain whether there was in reality any basis in careful exegesis for the radical conclusions of the school of Baur. All serious stu-dents of the New Testament of the time had to come to grips with the issues raised by the Tübingen critics. Where the conclusions of Baur and his disciples were rejected as unwarrantable and inade-quate, better solutions to the problems had to be suggested in their

---

[63] Schneckenburger lists the following parallels: 3.1–10 = 14.8–10; 9.32–34 = 28.8; 5.15 = 19.22; 8.18–24 = 13.6–12, 16.16–18, and 19.13–20; 5.1–11 = 13.6–12; 9.36–41 = 20.9–12; 5.13 and 10.25 = 28.6 and 14.11–13. In order to arrive at these parallels one has to ignore the chronological arrangement of the narrative. Considering the individual units in the order in which the author has placed them in the narrative, the parallelism between the two parts of Acts, following Schneckenburger's suggestion, would be: A = b; B = a; C and H = h and c; D = f; E = a, d and e; F = i; G = g. The case for the parallelism would be stronger if the order were A = a; B = b; C = c; etc.

J. C. Fenton, "The Order of the Miracles performed by Peter and Paul in Acts", *ExpT* 77 (1965/66), pp. 381–83, following M. D. Goulder, *Type and History in Acts* (London, 1964), has suggested a pattern of three chiasmuses in the order in which the miracles of Peter and Paul are paralleled. However, the suggested structure is much too complicated to have been the conscious inten-tion of the author of Acts. In addition, Fenton's arrangement leaves important gaps (e. g., he does not include Peter's conflict with Simon Magus, which, although no miracle is mentioned, is more closely parallel to the Elymas story than to the story of Ananias and Sapphira), which he himself admits. To quote C. S. C. Williams: If Luke had wanted to make the 'parallels' more explicit, he could have done so" (quoted in Fenton).

place, and evidence brought forward in support of the alternative views. This interaction of scholars with the Tübingen hypotheses resulted in the Book of Acts becoming one of the focal points of New Testament research for at least four decades. Indeed, the situation is somewhat analogous to the renewed interest by scholars in Lucan studies which has arisen from the application of *Redaktionsgeschichte* to the study of Luke-Acts in more recent years[64].

The suggestion is often made that Baur is chiefly responsible for the development of a "historical" or "objective" approach to the Book of Acts. The present writer would take exception to that view. First, the work of historical criticism was well underway by the time Baur came on the scene[65]. And, second, it is doubtful whether Baur's study of Acts was any more "objective" or "historical" than the most tradition-bound conservative. True, he came up with ideas that were strikingly new and original; but once he passed on to a further study of the text of the New Testament writings he was never able to free himself from reading the text in the light of his early hypotheses. In spite of the evidence against his original opinions he steadfastly refused to alter them to any significant degree. Whereas the traditionalist read the Book of Acts through the glasses of the older opinions concerning the problems of introduction, Baur read Acts through the glasses of his new "discoveries" concerning the true nature of early Christianity. His main contribution, therefore, was not his method of approach, but rather his raising of important critical issues. Scholarly research has occupied itself with many of these issues ever since.

The most serious criticism to be laid at the feet of the Tübingen critics is that their reconstruction of the nature of early Christianity was itself totally unhistorical. The antithesis between Jewish and Gentile Christianity, between the primitive apostles and Paul, was a figment of the imagination which existed only in the thought of the Tübingen critics. In none of the New Testament sources — neither in the Pauline epistles, nor in the traditions embedded in the Gospels, nor in the Book of Acts — do we have any evidence for the existence of a Jewish Christianity which differed from Judaism only in the acceptance of Jesus as the (Jewish) Messiah. Nor is there any evidence for the existence of any essential difference between the

---

[64] Cf. Chapter 10.

[65] Only Baur's essay on the Christ-party in the Corinthian churches (1831) precedes the commentary by H. A. W. Meyer, *Kritisch exegetisches Handbuch über die Apostelgeschichte* (Göttingen, 1835), which probably deserves to be recognized as the first critical commentary on Acts. (The work of Meyer is discussed in Chapter 3).

earliest apostles and Paul regarding the heart of the Gospel message, or the scope of its concern. Indeed, one of the main points which Paul stresses in Galatians is that the *Urapostel* were in ful agreement with the scope of his own ministry (esp. 2.9). Paul clearly states that Peter too had been conducting himself in the same manner as Paul until he changed his practice, and the implication is that this was temporary, due to his fear of the circumcision party (2.12 —14). There are undoubted difficulties in harmonizing the first two chapters of Galatians with Acts, but one of the points upon which both are clearly agreed is in the recognition of a basic harmony of opinion between Paul and the Jerusalem apostles. This is certainly one of the main points which Paul seems to be trying to get across to his readers. Furthermore, there is not a hint of any hostility between Paul and the primitive apostles in any of Paul's letters. Passages like 1 Corinthians 15.3—11 give the exact opposite impression.

The work of Baur and his followers illustrates the difficulty facing New Testament scholars when they attempt to "imagine" the background of a particular New Testament document. In theory, it is a noble aim to seek to understand a document in terms of its *Sitz im Leben;* to determine its true setting is much more difficult. Baur was not the first, and certainly not the last, to make the attempt to determine what a New Testament writer had in mind when he wrote, and to reconstruct a historical situation, when there is little or no material with which to work. The danger of his method is illustrated by the story told by C. R. Gregory of Baur's discussion of a book by Bernard Weiss which appeared in 1855[66]. "The most striking thing in the review", writes Gregory, "was the light it threw upon Baur's way of thinking". He applied the method of *Tendenzkritik* to Weiss's book and discovered a plan of operation in it. The matter grew more interesting when a view was attributed to Weiss, on the basis of the same principle, which he did not hold. When Weiss replied that he did not subscribe to that particular view, Baur insisted that he did. If Baur was so unable to determine the purpose in the mind of a scholar of his own day, concludes Gregory, he must have been much less able to tell what the writers of the New Testament thought[67].

---

[66] "Bernard Weiss and the New Testament", *AJT* 1 (1897), pp. 19—20; quoted in Mattill, *Luke as a Historian,* pp. 83—84.

[67] Cf. the observations of C. S. Lewis from his own experience as both a writer and a literary critic, *Christian Reflections,* ed. by W. Hooper (Grand Rapids, 1967), pp. 158—62. Among other things he writes: "The 'assured results of modern scholarship' as to the way in which an old book was written,

A study of the era of *Tendenzkritik* illustrates how difficult it is to be truly objective as a critic. No critic is without presuppositions, and it is those who pride themselves most in having no presuppositions who have to be watched most carefully. The Tübingen critics thought they were free of systems and *a priori* reconstructions of history when they abandoned traditional, supernaturalistic Christianity; they heaped scorn on their critics for being biased, prejudiced, and unhistorical. And yet the judgment of history is that they were deceived in their task and were guilty of taking this very stance themselves.

As has been pointed out already, it is probably an oversimplification to condemn Baur and his followers for creating their system simply by applying the principles of the Hegelian dialectic to the New Testament and the early Christian documents. The ideas of Hegel, and more particularly German idealism, of which Hegel was only one representative, did have an immense influence on his thought, as is especially evident from reading his more theological works. But it would be more accurate to say that the system which became the key to their understanding of the New Testament was Baur's brilliant conception of the nature of early Christianity which he developed in his earliest writings and which changed little from the time he first put it forward in 1831. This approach kept them from making any serious contribution to the cause of scientific exegesis. It is perhaps significant that Zeller's work is the closest that any of the Tübingen school ever came to producing a commentary.

---

are 'assured' . . . only because the men who knew the facts are dead and can't blow the gaff" (161).

Chapter III

THE CRITICS OF THE TÜBINGEN RECONSTRUCTION

The view of Baur and the Tübingen critics concerning the nature of primitive Christianity and the subsequent depreciation of the Book of Acts as a historical source provided the catalyst for scholarly debate during the immediately following decades of New Testament research in Germany. Although Baur still had his defenders[1], his opinions were attacked and rejected by the vast majority of scholars.

The conservatives rallied to defend the historical foundation of the Book of Acts, as they only shortly before had rallied to defend the historical truth of the Gospels against the attacks of David Strauss. Some of these writers were entirely dogmatic in their approach and, therefore, add very little to the history of criticism. Others, however, were challenged to a fresh examination of traditional views, and especially of the text of Acts itself — thus striking some telling blows against the Tübingen reconstruction, while at the same time making lasting contributions to the study of Acts.

In contrast to the conservatives there were others, such as Bruno Bauer and the so-called Radical Dutch School, who were critical of Baur for not going far enough in his criticism. True, Baur had recognized the issues, they said; but he did not follow them to their logical conclusions. The latter group are remembered chiefly for providing — unknowingly — the *reductio ad absurdum* of the Tübingen hypothesis.

This chapter is concerned primarily with those moderate critics in Germany who leveled their guns at Baur and his followers. The radical reaction leading to a rejection of the Tübingen position for entirely different reasons provides the subject of Chapter Four. The criticisms of British scholarship, which was practically united in its rejection of the views of Baur *in toto*, are discussed in Chapter Six.

---

[1] Notably, A. Hausrath, A. Hilgenfeld, and (in England) W. R. Cassels. H. J. Holtzmann was a representative of the Tübingen point of view for a time but later abandoned it.

For some strange reason it is usually the radical scholars who achieve fame in the history of New Testament criticism, while the lasting contributions are made by more moderate critics whose names are often forgotten. A scholar — usually a *German* scholar — publishes a book or an essay which puts forward a creatively new idea which causes the scholarly world to come to life. It is the Strauss, the Baur, or the Schweitzer, who challenges traditional views and demands a hearing. Then follow several decades of intensive examination of the issues raised by the new hypothesis. Traditional interpretations are re-examined, the new evidence which has been brought forward is carefully sifted, and a more moderate — and usually more adequate — position gains general acceptance; but the scholars who have done the more careful, if less creative, work remain largely unknown.

It was so in the era of *Tendenzkritik*. Every serious student of the New Testament is familiar with the name of Ferdinand Christian Baur, but few have ever heard of Matthias Schneckenburger. Yet there is little question but that the contribution of the latter to the study of the Book of Acts was of a higher quality and of a more lasting value than that of Baur. Schneckenburger received his inspiration from the radical suggestions of Baur, but the subsequent history of criticism has justified his more moderate position, while it has condemned that of his master[2].

So also in discussing the history of Acts-criticism it is customary to award the laurels to Baur for founding the modern critical study of Acts, even though others could more justly claim that honor. One could argue that it would be more accurate to give the award to de Wette for his *New Testament Introduction* of 1826 or, perhaps better, to Heinrich August Wilhelm Meyer (1800—73), founder of the internationally famous *Kritisch-exegetischer Kommentar über das Neue Testament*[3].

The first edition of Meyer's commentary on Acts appeared in

---

[2] Some would disagree with this evaluation; however, it is an important thesis of this study that these critics have "uncritically" accepted the views of Baur, while at the same time ignoring the work of other men who have demonstrated in many different ways that the Tübingen view was not only partly erroneous, but untenable in almost every detail.

[3] In addition to contributing the first two volumes of the series on the Greek text and German translation, which were published in 1829, Meyer wrote commentaries on the four Gospels, Acts, and eight Pauline epistles (excluding 1 and 2 Thess. and the Pastorals). These were published between 1832 and 1847 and were regularly revised up to the time of his death. In addition to his exegetical work, Meyer was a busy pastor and church official. Cf. *RE*[3] 12, pp. 39—42.

1835[4]. It was a sizable commentary of 345 pages in which he followed the principles of historical-grammatical exegesis as outlined
in the introduction to his Greek text of the New Testament[5]. The
first edition was published too early to take into account the views
of Baur, Schwegler, Zeller, and company; but in the second edition
of 1854 the Tübingen position is considered in detail and, generally,
rejected[6].

It should be emphasized from the start that Meyer's position is
not that of a dyed-in-the-wool traditionalist who is merely seeking
to uphold the tradition of the Church. He is as critical a scholar as
Baur — perhaps more so, if the word is given its essentially positive
meaning. He does not argue from the point of view of the inerrancy
of the Bible, or even of the Book of Acts. He meets the Tübingen
scholars on the ground of historical criticism, without being prejudiced, as they were, concerning the dialectical nature of early
Christianity, and without presupposing the results of his critical
inquiry.

Meyer allows that the Book of Acts contains various details which
must be corrected by the Pauline epistles, that even the history of
Paul is handled imperfectly on occasion, and that here and there in
the first part of the book legendary elements are unmistakable. Yet
none of these facts, he argues, are incompatible with the view that
the book is the work of a companion of Paul, who

nicht eher als Kap. 16 als solcher eingetreten, erst länger nach des Apo- [21]
stels Tode die Geschichtschreibung unternahm, und da, wo ihm die eigene
Zeugenschaft abging, an die mündlich und schriftlich ausgebildete Sage
und Überlieferung gewiesen war, weil er nicht *von vorne herein* die Absicht der Geschichtschreibung gehabt hat, und jetzt grossen Theils mit
demjenigen sich begnügen musste, was und wie es ihm die Tradition gab,
in deren Atmosphäre er selbst lebte (6).

The supposedly unpauline elements of the book and the imprint of
a definite tendency allegedly betraying a later stage of ecclesiastical
development were simply imputed to it by the Tübingen critics and
have no foundation in fact. Furthermore, the "we"-narratives, with
the living and direct impression of an eye-witness, will always remain a powerful witness in favor of a companion of the Apostle
Paul as the author of the whole work: to separate the "we"-narra-
tives from the work as a whole is a procedure of critical arbitrari-
ness.

---

[4] *Kritisch exegetisches Handbuch über die Apostelgeschichte* (Göttingen,
1835; 2nd ed., 1854; 3rd ed., 1861; 4th ed., 1870).
[5] *Das Neue Testament Griechisch ...* (Göttingen, 1829), pp. XXXI ff.
[6] The 2nd ed. is the one referred to in the text.

58

The approach of Meyer may be illustrated by his observations at various points. For example, he assumes that Luke's account of the ascension at the end of the Gospel (24.50–51) is based on a different tradition from that of the narrative of the forty days of Acts 1 (23). In the fourth edition of his commentary he attributes this diversity of tradition to a considerable interval of time occuring between the composition of the Third Gospel and Acts, during which the tradition of the forty days was formed, or at least, acquired currency[7].

Again, in his reference to the death of Judas (1.18–20), the author of Acts follows a different tradition from that of Matthew. This twofold form of the tradition does not, however, mean that the tragic end of Judas is unhistorical, "sondern nur die *Art und Weise* desselben unsicher" (30). Further, there is no real reason to reject the essentially historical character of the election of Matthias as a successor to Judas; Zeller, in his objections, simply assumes what he is attempting to prove[8].

The Pentecostal experience of Acts 2, *in the manner in which Luke narrates it,* is judged by Meyer to be unhistorical (43–47). Luke, he argues, clearly intends his readers to understand that persons possessed by the Spirit began to speak in languages which were foreign to them. This is neither logically possible nor psychologically conceivable. Nor does it correspond to the account of *glossolalia* in 1 Corinthians. This does not mean, however, that the Pentecostal experience is entirely unhistorical: only Luke's understanding of the details of what happened is incorrect.

[22]   Was aber das γλώσσοις λαλεῖν wirklich gewesen sei, haben wir aus der Hauptstelle darüber, aus 1. Kor. 12.14., zu entnehmen, nach welcher es . . . eine in höchster Exstase vor sich gehende Gebetsrede, für den Verstand einer Auslegung bedürftig, gewesen ist, nicht ein Reden in fremden Sprachen (45).

The occurrence of Acts 2 is to be recognized, therefore, as the phenomenon of *glossolalia* as it appeared for the first time in the Christian Church. It was subsequently elaborated by legend into a speaking in a foreign language, an experience far surpassing the subsequently frequent and well-known *glossolalia*. This is the view incorporated into the narrative by the author.

---

[7] Note on Acts 1.3 (4th ed.).

[8] In a footnote to the 4th ed., Meyer observes that Peter's assertion that the new apostle must have been associated with the apostles during the whole of the ministry of Jesus would hardly have been reported if the author had had the design imputed to him by Baur and his school, since this would not at all fit the case of Paul (on 1.22).

Meyer also argues for the historicity of the account of the Jerusalem conference of Acts 15, which he identifies with Paul's account in Galatians 2. He rejects the Tübingen attempt to set the two accounts in opposition to each other. He makes the following points: (1) Paul's account in Galatians is not in the form of a historical narrative (as is the case with Acts), but is rather a personal defense of his apostolic authority; therefore, Paul mentions only incidents and aspects of what happened in Jerusalem which were of special significance to him, but which do not necessarily exclude those mentioned by the author of Acts. Moreover, (2) the Tübingen critics seemed to have overlooked the basic fact that both Galatians 2 and Acts present the original apostles as being in basic agreement with Paul concerning the content of the Gospel and his ministry to the Gentiles. (3) In Galatians 2, Paul does not contrast himself with the primitive apostles in regard to doctrine, but in reference to the sphere of activity in the ministry of the same Gospel. (4) By κατ' ἰδίαν (Gal. 2.2), Paul indicates he had a private conference, which took place at the same time as the event of Acts 15, but which is not necessarily to be identified with the more public gatherings. (5) The absence of mention of the "decree" in Galatians is explained by the interim purpose of the recommendation (280).

Meyer argues further for the authenticity of the letter stemming from the Jerusalem meeting and that Paul would have been in full agreement with such, since it both guaranteed freedom from circumcision on the part of Gentile converts and, at the same time, provided for the maintenance of brotherly fellowship between the stricter Jewish Christians and the Gentile Christians (277–78, 280).

The speeches of Acts are regarded by Meyer as the author's recasting of traditional material which he had obtained through his personal contact with various members of the primitive Christian community (10). The resulting product bears the personal imprint of the author's thought and style, but they are not the author's special literary creations.

Meyer detects a combination of both oral and written tradition behind the narrative (10). The former would have been gained from personal conversation with οἱ ἀπ' ἀπχῆς αὐτόπται καὶ ὑπηρέται γενόμενοι τοῦ λόγου (Luke 1.2).

However, the writer has not merely strung the traditions together, as some would suggest, but has shaped them into an essential unity and has encased them in his own literary style. Even so, it is significant that the earlier part of the book bears a Semitic character, which is in keeping with the Aramaic traditions lying behind it.

What about the purpose of Acts? — the question which played

such an important role in the rise of the modern critical approach to the Book of Acts. Meyer begins his discussion of the purpose of Acts with the observation that the question of the aim of the author is often confounded with that of the contents, as, for example, when the author's purpose is defined in terms of writing a history of the expansion of the Church from Jerusalem to Rome (7). The Baurian conception of the apologetic purpose of the author is examined and rejected as erroneous (8—9), although Meyer himself fails to provide a better definition of the purpose. He sees Acts as a *Privat-schrift*, written for Theophilus according to the aim expressed in [23] Luke 1.1—4, "dem Theophilus nämlich den empfangenen christlichen Unterricht auf dem Wege der Geschichte zu bestätigen" (7).

[24]   Deshalb schrieb er diese Geschichte, und zwar in der theils durch das Bedürfniss des Theophilus, theils durch seine eigene paulinische Individualität bestimmten Auswahl und Beschränkung, das er nach der vorpaulinischen Geschichte, in welcher *Petrus* die Hauptperson ist, *Paulus* und sein Wirken bis an das Ende des Buchs so einnimmt und fast ausschliesslich in den Vordergrund stellt, das die Geschichte sogar biographisch wird und bleibt . . . (7—8).

As to the parallels between the two apostles, Meyer regards them as [25] "nicht *gemacht*, sondern geschichtlich *gegeben*". The account of Acts in this connection is like an extended commentary on Galatians 2.8 (7—8, n. 1). Other than these brief observations, Meyer adds little to the discussion concerning the purpose of Acts.

   Assuming that Luke 21.20—25 presupposes the destruction of [26] Jerusalem, Meyer dates Acts after that event. "Die Nichterwähnung der letzten dient nicht zum Beweise, daß sie noch nicht erfolgt gewesen, sondern führt darauf, daß sie schon einer längern Vergangenheit angehört habe" (11). Acts may have been written at the close of the seventh decade of the first century, most probably separated by some years from the time of the writing of the Third Gospel.

   In the early editions of his commentary, Meyer leaves the abrupt ending of Acts unexplained; but in the fourth edition he defends the thesis put forward by Credner and others that Luke intended to write a third volume, the simplest explanation of the author's failure to mention the death of Paul or the outcome of his trial[9].

   Johann August Wilhelm Neander[10] (1789—1850), professor of

---

[9] 4th ed., E. T., p. 16.
[10] Neander was born a Jew. He changed his name from David Mendel to Johann August Wilhelm Neander after his conversion to Christianity in 1806. On Neander, cf. K. R. Hagenbach, "Neanders Verdienste an Kirchen-

church history at Berlin for nearly four decades and founder of modern Protestant historiography, was a determined opponent of the Tübingen reconstruction of primitive Christianity. In his major contribution to the area of New Testament research, his two-volumed *Geschichte der Pflanzung und Leitung der christlichen Kirche durch die Apostel*[11], he defended the essential trustworthiness of Acts as a source to be put alongside of the Pauline epistles in reconstructing the history of the apostolic Church. In the fourth edition of his work, Neander singles out the views of Baur and his followers for special criticism. He does not add very much to the discussion in the way of exegesis. However, his work is of great value as the testimony of the leading church historian of the day against the Tübingen hypothesis, and as a model for future histories of the apostolic age. Considered as a positive and non-polemical work, which it essentially is, Neander's history is the best and by far the most comprehensive history of apostolic Christianity of the era.

Friedrich August Gottreu Tholuck (1799–1877) wrote a brief paper on the speeches of Paul in Acts as compared with his letters[12], in which he attempted to defend the author of Acts against the criticism of Baur. The title of his essay is a misnomer (perhaps it was intended to be the first of a series of essays?), since he limits his investigation to the narrative dealing with the city of Ephesus (especially Acts 19.11–41) and Paul's farewell address to the Ephesian elders on the beach at Miletus (20.17–35). He argues that the picture in Acts corresponds with what we know from other sources of the city, and that Paul's sermon bears the character of Paul as known from his letters. Tholuck is the first to point out that the sermon to the Ephesian elders is the only one that is really analogous to the Pauline letters, since it is the only one which is pastoral in nature (312). He argues not only that the general tone of the speech is in keeping with the Paul of the epistles, but also for specific points of contact with the Pauline epistles[13]. These points of

geschichte", *TSK* 24 (1851), pp. 543–94; P. Schaff, *August Neander: Erinnerungen* (Gotha, 1886); A. von Harnack, *Rede zum 100. Geburtstag von August Neander* (Berlin, 1889) = *Reden und Aufsätze* (Gießen, 1904) 1, pp. 193–218; and A. F. J. Wiegard, *Neanders Leben* (Erfurt, 1889).

[11] (Hamburg, 1832–33; 2nd ed., 1838; 3rd ed., 1841; 4th ed., 1847). Volume one is primarily historical; volume two is a compendium of the theology of the New Testament.

[12] "Die Reden des Apostels Paulus in der Apostelgeschichte, mit seinen Briefen verglichen", *TSK* 12 (1839), pp. 305–28.

[13] Among the various passages said to contain parallel thoughts to the thought of Acts 20.18–35 are 1 Thess. 2.10–12, 2 Cor. 6.3–4, 2 Cor. 1.12, 1 Cor. 11.1, Phil. 3.15, 2 Cor. 2.4, Phil. 3.18, 1 Cor. 15.32, 2 Cor. 1.18, and 1 Cor. 16.9.

contact stem from the fact that the author correctly represents the historical Paul; there is no evidence for any borrowing from the actual letters of Paul. The accumulative effect of a careful comparison of this speech with the letters of Paul demonstrates, in Tholuck's view, that it is at least in keeping with the character of the apostle as seen through his letters.

Perhaps the most effective critic of the Tübingen reconstruction was Albrecht Ritschl[14] (1822—89). His criticisms were no more telling than those of others; yet his rejection of the Baurian hypothesis concerning the nature of primitive Christianity makes it crystal-clear that it was not derived from the use of the historical-critical method, but was rather a brilliant scheme imposed on the historical materials by Baur. Ritschl, a former disciple of Baur and probably his most famous and influential pupil, was committed to the same basic method as his mentor; however, his study of the historical data led him to a decisive rejection of the Tübingen reconstruction.

His study on *The Origin of the Old Catholic Church*[15] is much broader, and his criticisms of Baur's views much deeper, than the part which is concerned with the subject of this thesis. It is, in fact, a criticism of the whole Tübingen reconstruction of the history of the Church in the first three centuries. Fundamental to the study, however, is his rejection of the Tübingen understanding of the nature of apostolic Christianity.

According to Ritschl, the Tübingen conception of early Christianity is both too simple and too complex. It is too simple in that if fails to make allowance for divergencies within both Gentile and Jewish Christianity. Early Christianity is far too complex to be understood in terms of a conflict between two monolithic parties, as Baur had supposed. The Tübingen critics failed to take into account the differences between the primitive apostles and the Judaizers, as well as between Pauline Christianity and that part of Gentile Chris-

---

[14] On Ritschl, cf. O. Ritschl, *Albrecht Ritschls Leben*, 2 vols. (Freiburg i. B., 1892); P. Hefner, *Faith and the Vitalities of History: A Theological Study Based on the Work of Albrecht Ritschl* (New York, 1966); and D. L. Mueller, *An Introduction to the Theology of Albrecht Ritschl* (Philadelphia, 1969). The first work is primarily biographical, but includes an account of his major books as well; the second is historical-theological, with a chapter devoted to Ritschl's criticism of Baur regarding the nature of early Christianity (pp. 12—44); the third treats Ritschl primarily as a systematic theologian.

[15] *Die Entstehung der altkatholischen Kirche* (Bonn, 1850; 2nd ed., 1857). In the first edition Ritschl is still very much under the influence of Baur, particularly in his acceptance of Baur's general conception of the antithesis between Pauline and Jewish Christianity. He deliberately and decisively casts off the mantle of the master in the second edition. The second edition of 1857 is, for this reason, the one referred to in the text.

tianity which was essentially independent of his influence (22—23). Not all Jewish Christians were Judaizers or opponents of Paul; not all Gentile Christians were Paulinists. The Tübingen view is guilty of circular reasoning when it first postulates that all Jewish elements in the New Testament are antithetical to Pauline Christianity and then uses the presence of these elements to demonstrate the existence of an anti-Pauline party (17).

On the other hand, the Baurian reconstruction is over-complex in that it fails to come to terms with the essential unity existing in apostolic Christianity. It posits an antithesis which, in fact, never really existed. The final reconciliation of Jewish and Gentile Christianity cannot be explained in terms of the Tübingen view. If the two parties had so little in common as Baur had supposed — only a common faith in Jesus, which meant one thing to Jewish Christians and another to Gentile Christians — there would have been no reason for them to have stayed together (18—20). A *rapprochement* would have been entirely impossible. However, in the New Testament itself, even in the Pauline epistles, there is sufficient evidence that the original apostles were in basic agreement with Paul in maintaining that faith in Christ was the only condition of salvation and in recognizing the right of both Jews and Gentiles to become members of the Church, and that this common conviction finds its roots in the teachings of Jesus (47—48). There are differences between Paul and the *Urapostel*, to be sure; but these are differences of expression and spheres of ministry, not differences of essential belief.

The Jewish Christianity represented in the Epistle of James, 1 Peter, and the Apocalypse provides evidence for the existence of a Jewish Christianity which was *un*-Pauline, but not *anti*-Pauline. The ideas of these writers are original, and therefore not specifically Pauline; however, contrary to the suppositions of Baur, there is no evidence to suggest that these ideas were developed in opposition to Pauline thought or are essentially contradictory to such (116—19). 1 Clement is another case in point which provides evidence for the existence of a Gentile Christianity which was independent of Paul (274—84).

Ritschl's discussion of the decision of the Jerusalem council in Acts 15 is important (128—40). According to Baur, the decision of the council represents a compromise between two warring parties which amounts to a recognition of two Gospels, one for Jews and another for Gentiles. For Ritschl, the decision is primarily sociological, rather than theological, in nature. It is recommended for Gentile Christians to observe certain parts of the Jewish proselyte law.

The reason for this has nothing to do with the question of salvation or admittance into the Church; it is intended to make social intercourse between Jewish and Gentile Christians possible. According to Ritschl, there is no reason to doubt that such an agreement would have been congenial to Paul (136) or to doubt the genuineness of the decision (138).

Ritschl was successful in pointing out the essential error of Baur's conception of the apostolic age: i. e., the failure to recognize the essential unity which, in fact, existed between Paul and the primitive apostles; but he failed to go into detail concerning the specific points of agreement. The latter was the subject of a prize-winning essay by Gotthard Victor Lechler[16] (1811—88) on *The Apostolic and Post-apostolic Age*[17], which was written in answer to the problem posed by the Teylerian Society of the Netherlands as to what constituted the differences and similarities between the teachings and practices of Paul and the primitive apostles[18].

Lechler begins his study with the observation that previous studies have usually concentrated on either the diversity or the unity of apostolic Christianity. The orthodox, in their attempt to maintain the view of apostolic Christianity as an undivided unity, overlooked the differences between the apostles themselves and between the various early Christian communities. The more recent criticism of the Tübingen School, having discovered the differences, has ignored the basic unity which existed in the primitive Church. Both groups have failed to come to grips with the fact that apostolic Christianity was marked by both unity and diversity and, therefore, have been unbalanced in their discussions of the evidence (2).

Lechler proceeds to call attention to the various similarities and dissimilarities between the teachings of the apostles. His attempt was not likely to convince any of the Tübingen persuasion, since he defends the historical reliability of the Book of Acts and the tradi-

---

[16] Lechler, author of a very influential book on the history of English Deism (*Die Geschichte des englischen Deismus* (Stuttgart and Tübingen, 1841)) and later professor at Leipzig, was one of the few German scholars of this period who interacted to any degree with British scholarship. He seems to be the first German commentator to be aware of the work of William Paley and James Smith. Lechler was also a former pupil of Baur (but never a disciple!).

[17] *Das apostolische und das nachapostolische Zeitalter. Mit Rücksicht auf Unterschied und Einheit in Lehre und Leben* (Haarlem, 1851; 2nd ed., Stuttgart, 1857; 3rd ed., Karlsruhe and Leipzig, 1885). The second edition is referred to in the text.

[18] The rather complicated, threefold statement of the problem posed by the society is contained in a footnote to the foreword of Lechler's study (III—IV, n. 1).

tional authorship of most of the New Testament writings. His work therefore is of value primarily as a compendium of the various strata of the theology of the New Testament — e. g., the theology of the Pauline epistles (45—145), the *kerygma* of the primitive Church in the early chapters of Acts (15—33), and the Pauline speeches in Acts (146—58) — and at most another scholarly testimony that the Tübingen hypothesis was essentially unconvincing. His study is marked by careful exegesis and analysis, but it fails to add very much toward the solution of the problems raised by Baur and his disicples.

One very important observation made by Lechler, however, concerns the significance of the destruction of Jerusalem in the development of early Christianity (434—41). Baur had undervalued the importance of the fall of Jerusalem and the dissolution of the Temple cult for Jewish and Gentile relations within the Church, since a recognition of its effect in this regard would have completely invalidated his late dating of the rise of Gentile supremacy in the Church. The events which Baur dated toward the middle of the second Christian century, argues Lechler, really took place in the eighth decade of the first century. The end of Jerusalem as a center of the Jewish cult marked the end of the influence of Jewish Christianity in the Church[19]. "Jewish Christianity", as understood by Baur, existed after this date only in small, isolated communities. The leadership of the Church was now permanently Gentile, as were also the future heresies. With this observation Lechler scores another point for the opposition against the Tübingen interpretation.

Two influential and widely-read histories of apostolic times were added to the growing number by Heinrich Wilhelm Josias Thiersch[20] (1817—85), Germany's most academically prominent convert to Irvingism, and Johann Peter Lange[21] (1802—84), the conservative substitute for D. F. Strauss as professor of theology at Zürich. Both of these works, however, are too theologically oriented to add very much to the critical discussion of Acts.

---

[19] Cf. "The fall of Jerusalem ... meant the final cleavage between Jews and Christians" (T. R. Glover, *The Ancient World* (London, 1944), p. 200).

[20] *Die Kirche im apostolischen Zeitalter und die Entstehung der neutestamentlichen Schriften* (Frankfurt a. M. and Erlangen, 1852; 2nd ed., 1858; 3rd ed., Augsburg, 1879). Thiersch wrote an earlier criticism of Baur's *Paulus* under the title, *Versuch zur Herstellung des historischen Standpunkts für die Kritik der neutestamentlichen Schriften* (Erlangen, 1845), to which Baur wrote a characteristic reply: *Der Kritiker und Fanatiker in der Person des Herrn H. W. J. Thiersch* (Stuttgart, 1846).

[21] *Das apostolische Zeitalter*, 2 vols. (Braunschweig, 1853—54).

If Baur and Zeller were normally inclined to take their conservative critics less than seriously, they must have been singularly unmoved by the attack of Michael Baumgarten (1812—89) on their interpretation of the Book of Acts. Baumgarten's three-volumed study of the Book of Acts[22] was one of the harshest criticisms of the Baurian hypothesis by any of the conservatives. It is extremely erudite and very thorough (running to nearly 1200 pages), but it is so obviously an attack upon the "unbelieving" attitude and conclusions of Baur and Zeller that it only served to confirm the Tübingen view of the hidebound position of their opponents.

Yet Baumgarten does add at least one point to the discussion by calling special attention to Paul's principle of Christian liberty[23].

The Tübingen scholars had interpreted Paul's defense of freedom from the Law as developed in Galatians and Romans as meaning [27] the "absolute Unvereinbarkeit des Judenthums mit dem Christenthum, des Gesetzes mit dem Evangelium, der Beschneidung mit dem Glauben an Christus"[24]. Galations 5.2 was interpreted in an absolute sense to mean that Paul would not allow circumcision any place at all in his religious thought, even as a custom for Jewish Christians. Therefore, of all Paul's Jewish practices mentioned in the Book of Acts, the circumcision of Timothy (16.3) was considered to be the most flagrant contradiction to Pauline doctrine. The Paul of the epistles could *never* have agreed to such action; of this the Tübingen critics were certain.

Baumgarten argues that such an absolutizing of the Pauline principle of freedom from the Law misunderstands Paul's concept of Christian liberty. In this way the Tübingen view transforms the [28] Pauline principle of freedom from the Law into a new law: "Bei solchem Eifer für die Freiheit die Freiheit selber wieder in eine Knechtschaft verwandelt" (II, 188). Paul was not one to substitute one bondage for another. The interpretation of Baur and Zeller of Galatians 5.2 is clearly contradicted by Paul's previous statement in 5.1. Paul was no legalist — even in his determined opposition to the Judaizers. Rather, has principle of Christian liberty was this: πάντα ἔξεστιν, ἀλλ᾽ οὐ πάντα συμφέρει· πάντα ἔξεστιν, ἀλλ᾽ οὐ πάντα οἰκοδομεῖ (1 Cor. 10.23).

[29] Nach diesem entscheidenden Ausspruch besteht die Freiheit darin, sich schlechterdings nicht von aussen bestimmen und beschränken zu lassen,

---

[22] *Die Apostelgeschichte; oder der Entwickelungsgang der Kirche von Jerusalem bis Rom*, 3 vols. (Halle, 1852).

[23] Mattill regards Baumgarten's discussion of Christian liberty as "the most valuable part of his work" (*Luke as a Historian*, p. 98, n. 1).

[24] Zeller, *Apostelgeschichte*, p. 445.

sondern lediglich von dem innern Urtheil. Wenn demnach also alles ge-stattet ist, so darf auch die Beschneidung nicht ausgenommen werden, als wäre diese Ausnahme vielmehr schon eine Beschränkung der Freiheit (II, 188).

Not only does Paul's general principle of Christian liberty contra-dict the limitations placed upon him by Baur, but he specifically applies this principle to the situation of Jewish missions and says, καὶ ἐγενόμην τοῖς Ἰουδαίοις ὡς Ἰουδαῖος, ἵνα Ἰουδαίους κερδήσω · τοῖς ὑπὸ νόμον ὡς ὑπὸ νόμον, ... ἵνα τοὺς ὑπὸ νόμον κερδήσω (1 Cor. 9.20).

Luther, the champion of Paul's concept of freedom from the Law, understood this clearly when he commented:

Gleich als wenn ich jetzt unter die Juden käme und sollte das Evange- [30] lium predigen, und sähe, dass sie schwach wären, wollte ich mich beschnei-den lassen, essen und mich enthalten wie sie thäten. Denn wo ich mich nicht nach ihnen richtete, so schlösse ich vor mir meinem Evangelio die Thüre zu (quoted by Baumgarten (II, 189)).

Furthermore, the Tübingen view fails to understand the complex social relations involved in a person's being a Jew. For Paul to have insisted that any Jew who accepted the message of his Gospel leave behind all his personal, social, and national ties with Israel — as the Baurian interpretation demands — would have not only been impractical, but inconceivable. If he were to maintain any con-tacts whatsoever with devout Jews, and there is much evidence in his letters that he did so, it would have been a necessity for him to have made some such accomodation[25].

The study which is in many ways the most valuable of the period was written by an otherwise unknown pastor by the name of Eduard Lekebusch. It is entitled *The Composition and Origin of Acts*[26]. Lekebusch is definitely conservative in his conclusions, yet his study is not marked by the same apologetic purpose as some of the other conservative writings. His study is not primarily a theological essay, but rather an exercise in literary criticism. It is not so much an at-tack on Baur and his followers as it is an attempt to take their views seriously and to see whether they stand up beside a careful analysis of the narrative of Acts.

---

[25] Another study of the period which was devoted primarily to a comparison of the account of Paul's activity according to Acts and the Pauline epistles is J. R. Oertel, *Paulus in der Apostelgeschichte* (Halle, 1868). In spite of the extremely apologetic stance of the author, the study is of value in showing that Paul in the Book of Acts and the Paul of the epistles are not quite so contradictory as the Tübingen critics supposed.

[26] *Die Composition und Entstehung der Apostelgeschichte* (Gotha, 1854).

Lekebusch's work can be best compared to that of Schneckenburger as one of the most cautious and painstakingly careful studies
of this era of criticism. His work differs from Schneckenburger's,
however, in that he is not out to demonstrate a thesis. He does not
state a hypothesis and then see if it fits the data; his aim is rather a
minute examination of the evidence, independently of hypotheses, in
order to determine the state of the case.

The major parts of Lekebusch's work are concerned with the
literary activity of the author of the Book of Acts (35–131) and
the purpose of Acts (189–386). Schleiermacher, Mayerhoff, and
Schwanbeck had attempted to isolate the sources of Acts by detect-
ing various literary features which indicated, in their opinion, the
various sources of the author[27]. The author was regarded as primarily a redactor who strung together a number of literary sources
without bothering to reshape them to any great degree, or to or-
ganize the whole work into a literary unity. Thus the presence of
the first person plural in the latter part of Acts (16.10–17; 20.5–
15; 21.1–17; 27.1–28.19) was regarded as a sign that the author
had used the diary of a companion of Paul — either Timothy
(Schleiermacher and Mayerhoff) or Silas (Schwanbeck) — rather than
that he himself was a companion of Paul. The presence of ἡμεῖς
in the narrative was considered to be an illustration of the carelessness of the author in failing to revise his sources thoroughly.

Building on the previous study of the literary style of Luke-Acts
by Zeller[28], Lekebusch engages in a careful examination of the language of Acts[29]. He finds that all parts of Acts, and to some degree
also the Gospel of Luke, are marked by the same characteristics of
language and style throughout. This can be seen especially in the
presence of words and expressions which are seldom found elsewhere in the New Testament in all parts of the Lucan writings, and
also in the use of the Septuagint in the Scripture citations[30]. Rather
than a collection of loosely strung-together sources, Acts is found
[31]   to be "ein von schriftlichen Quellen im Allgemeinen unabhängiges,
aus einer Feder geflossenes Originalwerk" (79). This leads to the
important conclusion — a conclusion which even those who deny

---

[27] For a convenient survey of their views, see Dupont, *Sources*.

[28] Zeller, "Die Apostelgeschichte, ihre Composition und ihr Charakter",
Theologische Jahrbücher 10 (1851), pp. 433–69; expanded in his *Apostelgeschichte*, pp. 387–452.

[29] His work in this connection was only superseded by the studies of H. J.
Cadbury; cf. *infra*, pp. 68–70.

[30] The recent researches of Max Wilcox (*The Semitisms of Acts* (Oxford,
1965)) show that this frequently made observation regarding the use of the
Septuagint in Acts is not entirely accurate.

that Acts could have been written by a personal acquaintance of Paul find it difficult to deny[31] — that the author of the whole narrative of Acts and the so-called "we"-narratives are the one and the same person (81). Lekebusch goes on to make his case almost water-tight by a careful examination of the inner connections of the narrative (82—131), which demonstrates that Acts is a carefully organized whole.

The longest section of Lekebusch's study is devoted to a consideration of the purpose of Acts (189—386). He insists upon the necessity of asking the question, even if it be decided that the Book of Acts is an essentially historical work, since almost all histories are written from a definite point of view with a specific purpose, or purposes, in mind (190). This preliminary observation is followed by an excellent historical survey of the discussion of the problem from the time of Michaelis, through the Tübingen criticism, up to the work of Bruno Bauer. He does not lightly dismiss either the Tübingen criticism or Bauer, but takes their views quite seriously. However, as a result of very careful analysis of their individual hypotheses and of the text of Acts, he finds them very wanting indeed. The conclusion of his research on the matter is this:

Die Apostelgeschichte ist keine Tendenzschrift, weder eine apologetische, noch eine conciliatorische, noch weniger eine judaistische, sondern, wofür sie selbst gehalten sein will, was auch nach dem Zugeständniss der neueren Kritik der erste Eindruck ist, den sie auf den Leser macht, eine rein historische Schrift, in welcher der allmälige Entwicklungsgang der christlichen Kirche, wie sie sich vom paulinischen, universalistischen, mit Einem Worte — vom christlichen Standpunkt aus darstellt, von ihrer Entstehung zu Jerusalem an bis zu dem Momente, wo der grosse Heidenapostel im Mittelpunkte des Heidenthums, zu Rom, auftritt, im ununterbrochener Reihenfolge beschrieben wird. Die Apostelgeschichte ist keine Parteischrift. Aber wenn man sie durchaus auf ein Partei-Interesse zurückführen wollte, so könnte man nur ein apologetisch-paulinisches in ihr vertreten finden ... Wie das dritte Evangelium von den Alten für das specifisch paulinische Evangelium ... angesehen wurde und auch jetzt noch als solches gilt, so trägt auch die Apostelgeschichte einen ächt paulinischen Character an sich, der sich am klarsten in der Thatsache bezeugt, dass sie von den Gegnern dieses Apostels verworfen und vom kirchlichen Gebrauch ausgeschlossen wurde (374—75). [32]

Lekebusch agrees with the other critics of the Tübingen criticism in finding in the Book of Acts an essentially trustworthy account of

---

[31] Even Zeller freely admitted that by the use of the first person plural the author intended to give the impression that he was a member of Paul's missionary *entourage*.

the history of apostolic times. This does not mean, however, that every story or item contained in Acts can be taken at face value simply because it has found its way into a "canonical book".

[33]   Wir verstatten vielmehr der Kritik ihr volles Recht, die Glaubwürdigkeit eines jeden ihrer Berichte vorurtheilsfrei zu prüfen und diesen oder jenen je nach seiner Beschaffenheit für unhistorisch oder mythisch zu erklären. Aber wir hegen die feste Überzeugung, dass alle Aussetzungen, welche man mit Recht an dem Inhalt unserer Schrift machen könnte, bei weitem nicht schwer genug wiegen, um deswegen die Identität ihres Verfassers mit jenem Begleiter des Paulus gegen ihre eigene Aussage in Abrede zu stellen (376).

A careful, unprejudiced criticism of Acts, argues Lekebusch, leads one to this inevitable conlcusion:

[34]   Die Apostelgeschichte ist wirklich das Werk jenes Apostelschülers und Begleiters Pauli, als den sich ihr Verfasser durch die augenzeugenschaftliche Erzählungsform eines grossen Theils seiner Geschichte und durch das ἡμῖν im Eingange seines ganzen Werks selbst bezeichnet (386).

In his discussion of the authorship of Acts, Lekebusch finds no better suggestion than the traditional view that both the Third Gospel and Acts were written by the Luke mentioned in the Pauline epistles (387—402). Arguing that Paul's words in his speech to the Ephesian elders in Acts 20.25 imply that he has died at the time of the author's writing, and that αὕτη ἐστὶν ἔρημος of 8.26 refers to Gaza (rather than to τὴν ὁδόν), which was destroyed at the beginning of the Jewish war, Lekebusch insists upon a date of composition shortly after the destruction of Jerusalem (413—28). He is unimpressed by the arguments put forward in support of the necessity of an earlier or a later date than this for the book.

The above discussion of the work of the critics of the Tübingen reconstruction has been much more favourable in its evaluation of their work than many discussions of the history of New Testament criticism[32]. I have been careful to point out that not all "conservatives" were reactionaries trying to defend traditional views from the standpoint of dogmatic presuppositions. Many of the "conservatives" were capable of a much more thoroughly historical approach than were Baur and his followers, and not all of the critics of the Tübingen position could even loosely be called "conservative"[33]. Moreover, it simply is not true that Baur and his followers were un-

---

[32] Mattill, *Luke as a Historian*, pp. 85—167, is an exception in this regard.

[33] Ritschl, at least, could not be thus classified, and it may be argued that there is a great difference between the position of a true "conservative", such as Baumgarten, and the others mentioned in this chapter.

prejudiced and scientific in their approach, in spite of their claims of objectivity. Admittedly, their work was free from the presuppositions of Church tradition, but in the place of tradition was placed a basic conception of the nature of primitive Christianity which, in effect, prejudged the results of their criticism.

The critics of the Tübingen hypothesis demonstrated beyond doubt that the Baurian conception of apostolic Christianity was not the result of a careful examination of the historical data, or of the use of the method of historical criticism. It was, rather, a brilliantly conceived system imposed upon the New Testament writings and the other early Christian documents. The Tübingen approach was in its own way as uncritical as traditional orthodoxy; it differed mainly in its substitution of Baur's more recent judgments for the older, traditional conceptions.

All of the critics were agreed that Baur was wrong in his conception of apostolic Christianity as consisting of two parties which were in constant conflict over their essentially different understandings of the nature of Christian faith, and they brought evidence which demonstrated both that there was a greater variety within early Christianity than merely two parties, and that there existed an essential unity between Paul and his followers and the *Urapostel* and the Jewish Christians. They were able to show that Paul himself, even in the four epistles recognized as genuine by the Tübingen critics, insisted that he and the earlier apostles were agreed upon the basic issues. Having pointed out the basic fact of the agreement between Paul and the primitive apostles, however, the critics of Baur were less successful in working out a convincing account of the details in which their agreement consisted[34].

Furthermore, the critics of the Tübingen reconstruction demonstrated that the evidence brought forward by Baur and his followers in argument against the essential historicity of Acts was not compelling. It seemed to them, quite rightly, that the Tübingen School had made up their minds in advance concerning the trustworthiness of Acts and then set out to demonstrate that they were right. The same held true for the supposed contrast between the Paul of the

---

[34] This may have been largely due to the lack of materials available for such a comparison. If one accepts the First Epistle of Peter as representing the teaching of Peter, or the essential accuracy of the primitive *kerygma* in the early chapters of Acts, as most of the critics of Baur did, then it is not too difficult to demonstrate that there is a considerable area of agreement between the theology of Paul and the *Urapostel*. However, where does one look for information concerning the theology of the primitive apostles when one excludes these two documents from the sources? Certainly not to the Clementine literature!

Acts and the Paul of the epistles, a contrast which the critics thought was greatly stretched by Baur. However, the critics of the Baurian hypothesis were unable to offer a detailed solution to these two important problems raised by the Tübingen scholars which would command general acceptance. They showed themselves much more capable of truly historical thinking than Baur and his school, but they did not have the equipment to examine the question of the historical value of Acts in a thorough manner. Historical research, and more specifically archaeology, was still in its infancy.

Chapter IV

RADICAL DESCENDANTS OF THE TÜBINGEN SCHOOL

The views of F. C. Baur and the Tübingen School by no means suffered annihilation because of the attacks of their opponents. More than once in the course of our study of the history of the criticism of the Book of Acts it will become apparent that many of the conclusions and underlying assumptions of the Tübingen critics continue to come to the surface of critical discussion, though in a modified form.

In addition to the more conservative critics of the Tübingen critics, there was another group of scholars who rejected the approach of *Tendenzkritik*, but for quite different reasons. They viewed themselves as the true descendants of the Tübingen criticism, although they were in some ways more extreme in their approach to the Book of Acts than Baur had been. This group of scholars includes Bruno Bauer, Ernest Renan, Franz Overbeck, W. C. van Manen and the so-called "Dutch Radical Critics", and P. W. Schmiedel. Because of their own peculiar reaction to the criticism of Baur and his followers, and because of their lasting influence (in some ways) on the subsequent history of New Testament criticism, it is worthwhile to pause to consider their views before passing on to the work of others who belong more to the mainstream of critical research.

Bruno Bauer[1] (1809—88) is one of the tragic figures in the history of New Testament interpretation. He began his academic career as a *Privatdozent* in Berlin as a conservative Hegelian and erstwhile follower of E. W. Hengstenberg. From this point of view he contributed a strong criticism of Strauss's *Leben Jesu* in the *Jahrbücher für wissenschaftliche Kritik* (1835—36). Toward the end of his time in Berlin he began to move swiftly to the left in his philosophical and theological views. This change of stance became quite evident

---

[1] On Bauer, see M. Kegel, *Bruno Bauer und seine Theorien über die Entstehung des Christentums* (Leipzig, 1908); E. Barnikol, *Das Entdeckte Christentum im Vormärz: Bruno Bauers Kampf gegen Religion und Christentum und Erstausgabe seiner Kampfschrift* (Jena, 1927); and E. Barnikol, "Bruno Bauers frühe Grundthese von der Entstehung des Christentums", *ThJ* (1956), pp. 87 ff.

in his work on the Gospel of John[2] and in this three-volumed study of the Synoptic Gospels[3], which were published during the brief interval he lectured at the University of Bonn (1839—42). The radical views put forward in these two works led to an uproar in the Church and to his enforced retirement as a university teacher of theology[4].

In his criticism of the Gospel history Bauer outdid even Strauss. Whereas Strauss had argued that many of the events narrated in the Gospels were the products of the creative imagination of the Christian community, Bauer attributed them to the creative imagination of the individual Gospel writers. He differed from F. C. Baur in that he often could see no definite purpose lying behind the author's invention of a particular event or saying placed in the mouth of Jesus.

In 1850 Bauer applied the same methods to the criticism of the Book of Acts, in what is perhaps the most radical study ever written on the subject[5]. His work was not taken very seriously by New Testament scholars of the day, since it was so obviously a work *ab irato*, written by a man who was obviously intent on disproving the truthfulness of the Christian faith[6]. Yet, in spite of its radical conclusions and the personal stance of the author, it is a very significant work in a number of ways.

Bauer begins his monograph on the Book of Acts by calling attention to the alleged difference between the Paul of the Acts and the Paul of the epistles, to which Schrader and Baur had drawn attention. Baur, assuming the incontrovertible authenticity of the so-called *Hauptbriefe* (i. e. Romans, Galatians, 1 and 2 Corinthians), had expressed the conviction "dass bei der grossen Differenz

[35]

---

[2] *Kritik der evangelischen Geschichte des Johannes* (Bremen, 1840).

[3] *Kritik der evangelischen Geschichte der Synoptiker*, 3 vols. (Leipzig, 1841 to 1842).

[4] On this period of Bauer's activity, see A. Schweitzer, *Von Reimarus zu Wrede* (Tübingen, 1906), 11.

[5] *Die Apostelgeschichte. Eine Ausgleichung des Paulinismus und des Judenthums innerhalb der christlichen Kirche* (Berlin, 1850). This work is often mistakenly referred to as a commentary. It is a one hundred and forty three page monograph.

[6] Bauer's work was, however, appreciated by a number of other scholars included in this chapter, specifically Overbeck and the Dutch Radicals. Nietzsche also singled out his work for praise and expressed essential agreement. (Cf. E. Barnikol, *Op. cit.*, pp. 78—79). His later work, *Christus und die Cäsaren* (Berlin, 1877) became the more or less authoritative interpretation of early Christianity from the Marxist-Socialist point of view through the influence of his one-time followers and friends, Karl Marx and Friedrich Engels.

der beiderseitigen Darstellungen die geschichtliche Wahrheit nur entweder auf der einen oder auf der andern Seite seyn kann"[7]. Bauer suggests that this is a false assumption on the part of Baur. There is another alternative which the Tübingen professor failed to consider: it is possible that *both* Acts and the so-called genuine epistles of Paul are unhistorical. The assumption that Galatians, Romans, and the Corinthian epistles are genuine works of Paul was purely arbitrary on the part of the Tübingen critics.

Können nicht beide Darstellungen demselben Boden der absichtlichen Reflexion entsprossen seyn und auf diesem Boden immer noch ihren Unterschied behaupten, ja, nun erst ihren Unterschied mit voller Kraft geltend machen? (V) [36]

F. C. Baur had made the suggestion that the relationship between the Paul of the Acts and the Paul of the epistles was similar to that of the Jesus of the Fourth Gospel and the Jesus of the Synoptics. Bruno Bauer accepts the comparison as valid, but, having earlier argued that both the Synoptics *and* the Gospel according to John are essentially unhistorical, he refuses the either-or alternative which Baur lays down as a basis for the criticism of Acts[8].

The portrayal of Paul as a miracle worker and magician ("Wunderthäter und Zauberer") is regarded by Bauer to be the primary feature of the Pauline part of Acts (8—9). He calls attention to the same parallelism between the miracles performed by Peter and Paul which had been suggested by Schneckenburger, Zeller, and others (9—11). Whereas Schneckenburger had assumed that the author of Acts had selected certain events (especially miracles) from the life of Paul which were more or less parallel to events in the life of Peter, the latter being a part of the tradition of the early Church, Bauer argues that the miracle-working activity of both is modelled after the life of Jesus.

Das Original des Petrus und des Paulus der Apostelgeschichte ist der Jesus der synoptischen Evangelien. Der Verfasser der Apostelgeschichte hatte die letzten ... vor Augen, als er ihnen die Züge entlehnte, aus denen er das Bild beider Apostel zusammensetzte (12). [37]

He continues in the attempt to show verbal similarities between the miracle stories of Acts and the miracle stories of the Gospels (13

---

[7] *Paulus*, p. 5.

[8] In his three-volumed work on the Pauline epistles (*Kritik der paulinischen Briefe* (Berlin, 1850—52)), Bauer argued against the authenticity of the *Hauptbriefe*, as well as the other Pauline letters.

—21)[9]. These he regards as demonstrating conclusively that the narrative of Acts is a product of the free imagination of its author.

Bauer's study is not very original until he comes to consider the question of the purpose of Acts. And it is here that he touches on a weak point in the Tübingen theory[10].

The author, according to Bauer, has an apologetic purpose; but it is not the one imagined by F. C. Baur. Rather, the author is trying to show how it came to be that Christianity, which was first a Jewish sect, became a universal religion, dominated by Gentiles. In order to accomplish his purpose he has the apostle Paul constantly preaching to Jews — even though he was commissioned by the Lord to be the apostle to the Gentiles — who, in turn, constantly reject his message. As a result, Paul turns to the Gentiles: thus Christianity becomes a universal religion, almost as if by accident (110—14).

Far from being a *Tendenzschrift* to bring about harmony in the Church between the Jewish and Gentile factions, the Book of Acts was written at a time when all such strife was past. The writer assumes a basic harmony in the Church, and his story only makes sense under such circumstances.

[38]   Als die Apostelgeschichte geschrieben wurde, war die Spannung der Parteien zusammengefallen, war der Gegensatz schon verschleiert, die Differenz verwischt, hatte sich der Friede schon gemacht — die Apostelgeschichte ist nicht ein Friedensvorschlag, sondern der Ausdruck und Abschluss des Friedens und der Erschlaffung (121).

He finds the Tübingen interpretation wholly incredible. It is impossible to think in terms of unreconciled parties in the Church at the middle of the second century (118—19). Furthermore, the book itself reflects a time when the members of the Church had lost touch with the Jewish heritage of the faith and needed to have it explained to them; that is, it assumes an essentially Gentile Christianity (120—22).

---

[9] Cf. Acts 3.6 and 9.33—34 with Mk. 2.11; Acts 3.10 with Mk. 2.12; Acts 28.9 with Mk. 1.32; Acts 28.8 with Mk. 1.30; Acts 5.15—16 with Mk. 6.55—56; Acts 16.17 with Mk. 3.11; Acts 9.36—40 with Mk. 5.40; Acts 9.40—41 with Lk. 7.15; Acts 20.10 with Mk. 5.39. Bauer attempts to show that not only has the author created his stories on the basis of the Gospel stories, but he has misunderstood the Gospel stories as well!

[10] Cf. the statement by McGiffert concerning Bauer's work: "It exposes the weakest point in the Tübingen theory, the notion that the conflict between Judaisers and Paulinists continued long after Paul's death and supplied the occasion for the composition of Acts and other irenic writings" (*BC* 2, p. 378).

In this connection Bauer makes a suggestion which is very significant in the history of German New Testament criticism. He interprets Catholicism, of which Acts is representative, as the development of the Jewish or conservative spirit *within Gentile Christianity,*
rather than (as Baur had argued) as a compromise between Jewish
and Gentile Christianity. The Book of Acts was of supreme influence in the process of Catholicization.

Sie half die Kette, die die Gemeinde mit der jüdischen Welt verband,   [*39*]
schliessen und die Kirche hielt an der Apostelgeschichte fest und erkannte
sie als kanonischen Ausdruck ihres Bewusstseyns an, weil sie diesem Bund
mit dem Judenthum und diese jüdische Vermählung mit der Vergangenheit und mit dem Himmel haben wollte (122).

However, the Judaism represented by the Book of Acts was not his-
toric Judaism. Nor was it "Jewish Christianity". It had not the
slightest thought of denying freedom to Gentile Christians, nor of
imposing on them the yoke of the Law. When this "Judaism" prevailed, the freedom of Gentile Christians and the universal nature
of the Christian faith were taken for indisputable facts.

Das Judenthum, von dem wir sprechen, ist vielmehr eine Macht, die,   [*40*]
wenn auch unter wechselnden Formen, bis in die neueste Zeit ihre Herrschaft behauptet hat ...
Judenthum nennen wir diese conservative, ausgleichende, counterrevolu-
tionäre und bei alle de mden Gewinn der Revolution sicher stellende Macht,
weil sie im Alten Testament, in der alttestamentlichen Unfähigkeit zur
Anschauung der geschichtlichen Unterschiede, in der jüdischen Umwand-
lung des später geschichtlichen Products zu einer gottgewirkten Tradition
— kurz, im jüdischen Theismus, der den geschichtlichen Schöpfer zur Ohn-
macht verurtheilt und dem Himmel die Prärogative der Offenbarung
übergibt, ihren classischen Ausdruck erhalten hat und allerdings auch
durch das ursprüngliche Erbtheil, welches die neue Gemeinde am Alten
Testament besass, in der Kirche ihren Einfluss beibehielt, ja für denselben
nur noch ein grosseres Terrain gewann (123—25).

At this point Bauer begins to preach and is both too negative and
too obviously angry with the Church to be taken very seriously.
The name of Ernest Renan[11] (1823—92), who forsook his studies at the Roman Catholic seminary of St. Sulpice in Paris because
he could no longer harmonize his critical views concerning the
Bible with an acceptance of the Christian faith, rightly belongs
among the "radical" New Testament critics, even though he was

---

[11] On Renan, see Schweitzer, *Von Reimarus zu Wrede,* Ch. 13; H. Knight,
"Ernest Renan", *Theology* 48 (1945), pp. 224—31. Many biographies and
studies of Renan have been written; see *EB* or *RGG*[3] for further bibliography.

not nearly so negative in his criticism of the Book of Acts as was
Bruno Bauer. The work of Bauer was the work of an angry man
who was bitter in his oppositions to his opponents and who could
see only evil and error in the Christianity they represented. Renan,
on the other hand, was not so much a bitter opponent of Christianity as a man who wanted desperately to believe but who could
not bring himself to do so. He attempted to save the best and the
highest virtues and ideals of Christianity by combining them with an
evolutionary optimism and a faith in the supreme value of modern
science, while rejecting the essential foundations of the Christian
faith as unhistorical.

Renan set before himself the goal of tracing and explaining the
evolution of the higher spiritual consciousness of mankind, seeking
to understand the secret of the creative epochs of human history. As
fundamental to this task he conceived and published a seven-vol-
umed *Histoire des origines du Christianisme*[12], the first volume of
which was his famous *La Vie de Jésus*[13]. The second and third volumes of his history are concerned primarily with the Book of Acts[14].

In sharp contrast to Bruno Bauer, as well as to the Tübingen
scholars, Renan returned to the traditional view that the author of
Acts was really Luke, the disciple of Paul. He could neither reject
the striking evidence of the "we"-narratives (X—XVI) nor deny the
improbability that the book would have been attributed to an otherwise obscure companion of Paul unless he were actually the author
(XVI—XVIII)[15]. Added to this is the fact that, by attributing the
book to a companion of Paul, two important peculiarities are explained:

[41] d'une part, la disproportion des parties de l'ouvrage, dont plus des trois
cinquièmes sont consacrés à Paul; de l'autre, la disproportion qui se
remarque dans la biographie même de Paul, dont la première mission est
exposée avec une grande brièveté, tandis que certaines de la deuxième

---

[12] (Paris, 1863—81).

[13] The other volumes are *Les Apôtres* (1866), *Saint Paul* (1869), *L'Anté-
christ* (1873), *Les Evangiles* (1877), *L'Chrétienne* (1879), and *Marc Aurèle
et la fin du monde antique* (1881).

[14] References in the text which follow are to *Les Apôtres*, to which he contributed a detailed introduction explaining his critical views concerning Acts.

[42] [15] "Inscrire un nom célèbre en tête d'un écrit, comme on le fit pour la
deuxième épître de Pierre, et très-probablement pour les épîtres de Paul à Tite
et à Timothée, n'avait rien qui répugnât aux habitudes du temps. Mais inscrire
en tête d'un écrit un faux nom, obscur d'ailleurs, c'est ce qui ne se conçoit plus"
(XVII). Renan goes on to ask why, if it was the intention to invest the book
with the authority of Paul, it was not attributed to Paul himself, or at least to
Timothy or Titus, who were so much better known than Luke.

et de la troisième mission, surtout les derniers voyages, sont racontés avec de minutieux détails. Un homme tout à fait étranger à l'histoire apostolique n'aurait pas eu de ces inégalités. L'ensemble de son ouvrage eût été mieux conçu (XV).

Renan dates Acts about the year 80, finding in the author's attempt to show how the Roman authorities were favourable to the Christian religion a reflection of the situation of the age of the first Flavians (XXII–XXIII).

Having defended the traditional view concerning the authorship of Acts and a rather conservative opinion regarding the date it was written, Renan parts company with the conservative critics. Although the author was a friend and companion of Paul, he is a partisan who has little concern for historical accuracy. He is an apologist at any cost. He is the first of a long series of ecclesiastical writers who are "béatement satisfaits, décidés à trouver que tout dans l'Église se passe d'une façon évangélique" (XXIV). [43]

Trop loyal pour condamner son maître Paul, trop orthodoxe pour ne pas se ranger à l'opinion officielle qui prévalait, il effaça les différences de doctrine pour laisser voir seulement le but commun, que tous ces grands fondateurs poursuivirent en effet par des voies si opposées et à travers de si énergiques rivalités (XXIV). [44]

Renan calls attention to the way the author has, in the Gospel of Luke, distorted the historical tradition to a much greater degree than have Matthew and Mark (XXVI)[16]. Is it not likely, he argues, that he has done the same thing in the Book of Acts? The answer is, quite naturally, a strong affirmative.

Still, Renan makes a basic distinction between the first part of the Book of Acts (chs. 1–12) and the second (chs. 13–28) in regard to their historical value (XXVI–XXVIII). The first part of the book is extremely unreliable, since the author is a Greek who has little feeling for or an understanding of things Jewish, and since sources of information were largely legendary. However, in the second part, he himself was an eyewitness to a part of what he narrates: and even where he was not an eyewitness his sources of information were excellent.

---

[16] It is interesting to note that, while those who are concerned to demonstrate the unreliable nature of the narrative of Acts point out the author's allegedly arbitrary use of his sources in the Gospel, those who are concerned to demonstrate the trustworthy nature of the history of Acts make the observation that the author's careful use of his sources in the Gospel is a sign of his essential trustworthiness as a historian! Many examples could be given; however, it is sufficient to suggest that the data are ambiguous and can be used according to the presuppositions of the individual critic.

[45]   Vers la fin surtourt, le récit prend un caractère étonnant de précision. Les dernières pages des *Actes* sont les seules pages complètement historiques que nous ayons sur les origines chrétiennes. Les premières, au contraire, sont les plus attaquables de tout le Nouveau Testament (XXVII)[17].

Having said this, however, Renan goes on to lay stress on the unhistorical part of the book. Here he stresses the alleged contradictions between the Pauline epistles, especially Galatians, and Acts, which the Tübingen critics had emphasized (XXIX—XXI). He adds nothing of real importance to the discussion, other than an eloquent statement of his opinion that the author's "tendency" is to support the opinions of the orthodoxy of his time by smoothing over the conflicts of the earlier age and by selecting from the tradition circulating in the Church materials which were partly legendary and partly historical.

[46]   Les *Actes,* en un mot, sont une histoire dogmatique, arrangée pour appuyer les doctrines orthodoxes du temps ou inculquer les idées qui souriaient le plus à la piété de l'auteur. Ajoutons qu'il ne pouvait en être autrement. On ne connaît l'origine de chaque religion que par les récits des croyants. Il n'y a que le sceptique qui écrive l'histoire *ad narrandum* (XXIX).

Renan concludes his introduction to the Book of Acts with a twenty-two page (more than one-third of the introduction!) attack upon the belief in miracles and an *apologia* for his rejection of orthodox Christianity (XLIII—LXIV)[18]. Although this makes interesting reading, it adds little to the study of the Book of Acts.

A good case could be given for including the name of Franz Camille Overbeck[19] (1837—1905), professor of New Testament

---

[17] It should be noted in passing that Renan was one of the first to argue for the so-called "South Galatian hypothesis", i. e. for the identification of the "Galatia" of Paul's epistle with the cities of Pisidian Antioch, Iconium, Lystra, and Derbe, which are mentioned in the Book of Acts (see his *Saint Paul,* pp. 22—56, 118—34, 311—28). This point of view was taken up later by Sir William M. Ramsay and will be discussed in chapter seven. It may be of special significance that Renan was probably the first person to write on the subject who could speak from a firsthand acquaintance with the geography and archaeology of Asia Minor.

[47]   [18] Cf. "Les douze premiers chapitres des *Actes* sont un tissu de miracles. Or, une règle absolue de la critique, c'est de ne pas donner place dans les récits historiques à des circonstances miraculeuses" (XLIII).

[19] On Overbeck, see W. Nigg, *Franz Overbeck: Versuch einer Würdigung* (München, 1931); P. Vielhauer, "Franz Overbeck und die neutestamentliche Wissenschaft", *EvTh* 10 (1950/51), pp. 193—207; E. Stähelin, *Overbekiana: Teil 1* (Basel, 1962); M. Tetz, *Overbekiana: Teil 2* (Basel, 1962); and B. Müller, *Glaube und Wissen nach Franz Overbeck* (Berlin, 1967). Both Nigg and Vielhauer are, in my view, too uncritical in their enthusiasm for Overbeck's work.

and early Christian history at the University of Basel from 1870 to 1897, among the authors who might be described as belonging to the mainstream of German biblical criticism, rather than among the "radicals". His work is in many ways more substantial than any of the others mentioned in this chapter and has always been taken more seriously by scholars[20]. However, because of the similarity of his position to that of Bruno Bauer[21], and because of the increasingly negative stand he came to take in regard to the Christian faith and the New Testament documents as a whole[22], he is best grouped with the company of scholars included in the present chapter. The length and erudition of his work does not make it therefore less extreme in its opinions.

Overbeck's important work on the Book of Acts is the greatly expanded revision of W. M. L. de Wette's commentary, which he published in 1870[23]. This was essentially a new work[24], even though this fact is partially obscured by the retention of de Wette's name on the title page, as though he were the chief author, and by the curious way in which the author places his own views alongside de Wette's — even when, as is often the case, they are mutually contradictory[25].

In general, Overbeck's views are much more dependent upon the work of F. C. Baur and his followers, in particular Eduard Zeller, than upon the work of de Wette. Indeed, his views are often in sharp contrast to the original author of the commentary. This is especially true in the way he takes a much more negative stance concerning the historical value of Acts. De Wette, as we have seen,

---

[20] Cf. "Overbeck's work was far and away the most important discussion of the subject that had appeared since Zeller's and still remains in many respects the best commentary we have" (McGiffert, *BC* 2, p. 381); cf. also Haenchen, *Die Apostelgeschichte*, pp. 19–20.

[21] Cf. McGiffert, *BC*, p. 382 n. Interestingly enough, the copy of Bauer's monograph on Acts (an exceedingly rare work) which I used as a basis for my summary of his position was once owned by Overbeck.

[22] Overbeck was a close friend of Friedrich Nietzsche and also became an atheist, although he kept his position as a theological professor at Basel. Cf. C. A. Bernouilli, *Franz Overbeck und Friedrich Nietzsche*, 2 vols. (Jena, 1908).

[23] *Kurze Erklärung der Apostelgeschichte*, Von W. M. L. de Wette, Vierte Auflage bearbeitet und stark erweitert von Franz Overbeck (Leipzig, 1870).

[24] He regards de Wette's commentary on Acts as "die schwächste Arbeit seines exegetischen Handbuches" (X).

[25] The situation is further confused by the English translator of the preface to Overbeck's commentary (printed in the E. T. of Zeller's *The Contents and Origin of the Acts of the Apostles* (London and Edinburgh, 1875), pp. 1–81), who gives no indication of the source of any given statement. Thus one finds mutually contradictory statements side-by-side as if both were from the pen of Overbeck!

judged the Book of Acts to be unhistorical in various places, especially in the earlier chapters; but in general he considered it to be a good deal more reliable as a source of early Christian history than did Baur. Overbeck, on the other hand, considers the essential unreliability of the book to be an established fact of criticism, "in the whole and in the part", and hardly worthy of discussion (XVIII, LIX). Even though he admits that items here and there in the Pauline section of Acts may have had a historical basis of some sort, he is unwilling to give even this part of Acts anything like the value given to it by de Wette (XXIX—LII).

Although Overbeck espouses a number of important views in common with Bruno Bauer, he does not seem to have been greatly influenced by his work in regard to detail. Rather, his commentary bears a more important relationship to that of Zeller, who is probably the most frequently quoted author and with whom he expresses general agreement. If Overbeck did not differ from the Tübingen critics in one important way, it might be justifiable to refer to his work as the one commentary on Acts which was written from this point of view. However, there is a major difference: Overbeck rejected the Tübingen formulation of the purpose of Acts.

He agrees with Baur and Zeller that the Book of Acts is a *Tendenzschrift*; but its *Tendenz* is a different one from that suggested [48] by the Tübingen scholars. It is not "der Entwurf eines Friedensvorschlags von paulinischer Seite den Judaisten vorgelegt[26]" which "die Anerkennung des Heidenchristenthums von Seite der Judenchristen durch Zugeständnisse an den Judaismus erkaufen und in diesem Sinn auf beide Parteien wirken will"[27]. No, it could not have been intended to exercise a conciliatory influence upon Jewish Christians. This is especially evident when one takes note of the "nationale Antijudaismus" of the Book of Acts, its antagonism to the Jews as a nation (XXX). The author constantly attributes the development of the Christian Church to the steadfast unbelief of the Jews. In fact, he betrays a zealous endeavour to separate the cause of the [49] Christians from that of the Jews (XXXI)[28]. Overbeck writes, "Nichts kann vielmehr evidenter sein, als dass die AG. das jüdische Christenthum als solches preisgibt und auf einem Standpunkt geschrieben ist, welchem das Heidenchristenthum als das in der Gemeinde durchaus vorherrschende Element gilt" (XXXI). In short, there was no real need to reconcile the Judaizers and the Paulinists; for when Acts

---

[26] Zeller, *Die Apostelgeschichte*, p. 358.

[27] *Ibid.*, p. 363.

[28] Cf. his comments, pp. 293—97, 323—27; also, on the secondary, political purpose of Acts, *infra*, pp. 83—84.

was written all such conflict was a thing of the past, and Gentile Christianity clearly had the upper hand in the Church.

The Gentile Christianity of the Book of Acts is not Pauline Christianity; neither is the Jewish Christianity of Acts to be identified with that of the *Urapostel*. "Vielmehr muss das Judaistische der AG. schon ein Bestandtheil des Heidenchristenthums sein, welches sie selbst vertritt ..." (XXXI). Therefore, Acts is to be interpreted not as

[50]

ein Friedensvorschlag zwischen jenen urchristlichen Parteien, sondern der Versuch eines selbst vom urchristlichen Judaismus schon stark beeinflussten Heidenchristenthums sich mit der Vergangenheit, insbesondere seiner eigenen Entstehung und seinem ersten Begründer Paulus auseinander zusetzen (XXXI).

[51]

The Book of Acts represents a Gentile Christianity which has given up the essential features of Paulinism, with the single exception of universalism. However, this is not the result of a concession being made to a party outside of its own circle, but rather the result of its own conception of Paul, a conception which stems from the Judaistic influences which were at work in the Church from the very beginning and from the natural inability of Gentile Christianity to grasp the original Pauline theology. In short, it is that theology which came to dominate what church historians call the Old Catholic Church (XXXI–XXXII).

The primary purpose of the author, then, is to explain the (Gentile) Christianity of his day — which Overbeck regards to be that of the second or third decade of the second century (LXIV)[29] — in terms of its past. But there is also, in Overbeck's view, a secondary aim of the author: a political apologetic (XXXII–XXXIII).

In this connection Overbeck regards the author of Acts as writing with his eyes on the Romans. The author tries to win the favor of the state authorities for the Christian cause by the consistent representation of the friendly relations which the Christian leaders of the apostolic age, especially Paul, had with the Roman state and its officials. For example, prominent Roman officials are among those Gentiles converted by Peter and Paul (10.1–47; 13.7–12; cf. also 28.7–9). In addition, the groundlessness of the political indictments against Paul is repeatedly urged[30], the authorities always offer him their protection (18.12–17; 19.35–41); or, when they have mistakenly shown him any lack of respect, they recognize the claim which he has as a Roman citizen to their protection (16.37–39; 22.22–29). The trial of Paul gives the Roman authorities a special

---

[29] Cf. *infra*, pp. 85–86.   [30] Cf. his comments, pp. 270–71.

opportunity to show a favorable opinion of him[31]; even as a pris-
oner in Rome he is able to fulfill his apostolic duties for a time,
under the shelter of the Roman law (28.30—31). In the light of
these facts, Overbeck concludes:

[52] Man kann in dieser Darstellung ... die Absicht einer Abweisung politi-
scher Verdächtigungen des Christenthums nicht verkennen, und sie kann,
wie sie in der AG. ausgeführt ist, nicht wohl an eine andere Adresse ge-
richtet sein, als an die ausserh. der Gemeinde stehenden Heiden (XXXIII).

The Book of Acts, then, is the immediate forerunner of the apologetic literature which flourished at a slightly later time in the
Church's development (LXV).

As has already been noted, Overbeck is in general agreement
with the Tübingen critics regarding the historical value of Acts. The
main difference between his view and theirs is that, whereas the
Tübingen critics attributed the historical inaccuracies to the deliberate falsification by the author as a result of his *Tendenz*, Overbeck attributes the inaccuracies as due, in a large measure, to the
author's ignorance. He is not so much trying to alter the facts to fit
his case as he is writing at a time and in a position where he is no
longer aware of many of the original facts. Therefore, he can only
fall back on the resources of his own imagination in filling in the
details of the fragmentary sources of information which he has at
his disposal. Since he possesses little truly reliable information, he
can only attempt to reconstruct the events of the early age in terms
of what he *thinks* they were like. Thus his reconstruction is influenced in a large measure by the nature of the Christianity of his
own age.

But what, then, of the ἡμεῖς-sections? Are these not evidence
that the author was an eyewitness of at least some of the events
which he narrates? This question Overbeck answers with an emphatic negative (XXXIX—LII). He argues on the basis of certain
peculiarities of the narrative that the "we"—sections are the result
of the author's having used a written source of some sort, possibly
a memoir of a former travelling companion of the Apostle. In its
original form it was more than merely a travel-diary or itinerary
(XLVI). However, in the form we now have it it has been almost
totally rewritten by the author, who has introduced a large amount
of unreliable information into the narrative. Side by side with a few
items taken from his source which may be accepted as more or less
trustworthy lie parts of the narrative which belong to the most unreliable strata of the Book of Acts. For example, the narratives of

---

[31] Cf. his comments, pp. 367—68.

the arrest and release of Paul and Silas in Philippi (16.18–40), the note in 20.16, Paul's Miletus speech (20.17–35), the account of Paul's purification (21.18–26), and his meeting with the Jewish leaders in Rome (28.17–25) — each of which Overbeck assigns to the category of the unreliable (XLVIII–XLIX)[32] — immediately follow the text of the original ἡμεῖς-sections.

Why, then, has the author retained the ἡμεῖς? Is this merely accidental, an oversight on his part? The retention of the ἡμεῖς can only be explained as due to the author's special design, argues Overbeck. He desires to pass himself off for one of Paul's companions (XLV), probably the Luke of the Church's tradition (LI).

As far as the use of other sources by the author of Acts, Overbeck argues that the author may have used them but that he has handled them with such freedom that they are scarcely discernible, if at all (LVII–LVIII). He specifically rejects de Wette's suggestion that the letters of 15.23–29 and 23.26–30 and the speeches bear evidence of being based on sources which might be quite reliable (LII–LV).

Concerning the date of the Book of Acts, Overbeck contends that it could not have been written during the apostolic age, or even as early as the last two decades of the first century.

Ein Buch, das wie dieses (namentl. im 1. Theil) schon so stark unter dem Einfluss der Sage steht und (namentl. im 2. Theil) die Dinge, über die es berichtet, schon in so fremdartiger Verschiebung erscheinen lässt, müsste entweder eine vollkommen sinnlose Fälschung sein, oder es setzt zwischen sich und seinem Object eine längere Zeit voraus, welche einerseits der absichtsloseren Sage, anderseits den Verhältnissen, welche die Vergangenheit schon einer sie so stark modificirenden Betrachtungsweise unterwarfen, Raum zur Entwickelung lässt. Ganz besonders die Thatsache, dass Paulus der Held der AG. ist und sein Bild doch nur in so starker Entstellung darin vorliegt, setzt eine Geschichte voraus, welche nicht wohl innerhalb der Grenzen des apostol. Zeitalters schon zu solchen Resultaten geführt haben kann (LXIV). [53]

While one cannot be too certain concerning all the details of this history, there nevertheless appears to be sufficient reason to seek the date as late as the external testimony in regard to the Third Gospel will allow, viz. the second or third decade of the second century.

Overbeck finds five items which argue for the appropriateness of this time in the Church's history for the origin of Acts (LXIV to LXV): (1) The political-apologetic aspect of Acts presupposes a reasonably advanced maturity and settled state of affairs in the

---

[32] Cf. his comments, pp. 261–68, 336–54, 364–90, 472–81.

Church, and particularly the absence of those questions concerning the relationship between Christianity and Judaism which dominated the life of the Church in its earliest days. The Church has already achieved its independence, even though it recognizes a debt to Judaism. (2) As had already been observed, the apologetic nature of Acts gives it the character of an immediate forerunner of the apologetic literature which flourished a few years later. (3) The author regards the *parousia* as an event belonging to the indefinite future. (4) The traces of the beginning of a hierarchical constitution of the Church (1.17, 20; 8.14—17; 15.28; 20.17, 28)[33] and of (5) a polemic against Gnosticism (20.29)[34] also point in this direction.

Asia Minor, probably Ephesus, rather than Rome, is suggested as the likely place of origin of the Book of Acts (LXV—LXIX). In defence of this view it is argued that Marcion may have become acquainted with the Lucan writings there, rather than in Rome; that the use of Luke's Gospel in the Gospel of John points in this direction; that Acts shows a special interest in Asia Minor; that it was here that Pauline Christianity began, struggled for its existence against the Christianity which adhered to the theology of the primitive apostles, and in all probability became victorious (though not without change); and that the political character of Acts also points to Asia Minor, where, during the reign of Trajan, Christianity first independently confronted the Gentile state, and where the oldest apologetic literature originated.

Willem Christiaan van Manen[35] (1842—1905), professor of early Christian history and New Testament exegesis at Leyden, the leading representative of the so-called Dutch Radical School of New Testament criticism, was more dispassionate in his criticism than the other "radicals". His tone is at all times reasonable and cool. One does not detect the same spirit of bitterness toward orthodox theology or traditional opinion which is all too obviously present in the writings of Bauer, Renan, Overbeck, or the earlier Tübingen critics. If there is a note of bitterness in what he wrote, it is directed

---

[33] Cf. his comments, pp. 12—14, 122—24, 236—42, 244—45, 339, 347—48.

[34] Cf. his comments, pp. 348—51.

[35] On van Manen and the Dutch radicals, see H. J. Hager, *The Radical School of Dutch New Testament Criticism* (diss. University of Chicago, 1935). The views of van Manen are expounded in detail and defended by T. Whittaker, *The Origins of Christianity* (London, 1904; 2nd ed., 1909; 3rd ed., 1914; 4th ed., 1933), and G. A. van den Bergh van Eysinga, *Radical Views about the New Testament* (E. T., London, 1912).

toward the critical establishment in Germany, who failed to give his views the careful attention he felt they deserved[36].

Building on the work of his immediate predecessors in the Netherlands — A. Pierson, S. A. Naber, and A. D. Loman — as well as on the work of the earlier Tübingen critics[37], van Manen became the best known exponent of the Radical Dutch point of view. Between 1890 and 1896 he published a three-volumed work on Paul in which he set out his views in detail. The first volume was devoted to the Book of Acts[38]. His views became widely known in the English-speaking world in 1902 through his famous article on Paul which was written for the *Encyclopaedia Biblica*[39].

The Dutch radicals agreed with F. C. Baur in their interpretation of early Christianity as essentially Jewish. However, they recognized that the Pauline epistles, especially Galatians and Romans, emphasize the continuity between the theology of Paul and that of the earliest apostles. In view of the developed theology of the Pauline epistles — even in the so-called *Hauptbriefe* — they felt it was impossible to maintain this identity. Thus follows the further conclusion that *none* of the Pauline epistles is genuine. The Pauline letters — too impersonal to have been real letters written to specific congregations, and too theologically developed to have been written in such close proximity to the historical Jesus — were then attributed to a "Paulus Episcopus"[40], a second century bishop who combined various Jewish and Christian fragments with his own theological convictions and published them under the name of a legendary early missionary.

In his examination of the Book of Acts — an examination which, in the light of the evidence advanced against the genuineness of the Roman, Galatian, and Corinthian epistles, he insists must be made independently of the Pauline letter corpus — he detects an essential

---

[36] See his article, "A Wave of Hypercriticism", *ExpT* 9 (1898), pp. 205—11, 257—59, 314—19.

[37] Hager refers to the Dutch Radical School as "the left branch of a stream (*sc.* the Tübingen criticism) which divided almost at its source" (*Op. cit.*, p. 1). Bruno Bauer certainly belongs to "the left branch" too, and possibly also Overbeck.

[38] *Paulus I. De Handelingen der Apostelen* (Leiden, 1890). A convenient condensation for English readers is contained in T. Whittaker, *Op. cit.*, pp. 73 —110. *Paulus II* is a study of Romans; *Paulus III*, of 1 and 2 Corinthians.

[39] *EncBib* 3 (1902), cols. 3603—38. Sections 4—32 are by Edwin Hatch and are taken from his article on Paul in the ninth edition of *Encyclopedia Britannica* (vol. 18, 1885).

[40] Cf. W. C. van Manen, "Paulus Episcopus", *JPT* 13 (1887), pp. 395—431.

unity of the work[41]. The fact that one can observe a definite order
and plan, as well as an essential unity of literary style, is evidence
in favor of a single author. Acts gives evidence of imaginative reconstruction — as, for example, the unity it assumes between the
messages of Peter and Paul, Paul's submissive relationship to the
authority of the Jerusalem church, and so forth — but it is not an
entirely free composition throughout. This is shown by the intermingling of inconsistent traditions, as one observes, for example, in
connection with the gift of tongues and the passages relating to the
reception of the Holy Spirit. Furthermore, there is clear evidence of
the author's use of sources.

Van Manen lists five possible sources used by the author: the
"Pauline" letters, the itinerary-document, an "Acts of Paul", an
"Acts of Peter", and the writings of Josephus. The only use of the
Pauline letters which seems to him probable is the author's use of
Galatians 2 in his account of the so-called Jerusalem council of
Acts 15. The similarities, he contends, are too numerous to be the
result of coincidence; and it is most improbable that the author of
Galatians would have neglected to mention James' support of the
decision of the Jerusalem council if he were dependent on the Book
of Acts.

The so-called "we"-narratives are regarded as possibly based on
a diary or story of a single journey of Paul, which may have been
historical even if we cannot be sure of the exact details. The "Acts
of Paul" (περίοδοι or πράξεις παύλου) and the "Acts of Peter" (περίοδοι or πράξεις πέτρου) are two documents which he finds underlying the basically Pauline (chs. 13—28) and Petrine (chs. 1—12)
parts of the book. The former, which probably also included the
earlier itinerary-document, was probably written by a "Paulinist"
towards the end of the first century; it is a collection of various
legends and traditions about an early missionary-hero of the Gentile
churches. The latter was apparently written as a counterpart to the
older Acts of Paul: this, then, is the reason for the deliberate parallelisms between the two documents, as well as for the exaggerations
of the legendary and miraculous elements in the earlier part of the
book. Evidence for the dependence on Josephus by the author of
Acts is found in the parallelism existing between the phenomena
said to have accompanied the outpouring of the Holy Spirit on the
day of Pentecost and the portents described by Josephus as preceding the destruction of Jerusalem[42], the mention of Theudas and

---

[41] The statements which follow are based on T. Whittaker's summary (n. 38)
and on the article in *EncBib* (n. 39).

[42] Cf. Acts 2.1—4 with *BJ* 6.5,3.

Judas the Galilean in Gamaliel's speech (due evidently to an imperfect recollection of what the author had read in Josephus)[43], the reference to the "Egyptian" who led four thousand σικάριοι into the wilderness in revolt against Rome[44], and the chief personages connected with Paul's imprisonment and trial — Felix, Drusilla, Festus, Agrippa, and Bernice[45].

Van Manen is critical of the Tübingen definition of the purpose of Acts. The author, he argues, did not need to begin the reconciliation of the Petrinists and Paulinists, since others, notably the author of the Acts of Peter, had preceded him in this. It would be an error to describe one single aim as the author's predominant aim. One may observe an apologetic aim with regard to the Romans[46], i. e., to encourage them to continue their protective attitude toward Christianity which, according to the story, they had taken from the beginning; yet the author combines this with other purposes, such as the drawing clearly of the line between Judaism and Christianity, the smoothing over of existing doctrinal differences in the Church, and so forth. In the end it would be unjust not to recognize that his essential purpose is correctly described by himself at the beginning of the Third Gospel, of which Acts, according to his own statement, is a continuation. What he primarily had in view was to give more exact instruction to Christian converts as to the events on which their faith was founded. His purpose was to write

---

[43] Cf. Acts 5.36—37 with *Ant.* 20.5,1—2.

[44] Cf. Acts 21.38 with *Ant.* 20.8,6; *BJ* 2.13,5. Van Manen points out that the word σικάριος, which is found nowhere else in the New Testament, occurs often (seventeen times) in Josephus and apparently in no other Greek writer. The term is found, however, in the Talmudic literature in reference to the terrorists during the last siege of Jersualem (see M. Jastrow, *A Dictionary of the Targumim* ... (London, 1903), p. 986) and in the *Lex Cornelia de Sicarii*, and in Cicero in the general sense of bandits (see Hug, "Sica", *P—W²* 4 (1923), p. 2184). See the index to the Loeb edition of Josephus for a complete list of the references in Josephus.

[45] Van Manen adds a further item of evidence: In making Paul predict that God shall "smite" the high priest Ananias (23.3), the author of Acts probably had in mind the fact that the same high priest — whose slaves used to "smite" those who would not willingly give him tithes from the threshing floor (*Ant.* 20.9,2), just as he commanded that Paul should be smitten (23.2) — had died a violent death (*BJ* 2.17,3).

[46] This is given as the reason why the death of Paul is not mentioned in Acts: the writer did not wish to arouse prejudice on the part of the Romans, whom it was his object to prepossess in favor of Christianity. Another example of the way this aim of the author is maintained is found in the way the Jews are represented as rejecting and actively persecuting the new "Way", while the Romans are always benevolently disposed toward it.

history, in a sense: "sacred history" would perhaps be the best description.

What is there of historical value which remains when the sources have been evaluated and sifted? What, in particular, remains of the historical Paul, when radical criticism has done its work? Here is the basic outline in terms of van Manen's principles:

Paul was the somewhat younger contemporary of Peter and the other disciples of Jesus, and probably a Jew by birth, a native of Tarsus in Cilicia. At first his attitude towards the disciples was one of hostility. Later, originally a tentmaker by calling, he cast in his lot with the followers of Jesus, and in the service of the higher truth revealed through them, spent the remainder of a life of vicissitude as a wandering preacher. In the course of his travels he visited various lands: Syria, Asia Minor, Greece, and Italy ... With regard to his journeys, we can in strictness speak with reasonable certainty and with some detail only of one great journey which he undertook towards the end of his life: from Troas to Philippi, back to Troas, Assos, Mitylene, Samos, Miletus, Rhodes, Patara, Tyre, Ptolemais, Caesarea, Jerusalem, back to Caesarea, Sidon, Myra, Fair Havens, Melita, Syracuse, Rhegium, Puteoli, Rome (Acts 16.10–17; 20.5–15; 21.1–18; 27.1-28.16).

Perhaps at an earlier date he had been one of the first who, along with others of Cyprus and Cyrene, proclaimed to Jews and Gentiles outside of Palestine the principles and hopes of the disciples of Jesus (Acts 11.19 f.). Possibly, indeed probably, we may infer further details of the same sort from what Lk. and the authors of the epistles have borrowed from the 'Acts of Paul', as to the places visited by Paul, and the measure of his success in each; in which of them he met with opposition, in which with indifference; what particular discouragements and adventures he encountered; such facts as that he seldom or never came into contact with the disciples in Palestine; that even after years had passed he was still practically a stranger to the brethren dwelling in Jerusalem; that on a visit there he but narrowly escaped suffering the penalty of death on a charge of contempt for the temple, which would show in how bad odour he had long been with many[47].

But, he immediately adds: "As regards all these details, however, we have no certain knowledge."

In spite of his rather consistent historical skepticism, van Manen is in at least one way more conservative than the Tübingen critics: he regards the "Jewish" Paul of the Book of Acts as having been the real Paul. Acts has erred not in making Paul appear too Jewish, but rather in making him out to be too Gentile, or, perhaps better, too Christian. He was and remained a faithful Jew.

---

[47] "Paul", *EncBib* 3, cols. 3631–32.

It may be that Paul's journeyings, his protracted sojourn outside of Palestine, his intercourse in foreign parts with converted Jews and former heathen, may have emancipated him (as it did so many other Jews of the dispersion), without his knowing it, more or less — perhaps in essence completely — from circumcision and other Jewish religious duties, customs, and rites. But even so he had not broken with these. He had, like all the other disciples, remained in his own consciousness a Jew, a faithful attender of temple or synagogue, only in the one thing distinguished from the children of Abraham, that he held and preached 'the things concerning Jesus', and in connection with this devoted himself specially to a strict life and the promotion of mutual love[48].

There was no essential difference as regards faith and life between Paul and the other disciples. This was to come later with the development of the "theology of Paul".

Before bringing the chapter to a conclusion, one last writer following in the "radical" tradition of *Actaforschung* should be mentioned — Paul Wilhelm Schmiedel[49] (1851—1935), professor of New Testament exegesis at the University of Zürich from 1893 to 1923 and author of the essay on the Book of Acts in the *Encyclopaedia Biblica*[50].

Schmiedel's views concerning Acts are very similar to those of Overbeck. Thus he sees the basic "tendency" of Acts as this: "to justify the Gentile Christianity of himself and his time, already on the way to Catholicism, and he seeks to do this by means of an account of the origin of Christianity" (40). He sees also two subsidiary *Tendenzen*, a political and an aesthetic one. The political *Tendenz* is manifest in the author's "desire to say as little as possible unfavourable to the Roman civil power" (42)[51]. The aesthetic *Tendenz* is evident in the author's mode of narration: he aims at being graphic (42)[52].

---

[48] *Ibid.*, col. 3632.

[49] On Schmiedel, see the article by A. Meyer in *Protestantische Monatshefte* 25 (1921), pp. 161—67. Schmiedel is best known for his famous thesis concerning the nine "Pillar-passages" for "a truly scientific life of Jesus" (his words), which was set forth in his lengthy article on the "Gospels", which appeared in *EncBib* 2 (1901), cols. 1761—1898; cf. especially sections 139 and 140.

[50] *EncBib* 1 (1899), cols. 37—57. The author claims this tradition for himself when he lists the work of the Tübingen critics, Bruno Bauer, and Franz Overbeck as the most important landmarks in the history of Acts criticism (col. 57).

[51] He brings forth the passages mentioned by Overbeck in support of this view.

[52] This is the purpose of the "we" and the details, "otherwise purposeless", which are appropriated from the "Journey Record". This aim is also served by much of the detail of chapters 1—12, the speeches, and the miracle-narratives, all of which add vigor and color to the narrative.

As far as the historicity of the events which are narrated in Acts is concerned, Schmiedel finds inaccuracies which are generally un-influenced by the author's purposes[53], as well as (more numerous) errors due to the author's primary "tendency". "A whole series of demonstrable inaccuracies", belonging to this latter category, stem from the fact that the author never allows Paul to come into con-flict with the original apostles or their followers as he does in his epistles[54]. On the other hand, Paul brings forward no new doctrine, nothing whatever in which the *Urapostel* had not led the way. "Far from going beyond them at all, he appears to be entirely dependent on them" (41). To substantiate this point of view, Schmiedel brings forth no new material; he simply points to the same date emphasized by the Tübingen critics.

Schmiedel agrees with Overbeck regarding the reasons for many of the inaccuracies of Acts. In the majority of cases these are ex-plained

simply by the assumption that the writer was not in possession of full information, and that, in a naive yet still unbiassed way, he first repre-sented to himself the conditions of the apostolic age, and afterwards de-scribed them, as if they had been similar to those of his own . . . . (42).

A general principle to be observed in determining the trustworthi-ness of the Book of Acts is this:

Apart from the "we" sections no statement merits immediate acceptance on the mere ground of its presence in the book. All that contradicts the Pauline epistles must be absolutely given up, unless we are to regard these as spurious. Positive proofs of the trustworthiness of Acts must be tested with the greatest caution (46).

Concerning the speeches of Acts, Schmiedel regards it as "beyond doubt" that the author constructed them in each case according to his own conception of the situation, in the manner of other ancient historians (47)[55]. The speeches of Paul, therefore, contain a theol-

---

[53] Belonging to this category he lists such details as the contradictions be-tween the three accounts of the manifestation of the Risen Lord to Paul (9.7: 22.9: 26.12—18), the explanation of the departure from Jerusalem in 9.26—30 with 22.17—21, the explanation of the offering in 21.20—26 with that in 24.17—18, and the occasion of the appeal to Caesar in 25.9—11 with that in 28.18—19.

[54] Evidence cited for Paul's alleged conflict "with the original apostles *or their followers*" (the last phrase is the significant one): Gal. 4.17; 5.7, 10, 12; 2 Cor. 10.14—15; 11.13—15, 18—32.

[55] Here Schmiedel refers to Thucydides' celebrated statement in his "History of the War between Athens and Sparta" (1.22.1).

ogy quite different from that of his epistles[56], and the most characteristically Pauline utterances come from Peter (15.7—11) and James (15.19). Yet he does attach a high degree of historical importance to the Christology of the Petrine speeches. Here Jesus is called παῖς θεοῦ — "not 'son', but 'servant' of God" (3.13, 36; cf. 4.25) — holy and righteous (3.14; 4.27; 2.27); he was not constituted Lord and Messiah before his resurrection (2.36); his death is regarded as a calamity for which the Jews are ultimately guilty, rather than as a divine arrangement for the salvation of men (3.13 —15; 5.30); he was anointed by God (4.27) with "holy spirit and strength"; he went about doing good and healing people, although Acts 10.38 indicates that he healed only demoniacs; his qualification for healing was the fact that God was with him (10.38); indeed, it is God who performed the miracles through him (2.22).

A representation of Jesus so simple, and in such exact agreement with the impression left by the most genuine passages of the first three gospels [sc. Schmiedel's "pillar-passages"], is nowhere else to be found in the whole New Testament. It is hardly possible not to believe that this Christology of the speeches of Peter must have come from a primitive source (48).

In conclusion, what was the significance of the work of the radical critics? Some would find the significance in their providing the *reductio ad absurdum* of the Tübingen position and, therefore, demonstrating most clearly the untenable nature of this hypothesis. The present writer, however, would find the significance in the influence of the radicals, either directly or indirectly, on subsequent criticism. Views which were first developed by the extreme critics — by men whose work was seldom taken seriously by mainstream criticism — later come to be part and parcel of what some scholars would regard as "the assured results of criticism". Some of these points may be mentioned here.

The first item of significance is the emphasis laid by the radicals on the creativity of the author of Acts in his narration of events. The book thus comes to be regarded primarily as "ein Werk der Dichtung und Reflexion", much of it the result of the "freie Schöpfung des Verfassers"[57]. This view has a very negative connotation in Bauer and Overbeck, but it comes to be stated more positively   [54]

---

[56] "A thought like Acts 17.28 is nowhere to be found in the epistles. Paul derives idolatry, not, as in Acts 17.29 f., from excusable ignorance, but from deliberate and criminal rejection of God (Rom. 1.18—32). Only in Acts 13.38 f., 16.31, 20.28, do some really Pauline principles begin to make themselves heard" (48).

[57] B. Bauer, *Die Apostelgeschichte*, pp. 141, 116.

by Schmiedel in his attributing an "aesthetic tendency" to the author[58].

Possibly the most significant change from the earlier Tübingen criticism was the stress by the radicals on the author's inability to know and, when knowledge was available, to understand the facts of the apostolic age, rather than his deliberate misconstruing of the facts as the result of a special *Tendenz*[59]. Although the author of the Book of Acts may have had a "tendency" or "tendencies", these did not affect the book in the thorough-going fashion that Baur and his followers had imagined. Yet, although the radicals assigned a different reason for it, they stood united in their agreement with the Tübingen critics that the narrative of Acts was essentially untrustworthy as a source of early Christian history.

A further important development was in connection with the understanding of the viewpoint of the author of Acts. Whereas Baur and his disciples had described the author as a "Paulinist" and attributed to him a conciliatory purpose, aimed at the reconciliation of the Jewish and Gentile elements, the radicals placed the author at a time when all such conflict was past history. They did not actually date the Book of Acts any later chronologically; rather, they pointed out the impossibility of the supremacy of Jewish leadership in the Church continuing until such a late date. The position of the author of Acts is that of *Frühkatholizismus;* the "Jewish" elements which find their way into the Book of Acts are not the result of a compromise with the Jewish-Christian party, but are elements which had already been incorporated into Gentile Christianity from Judaism as a result of the failure of the later generation to understand the teaching of Paul.

The purpose of Acts now comes to be thought of in much more general terms than that suggested by Baur. Now it is regarded as the attempt of Gentile Christianity to explain its Jewish origins and how it came to be an essentially Gentile movement; it was written at a time when Gentile Christians had lost touch with the Jewish heritage of the Church and needed to have it explained to them. Acts answers the question of why an originally Jewish movement changed into a Gentile movement by pointing to the steadfast rejection of the message of the Gospel by the Jews, which, in turn, led to the preaching of the Gospel to non-Jews.

---

[58] *Supra*, p. 91.

[55] [59] Cf. H. J. Holtzmann's statement: "Wo er [*sc.* der Verfasser der Apostelgeschichte] nach der Tübinger Kritik nicht sehen wollte, da konnte er der neueren Auffassung gemäss vielmehr meist nicht sehen" (*Hand-Kommentar zum Neuen Testament* 1 (Freiburg im Br., 1890), p. 308.

Most of the radicals found a secondary, political-apologetic aim of the author of Acts: to win the favor of the Roman authorities, or possibly Romans in general, for Christianity by emphasizing the friendly relationship which existed in the early days of the Church between the Church's leaders — primarily Paul — and the Roman officials. This had been suggested earlier by Schneckenburger, with whom Zeller had concurred, but had been generally overlooked in the discussion which centered around the debate concerning the main thesis of the Tübingen critics. Overbeck and others brought this feature of Acts to prominence once again, although they did not develop this to any great degree.

In this way, then, the radical descendants of the Tübingen School laid down certain guidelines which were to become very influential in the subsequent history of the study of the Book of Acts, especially in Germany. Nearly all scholars would give lip-service to the fact that the radicals were extreme and that most of their views were untenable. Yet, as also in connection with the original Tübingen criticism, seed sown by Bauer, Overbeck, and company will be seen to re-appear time and time again in the writings of the many scholars who often seem to be unaware of the origins of their own opinions.

Chapter V

GERMAN CRITICISM AT THE END OF THE CENTURY

By the end of the nineteenth century the Book of Acts had ceased to occupy the important place in scholarly debate which it had had a few decades earlier under the influence of the then-dominant Tübingen criticism. *Tendenzkritik* was uniformly rejected by all scholars of any importance and, as a result, was assigned to the junkheap reserved for all temporary fads of biblical criticism. Although, as we shall see later, certain basic assumptions of the Tübingen reconstruction of early Christianity had been assimilated by the dominant critical tradition, the reign of Baur (overtly, at least) was over.

Scholars were now devoting themselves, for the most part, to such problems as the "quest of the historical Jesus" and the relationship between Jesus and Paul, rather than to the Book of Acts and its special problems. The majority of those who were concerned with Acts at all were lost in the Stygian darkness of source criticism[1], where, with no documentary guidelines (as in the case of the Synoptic Gospels), they demonstrated the futility of their task by the extreme diversity of their conclusions[2]. A few others were attempting to solve the problem of the so-called "Western" text of Acts,

---

[1] The history of the source criticism of Acts lies outside of the scope of this study. Cf. Dupont, *Sources, passim;* O. Zöckler, "Die Apostelgeschichte als Gegenstand höherer und niederer Kritik", in *Greifswalder Studien: Theologische Abhandlungen H. Cremer zum 25jährigen Professorenjubiläum dargebracht* (Gütersloh, 1895), pp. 107–29; and R. J. Knowling, *EGT* 2, pp. 16–34, for a discussion of the significant contributions in this area in nineteenth century Germany.

[2] The most important attempts at isolating the sources of Acts were Bernhard Weiss, *Lehrbuch der Einleitung in das Neue Testament* (Berlin, 1886); Martin Sorof, *Die Entstehung der Apostelgeschichte* (Berlin, 1890); Paul Feine, *Eine vorkanonische Überlieferung des Lukas im Evangelium und Apostelgeschichte* (Gotha, 1891); Friedrich Spitta, *Die Apostelgeschichte: ihre Quellen und deren geschichtlicher Wert* (Halle, 1891); Carl Clemen, *Die Chronologie der paulinischen Briefe aufs Neue untersucht* (Halle, 1893) and "Die Zusammensetzung von Apg. 1–5," *TSK* 68 (1895), pp. 297–357; Johannes Jüngst, *Die Quellen der Apostelgeschichte* (Gotha, 1895); and Hans Hinrich Wendt, *Die Apostelgeschichte, KEK* 8th ed. (Göttingen, 1899).

while others were gathering evidence in support of an alleged polit-ical-apologetic aim in Acts. The important issues raised by the Tü-bingen scholars tended to recede into the background of the discussion.

The attempted solutions of the problem of the "Western" text of Acts was hardly more successful than the efforts to isolate the sources of Acts. Yet the textual criticism of the period did lead to the ingenious, if not enduring, hypothesis of the distinguished gram-marian, Friedrich Wilhelm Blass (1843—1907) — a theory which was accepted, with some modification, by Theodor Zahn[3] and Eber-hard Nestle[4].

One of the thorny problems which has troubled textual critics is the existence of two strikingly divergent textual traditions which characterize the text-history of the Book of Acts, represented by the general agreement of the older Greek uncials (א ABC) on the one hand, and what Westcott and Hort designated the "Western text"[5]. Generally speaking, the "Western" text is longer than that repre-sented by other manuscripts, so that as a whole it is nearly ten per cent longer than the "Alexandrian" text. The extra length of the "Western" text has generally been accounted for by scholars as due to scribal additions or interpolations; for this reason it is regarded to be of dubious value, although no generally recognized explana-tion of the divergencies has yet been offered.

The seventeenth-century Dutch theologian, J. Clericus, seems to have been the first to make the suggestion that the author of Acts himself may have been responsible for the two varying textual tra-ditions; however, he rejected this theory, which he viewed as im-probable (though possible), in favor of the view that the distinctive features of the "Western" text are due to scribal interpolation[6]. In

---

[3] Zahn had made the suggestion, independently of Blass, as early as 1885, that the "Western" text represented either the first draft of the author's work or a copy which contained supplementary marginal notes from the pen of the author. In his monograph, *Die Urausgabe der Apostelgeschichte des Lucas* (Leipzig, 1916), he defends what is essentially the same theory as the one suggested by Blass. All too much space is taken up by the discussion of the same theory in his two-volumed commentary on Acts in his *Kommentar zum Neuen Testament* (Leipzig, 1919 and 1921).

[4] See his "Eine neue biblische Entdeckung", *Die christliche Welt* 9 (1895), pp. 304—8, 332—33, 352—53; and "Einige Beobachtungen zum Codex Bezae", *TSK* 69 (1896), pp. 102—13.

[5] See Bruce, *Acts*, pp. 40—49, for an accurate account of the main features of the problem. Cf. also E. J. Epp, *The Theological Tendency of Codex Bezae Cantabrigiensis in Acts* (Cambridge, 1966), pp. 1—34.

[6] Cf. Clark (n.9), p. xxi.

the middle of the nineteenth century F. A. Bornemann[7] advanced the view that the longer text represents the original version of Acts, while the shorter stems from a very early copy; the former was deposited in the archives of the Jerusalem church, while the latter was made for publication at a slightly later date. Blass, however, was the first to make a careful study of the textual variants of the two major traditions as a whole. As a result of his examination he revived the view that had been rejected by Clericus, that is, that the author of Acts published his work in two different editions[8].

Blass argues that the two divergent recensions are remarkably similar in style and that, in spite of their differences, the two never really contradict each other. In his view the "Western" text (which he calls R[omana]) represents Luke's first draft of his work, while the non-"Western" tradition (which he calls A[ntiochena]) represents a more concise and carefully polished edition, the result of the author's eagerness to present his work to the distinguished Theophilus in as polished Greek as possible. The earlier, unrevised edition was given to the Roman church, since the more polished version had been sent to Theophilus in the East and was, for this reason, not readily available.

With the notable exceptions of Nestle and Zahn[9], Blass did not succeed in convincing very many scholars of the correctness of his "solution" of the problem of the "Western" text of Acts[10]. He did succeed, however, in pointing out the problem and offering the first major discussion and attempted answer to the problem, even if he was unable to provide a generally acceptable explanation of the origin of the two divergent recensions. His failure in this regard should not be regarded as casting too great a shadow over his scholarly reputation, since no one since his day has been successful in finding an alternative solution to the problem of the origin of the "Western" text of Acts which has commended itself to a majority

---

[7] *Acta Apostolorum ab sancto Luca* ... (Grossenhain and London, 1848).

[8] "Die Textüberlieferung in der Apostelgeschichte", *TSK* 67 (1894), pp. 86--119; "Über die verschiedenen Textesformen in den Schriften des Lucas", *NKZ* 6 (1895), pp. 712--25; *Acta Apostolorum sive Lucas ad Theophilum* ... (Göttingen, 1895); *Acta Apostolorum secundum formam quae videtur Romanam* (Leipzig, 1896). His view is summarized in his *Philology of the Gospels* (London, 1898), pp. 96--137.

[9] In a different way from Blass, A. C. Clark, *The Acts of the Apostles* (Oxford, 1933) argues for the originality of the "Western" text, the shorter recension being a second-century revision.

[10] The major answer to Blass was B. Weiss, *Der Codex D in der Apostelgeschichte*, *TU*, N. F. 2, 1 (Leipzig, 1897). The classic defense of the shorter, non-"Western" text is J. H. Ropes, *The Text of Acts* = *BC* 3 (New York, 1926), a work which is regarded by most scholars as convincing.

of critics, even though all would be agreed in rejecting Blass's theory of two original recensions.

The question of the purpose of Acts was raised once again at the end of the century. Most German critics, although strongly influenced by Overbeck, were not entirely satisfied with the vagueness of his conception of the aim of the author of Acts. It had become obvious that the Tübingen understanding of the purpose of Acts, i. e., that the author was concerned to defend Paul, while at the same time to conciliate the Jewish Christian party of the second or third decade of the second century, was historically improbable, if not impossible; but a more precise conception of the purpose than that offered by Overbeck was sought after. In this way the secondary, apologetic aim which had been suggested earlier by Schneckenburger and Zeller, and had been acknowledged even by Overbeck, came to be regarded as the dominant aim by a number of critics. In the words of Johannes Weiss (1863—1914), whose sixty-page brochure *Concerning the Aim and Literary Character of Acts*[11] is classic exposition of this view, Acts is

eine Apologie der christlichen Religion vor Heiden gegen die Anklage der Juden, welche zeigt wie es gekommen, dass das Judentum durch das Christentum in seiner Weltmission abgelöst ist (56). [56]

According to this view the author is concerned to show that Christianity is not a political threat to the Empire: thus he shows (1) that Roman officials have been uniformly friendly to the Christian faith in its spread throughout the Empire, chiefly in their dealings with its chief respresentative, Paul; and (2) that any trouble which has been caused in connection with the spread of Christianity has been due to the stubbornness and irrational opposition of the Jews, who, having rejected their Messiah and the Word of God, have been replaced by the predominantly Gentile Christian Church, which is "the new Israel" and heir to the promises of God. A similar understanding of the aim of Acts is found in the writings of Otto Pfleiderer, Carl Weizsäcker, Hermann von Soden, and others.

The important fact to take note of in connection with the state of *Actaforschung* in Germany at the end of the century is that, although New Testament critics had ostensibly rejected the views of *Tendenzkritik*, two important items of the Tübingen critical theory had become a part of the accepted tradition of that stream of German criticism which we may refer to as "critical orthodoxy". First, critical orthodoxy continued to assume the dichotomy between Paul

---

[11] *Über die Absicht und den literarischen Character der Apostelgeschichte* (Marburg and Göttingen, 1897).

and the *Urapostel* and, therefore, between Jewish and Gentile Christianity, although the reconciliation of the two points of view was generally dated a few decades earlier than Baur had dated it. And, secondly, these critics accepted without re-examining the evidence the negative judgement of Baur and his followers concerning the historical value of Acts.

There were exceptions, such as Bernhard Weiss (1827—1918), who steadfastly maintained the connection between Paul and the Jerusalem apostles and the essential reliability of the Book of Acts as a source of early Christian history[12]; but such men were seldom taken very seriously by those scholars who, as successors of Baur and Overbeck, regarded themselves as more authentically "critical" and "objective" than "conservatives" like the elder Weiss. The representatives of this school of criticism followed the Tübingen critics in emphasizing the differences between the Paul of Acts and the Paul of the Epistles, the creative role of the author in the composition of the speeches, the unhistorical portrayal of the missionary stance of both Peter and Paul, the smoothing over of the real differences which existed in the early Church, the Gentile-Christian standpoint of the author, and the "catholic" character of the theological and ecclesiastical motifs of the Book of Acts.

The newer criticism differed, however, from *Tendenzkritik* in its understanding of the reason for these imperfections. Contrary to the opinion of Baur and Zeller, the inaccuracies and inadequacies of Acts were not due to the author's deliberate falsification of the facts. Rather, they were, as Overbeck and the radical critics had suggested, due to the position of the author, who was writing at a place removed by both time and theology from the events of A. D. 30—60 and was simply unable to understand the true nature of the apostolic age. To use the celebrated quotation from Heinrich Julius Holtzmann (1832—1910), who was a typical representative of this [57] point of view: "Wo er nach der Tübinger Kritik nicht sehen wollte, da konnte er der neueren Auffassung gemäss vielmehr meist nicht sehen."[13]

The views expressed by Adolf Jülicher (1857—1938) in his *Introduction to the New Testament*[14] are representative of the newer

---

[12] Cf. his *Einleitung*.

[13] "Die Apostelgeschichte", *Hand-Commentar zum Neuen Testament* 1 (Freiburg i. B., 1899), p. 308. Cf. Mattill, *Luke as a Historian*, pp. 168—206, for a detailed account of the treatment of Acts by the chief representatives of German critical orthodoxy.

[14] *Einleitung in das Neue Testament* (Freiburg i. B. and Leipzig, 1894), pp. 259—70.

criticism. Acts is dated just after the beginning of the second century (262). Factors which are regarded as pointing to this late date include the idealization of the apostolic age by the author, the silence concerning many important events which are important for the authentic history of Paul, and the existence of organized Christian communities (Acts 11.30; 14.23; etc.). Whereas the Tübingen critics attributed the errors of historical fact and theological perspective of the book to the author's intentions, Jülicher ascribes these to "Unkenntnis ... Lückenhaftigkeit der Quellen und Unfähigkeit sich in die Art einer vergangenen Zeit zurückzuversetzen" (263). The parallelism between Peter and Paul, such as it is, is due partly to historical fact and partly (especially the speeches) to the author's own perspective. It is in this connection that Jülicher's famous dictum is found: "Nicht Paulus wird judaisiert, nicht Petrus paulinisiert, sondern Paulus und Petrus lucanisiert d. h. katholisiert" (263). That is, due to the author's lack of information concerning the theology and practice of the apostolic age he reads the views and practices of his own age back into the earlier period of the Church's history. He assumes that the Church of his own day is essentially the same as the Church of the first generation. Taking such an unhistorical point of view — which is, of course, all that could be expected of a writer of the time — he thus makes many serious blunders in his account of early Christianity.

In the tradition of Overbeck, Jülicher opts for a more general understanding of the author's purpose:

> Man thut der Apgsch. Unrecht, wenn man ihre harmlose Freude am Erzählen verkennend, allerwärts eine Tendenz wittert nicht bloss wo sie wahrscheinlich etwas zur Tradition frei hinzufügt, sondern auch wo sie lediglich die Überlieferung wiedergibt oder wo sie Ereignisse, die wir sonsther kennen, übergeht (264).

The author's purpose is primarily to write an edifying account of "die Geschichte der Kraft Gottes in den Aposteln" (264). There may possibly be a secondary, apologetic purpose (i. e. to demonstrate that Christianity is a politically harmless movement with strictly religious aims), but this is merely the indirect result of following the practical purpose so clearly expressed in Luke 1.4.

Jülicher, in common with other nineteenth-century German critics, has a slightly better opinion of the historical value of Acts than had either the Tübingen critics or the radicals. In his view Acts contains a mixture of materials, ranging from the faultless to the worthless. The "Wirquelle" of the Pauline part of Acts is especially valuable, possibly coming directly from the hand of a travel-

[58]

[59]

[60]

[61]

ling companion of Paul who from time to time recorded, in the rich colors of actual experience, the events in which he himself had taken part (268). Other sections, such as the account of the primitive Jerusalem community of Acts 1—6 and the Jerusalem council of Acts 15, are of very slight historical worth.

In short, the Book of Acts is the result of the desire for the Gentile Church of the second century to record "ihr bestes Wissen um die erste Periode ihrer Geschichte" (270). That best was far from perfect. But it is the best account we have, since it is the only writing we have in the New Testament which purposes to give a historical account of the apostolic age. For this reason it is a work of inestimable value to the student of Christian origins, though it must be handled with care.

[62]

There were a few scholars, such as Johannes Weiss, whose views lay somewhere in between the more extreme criticisms of Jülicher and the conservative opinions of the elder Weiss. J. Weiss, for example, argued that the differences between Paul and the Jerusalem apostles were not as great as the Tübingen critics had imagined, nor is Acts as untrustworthy a source of early Christian history as they had suggested. Even in the early chapters of Acts there are embedded reliable bits of information, as, for example, in the elements of the theology of the primitive church which are found in the speeches of Peter[15]. Yet even in the writings of those representing this mediating position the overall impression remains that the Tübingen critics, with the exception of their definition of the *Tendenz* of Acts, were, in the main correct in their conclusions.

The major commentary of this era of Acts-criticism in Germany is the revision of H. A. W. Meyer's commentary by Hans Hinrich Wendt[16] (1853—1928). In his basic stance Wendt occupies much the same position as that occupied by Johannes Weiss, although he does not follow him in his special understanding of the purpose of Acts (17). According to Wendt the author seems to betray a major and a minor purpose. His main purpose, as he himself emphasizes in his preface to the third Gospel (Luke 1.1—4), is a historical one: he wishes to pass on historical information concerning the early development of the Church in the apostolic age (15). The only reason scholars have found it necessary to deny this fact is that they have concluded that the writer's account is unhistorical in places

---

[15] Cf. his article on the Book of Acts in *HDCG* 1 (1906), pp. 25—28.

[16] *Die Apostelgeschichte*, KEK, 5th — 9th eds. (Göttingen, 1880—1913). The fifth through seventh editions are a mixture of Meyer and Wendt. From the eighth edition onward the work belongs entirely to Wendt. The eighth edition (1899) is cited below.

and have, as a result, inferred that he has no concern for the historical facts. But this is to judge the author in terms of a later, scientific understanding of the nature of historical writing and is a mistaken inference. Whether or not he has achieved his purpose to the satisfaction of modern critics is debatable; however, it is difficult to deny that he conceived of his aim in this manner.

A secondary purpose of the author is edification (15—16). The author of Acts is a preacher as much as he is a historian, as are the other biblical writers. He does not aim to present a purely objective account of the events, but rather an interpretative one. He is writing to inspire faith in his readers, and he attempts to do this by telling them the story of the foundation of the Church in a manner which will both strengthen their religious convictions and hold their interest. For this reason he emphasizes the positive aspects of the life of the early Church and passes over most of the negative aspects. He idealizes the primitive Christian community and harmonizes its factions. And as a result he falls far short of the modern view of the task of a historian. But, since he was not modern, this is exactly what one would expect.

How well, then, does the author succeed in fulfilling his aim to write history?

Man kann nicht ein allgemeingültiges Urteil über die Glaubwürdigkeit [63] oder Unglaubwürdigkeit der AG. im Ganzen oder auch nur bestimmter grosser Partheien in ihr, etwa der auf die Urgemeinde oder der auf Paul bezüglichen Stücke oder der Reden in ihr, fällen (33).

One must make a judgment concerning each individual point by itself. In general one may assume that the parts of the narrative which stem from the author's main source — which Wendt regards as the work of an eye-witness and which lies behind the major portion of chapters 13—28 — are wholly trustworthy. However, side by side with this authentic material lie traditions which have been so embellished by legend that it is difficult, if not impossible, to discern the kernel of truth contained in them, as well as additional trimmings added by the author which only reflect the views of the Church of the post-apostolic age of which he is a part.

The view that the author of Acts is dependent on the writings of Josephus has been discussed seriously from time to time since the latter part of the nineteenth century. A number of scholars, including Holtzmann, M. Krenkel[17], and Schmiedel, have argued positively for the author's literary dependence on the Jewish historian.

---

[17] Krenkel's *Josephus und Lucas: Der schriftstellerische Einfluss des jüdischen Geschichtsschreiber auf den christlichen nachgewiesen* (Leipzig, 1894) is the

In the earlier editions of his commentary, Wendt had maintained the view that the points of contact between Josephus and Luke are too general to justify the opinion that there was any literary dependence. Since the author of Acts and Josephus were both historians who lived at the same time, they would quite naturally possess independent knowledge of the same events and people. The fact that they both sometimes refer to the same incidents involving the same people, or often use the same vocabulary, is no proof of literary dependence. The differences between the two, even in their accounts of identical incidents, were regarded by Wendt in his earlier edition to be proof of the independence of the two historians.

However, in the 1899 edition Wendt changes his mind and argues for the dependence of the author of Luke-Acts on the writings of Josephus in at least one place (Acts 5.36—37)[18]; and he suggests that there is a high degree of probability of dependence in a few other cases, e. g. the references to the tomb of David in Jerusalem (2.29)[19], the Beautiful Gate of the Temple (3.2)[20], and the famine in the time of Claudius (11.28)[21]. (He sees no evidence for any dependence of Luke on Josephus in the Gospel.) Yet even in the case of the passage which Wendt regards as proof of definite dependence on Josephus, he suggests that the influence did not consist in "genauen Vertrautsein mit den Werken des Jos. und in sorgfältiger Ausbeutung ihres Stoffes, sondern in oberflächlichen Erinnerungen an eine frühere Lektüre" (38). Thus "Luke" makes the serious error of reversing the chronological order of the rebellions under Theudas and Judas[22].

[64]

Although Wendt's revision of Meyer's commentary was the major commentary of the era, it fell far short of the high standard set by its predecessor and the quality of the work of its successor[23]. It lacks the originality and authentically critical acumen of Meyer and

---

classic argument for this point of view. He falls into the same error as Hobart in his attempt to demonstrate the medical vocabulary of Luke and is quite uncritical in his selection of the evidence. For example, he quotes words and phrases which are used by both writers, but he fails to show that the same words and phrases were *not* used by other writers.

[18] Cf. *Ant.* 20.5.1—2.

[19] Cf. *Ant.* 7.15.3; 13.8.4.

[20] Cf. *BJ* 5.5.3.

[21] Cf. *Ant.* 3.15.3; 20.2.5; 20.5.2.

[22] The discrepancies between this and the other points of contact between Josephus and the author of Acts have led most scholars to the conclusion that the two historians are writing independently of each other. As Emil Schürer has commented: "Either Luke had not read Josephus, or he had forgotten all about what he had read." (*ZWT* 19 (1876), p. 582; quoted in Bruce, *Acts*, p. 25).

[23] The 10th—13th editions are by Ernst Haenchen. Cf. below, pp. 235—47.

the careful concern for detail and theological interpretation of Haenchen. Its significance for the history of New Testament criticism is mainly due to the fact that it illustrates both the strengths and weaknesses of the approach of nineteenth-century critical orthodoxy.

German criticism at the end of the nineteenth century, as we have already had occasion to observe, failed to add very much to the history of the study of the Book of Acts — with the exception of a variety of creative, if unconvincing, theories concerning the sources of Acts and the eccentric hypothesis of Blass concerning the twofold textual tradition of Luke-Acts. The study of this period is of value chiefly because it illustrates the stalemate which was reached in the area of *Actaforschung* in the generation of New Testament scholarship following the Tübingen criticism, and because it provides the background for the more radical stream of German criticism in the twentieth century.

As has been indicated above, the conclusions of the Tübingen critics concerning the historical value of Acts and the alleged dichotomy between Paul and the earliest apostles were accepted as part of the "assured results" of criticism by the representatives of critical orthodoxy at the end of the century, without serious reconsideration of the evidence. The views of those contemporaries of the Tübingen critics who exposed the unhistorical nature and untenableness of the Tübingen criticism of Acts[24] were ignored, and the work of those who represented a similar point of view at the end of the century were dismissed as "uncritical" or merely "traditional". In this way radical German criticism of the New Testament became as dogmatic and tradition-bound in its own way as the earlier theological orthodoxy had been.

Furthermore, the work of Lightfoot and other nineteenth-century British exegetes, who also took a quite different view of Acts and the nature of early Christianity, were ignored by this school of German criticism. If one had access only to the writings of German critics in the Baur-Overbeck-Jülicher tradition, one would scarcely be aware that any research was being carried on outside of Germany; British scholarship is not normally mentioned, much less interacted with[25]. Yet, as we shall see in subsequent chapters[26], some of the most lasting work was being done in the British Isles.

It would not be far amiss to say that a new theory of criticism had evolved in Germany at the end of the nineteenth century. No one calls special attention to its existence in so many words; and, if

---

[24] Cf. chapter 3.
[25] The reverse is *not* true!
[26] Cf. chapters 6 and 7 (on Ramsay).

its ruling influence over the work of New Testament criticism were pointed out to Johannes Weiss or to Jülicher or to Wendt, it would probably be disowned. However, it was clearly understood and practiced by most of the writers who have been discussed in the present chapter.

Rather than stressing the study of the New Testament writings themselves against the background of the historical setting of the Graeco-Roman world of the first Christian century, emphasis came to be placed on the study of the writings of other (*sc.* radical) New Testament critics. New Testament criticism became a "science" in its own right, entirely independent of the work of the ordinary literary critic or historian of antiquity; and there developed a body of "assured results of criticism", based on the principles of "scientific" exegesis, which was accepted as authoritative. *Neutestamentler* began to understand their task as that of adding to the work of previous scholars, rather than starting on the basis of inductive exegesis. New Testament research came to be regarded as *new* discovery, each successive scholar re-working the material of his predecessor, accepting the bulk of his conclusions (*if* he happened to be in the right critical tradition!) and adding a new point or two — thus advancing the cause of scientific exegesis. In adding to the superstructure of critical opinion in this way the important question concerning the stability of the foundation was overlooked. And in the case of the Tübingen criticism the foundation which had been laid was quite unstable indeed!

A radically different tradition of criticism had been developed by this time in Britain, where New Testament criticism had been based on the foundation of the study of classical philology and Graeco-Roman history. There the task of the New Testament critic was regarded as to study the New Testament documents; and the concrete materials of history — the other Greek writings of the surrounding centuries, inscriptions, coins, archaeological remains, and (at the end of the century) the papyri — were considered to be tools which were essential in carrying out this task.

It is to this tradition of criticism which we turn in the chapter which follows.

Chapter VI

NINETEENTH CENTURY BRITISH WORK ON ACTS

The rise of historical criticism in the British Isles is in many respects a quite different story from that of the parallel movement in Germany[1]. The word "parallel" is used advisedly; because, although the best British scholars were in touch with Germany and were quite aware of the course criticism was taking there[2], biblical criticism in the United Kingdom was to a large degree independent of continental influence.

For one thing, the process in Britain was much slower than in Germany. One cannot really date the rise of criticism; it came to be accepted more or less imperceptibly. Although there were a few outcries when traditional views were challenged, there was no great crisis in the Church and in the theological colleges, as was the case in Germany. When one comes to the last couple of decades of the nineteenth century, the principles of criticism are simply there; one does not ask how or when they got there.

One of the factors which led to the acceptance of criticism in England without a fight, so to speak, was that, contrary to the situation in Germany, there was never a division between orthodox theology and criticism.

There was no fundamentalist controversy, no conservative-liberal cleavage to any great degree. Historical criticism was accepted as

---

[1] On the rise of historical criticism in Britain, see L. E. Elliott-Binns, *English Thought 1860–1900: The Theological Aspect* (London, 1956), especially pp. 93–174; and W. B. Glover, *Evangelical Nonconformists and Higher Criticism in the Nineteenth Century* (London, 1954).

[2] German books were reviewed regularly in such periodicals as *The British and Foreign Evangelical Review* and *The Contemporary Review*, and the most important books, by both liberal and conservative critics, were translated into English. A very important series of translations was T. & T. Clark's "Foreign Theological Library". Of the works mentioned in chapters 2 and 3, for example, the majority of Baur's writings and Zeller's *Acts* appeared in English translation, as well as those of conservatives such as Neander, Lechler, Baumgarten, and the like. In addition, many British theological students, especially Scottish and Nonconformists, studied in Germany.

a necessary and useful tool by scholars of orthodox and evangelical faith[3]. This important factor led to a somewhat different understanding of what is meant by the term "historical criticism" in Britain from that which prevailed in some circles on the continent[4]. And, one might add, this factor is of fundamental importance even today for understanding the different emphases of what, for lack of better terms, one may refer to as mainstream British and German criticism[5].

An important feature of early British criticism is that it was rooted firmly in historical study. Those who became the leading New Testament critics had received their preparation for this task by a careful and minute study of the classics and ancient history. This underlined for them the importance of the true environment of the New Testament writings, *viz.* the Hellenistic world at large. It also prepared them to recognize the important contribution of archaeological research to the study of the New Testament as soon as this new science appeared on the scene.

In contrast to criticism in Germany, British biblical scholarship was never the handmaid of philosophy. In spite of their claims to the contrary, the Tübingen critics were and remained primarily philosophers and never really understood the true nature of historical research[6]. On the other hand, the early British critics were not even primarily theologians, but rather historians, philologists, and (a little later) archaeologists. Here one thinks especially of J. B. Lightfoot, the greatest of the early critics, a scholar who personifies the

---

[3] Cf. Glover, *Op. cit.* See H. D. McDonald, *Theories of Revelation: An Historical Study, 1860—1960* (London, 1963), pp. 99—132, however, for an account of what controversy there was.

[4] One need only compare the article by A. Kuenen on "Critical Method", appearing in the first volume of *The Modern Review* (1 (1880), pp. 461—88, 685—713), with one by B. F. Westcott, appearing in the first volume of *The Expositor* ("Critical Scepticism", *Expos.* 1 (1875), pp. 211—37), to see the importance of this observation. Cf. also the comments of J. B. Lightfoot, *Essays on the Work Entitled "Supernatural Religion"* (London, 1889), pp. 23—26.

[5] Cf. Elliott-Binns, *Op. cit.*, pp. 118, 173—74; Glover, *Op. cit.*, pp. 25—30, 36—70, 97—104, 283—84; and W. Robertson Nicoll, *The Church's One Foundation: Christ and Recent Criticism* (London, 1901). This difference of perspective can be seen very clearly by comparing the two histories of New Testament criticism by W. G. Kümmel [*Das Neue Testament: Geschichte der Erforschung seiner Probleme* (Freiburg, 1958)] and S. Neil [*The Interpretation of the New Testament, 1861—1961* (London, 1962)].

[6] Baur's early studies and lectures were in philosophy, and his major emphasis was always the philosophy of religion; his disciples, Schrader, Schwegler, and Zeller later gave up theological study for philosophy.

characteristic greatness (some would say *weakness*!) of British New Testament criticism[7].

The first British scholar to be singled out for special mention was not a theologian, but a layman. James Smith of Jordanhill (1782–1867), a Scot and a Fellow of the Royal Society, was enabled by his considerable means to travel widely and to devote himself to original geological and geographical research. He was also an amateur archaeologist — in those days nearly all archaeologists were "amateurs". His travels led him to Malta, where he resided during the winter of 1844–45. Here the yachtsman of thirty years' experience who had already done a great deal of research into ancient nautical matters was able to combine a firsthand investigation of the region, as well as sailing conditions in the Eastern Mediterranean, with a careful study of the narrative in Acts 27 of the journey and shipwreck of Paul and his company on the way to Rome. This was followed up by research in the important libraries and museums of Europe. The results of his investigations were published in a volume entitled, *The Voyage and Shipwreck of St. Paul*, which was published in 1848[8]; this remains the classic study of the subject up to the present day[9].

Smith's study contains a careful analysis of the narrative of Acts 27–28.16 in the light of geography, archaeology, and the author's personal knowledge of seamanship, both ancient and modern (61–158). This is followed by several valuable essays apropos of the narrative in Acts, the most important being "On the Ships of the Ancients" (181–236), which ranks among the best of the early studies of this subject.

It would occupy too much space in an already too lengthy study to examine Smith's monograph in detail. It is sufficient to note that this study has rendered forever implausible (to most British and American scholars, at least) the suggestion that Luke's account of the journey and shipwreck of Paul is merely a literary device based on the example of Greek authors such as Homer, Josephus, or Lucian. Smith has this to say concerning Luke's description of the nautical matters contained in the narrative:

---

[7] Cf. Elliott-Binns, *Op. cit.*, p. 119.

[8] (London, 1848; 4th ed., 1880). The fourth edition is cited in the text.

[9] In 1949, F. F. Bruce referred to Smith's study as "a work which remains indispensable on the subject, and which certainly ought to be reprinted" (*Acts*, p. 17).

[10] But see E. Norden, *Agnostos Theos* (Leipzig, 1912; repr. Stuttgart, 1956), pp. 313–14; M. Dibelius, *Aufsätze zur Apostelgeschichte* (Göttingen, 1951), p. 174; E. Haenchen, *Die Apostelgeschichte*, pp. 634–36; and H. Conzelmann, *Die Apostelgeschichte* (Tübingen, 1963), pp. 146–47.

(His) style ... though accurate, is unprofessional. No sailor would have written in a style so little like that of a sailor; no man not a sailor could have written a narrative of a sea voyage so consistent in all its parts, unless from observation. This peculiarity of style is to me, in itself, a demonstration that the narrative of the voyage is an account of real events, written by an eyewitness. A similar remark may be made on the geographical details. They must have been taken from actual observation, for the geographical knowledge of the age was not such as to enable a writer to be so minutely accurate in any other way (xlvi-xlvii)[11].

In this manner, James Smith, a layman, typifies what was to become the approach of British scholars to the problems arising from a critical study of the Book of Acts. The emphasis was to be always on the solid facts of historical research, including the study of ancient writings and firsthand archaeological and geographical investigations, in order to seek to understand the New Testament writing in its broader environment, that is, in the ancient world.

The first important British contribution to the modern study of the Book of Acts by way of a commentary was made by Henry Alford[12] (1810—71). Alford, an all-round Victorian in the *best* sense of the word, hymn writer and popular preacher, Fellow of Trinity College, Cambridge, minister of a large London congregation and later Dean of Canterbury Cathedral, was "the first to import the results of German exegesis into many circles in England"[13]. He had spent time in Germany in order to perfect his German so that he could make full use of the work of German exegetes in the preparation of his famous *Greek Testament*[14]. His attitude toward German scholarship is demonstrated by the following quotation from a letter to a friend:

---

[11] Cf. also pp. 20—23. Smith goes on to argue that the narrative implies considerable experience at sea travel by the author, though not as a sailor. He makes the interesting, though of necessity unprovable, conjecture that Luke had served as a ship's doctor for a period of time (21).

The other major work on the subject agrees with Smith's judgments, although it differs in regard to various technical details: A. Breusing, *Die Nautik der Alten* (Bremen, 1886). Cf. especially Breusing's striking testimony, p. XIII.

[12] On Alford, see the introduction to the recent reprint of his *Greek Testament* (Chicago, 1958), pp. v—xiv, by E. F. Harrison.

[13] W. Sanday and A. C. Headlam, *Romans*, ICC, 5th ed., (Edinburgh, 1902), p. cvii.

[14] The work appeared in four volumes between 1849 and 1861: voume II, containing Acts-2 Corinthians, appeared first in 1852 and went through seven editions in his lifetime. A new edition, based on the 7th ed. of vols I and II and the fifth ed. of vols III and IV, was published in Chicago in 1958 and is cited below.

I am fully prepared ... to cast in my lot among those who are digging in
the soil of Scripture for the precious truth that lies beneath; and I cannot
feel grateful enough to those German writers who have done so much of
the heaviest earthwork before me — some, I own, in the wrong direction
and leading only to disappointment; but some also in the right one, and
that untried before. I have been painfully struck, as I have advanced in
my work, with the dishonesty of our English commentators in concealing
difficulties, or solving them in a manner which must be even to themselves
unsatisfactory[15].

Alford's commentary on the Greek New Testament is marked by
a vigorous and clear literary style, careful discernment, and sound
scholarship, especially from the publication of the second volume
onward. Probably rightly regarded as the first truly modern British
commentary, it is certainly the most important one-man commentary
on the New Testament of the nineteenth century; and, as such, it set
the pattern for future British commentaries.

His commentary on Acts, comprising 310 double-columned pages
of small print, is prefaced by a rather full and judicious introduction (II, 1*—31*). Here he upholds more or less traditional views,
but he includes a detailed discussion of the arguments advanced in
favor of other views[16]. He accepts the traditional Lucan authorship, though he gives due consideration to the Silas- and Timothy-
hypotheses. Dividing Acts into the usual two parts, chapters 1—12
dealing with Peter and (primarily) the Jerusalem church and chapters 13—28 narrating the activities of Paul, Alford argues that the
author is dependent on personal experience and on Paul for information concerning the latter and on the leaders of the Jerusalem
church and other members with whom he had talked during his
time in Palestine while Paul was in prison at Caesarea for the former (II, 8*—15*)[17]. He believes he can trace evidence in Acts 17.
16—18.5 of the influence of Paul upon the literary form of the narrative (II, 12*), even though the final form of the narrative is due
to the author of the entire work. The speeches he regards as reliable
summaries of the actual preaching, although they have been carefully re-written by Luke (II, 9*—10*, 11*—15*); a number of strik-

---

[15] Quoted in Harrison, *Op. cit.*, p. vii.
[16] Cf. especially his discussion of the problem of authorship (II, 1*—7*) and
the purpose of Acts (II, 15*—19*).
[17] He considers the "we"-narratives as conclusive proof of the presence of
the author as a companion and fellow missionary with Paul. See, for example,
his observation, in connection with the variation between the accounts of the
death of Herod Agrippa I by Josephus and Luke, that Luke had spent a week
in Tyre (Acts 12.20—22) and was undoubtedly better acquainted with the facts
than Josephus (II, 11*, 136—37).

ing differences in the theology and diction of the speeches points in the direction of the former conclusion, while the general uniformity of style indicates the latter.

Alford emphasizes the importance of a consideration of the preface to the Third Gospel (Luke 1.1—4) in determining the purpose of the author's writing. From this one learns that it is probable that the clause, ἵνα ἐπιγνῷς περὶ ὧν κατηχήθης λόγων τὴν ἀσφάλειαν, is to be understood as the purpose behind his δεύτερος, as well as his πρῶτος λόγος (II, 15*). Any view which attributes a primary purpose of the author beyond a faithful narration of such facts as will edify his (Christian) readers, Alford regards as mistaken (II, 17*). There are undoubtedly many other purposes of the book, but these are probably not the result of the conscious deliberation of the author.

While carefully considering the arguments of German critics to the contrary, Alford argues strongly for a date of A. D. 63, i. e., at the end of the two years described in the last verse of chapter 28 (II, 8*, 17*—19*). His comment on the interpretation of Luke 21.24 as a *vaticinium ex eventu* underlines one aspect of the existing gap between British and German criticism in the nineteenth century.

The prevalent opinion of recent critics in Germany has been, that the book was written much later than this. But this opinion is for the most part traced to their subjective leanings on the prophetic announcement of Luke xxi. 24. For those who hold that there is no such thing as prophecy (and this is unhappily the case with many of the modern German critics), it becomes necessary to maintain that the verse was written after the destruction of Jerusalem. Hence, as the Acts is the sequel to the Gospel, much more must the Acts have been written after that event. To us in England, who receive the verse in question as a truthful account of the words spoken by our Lord, and see in them a weighty prophetic declaration which is even now not wholly fulfilled, this argument at least has no weight (II, 17*—18*).

Alford's *Greek Testament* was probably the most widely studied and influential commentary in the nineteenth century. Another work which was as widely studied and perhaps even more influential was *The Life and Epistles of St. Paul* by William John Conybeare (1815 —1857) and John Saul Howson (1816—85)[18]. Indeed, it has been

---

[18] 2 vols. (London, 1852; 2nd ed. 1856; 3rd ed. 1862; 4th ed. 1864). A one-volumed edition was issued in 1892 and has been reprinted many times, most recently in 1959 (Grand Rapids).

Howson was chiefly responsible for the historical, geographical, and archaeological aspects of the work and authored chapters 1—12, 14, 16, 20, 23—24. Conybeare provided the translation of the epistles and speeches of Paul and

justly claimed that this work "marked the beginning of the modern understanding of Paul in the English-speaking world"[19].

The first edition of "Conybeare and Howson" — to use the name by which the work has been known to students for more than a century — was a beautifully produced work of more than a thousand pages, containing many excellent plates (maps and drawings of the important cities of Paul) and valuable illustrations (especially coins). The aim of the authors was to provide the student with a summary of the most important results of the researches of scholars up to that time in the areas of history, archaeology, and geography of Palestine, Asia Minor, and Greece, especially inasmuch as it could be seen to throw light onto the pages of the Book of Acts and the epistles of Paul. The goal was achieved in a magnificent way.

Although *The Life and Epistles of Paul* is now very much out of date, it would be false to say that it has ever been surpassed; certainly it has never been replaced. Following the lead of James Smith, Conybeare and Howson place Paul in his authentic *Sitz im Leben:* the eastern part of the Roman Empire, the middle decades of the first century A. D. They demonstrate in a brilliant manner that a knowledge of the history of such cities as Tarsus, Ephesus, and Corinth, the general life and culture of the time, extra-biblical Greek literature, combined with a careful and contextual analysis of the text of the books themselves, is much more important for an accurate understanding of the Book of Acts and the letters of Paul than is a knowledge of alleged internecine rivalries in the primitive Christian community, or of theological *Tendenzen*.

In this way Conybeare and Howson add to the work of Smith and Alford, and together they set the trend of future British and (to a large degree) American scholarship. They assured the close connection between New Testament criticism and historical research, broadly understood, which has been the order of the day in Britain; and they pointed to the valuable contributions which students of the New Testament could expect to arise from the researches of the archaeologists. And in so doing, without having an apologetic motive in view, they indicated the ground on which the Tübingen criticism could be effectively attacked and defeated.

Future British scholars, having thus come to the study of Acts from a historical perspective, and having observed at firsthand its many specific contacts with historical reality, would be unable to accept the view that the Book of Acts was a *pia fraus*, the imagina-

himself wrote chapters 13, 15, 18—19, 25, 27—28, as well as the introduction and appendices. Chapters 17, 21, 22, and 26 are by joint authorship.

[19] *ODCC*, p. 340.

tive creation of a second-century apologist for Pauline (or any other kind of) Christianity. And, in case they had lingering doubts, they were to have J. B. Lightfoot to settle the matter for them once and for all.

The first person to advocate a Tübingen interpretation of Early Christian history on British soil was Samuel Davidson (1806—98), a Nonconformist scholar. In the second edition of his *Introduction to the Study of the New Testament*, which was published in 1868[20], he abandoned the traditional views which he advocated in the first edition[21]. His work, representing a total "conversion" to the Tübingen point of view, in some ways impressively erudite, is essentially a compendium of largely undigested opinions, with copious quotation of German authors, and was of no great influence on British scholarship.

A more influential work, however, was the study entitled, *Supernatural Religion: An Inquiry into the Reality of Divine Revelation*, which was published anonymously in 1874[22]. The work became an immediate *succès de scandale*, virtually the *Honest to God* of the Victorian Era. Its author was Walter Richard Cassels[23] (1826—1907), a thinker of little originality whose name would not belong to the history of New Testament criticism except for the widespread popularity his opinions achieved and — even more important — the reply they elicited from Lightfoot.

The major thesis of Cassels' work is that the ethical and supernatural content of Christianity can easily be separated, and that it would be of advantage to the Christian faith to be everlastingly rid of the latter. The view was, of course, not new; its roots lay deep in the Deism of an earlier age. But Cassels added a new twist to the argument by seeking a scholarly foundation for his thesis in the reconstruction of early Christian history which had been advanced by F. C. Baur, who, incidentally, would have agreed with his major thesis, but would have been much more sophisticated in his approach and infinitely more careful in his handling of his material.

Cassels's work comprises three main parts. In the first, following the suggestions of the philosopher, David Hume, he seeks to prove that miracles are not only highly improbable, but antecedently in-

---

[20] 2 vols. (London, 1868); his views on Acts are found in vol. 2, pp. 196—290.
[21] 3 vols. (London, 1848—51). In the earlier edition he even defends the Pauline authorship of the Epistle to the Hebrews!
[22] 2 vols. (London, 1874; 2nd-4th eds. 1874; 5th—6th eds. 1875; "Complete ed. in 3 vols." 1879; "Popular edition" (abridged), 1902). The 1902 ed. is cited below.
[23] Wrongly given the initials "J. A." by S. Neill, *Interpretation*, p. 36.

115

credible; so that no amount of evidence can overcome the objections to them. In the second part he examines the actual witnesses themselves, i. e., the four Gospels, Acts, and the Pauline letters, in order to give the *coup de grâce* to the supernatural claims of Christianity. He concludes with a discussion of the heart of the matter, the resurrection and ascension of Christ.

In the historical section (i. e. the second part) his purpose is to demonstrate that the Gospels and Acts, as well as most of the Pauline epistles, are entirely devoid of evidence which is sufficient to demonstrate their first century date and traditional authorships. Here he concerns himself chiefly with examining the external witnesses to the authenticity and genuineness of the writings.

As for his treatment of Acts, following an attempt to prove that there is no evidence for the book's existence prior to the middle of the second century, the author draws at random from the writings of the Tübingen critics, and any others who are thought to support his views, in his attack on traditional opinion. He points to such familiar items as the (mis-)use of Josephus by the author, the tendentious parallelization of Peter and Paul in both their actions and sermons, the (false) picture of primitive Christianity given in the early chapters of Acts, the "contradictions" between Acts and the letters of Paul, and so forth. His conclusion concerning Acts is indicative of the tone of the book as a whole:

The phenomena presented by the Acts of the Apostles become perfectly intelligible when we recognize that it is the work of a writer living long after the occurrences related, whose pious imagination furnished the Apostolic age with an elaborate system of supernatural agency, far beyond the conception of any other New Testament writer, by which, according to his view, the proceedings of the Apostles were furthered and directed, and the infant Church miraculously fostered. On examining other portions of his narrative, we find that they present the features which the miraculous elements rendered antecedently probable. The speeches attributed to different speakers are all cast in the same mould, and betray the composition of the same writer. The sentiments expressed are inconsistent with what we know of the various speakers, and when we test the circumstances related by previous or subsequent incidents and by trustworthy documents, it becomes apparent that the narrative is not an impartial statement of facts, but a reproduction of legends or a development of tradition, sharpened and coloured according to the purpose of the pious views of the writer.

Written by an author who was not an eye-witness of the miracles related; who describes events not as they really occurred, but as his pious imagination supposed they ought to have occurred; who seldom touches history without distorting it by legend, until the original elements can scarcely be distinguished; who puts his own words and sentiments into the mouths of the Apostles and other persons of his narrative; and who represents almost every phase of the Church in the Apostolic age as influenced, or directly produced, by supernatural agency — such a work is of no value as evidence for occurrences which are in contradiction to all experience. The Acts of the Apostles, therefore, is not only an anonymous work, but upon due examination its claims to be considered sober and veracious history must be emphatically rejected. It cannot strengthen the foundations of super-natural religion, but, on the contrary, by its profuse and indiscriminate use of the miraculous, it discredits miracles, and affords a clearer insight into their origin and fictitious character (750—52).

Whether or not the narrative of the Book of Acts is marked by an all-pervasive *Tendenz* may remain debatable, but it is certain that the author of *Supernatural Religion* is no unbiased historian! Under normal circumstances the work would neither have deserved nor gained the serious attention of a scholar of the stature of J. B. Lightfoot. However, unfortunately for its author, it achieved just that, and thereby attained immortal notoriety[24].

The reputation of Joseph Barber Lightfoot[25] (1818—89), who still casts his long shadow across the well-worn path of British New Testament criticism, does not depend on his criticism of *Supernatural Religion*, but is altogether independent of it. He was never one to seek out controversy. One of the impressive features of his commentaries is the courteous and dispassionate way he deals with the views of those scholars with whom he disagrees; there is no emotional oratory, no sophistical formulae, no negative pigeonholing of his opponents and their views. Ordinarily he would have thought it unnecessary to raise his voice in opposition to the extreme views of a critic like Cassels. However, two factors compelled him to speak out, in spite of his natural reluctance to do so.

First, the anonymous author of *Supernatural Religion* had made the grave mistake of going out of his way to impugn the honesty of B. F. Westcott, Lightfoot's friend and former tutor, charging him with "what amounts to a falsification of the text". This, coupled

---

[24] Lightfoot reviewed the work for *The Contemporary Review* in December 1874, and followed this up with a series of articles criticizing the major premises of Cassels' critical theories (1875—77); he limited his criticism solely to the allegedly historical part of the work, rather than the philosophical. His essays were reprinted as a separate volume, *Essays on the Work Entitled "Supernatural Religion"* (London, 1889); this work is cited below.

[25] On the significance of Lightfoot, see G. R. Eden and F. C. MacDonald (eds.), *Lightfoot of Durham* (London, 1932); Neill, *Interpretation*, pp. 33—57; P. H. Richards, "J. B. Lightfoot as a Biblical Interpreter", *Interp.* 8 (1954), pp. 50—62; L. W. Barnard, "Bishop Lightfoot and the Apostolic Fathers", *ChQR* 161 (1960), pp. 423—35; and C. K. Barrett, "Joseph Barber Lightfoot", *The Durham University Journal* 64 (1972), pp. 193—204.

with the fact that a half dozen or so reviewers had been taken in by
the author's pretentions to great learning and had written reviews
which were quite positive, was just enough to cause him to put pen
to paper in reply to Cassels. (The reviews called forth the sarcastic
comment from Lightfoot that the reviewers must have been "dealing with some apocryphal work, bearing the same name and often
using the same language, but in its main characteristics quite different from and much more authentic than the volumes before
me" (3)!)

Lightfoot had no difficulty in exposing the shallowness of Cassels' assumed scholarship. He began by pointing out numerous
gross errors in the work which indicated quite clearly the inadequacies of the author's knowledge of the basic elements of Greek and
Latin grammar. Moreover, the author, whose name Lightfoot neither knew nor cared to learn, was guilty of the devious practive of
lifting groups of references from the pages of other people's works
and quoting them to back up his various speculations[26]. All too
often the opinions of the authors cited by Cassels were the exact
opposite to his own — thus demonstrating that he had not even
read them!

The details of Lightfoot's devastating criticism of the work entitled *Supernatural Religion* need not concern us here, since they
are so well-known. Cassels' work is mentioned primarily because it
was the major attempt to establish the respectability of the Tübingen conception of Christian origins on British soil; and Lightfoot's
criticism, as the main reason the attempt was singularly unsuccessful.

However, Lightfoot's book written in controversy with the author
of *Supernatural Religion* was not his main contribution to New Testament research and the date concerning the nature of primitive
Christianity. His main contribution was made through his non-
polemical works — his commentaries on the Pauline epistles[27] and
his studies of the Apostolic Fathers[28]. And it was in this context
that he demonstrated most clearly the unhistorical nature of the
Tübingen theory.

---

[26] The author judiciously removed most of the references to the scholarly
literature from the one-volumed edition of his work.

[27] *Galatians* (London, 1865), many editions; repr. most recently Grand
Rapids, 1962; *Philippians* (1868), many editions; repr. Grand Rapids, 1963;
Colossians and Philemon (1875), many editions; repr. Grand Rapids, 1961.

[28] *The Apostolic Fathers*, 5 vols. (London, 1885–90); includes only Clement
of Rome, Ignatius, and Polycarp. An earlier edition of Clement was published
(1869 and 1877), but this was thoroughly revised in 1890.

The overall effect of Lightfoot's work was to show that Baur and his followers had simply built a castle in the sky, basing their interprepation mainly on a prior interpretation of the pseudo-Clementine literature and forcing the other early Christian writings into a mold of their own making. In his monumental studies of the Apostolic Fathers, Lightfoot established the genuineness of the First Epistle of Clement (written ca. A. D. 96) and the seven letters of Ignatius of Antioch (written between A. D. 98—117)[29], in which there is not the slightest trace of even the remnant of a Petrine-Pauline conflict. On the contrary, both Paul and Peter are held in honor by Clement and Ignatius[30]. Thus a major prop is knocked out from under the arguments of the Tübingen critics, who found it necessary to deny the authenticity of these two groups of documents.

In his commentaries — each one a model of careful scholarship — Lightfoot pushed his opponents back even further against the wall by arguing that the Pauline epistles too showed no evidence of a division of opinion between Paul and the *Urapostel*. He has no axe to grind, no apologetic aim in view. His aim is strictly positive — to understand the text of the New Testament writings. The underlying presupposition of his work is that "the only safe way to the meaning of a great writer lies through faith in his language, and therefore through exact investigation of grammar and vocabulary"[31]. In pursuing this objective Lightfoot arrives at an alternative interpretation of early Christian history which has always impressed the world of British scholarship as being so much more historical than the arbitrary views advanced by the Tübingen critics[32].

Lightfoot had looked forward one day to writing a commentary on Acts; but this wish, along with many other ambitious plans of this great scholar, was to remain unfulfilled. Two items, however, give us a partial glimpse into what it would have contained if it had been written.

The first of these is his essay entitled, "Discoveries Illustrating the Acts of the Apostles", which was first published in 1878 and later added as an appendix to his *Essays on* ... *"Supernatural Religion"* (291—302), in which he surveys some of the recently published findings of archaeological research in Cyprus and Ephesus.

Lightfoot begins the essay by drawing attention to the great difficulty of a writer's being accurate when writing about the govern-

---

[29] F. J. A. Hort, *DNB* 33 (1893), p. 237.
[30] Cf. especially 1 Clement 5 and Ignatius, *To the Romans* 4.3.
[31] *DNB* 33, p. 238.
[32] His most important contribution in this connection is his commentary on Galatians, especially the lengthy essay on "Paul and the Three".

ment of the Roman provinces. From the time of Augustus' reorganization of the empire, there were two types of provincial governors. Provinces which were adminstered by the Senate, because they did not require a standing army, were ruled by a proconsul (ἀνθύπατος). The representatives who ruled a province on behalf of the emperor bore the name of propraetor (ἀντιστράτηγος) or legate (πρεσβυτής), a usage quite different from that of republican times. Moreover, the original subdivision of the provinces between the emperor and Senate underwent constant modifications. Thus "at any given time it would be impossible to say without contemporary, or at least very exact historical knowledge, whether a particular province was governed by a proconsul or propraetor" (292). The province of Achaia is a case in point. A few years before Paul's visit to Corinth, and some years after, Achaia was governed by a propraetor. At the time of his visit, however, it was ruled by a proconsul on behalf of the Senate, just as it is represented in the Book of Acts[33].

Cyprus is another example. Earlier scholars, basing their views on Strabo, accused Luke of an incorrect use of terminology in referring to Sergius Paulus as ἀνθύπατος when Paul visited that island (Acts 13.17). Contemporary records, mainly inscriptions and coins, make it clear that Cyprus was under the rule of the Senate and was therefore governed by a proconsul during the time of Paul's visit, even though at a later date the situation was quite different. Lightfoot calls attention to a newly discovered inscription, dated "in the proconsulship of Paulus", which may refer to the Sergius Paulus of Acts 13[34].

Discoveries at Ephesus by J. T. Wood and others bring to light even more illustrative matter. The main feature of the narrative of Acts 19 is the manner in which the cult of the Ephesian Artemis dominates the scene, a fact to which there is abundant inscriptional evidence. Some of the inscriptions almost form a running commentary on the excited appeal of Demetrius and the concern of the crowd. Important references include the description of Artemis as "the great goddess Artemis", as in Acts, as well as to the fact that the theater was the recognized place of public assembly. Nor is Luke

---

[33] Even more important than this was to be the Delphi inscription, first published in 1905, which mentions L. Junius Gallio (Acts 18.12–17), the brother of Seneca the philosopher, which offers one of the virtually certain dates for Pauline chronology. Cf. *BC* 5, pp. 460–64; A. Deissmann, *Paul*, E. T., 3rd ed. (London, 1927), pp. 261–86.

[34] Lightfoot was probably wrong in this identification; cf. *BC* 5, pp. 455–57; and B. Van Elderen, "Some Archaeological Observations on Paul's First Missionary Journey", in *Apostolic History and the Gospel*, ed. W. W. Gasque and R. P. Martin (Exeter, 1970), pp. 151–56.

120

less careful in his reference to the governing officials. Ἀνθύπατος (the Roman proconsul)[35], γραμματεύς (the chief magistrate of the city), and Ἀσιαρχαί (deputies of the κοινὸν Ἀσίας, the league of cities of the province of Asia)[36] — all appear again and again in the inscriptions. In addition, there is inscriptional evidence for the use of ἱερόσυλος (19.37) for one who is guilty of certain offenses against the goddess, for the description of the city as νεωκόρος (guardian) of the temple of Artemis[37], and for the technical use of ἔννομος ἐκκλησία to refer to assemblies which were held on stated days already predetermined by the law (as opposed to those which would be called together on account of emergency situations).

Lightfoot sampled only a small part of the material which was then beginning to be brought to light by archaeologists and historians who were concerned with Asia Minor and Greece. In this brief essay, however, he indicated the area where the student of early Christian history might expect to receive more light in the future for an accurate understanding of the narrative of Acts. In this essay, he expresses the conviction concerning the Book of Acts which was to become even clearer in the next three decades of research: "No ancient work affords so many tests of veracity; for no other has such numerous points of contact in all directions with contemporary history, politics, and topography, whether Jewish or Greek or Roman" (291).

Lightfoot's second contribution in lieu of his commentary on Acts which failed to appear is in the form of an article contributed to the second edition of Smith's *Dictionary of the Bible*[38]. Here we have the mature conclusions of the *doyen* of nineteenth century British exegetes and patristic scholars on our subject.

His conclusions are, generally speaking, traditional, though his judgment is marked by careful criticism and historical investigation, rather than by a simple assumption of traditional views. He argues forcefully for an identification of the author of the "we"-narratives

---

[35] The plural ἀνθύπατοι in Acts 19.38 may be a generalizing plural, reflecting the fact that the proconsul of Asia had recently been assassinated (October A. D. 54) and his successor had not yet arrived on the scene; or it may even refer to the two assassins, who were at that time in charge of the emperor's affairs in Asia.

[36] There is evidence that the term "Asiarch" is a rather broad term, including many men of wealth and public influence, religious leaders and civic benefactors; thus there would be a number of Asiarchs in a city like Ephesus at any given time.

[37] The term is normally used, in Ephesus or elsewhere in Asia, in reference to the imperial cult.

[38] Vol. 1 (London, 1893), pp. 25—43.

with the author of the book as a whole (31—33), and that he is probably the traditionally recognized Λουκᾶς ὁ ἰατρὸς ὁ ἀγαπητός (Col. 4.14). Lightfoot dates the time of writing as probably sometime in the early seventies, although he rejects the (to him, false) interpretation of Acts 8.26 and Luke 21.20—24 as demanding a date of this time (40—41).

What about the objections of the Tübingen critics and their critical offspring that the author of Acts presents a very unhistorical picture of the early Church when he portrays Peter and the *Urapostel* as being in essential agreement with Paul? Does this not demonstrate conclusively that the author could not have been a friend and former travelling companion of the Apostle? Lightfoot's opinion is forthright:

We can only say that to ourselves such passages an I Cor. i. 12 *sq.*, 23; Gal. i. 18, ii. 6 *sq.*, 14 *sq.*, seem to indicate a substantial harmony in principle between the two supposed antagonists; that they are placed on the same level by the two earliest of the apostolic Fathers (Clem. Rom. 5; Ignat. *Rom.* 4), and are quoted as of equal authority by the third (Polyc. *Phil.* 2, 5, 6 &c.); that the main stream of Christian history betrays no evidence of this fundamental antagonism as the substratum of the Catholic Church; and that the first distinct mention of it occurs in an obviously fictitious narrative, which cannot date before the second half of the second century, though doubtless even from apostolic times there were some extreme men who used the names of the two Apostles as party watchwords (37).

A number of items are adduced as evidence in favor of the essentially trustworthy character of the Book of Acts. First, there are the incidental points of contact between the narrative of Acts and the epistles of Paul which Paley had pointed out a hundred and three years earlier (34). Secondly, a comparison of the speeches ascribed to the different apostles in Acts — James, Peter, and Paul — with the epistles attributed to them betray striking and unexpected similarities of thought and diction (34—35). However, the most significant evidence comes from the recent researches concerned with geography, history, and archaeology.

If, for instance, we confine ourselves to geography, we accompany the Apostle by land and by sea; we follow him about in Jerusalem, in Palestine and Syria, in Asia Minor, in Greece, in Italy. The topographical details are scattered over this wide expanse of continent, island, and ocean; and they are both minute and incidental. Yet the writer is never betrayed into an error (35).

When we turn from geography to history, the tests are still more numerous, and lead to still more decisive results. The laws, the institutions, the manners, the religious rites, the magisterial records, of Syria and Palestine, of Asia Minor, of Macedonia and Greece, all live in the pages of this narrative (35).

To the material relating to Cyprus, Corinth, and Ephesus, which he had cited in his earlier essay, he adds further data concerning the historical situation at Philippi, and Athens, as well as additional material concerning Corinth and Ephesus (35—36).

Paul's visits to the two Macedonian cities of Philippi and Thessalonica, neither of which had political constitutions following the normal type of Greek city, are illustrative. Philippi was a Roman colony (16.12); accordingly, we find all the apparatus and coloring of a colony, which was a miniature reproduction of Rome itself. There are the local magistrates, the *duumviri*, who in typical fashion arrogate to themselves the title of στρατηγοί (16.20, 22, 35—36, 38)[39] and their *lictores* (ῥαβδοῦχοι, 16.35, 38). The majesty of Rome is appealed to again and again (16.21, 37—38). But, turning to Thessalonica, the picture is changed, for Thessalonica was a free city with a magistracy all its own. Here the magistrates are called πολιτάρχαι (17.6, 8), a designation which was unknown in the whole of Greek literature[40] before the discovery of inscriptions found at Thessalonica itself[41], which illustrates the careful accuracy of the author of Acts. The reference to a popular assembly (δῆμος, 17.5) is likewise in keeping with the special character of the city.

Luke's precision is further illustrated by his careful individualization of Athens, "the most Hellenic of all the cities, the heart and citadel of Greece", and Ephesus, where there was a strong mixture of oriental ideas and institutions with the mainstream of Hellenism. The difference between the two cities can be seen in the conflicts of Paul with the populace of either.

One is inquisitive, philosophical, courteous, and refined; the other fanatical, superstitious, and impulsive ... At Athens ... we are confronted with some of the main topological details of the city — the Areopagus and the agora. There are the representatives of the two dominant philosophical schools, the Stoics and Epicureans. There is the predominant attitude of inquiry in this metropolis of newsmongers, and here even the characteristic Athenian term of abuse (σπερμολόγος) finds its proper place ... There is

---

[39] This term, though not quite officially correct, occurs in a number of inscriptions with reference to Philippi.

[40] Lightfoot notes that πολίταρχος appears, in a general sense, in an obscure passage of Aeneas Tacticus.

[41] Inscriptions have been found also in connection with a number of other cities in Macedonia, from which it appears that the term was the special designation of members of the city council of Macedonian towns.

the reference to the numerous images and temples which thronged the city; to the boastful pride of the citizens in their religious devotion to the gods, consistent as it was with no small amount of theological scepticism; to their jealousy of the introduction of strange deities, as manifested in the case of Socrates and at various points in their history; to their practice of propitiating the offended powers after any plague or other infection, by erecting an altar to "an unknown god" or "unknown gods"; to their custom of deifying attributes of character, frames of mind, and conditions of body, so that "Resurrection" (Anastasis) would seem to them to be only another addition to their pantheon ... Lastly, there is an appropriate allusion to τὸ θεῖον, an expression which would commend itself to his philosophical audience, but which occurs nowhere else in the New Testament; and an equally appropriate appeal to the sentiment of the Stoic poets Aratus and Cleanthes (τῶν καθ᾽ ὑμᾶς ποιητῶν), who had proclaimed the universal fatherhood of Zeus (36)[42].

Although the historical materials are not so plentiful in regard to the situation in Jerusalem and Palestine, Lightfoot argues that where it can be tested the picture drawn by the author is faithful to the historical reality (36—37).

What about the purpose of Acts? Here Lightfoot reverts to the old view that the author "merely purposes to give for the edification of his readers a history of the Christian Church from its foundation to its establishment in the metropolis of the world" (41). If there is a theological principle behind the narrative, it is "the continued working and presence of Jesus, no longer in the flesh, but in the Church" (41). He finds no evidence in favor of a special apologetic or conciliatory purpose.

Frederic William Farrar (1831—1903) deserves at least passing notice for writing one of the most influential works of the time (next to that of Conybeare and Howson) on Paul. His *The Life and Work of St. Paul*[43], dedicated to Lightfoot, his former teacher, is built on the assumption that one can obtain a historically accurate picture of Paul by combining the information of the Pauline section of Acts and of the epistles, with the results of historical research into the life and thought of the first century. His work, although popular in style, is based on a wide scholarship. Thoroughly conversant with the work of the German scholars who defend the opposing view, Farrar sides with his great mentor in defending the historical reliability of Acts.

---

[42] The local color of Ephesus is discussed in his "Discoveries Illustrating the Acts of the Apostles".

[43] 2 vols. (London, 1879); reprinted many times.

An even more influential work is the classic study of *The Medical Language of St. Luke* by William Kirk Hobart[44] of Trinity College, Dublin.

Luke, the traditional author of the Third Gospel and Acts, is referred to in Colossians 4.14 as ὁ ἰατρὸς ὁ ἀγαπητός. As early as the eighteenth century some attention had been given to the language of Luke-Acts, in order to determine what (if any) influence the author's profession may have had upon his diction. Wettstein and Bengel, among others, listed a number of illustrations which they thought betrayed the author's special medical knowledge; these, in turn, were taken over into subsequent commentaries and used as another argument for the Lucan authorship of the two books[45]. In 1841 a paper appeared in *The Gentleman's Magazine*[46], listing a selection of expressions used by Luke which were alleged to show his professional bias. The suggestions of this author were greatly enlarged upon by Hobart.

Hobart lists examples of words or phrases which are unique, among New Testament writings, to Luke-Acts; or which are used more frequently by Luke than by other New Testament writers. By reference to the Greek medical writers, specifically Hippocrates, Galen, Dioscorides, and Aristaeus, he seeks to demonstrate that these were typically medical words and were the result of the author's special training as a physician.

Hobart's work is thorough, but rather uncritical. He overlooked, for instance, the fact that more than eighty percent of his list of four hundred words are found in the Septuagint, which certainly would have had as much an influence on the author's vocabulary as an alleged medical training. Furthermore, at least ninety percent of the words listed by Hobart occur in Josephus, Lucian, and Plutarch — none of whom had any special medical training. In short, although Hobart shows clearly that the words he lists are used by medical writers, he fails to prove that they were *not* used by other authors who are not medically trained. Nevertheless, allowing for both exaggeration and an uncritical handling of the data, many scholars have been convinced that there remains a residue of expressions in the Lucan writings which may very possibly reflect a doctor's way of looking at things. Whether or not it is an evidence of the author's profession may remain debatable; but these scholars,

---

[44] (Dublin and London, 1882; repr. Grand Rapids, 1954).

[45] Cf. G. F. Moore's editorial note to H. J. Cadbury's *The Style and Literary Method of Luke* (Cambridge, Mass., 1920), pp. 51—54; also R. J. Knowling, *Acts* in *EGT* 2 (Repr. Grand Rapids, 1961), p. 9.

[46] (June 1841), pp. 585—87; the author was J. K. Walker.

reaching the conclusion for other reasons that the author is Luke the friend and companion of Paul, consider these expressions to be at least illustrative of his profession[47].

The two commentaries by Joseph Rawson Lumby[48] (1831—95) in the Cambridge series reflected generally the views of contemporary British scholarship. They were, in the context of their limited aim, in some ways, quite good; but they were hardly brilliant. And they scarcely added anything new to the critical discussion.

The commentary by Thomas Ethelbert Page[49], the classical scholar, was of a different nature. Based on the Greek text of Westcott and Hort and aimed at "pure exegesis, without diverging into doctrinal controversy on the one hand or homiletic eloquence on the other" (ix), Page's work is a model of concise comment and careful exegesis. He does not clutter the pages with reference to the scholarly literature (which he has read), but rather concentrates on a careful examination of the Greek text of Acts. Neither does he waste precious space and time examining every possibility of interpretation; rather, he presents the results of his own careful exegesis, pausing only to note cases where there is a great deal of uncertainty involved. One of the strong points of Page's commentary is his careful grammatical comments; this is combined with carefully selected references to Greek literature, the Old Testament, and historical matters.

Page belongs to the mainstream of British interpreters, in the Lightfoot tradition; yet he adds one or two points to the discussion. First, he argues that the Lucan writings must be dated post-A. D. 70 (xvii—xviii). This is not due to the necessity of interpreting Luke 21 as a *vaticinium ex eventu*, but rather is deduced from the way Luke *interprets* the saying of Jesus (cf. Mark 13.14 and Matt. 24.15 with Luke 21.20). According to Page, it seems clear that Luke modifies the words τὸ βδέλυγμα τῆς ἐρημώσεως (in Mark and Matt.) so as to make them intelligible to Gentile readers; and he modifies them with reference to a definite historical fact of which he had knowledge, viz. the siege of Jerusalem in A. D. 70. In addition, his state-

---

[47] Harnack and Zahn were more cautious and critical in their approach than was Hobart, but they came to similar conclusions. Cadbury, on the other hand, subjected Hobart's thesis, as well as the data produced by Harnack and Zahn, to searching criticism, arguing that the data prove nothing more than that the author was a reasonably well-educated Greek of his day (*Op. cit.*, pp. 39—72).

[48] *The Acts of the Apostles* in *The Cambridge Bible* (Cambridge, 1882) and *The Cambridge Greek Testament* (Cambridge, 1894); both works have been reprinted many times.

[49] *The Acts of the Apostles* (London, 1886); reprinted many times. An introduction was added in 1895; the 1900 (= 1895) printing is cited below.

ment that many other attempts had been made to give an account περὶ τῶν πεπληροφορημένων ἐν ἡμῖν πραγμάτων (Luke 1.1) strongly suggests a date somewhat later than A. D. 70.

A real clarification of the problem of the purpose of Acts is made by Page in a commonplace-sounding observation — which is, surprisingly enough, far from commonplace in the writings of New Testament scholars — that a work such as Acts *"must necessarily be influenced by more than one motive or tendency, and cannot be fully described by any single phrase"* (xxii)[50]. Thus the Book of Acts is neither bare history, nor a dogmatic treatise, nor a biography — but a combination of all three. It seems strange that so many scholars have overlooked this almost self-evident fact; yet they have. A clear recognition of this basic principle would have saved many scholars much paper and ink.

Page also makes some interesting observations concerning some of the theological concerns of the author. The first of these concerns the importance of the motif of witness in Acts[51]. The author is occupied with the work of bearing witness to Christ (1.8) and thus extending the Church. Page, also, seems to be the first to note the importance of summary notes concerning the growth of the Church at various stages in the course of Luke's narrative (2.41; 2.47; 4.4; 6.1; 6.7; etc.). From a small band of disciples in Jerusalem the Church grows, through persecution as well as preaching, as a result of the testimony of an ever widening circle of "witnesses", until it is established in some of the important centers of the Gentile world. Thus a triumphant note is struck by the report of the ways the "word of God grew and multiplied" (12.24).

Other important theological themes of Acts singled out for special mention by Page include emphasis on the preaching of the resurrection[52], faith in Jesus (often connected with baptism and/or the gift of the Holy Spirit)[53] and the universal character of the Gospel[54].

---

[50] Emphasis mine.

[51] Cf. 1.22; 2.32; 3.15; 4.33; 5.32; 10.39—43; 13.31; 22.15; 26.16. "The motive for the triple repetition of the account of Paul's conversion is clearly not merely the personal interest of the writer in him, but the importance attached to his 'witness' to the resurrection" (xxviii).

[52] Cf. 4.2; 17.18; 23.6; 26.23.

[53] Cf. 2.38; 3.16; 8.12, 13, 17, 37; 10.47; 16.31—33; 18.8; 19.1—6. Cf. also the phrases πλήρης πίστεως καὶ πνεύματος ἁγίου (6.5) and πλήρης πνεύματος ἁγίου καὶ πίστεως (11.24).

[54] Cf. 2.39; 3.26; the careful repetition of Peter's vision (10.10—16; 11.5,10); 10.34—43; 11.18; 14.27; and, of course, ch. 15.

Many scholars before had referred to a passage in Thucydides (1.22) as a proof that it was customary for Greek historical writers to compose speeches quite freely and to insert them in their narrative. Page pauses to see *what* Thucydides actually said, and quotes the statement in full:

And as regards speeches, ... it was hard to record the exact words spoken, both in cases where I was myself present, and where I used the reports of others. But I have used language in accordance with what I thought the speakers in each case would have been most likely to say, *adhering as closely as possible to the general sense of what was actually spoken*[55].

Whatever the general practice of Greek historians may have been — and it is probable that other historians were much less scrupulous than Thucydides — Thucydides, at least, makes the claim that he did *not* freely compose speeches. And it is possible that Luke may have followed in this tradition. If this is so, the speeches in Acts would then be the author's summaries of what was said on particular occasions, insofar as Luke was able to determine this[56].

The end of the century saw the appearance of a number of very important works in Britain. The first volume of the monumental *Dictionary of the Bible,* edited by James Hastings, included an article by Arthur Cayley Headlam (1862—1947) in which he summed up the results of British research into the problems related to the Book of Acts[57]. The same volume also included a very significant essay on the chronology of the New Testament by Cuthbert Hamilton Turner[58] (1860—1930), in which he made what is probably the most useful suggestion yet to be made concerning the arrangement by Luke of his material in Acts (421).

Turner calls attention to the importance of six summary statements of the progress of the Gospel in Acts (6.7; 9.31; 12.24; 16.5; 19.20; and 28.30—31). Each statement marks the end of one stage and the beginning of a new stage in the expansion of the Church in Acts, emphasizing the fact of growth and blessing in spite of persecution. Taking these summaries as his key, Turner suggests the following six-panel outline of Acts:

1.1—6.7. The first period, centering in the Jerusalem Church and the preaching of Peter. This is followed by the summary in 6.7: καὶ

---

[55] Italics Page's; the Greek text is cited in a footnote.
[56] Cf. T. F. Glasson, "The Speeches in Acts and Thucydides", *ExpT* 5 (1965), p. 165; A. W. Gomme, *A Historical Commentary on Thucydides* (Oxford, 1945) 1, pp. 139—48; and below, pp. 225—28.
[57] "Acts of the Apostles", *HDB* 1 (1898), pp. 25—35; *infra,* pp. 133—34.
[58] *HDB* 1 (1898), pp. 403—425.

128

ὁ λόγος τοῦ θεοῦ ηὔξανεν, καὶ ἐπληθύνετο ὁ ἀριθμὸς τῶν μαθητῶν ἐν Ἰερουσαλὴμ σφόδρα, πολύς τε ὄχλος τῶν ἱερέων ὑπήκουον τῇ πίστει. *6.8—9.31.* Second period, marking the extension of the Church in Palestine, the preaching of Stephen, and conflict with the Jewish authorities. Summary: Ἡ μὲν οὖν ἐκκλησία καθ᾽ ὅλης τῆς Ἰουδαίας καὶ Γαλιλαίας καὶ Σαμαρείας εἶχεν εἰρήνην οἰκοδομουμένη, καὶ πορευομένη τῷ φόβῳ τοῦ Κυρίου καὶ τῇ παρακλήσει τοῦ Ἁγίου Πνεύματος ἐπληθύνετο.

9.32—12.24. Third period, the extension of the Church to Antioch, the conversion of a Roman army officer, and further conflict with the Jewish authorities. Summary: ὁ δὲ λόγος τοῦ Κυρίου ηὔξανεν καὶ ἐπληθύνετο.

12.25—16.5. Fourth period, the extension of the Church to Asia Minor. Summary: Αἱ μὲν οὖν ἐκκλησίαι ἐστερεοῦντο τῇ πίστει καὶ ἐπερίσσευον τῷ ἀριθμῷ καθ᾽ ἡμέραν.

16.6—19.20. Fifth period, the extension of the Church to Europe, centering in Paul's missionary work in the great centers, such as Corinth and Ephesus. Summary: Οὕτως κατὰ κράτος τοῦ Κυρίου ὁ λόγος ηὔξανεν καὶ ἴσχυεν.

19.21—28.31. Sixth period (and longest section of the Book of Acts), carrying on the story until Paul arrives in Rome. The last two verses form the summary of this section and the end of the book: Ἐνέμεινεν δὲ διετίαν ὅλην ἐν ἰδίῳ μισθώματι, καὶ ἀπεδέχετο πάντας τοὺς εἰσπορευομένους πρὸς αὐτόν, κηρύσσων τὴν βασιλείαν τοῦ θεοῦ καὶ διδάσκων τὰ περὶ τοῦ Κυρίου Ἰησοῦ Χριστοῦ μετὰ πάσης παρρησίας ἀκωλύτως. It is further noted that the first three panels belong to the part of the book in which Peter is the chief actor; and the last three, Paul.

It is doubtful whether the author of Acts had this or any other definite outline before him as he wrote. Yet, while recognizing the limitations[59], it may be accepted as the most natural outline so far suggested[60].

In his celebrated monograph, *Horae Synopticae: Contributions to the Study of the Synoptic Problem,* Sir John Caesar Hawkins[61] (1837—1929) included an important discussion of the linguistic re-

---

[59] F. V. Filson, *Three Crucial Decades* (London, 1964), p. 13, points out that neither this outline nor any other gives proper expression to the important role of the speeches in Acts.

[60] It may also be noted that the presence of these summaries, leading up to the final one at the end of the book, tells against the theory that the book was left unfinished. From this point of view Acts 28.30—31 forms a fitting conclusion to the book as a whole.

[61] (Oxford, 1898; 2nd ed. 1909).

lations between the Gospel according to Luke and the Book of Acts
(2nd. ed., 174—93). His careful study is generally recognized as
demonstrating that the style and language of the "we"- sections cannot be distinguished from those of the rest of the Book, and that
both in turn cannot be distinguished from that of the Third Gospel[62]. In addition to the agreements, however, he points to a number of significant stylistic *differences* between the Gospel and Acts
(177—82). These differences in vocabulary and phraseology, though
insufficient to destroy the argument for the unity of authorship, lead
Hawkins to the inference that "the two books, though the works of
the same writer, could not have proceeded from him at the same
time, or very nearly the same time" (180).

The turn of the century saw the appearance of two very important commentaries on Acts, by Richard John Knowling (1851—1919)
and Richard Belward Rackham (1868—1912), which would appear
on anyone's list of the half dozen most important commentaries on
the book which have appeared in English. These two works, in their
own very different ways, were the most careful and thorough studies
of Acts to appear up to that time. That both are still in print nearly
seven decades later is an evidence of their abiding value to the
present day.

Knowling's volume appeared in 1900 as a part of the famous
Expositor's Greek Testament, edited by W. Robertson Nicoll[63]. It
is very much the sort of commentary that Lightfoot would have
written had he been able to fulfill his wish. It contains a lengthy introduction, discussing the most important research, with a heavy
emphasis on the work of German scholars (1—48). Knowling is the
one commentator of the time who is equally conversant with the
work of both German and British scholarship — an all too rare
occurrence even today.

The commentary itself is full of the sort of historical material to
which British critics before him had pointed; but it is more thorough, as well as more carefully sifted, than any of the earlier studies.
It is especially valuable for its careful discussion of points of grammar and philology, and for its careful consideration of the historical problems arising from a critical study of Acts.

---

[62] The only really significant attempt to demonstrate that the Gospel according to Luke and the Book of Acts were written by two different authors
was made by another British scholar, A. C. Clark, *The Acts of the Apostles*
(Oxford, 1933), pp. 393—408, an extremely eccentric piece of work. See, however, the careful critisism of W. L. Knox, *The Acts of the Apostles* (London,
1948), pp. 3—15, 100—09.

[63] *The Acts of the Apostles*, EGT (Edinburgh, 1900) 2, pp. 1—554.

130

The author is conservative in his conclusions, although he does not fail to consider any significant contrary opinion advanced by other scholars. He affirms the high value of the Lucan writings as historical sources (here he has the benefit of the work of Ramsay)[64] and the traditional authorship, although he leaves the question of date open. Arguing that none of the source-critical theories advanced by German scholars could be regarded as really successful to any great degree, Knowling advances the view that the author's sources are primarily personal (16—34). His knowledge of the events narrated in the latter portion of Acts would have been gained from a personal sharing in the experiences and from conversation with Paul and in hearing him relate minutely, as was his habit[65], what God had done through him. His sources for the earlier sections may have been John Mark[66], Barnabas and other members of the Jerusalem church who were at Antioch[67], Mnason, ἀρχαῖος μαθητής (21.16)[68], Philip the evangelist and his daughters (21.8—12)[69], Silas (ch. 16)[70], as well as other members of the Jerusalem church (21.18). While it may be that Luke made use of some written documents, for example, in his account of the speeches of Peter and Stephen and in connection with the early days of the Church in Jerusalem (18), the identification of the author of the whole book with the author of the "we"-narratives brings the author into close enough contact with eyewitnesses of the earlier events to have obtained his information from face to face interrogation. And from this point of view the question of sources becomes a less important one[71].

---

[64] See chapter 7.

[65] Cf. Acts 21.19; 14.27; 15.3, 12, 26; Gal. 2.2, 7—9.

[66] The vivid and circumstantial details of Peter's escape from prison and return to the house of the mother of John Mark in chapter 12 are regarded by Knowling as best explained in this way (16—17, 272—78), as well as the other incidental details connected with John Mark himself.

[67] Knowling regards the Western text of 11.27—28 as representing a reliable tradition connecting Luke with Antioch, if not authentic (17, 269—70).

[68] "It is very likely that, like Philip's daughters, he receives explicit mention because, as an early disciple, he could give information about the early days of the Church" (Bruce, *Acts*, p. 390).

[69] This suggestion was to be developed by Harnack, who saw in Luke's contact with the daughters of Philip the evangelist the reason for the special emphasis given to women, prophecy, and Samaritans in Luke-Acts (*Lukas der Arzt* (Leipzig, 1906), pp. 109—15). He also argued for Luke's dependence on Mark for much of the Petrine material.

[70] Silas is mentioned in 15.22 as one of the chief among the brethren of Jerusalem.

[71] Cf. J. Dupont, *The Sources of Acts*, E. T. (London, 1964), p. 167; and Bruce, *Acts*, pp. 21—22.

The strong point of the commentary by R. B. Rackham[72] is also the source of its weakness — it is essentially a theological commentary. In a way it is a good complement to Knowling, who devotes little space to the discussion of the theology of Acts; yet it lacks the careful historical perspective of the former. The theological discussion — although rightly emphasizing such features as the emphasis of the Lucan writings on women (xxxii—xxxiii), the brotherly oneness of the primitive Church (xxxiii—xxxv)[73], the Risen Lord at work in the Church (xxxv, lxx), prayer (xxxv—xxxvi), joy in the Spirit (xxxvi), and the work of the Holy Spirit (xxxvii—xli, lxx—lxxi, lxxiv—lxxvi) — is written too much from the point of view of the subsequent theology of the Church, marked by Rackham's own High Church position. Still, it remains one of the great English commentaries.

In an article published in the first issue of the *Journal of Theological Studies*[74], the main points of which are summarized in his commentary (l—lv), Rackham offers the classic defense of the early date of Acts. His argument is basically this:

An ordinary reader, finding that the book ends without any mention of the results of the appeal to Caesar and that it leaves Paul working at Rome for two years in a kind of 'free custody', would naturally conclude that the author had written his book in those two years and come to an end because he had no further information to give. If the reader was further aware that shortly after these two years not only S. Paul but S. Peter also was put to death in a fierce outburst of persecution at Rome, and knew that the account of their deaths (which would have formed the natural close of the book) would have been of intense interest not only to their contemporaries but to all future generations of Christians, his conclusion that the Acts was written before the martyrdom took place would become an irresistible conviction (1).

---

[72] In the *Oxford Commentaries* = *Westminster Commentaries on the Revised Version, The Acts of the Apostles* (London, 1901); repr. many times.

[73] Contrary to the Tübingen view that the author of Acts sought to gloss over the difference of opinion in the Church in order to conceal the true situation, it is observed that "with all his desire for unity S. Luke did not conceal unwelcome facts. The murmuring in the Church, the reluctance of the Brotherhood to receive a new brother, the Pharisaic spirit which criticized the chief apostle and which would have excluded the Gentiles, the 'no small dissension and questioning' which arose in the Church on the matter of circumcision — all these are duly recorded. Most painful of all was the 'sharp contention' which arose between the two great apostles and fellow-workers, Paul and Barnabas" (xxxiv—xxxv).

[74] "The Acts of the Apostles: A Plea for an Early Date", *JTS* 1 (1899/1900), pp. 76—87.

In support of this conclusion he offers the following arguments: (1) There is no allusion to any events which happened after the two years of the closing narration. And yet within a few years there occurred very important events which had great significance for the story told in Acts: for example, the martyrdom of James, the persecution of Christians under Nero in Rome and the martyrdom of Peter and Paul, and the destruction of Jerusalem and the Temple in A. D. 70. (2) There is no word of the death of Paul[75], which seems incredible if the event had been known to the author or his readers[76]. (3) Luke probably would not have left Acts 20.25 and 38 as it stands had he been aware that Paul (as we know from the Pastorals) had visited Ephesus again. (4) Acts presents a situation which could only have existed before A. D. 64.

The attitude of Rome to the church in the Acts is evidently still undecided, not to say favourable; and S. Luke is writing a defence of Christianity with good hopes of success. But all this was dashed to the ground by the great fire of 64 and Nero's persecution. From that time the relation of the empire to the church is better painted by the Revelation (lii).

At any rate, if Luke wrote after the disaster of A. D. 64, his peaceful and joyful optimism would be hard to understand[77]. Similarly (5) the description of Judaism in Acts is certainly pre-A. D. 70. Thus we read that μυριάδες εἰσιν ἐν τοῖς Ἰουδαίοις τῶν πεπιστευκότων (21.20) in the Holy City itself. And there is no hint of the fact of the destruction of the Temple, an event which was the final solution to the discussion of chapter 15, or of the fact that the members of the Jerusalem church are at the moment in exile at Pella. Two -further arguments are given: (6) Acts faithfully reflects the ideas and theology of the early Church; and (7) the author makes no use of the Pauline letters to supplement his knowlege of Paul and his theology[78].

---

[75] Rackham sees no allusion to Paul's death in 20.25 and 38.

[76] This is especially significant in the light of the parallelism, which Rackham observes, between the Gospel and Acts.

[77] Cf. "It is not often stated, yet perhaps it is the fact, that the best short general picture of the *Pax Romana* and all that it meant — good roads and posting, good police, freedom from brigandage and piracy, freedom of movement, toleration and justice — is to be found in the experience, written in Greek, of a Jew who happened to be a Roman citizen — that is, in the Acts of the Apostles" (Lord Hewart in *The Proceedings of the Classical Association* 24 (1927), p. 26; quoted in A. C. Clark, *Acts*, p. 390).

[78] "While he had access to the living apostle, there was no need of his letters. ... The Acts in itself suggests living intercourse with the apostle" (lii—liii).

The only real argument against an early date for Acts is, in Rackham's view, that based on the opinion that Luke's version of Jesus' prophecy of the destruction of Jerusalem (Luke 21.20—24; 19.43 —44) is written from the point of view of the destruction having already taken place. Several considerations, however, rob this argument of its force: (1) It is in any case certain that Jesus himself predicted, and that the early Christians expected, the destruction of Jerusalem. (2) Luke's account can be understood as a clarification of the words of Jesus with a Gentile audience in view. (3) The detailed language used by Luke is nothing more than that implied in the destruction of a city, an experience which was not new for Jerusalem. Twice in the preceding century and a half, and earlier under Antiochus Epiphanes, and earlier still under Nebuchadnezzar, the city had been "surrounded by armies" and the Temple desecrated. (4) The Old Testament itself provides parallels for nearly all the details of the passage[79].

Rackham seems to have been the first English author to suggest a two-fold parallelism in Luke-Acts (xlvii—l). First, there is a general parallelism between the Gospel and the Acts, including an introductory period of Waiting and preparation (Luke 1—2; Acts 1), a baptism of the Spirit (Luke 3; Acts 2), followed by a period of active ministry. This is concluded by a "passion" or period of suffering, which occupies a large proportion of the space of each volume. After early anticipations (Luke 9.51; Acts 19.21) and a detailed journey up to Jerusalem (Luke 17.11—19.48; Acts 20.1 to 21.17) with the "last words" of the sufferer (Luke 20—21; Acts 20.17—38), there follows the passion proper (Luke 22—23; Acts 21.17—28.31). Secondly, there is a similar parallelism between the two parts of Acts (i. e. between chs. 1—12 and chs. 13—28). Here Rackham points to the material first suggested by Schneckenburger — and, we might add, succeeds in outdoing even the Tübingen critics in finding parallels between the ministries of the two chief apostles! He dissents, however, from their negative judgment concerning the historicity of the parallels, arguing that "the parallelism arises out of the facts" (xlix).

The words of A. C. Headlam might be quoted in summing up the major conclusions of nineteenth century British scholarship in regard to the Acts of the Apostles:

---

[79] Cf. Jer. 20.4; Dt. 28.64; 1 Kg. 8.46; Isa. 5.5; 58.18; Dan. 8.13; Zech. 12.3; 1 Macc. 4.60; Isa. 29.3; 37.33; Jer. 6.6; 52.4—5; Ezk. 4.1—3; Ps. 137.9; Hos. 13.16. See C. H. Dodd, "The Fall of Jerusalem and the 'Abomination of Desolation'", *JRS* 37 (1947), pp. 49—50 = *More New Testament Studies* (Manchester, 1968), pp. 75—79.

1. The Third Gospel and the Acts of the Apostles are the work of the same person; and all tradition and argument suggest that the author was St. Luke, the companion of St. Paul.

2. He wrote the Gospel to describe as accurately as he could the life and preaching of Jesus; he wrote the Acts to describe the growth and spread of the Christian Church.

3. He had formed a clear idea in his mind of the steps and course of this growth, and arranged his work so as to bring out these points. The object he had in view would influence him in the selection of his materials and the proportional importance he would ascribe to events; but it would be taking far too artificial a view of his work not to allow some influence to various less prominent ideas, and even to the accidental cause of the existence or non-existence of information on different points . . .

4. Although he had a definite aim, and constructed a history with artistic unity, there is no reason for thinking that the history is therefore untrustworthy. He narrated events as he believed they happened, and he gives a thoroughly consistent history of the period over which it extends.

5. The exact degree of credibility and accuracy we can ascribe to him is dependent on his sources of information. From ch. 12 onwards his source was excellent; from ch. 20 onwards he was an eye-witness. For the previous period he could not in all cases attain the same degree of accuracy, yet he was personally acquainted with eye-witnesses throughout, and may very probably have had one or more written documents. In any case, his history from the very beginning shows a clear idea of historical perspective, and of the stages in the growth of the community, even if certain characteristics of the primitive Church in Jerusalem have been exaggerated[80].

Various factors led British scholarship in the direction of these conservative conclusions. The pace was set by Lightfoot, who, although he founded no "school" in the German sense, gave to other scholars an example to follow. In contrast to the speculative criticism of Baur, Lightfoot's work was historical in the fullest sense of the word. Instead of attaching his ideas to various isolated passages in the New Testament and early Christian literature, he emphasized the importance of both the immediate and larger contexts. Rather than forcing the New Testament into the mold of a prior understanding of the nature of primitive Christianity derived from a study of writings far removed from the mainstream of both canonical and post-canonical Christian documents, he sought to gain a clear understanding of what primitive Christianity was really like from a study of the minute details of exegesis. Thus British scholars who followed in the Lightfoot tradition were saved from the extravagancies which result from trying to discover what was in the mind of the writer, instead of what he put down on papyrus.

---

[80] *HDB* 1, p. 35.

Next to Lightfoot, the man who was most responsible for this positive (some would say, conservative) approach to the Book of Acts on the part of British scholars was Sir William M. Ramsay. His influential work on Paul appeared in 1895 and was immediately recognized as marking a new era in the history of the study of the Book of Acts. However, we must leave the discussion of his work until the following chapter.

Chapter VII

LUKE THE HISTORIAN DEFENDED

Lightfoot, as the last chapter indicated, was the major influence on nineteenth century British *Actaforschung*. He was the one who was chiefly responsible for pointing scholars like A. C. Headlam in the direction of a conservative view of the historical value of Acts. But toward the end of the century another important figure appeared on the scene, the influence of whose work can already be seen in the writings of the last three or four scholars to whom reference was made in chapter 6 — Sir William Mitchell Ramsay (1851—1939).

Ramsay was primarily a classical scholar and archaeologist, "the foremost authority of his day on the topography, antiquities, and history of Asia Minor in ancient times"[1]. Although his major contribution to the world of scholarship was in this area, he made an almost equally significant contribution to New Testament research[2].

When he first began his work in Asia Minor, Ramsay accepted, in general, the "Tübingen" approach to the Book of Acts. "I had read a good deal of modern criticism about the book", he later wrote,

and dutifully accepted the current opinion that it was written during the second century by an author who wished to influence the minds of people in his own time by a highly wrought and imaginative description of the early Church. His object was not to present a trustworthy picture of the facts in the period of about A. D. 50, but to produce a certain effect on his own time by setting forth a carefully coloured account of events and persons of that older period. He wrote for his contemporaries, not for truth. He cared naught for geographical or historical surroundings of the

---

[1] J. G. C. Anderson in *DNB 1931—1940*, p. 727.

[2] His most important works for the study of Acts are *St. Paul the Traveller and the Roman Citizen* (London, 1897); articles in *HDB* 1—5 (1898—1904); *Pictures of the Apostolic Church* (London, 1910); *The Bearing of Recent Discovery on the Trustworthiness of the New Testament* (London, 1915). See the complete bibliography and indexes of major subjects, passages of Scripture, and Greek words dealt with by Ramsay in W. W. Gasque, *Sir William M. Ramsay: Archaeologist and New Testament Scholar* (Grand Rapids, 1966).

period A. D. 30 to 60. He thought only of the period A. D. 160—80, and how he might paint the heroes of old times in situations that should touch the conscience of his contemporaries. Antiquarian or geographical truth was less than valueless in a design like this: one who thought of such things was distracting his attention from the things that really mattered, the things that would move the minds of men in the second century[3].

In his search for information bearing on the geography and history of Asia Minor, Ramsay at first paid slight attention to the early Christian authorities. He had the impression that these were quite unworthy of consideration by a historian; anything having to do with religion belonged to the realm of the theologians, not to that of the historians. When he spent time copying early Christian inscriptions in his earliest years of travel and exploration, he felt the time to be wasted — even though a sense of duty compelled him to make copies of them. Finally, in a desperate search for any information throwing light on the geographical and historical situation of that part of Asia Minor which scholars refer to today as "South Galatia", he began to study the journeys of Paul in this region as described in the Book of Acts. He hardly expected to find any information of value regarding the actual situation in the time of Paul. Rather he thought he would find material bearing on the second half of the second century of the Christian era, i. e., the age in which (he thought) the author of Acts lived and wrote.

In his book, *The Bearing of Recent Discovery on the Trustworthiness of the New Testament*, Ramsay tells how he came to change his mind[4]. The first thing that caused him to begin to doubt the conclusion which he had assumed was a careful study of the narrative of Acts 14, which he discovered to be meticulously accurate in regard to its professed historical setting[5]. This, in turn, led him to ask the further question: If the author of Acts proves to be carefully accurate in a matter of one detail, would it not be likely that he would prove to be the same in regard to others?

There is a certain presumption that a writer who proves to be exact and correct in one point will show the same qualities in other matters. No writer is correct by mere chance, or accurate sporadically. He is accurate by virtue of a certain habit of mind. Some men are accurate by nature; some are by nature loose and inaccurate[6].

His attitude toward the Book of Acts was now radically changed. Instead of assuming the book to be untrustworthy in regard to its

---

[3] *Bearing of Recent Discovery*, pp. 37—38.
[4] Pp. 39—52.   [5] Cf. Gasque, *Op. cit.*, pp. 25—26.
[6] *Bearing of Recent Discovery*, p. 80.

avowed historical situation, he began to approach Acts with an open mind that it might after all prove to be accurate in any given detail. He now realized, as F. F. Bruce has stated, that if an author's trustworthiness "is vindicated in points where he can be checked, we should not assume that he is less trustworthy where we cannot test his accuracy"[7]. Ramsay would at least give the author of Acts the benefit of the doubt.

Over the years the opinion gradually forced itself upon him that Luke's history of early Christian origins was unsurpassed for its accuracy. After more than thirty years of close study of the milieu of first century Christianity, he penned these words:

The more I have studied the narrative of Acts, and the more I have learned year after year about Graeco-Roman society and thoughts and fashions, and organization in those provinces, the more I admire and the better I understand. I set out to look for truth on the borderland where Greece and Asia meet, and found it here. You may press the words of Luke in a degree beyond any other historian's, and they stand the keenest scrutiny and the hardest treatment, *provided always that the critic knows the subject and does not go beyond the limits of science and justice*[8].

It is a great pity that the reputation of Ramsay was tainted by his willingness to don the mantle of a popular apologist in his later years, and particularly by his unwise controversy with James Moffatt[9]. However, it should be remembered that the judgments he popularized were

judgments which he had previously formed as a scientific archaeologist and student of ancient classical history and literature. He was not talking unadvisedly or playing to the religious gallery when he expressed the view that "Luke's history is unsurpassed in respect of its trustworthiness"; this was the sober conclusion to which his researches led him, in spite of the fact that he started with a very different opinion of Luke's historical credit[10].

And the majority of British and American New Testament scholars and historians of Greek and Roman antiquity — indeed, it may almost be said, *all* scholars who have studied Ramsay's work closely — have agreed that his major thesis has been proven[11].

---

[7] *Acts*, p. 17.
[8] *Bearing of Recent Discovery*, p. 89. The emphasis is mine and is very important.
[9] See Gasque, *Op. cit.*, pp. 56—59.
[10] F. F. Bruce, *The New Testament Documents: Are They Reliable?* (5th ed., London, 1960), pp. 90—91.
[11] See Gasque, *Op. cit.*, pp. 23—37, for a discussion of the major points bearing on the historical value of Luke-Acts. I am aware that the above

Another problem of New Testament criticism was closely related in the thought of Ramsay to the problem of the reliability of Acts: Who are the churches to whom Paul writes and whom he addressed as "Galatians" (Gal. 1.2; 3.1)? Is the reference to ethnic or political Galatia? That is, does it signify the central mountainous region of Asia Minor occupied by the descendants of the Gauls who emigrated from Europe in the third century B. C.? Or does it refer to the Roman province of this name, which was a much larger district (including "South Galatia")? In the latter case the epistle would be addressed to the churches of Pisidian Antioch, Iconium, Lystra, and Derbe (Acts (13.14—14.23; 16.1—5), founded on Paul's "first missionary journey".

The traditional view was to identify the Γαλάται with the descendants of the earlier Gallic invaders who had established a kingdom in "North Galatia"[12]. Thus Paul's Epistle to the Galatians would have been addressed to churches in the region of Ancyra, Tavium, and Pessinus, to which only passing allusion is made in the narrative of Acts (16.6 and 18.23, according to this interpretation). One or two scholars before Ramsay (e. g. Renan) had rejected the North Galatian theory, but it remained the dominant view until the end of the nineteenth century in both British and continental criticism[13]. The major defender of the North Galatian view in England was none other than J. B. Lightfoot[14], who argued that the natural in-

---

summary has been extremely brief and has merely stated conclusions, rather than offered proof. Conviction concerning the rightness of Ramsay's conclusion — or, for that matter, the rebuttal of it — can only come through a careful study of his writings or the use made of his work by F. F. Bruce and more recent British commentators. I have done this and can only state my conviction that Ramsay's conclusion concerning the historical reliability of the Book of Acts can be defended. Cf. the view of A. N. Sherwin-White, the most recent classical historian to study the problem of the historical value of Acts: "Any attempt to reject its (i. e., Acts') basic historicity even in matters of detail must now appear absurd" (Roman Society and Roman Law in the New Testament (Oxford, 1963), p. 189).

[12] The traditional view, according to Ramsay, was due to the fact that "the term Galatia ceased to bear the sense which it had to a Roman in the first century. The whole of central and southern Lycaonia was, before the middle of the second century, separated from Galatia, and formed into a province Lycaonia, which was united with Isauria and Cilicia under the title of 'the three Eparchies', and put under the command of a governor of the highest rank. From this time onwards the true sense of the term Galatia in St. Paul's time was lost . . ." (The Church in the Roman Empire, p. 111).

[13] The North Galatian view continues to be the dominant view in Germany; cf. W. G. Kümmel, An Introduction to the New Testament, E. T. (London, 1966), pp. 190—93 for a convenient summary of the arguments for this view.

[14] Galatians, pp. 1—35.

terpretation of the term would be to understand it in a regional-ethnic sense, and that the main characteristics of the Gauls as a people stand out in Paul's letters[15]. But Lightfoot did not have the advantage of the information gained by geographical and archaeological research at the end of the century. Had he lived a decade or so longer it is quite likely that he would have changed his mind on the subject.

When Ramsay began his study of the New Testament, he accepted the North Galatian view; but the more he studied the evidence the more he became convinced that this theory just did not coincide with the facts[16]. Several factors combined to compel him to abandon the older view. (1) There was a great difference between the rustic Gallic population of North Galatia, who were probably little affected by Greek manners and language, and the population of the cities, who were for the most part not Gauls[17]. If Paul followed his custom and worked in the cities of this area (assuming, for the sake of argument, that he did in fact do missionary work in North Galatia), then his converts, for the most part, would not have been Galatians in the ethnic sense. Therefore, "Galatians" would be no more appropriate as a term of reference to these people than to people of the South Galatian area. (2) Furthermore, it was Paul's general practice to work in cities which were to some degree Hellenized and where there has a Jewish population; this would not have been the case in North Galatia in the first century. (3) There is little evidence for the existence of Christianity in North Galatia until a much later time than the first century. On the other hand, (4) the simple name of "Galatians" would have been the ideal name to use in referring to the people of the cities of Pisidian Antioch, Iconium, Lystra, and Derbe. In fact, it is the *only* name that would have been apropos to the situation. They could not have been addressed as "the churches of Lycaonia" or "Lycaonians", because Antioch and Iconium were in the region of Phrygia. Furthermore, many of the inhabitants of these cities were not natives to the region: thus to describe them as Lycaonians or Phrygians would have been quite inappropriate — especially since some of them would

---

[15] *Ibid.*, pp. 13—17.

[16] Cf. Gasque, *Op. cit.*, pp. 29—34. Ramsay's views were first stated in *The Church in the Roman Empire before A. D. 170* (London, 1893), pp. 8—11, 16—111, further developed in *St. Paul the Traveller*, pp. 89—151, 178—93, and in his *Historical Commentary on St. Paul's Epistle to the Galatians* (London, 1899), pp. 1—234. A convenient summary of the relevant material will be found in his articles on "Galatia", etc. in *HDB* 2, pp. 81—93, which are of great value even today.

[17] *HDB* 3, p. 84.

have been Roman citizens (Antioch and Lystra were Roman colonies). In addition, the term "Phrygian" was a term with a very bad connotation[18], and it would not have been in good taste to use it in referring to the people of the region. The only all-inclusive term which was available for use in speaking of the members of the churches to which Paul founded in the region of South Galatia would be "Galatians"; and Paul, as a Roman citizen, would quite naturally follow the Roman provincial division and ignore those national distinctions which were opposed to the organized Roman unity[19]. It was Paul's practice to use the titles of the Roman provinces in his letters, rather than those of geographical or ethnic groups.

Space does not permit the listing of other arguments brought forward by Ramsay in support of the South Galatian view, nor to attempt to answer the objections of the advocates of the traditional view. It is possible only to observe that nearly all British and American scholars, and not a few German, have been convinced by Ramsay's research of the probability of the South Galatian view[20].

The usual view of the relationship between the two visits to Jerusalem mentioned by Paul in Galatians 1 and 2 and the visits to Jerusalem recorded in the Book of Acts is to equate the visits of Gal. 1.18 with Acts 9.26 and Gal. 2.1 with Acts 15. Thus Gal. 2.1−10 is taken to be Paul's account of the so-called Jerusalem council. Since it is difficult to harmonize the two accounts in all details — though not quite so difficult as some have thought — some critics, from de Wette onwards, have tended to give very little historical credit to the account in Acts 15. Emphasis on the alleged differences between the two accounts was, as we have seen, one of the main planks in the Tübingen attack on the historical reliability of Acts.

Ramsay put forward the view that the visit of Galatians 2 should not be equated with the visit of Acts 15, but rather with the famine-relief visit recorded in Acts 11.30[21] — a view which has been very influential among British New Testament critics.

---

[18] Φρύξ was used as a synonym for "slave" (cf. Aristophanes, *Vespae* 433) and as a byword for cowardice (cf. the proverb quoted in Strabo 1. 2. 30, δειλότερος λαγὼ φρυγός; also Lucian, *Dial. Mort.* 26 (15. 1: 399). See also *The Martyrdom of Polycarp* 4 and the references listed in Lightfoot, *Colossians*, p. 312.

[19] On the other hand, the author of Acts, being a Greek and not a Roman citizen, follows the common Greek usage and uses regional terms.

[20] However, not all have been convinced of his interpretation of the geographical references in Acts 16.6 and 18.23; cf. Gasque, *Op. cit.*, pp. 29−30, 33, with references.   [21] *St. Paul the Traveller*, pp. 54−64 *et passim*.

142

Why, then, did Paul not mention his third visit (i. e. Acts 15) to Jerusalem in his letter to the Galatian churches? In his earlier writings, Ramsay finds the answer difficult. He answers that it was beside the point of his argument. Paul "is engaged in proving that, *when he gave his first message to the churches of Galatia*, he had never received any charge from the older apostles"[22]. The third visit did not take place until after the Galatian churches were founded; therefore, it could find no place in the autobiographical retrospect of Galatians 1 and 2. A more satisfactory explanation was decided upon later: the Epistle to the Galatians was written *prior to* the events of Acts 15[23], thus making it the earliest of Paul's epistles[24]. This latter point has not gained the same widespread acceptance as has Ramsay's view of the South Galatian destination of the Epistle to the Galatians, but it has commended itself to many, especially in Great Britain.

Theodor Zahn (1838—1933), the conservative Lutheran scholar, is remembered by students of the Book of Acts chiefly for his refinement of Blass's theory of a two-fold recension of Acts, from the hand of Luke himself, and for his advocacy of the view that Luke intended to write a third volume. He arrived at the former conclusion independently of Blass[25], and he differed with him in regard to a number of details — chiefly in his rejection of Blass's extension of the theory to the Third Gospel. Still, with various modifications and refinements, he defended the view that the so-called "Western" text of Acts represented the author's first draft (plus a few early deteriorations), which was subsequently revised by the excision of matter which was unnecessary or which might be misunderstood. The later revision is in general agreement with what is usually designated the "Alexandrian" text of Acts.

This theory was first put forward in the second volume of his monumental *Introduction to the New Testament*[26], developed in a

---

[22] *St. Paul the Traveller*, p. 187; italics mine.
[23] See the preface which was added to the 14th edition of *St. Paul the Traveller* (London, 1920). Unfortunately this was not included in the American reprint of 1960 (= 3rd ed., 1897).
[24] If one accepts the South Galatian hypothesis, only two possible objections could be raised to this date: (1) Galatians is thus separated from the Epistle to the Romans, the Pauline letter to which it has the closest affinity, by about nine years; (2) Gal. 4.13 seems to require two visits by Paul to the churches addressed. The former of these is the weightiest of these objections, but neither is absolutely compelling. Cf. F. F. Bruce, "The Epistles of Paul", in *Peake's Commentary on the Bible*, M. Black and H. H. Rowley (eds.), (London, 1962), pp. 930—31.   [25] Cf. *supra*, p. 97, n. 3.
[26] *Einleitung in das Neue Testament*, 2nd ed., 2 (1900), pp. 339—60. Quotations and references which follow are from this vol. and edition.

special monograph on the subject[27], and reaffirmed in his great commentary on the Book of Acts[28]. He gives three main reasons in support of the originality of the two-fold text-tradition: (1) The data found in the "Western" text which are omitted from the "Alexandrian" are neutral in character[29]; they are quite untypical of scribal insertions or excisions. (2) In spite of the differences the "Western" and "Alexandrian" texts never really contradict each other. (3) Both recensions manifest the style which is characteristic of the larger part of the book which is common to both[30]. What is argued in brief in his *Einleitung* is argued at length — some would say, at much too great length — in his monograph and commentary. Few have been convinced of the correctness of his thesis, but his work remains as one of the most careful and comprehensive analyses and attempted solutions of the problem of the "Western" text of Acts; and it must be taken seriously by all who are engaged in New Testament textual criticism.

Some scholars, notably Ramsay[31] and Zahn[32], have found in the use of τὸν μὲν πρῶτον λόγον (in the place of the more correct τὸν μὲν πρότερον λόγον) an intimation from the author that he contemplated writing a τρίτος λόγος. In the words of Zahn,

Einem Schriftsteller, welcher fähig war, die stilistisch tadellose Periode [65] Lc 1, 1—4 zu schreiben, ist nicht zuzutrauen, das er da, wo er nicht älteren, hebräisierenden oder sonst schlecht geschriebenen Quellen folgt, sondern an der Spitze eines Buchs seinen Gedanken frei zum Ausdruck bringt, τὸν μὲν πρῶτον statt des richtigen τὸν μὲν πρότερον λόγον geschrieben haben sollte, wenn das Ev ein erstes von nur zwei und nicht vielmehr von einer grösseren Zahl von Büchern sein sollte (372)[33].

In favor of this view Zahn adduces the following: (1) Nothing is told about Paul's preaching in Rome or the outcome of his trial,

---

[27] *Die Urausgabe der Apostelgeschichte des Lucas*, Forschungen zur Geschichte des neutestamentlichen Kanons und der altkirchlichen Literatur IX. Teil (Leipzig, 1916).

[28] *Die Apostelgeschichte des Lukas*, KzNT, 2 vols. (Leipzig, 1918 and 1921).

[29] This has been denied by some scholars — most recently by E. J. Epp, *The Theological Tendency of Codex Bezae* (Cambridge, 1966) — but few have been convinced of a general "tendency" lying behind the Western text.

[30] *Einleitung* 2, p. 342.

[31] *St. Paul the Traveller*, pp. 23, 27—28, 351—52, *et passim*.

[32] *Einleitung* 2, pp. 370—73.

[33] It is probable, however, that πρότερος had been largely replaced by πρῶτος in Hellenistic Greek, very much as "first" is used for the more strictly correct "former" in modern English when only two things are in question. Cf. Bruce, *Acts*, p. 65; Bauer-Arndt-Gingrich, pp. 732—33, with bibliography; and Blass-Debrunner-Funk, sec. 62.

even though the reader has had his attention fixed on both earlier in the narrative (Acts 19.21; 23.11; 25.10—11, 21, 25; 27.24). "Ein ungeschickterer Schluss des Werks als dieser wäre kaum zu ersinnen" (370)[34]. (2) Luke's reference to an exact period of time (διετίαν ὅλην, 28.30) for the duration of Paul's imprisonment indicates that a change in Paul's condition had taken place at the time of writing. (3) In his prologue (Luke 1.1—4) the author states that he intends to write a history of Christianity up to the point of development reached in his own day, a plan which is by no means carried out if the story originally ended with Acts 28.

What would have been the contents of Luke's τρίτος λόγος? He certainly would have told more about Paul's preaching in Rome, suggests Zahn, and concerning the outcome of his trial. Perhaps he would have included more information about the course of missionary activity through others besides Paul, of the destruction of Jerusalem as prophecied by the Lord[35], and of the subsequent history of the Jerusalem church. Yet Luke either failed to write a third volume; or, less probably, the work was lost soon after it was written.

What, in Zahn's view, is the purpose of Acts? The author's aim, answers Zahn, is to set forth, after the manner of the Greek historians, the history of Christianity from its beginnings to the events of his own time (373). He aims to do this in a way that will impress a cultured Gentile who has heard much about the facts which were then current in the Christian Church, who has become interested in its history, and who is friendly toward Christians like the author. Theophilus (Luke 1.3; Acts 1.1) would be a man of high position, but who is not himself a Christian[36]. Luke is concerned primarily

---

[34] Other scholars, however, consider Acts 28.30—31 a very fitting ending to the book. Yet perhaps the majority would agree that the conclusion of the narrative is strange — unless, of course, it was completed at the end of the two years of 28.30 and the author knew no more — without accepting the hypothesis of an intended third book.

[35] Zahn suggests a date of ca. 75 for Acts (434—36). The author was the traditional Luke.

[36] The mode of address, κράτιστε Θεόφιλε (Luke 1.3), in the preface indicates not only the recipient's high rank, but also indicates that he was not (yet) a member of the Christian Church; there is no instance in the Christian literature of the first two centuries where a Christian uses a secular title in addressing another Christian, let alone a title of honor like this (361, 385 n.). Furthermore, there is no reason, argues Zahn, to interpret κατηχήθης in a technical sense ("instructed as a catechumen"), since (1) the word is not used in this way until a later time, and (2) this idea is out of character with Luke's aim to give to Theophilus a conviction of certainty concerning the trustworthiness of the λόγοι which he had heard. On the other hand, the fact that Luke's work is

to commend the Christian message to Theophilus; but the recipient's position was also a guarantee that the work, when it had accomplished its immediate aim, would gain a wider circulation.

Zahn defends the historical trustworthiness of Acts, along the lines of British scholarship, noting that

> Während die Theologen auf Schritt und Tritt den Lc mit Vorwürfen [67] wegen seiner Unkenntnis der geschichtlichen Verhältnisse und Personen, die er berüht, verfolgt haben, ist namentlich die AG von Historikern und Altertumsforschern ersten Rangs, welche sich eingehender mit ihr beschäftigt haben, durchweg als ein bedeutendes und überwiegend glaubwürdiges Geschichtswerk beurteilt worden (430).

In addition to the confirmatory material brought to light by the classical archaeologists, a strong proof of Luke's thorough acquaintance with the facts he narrates is that, without actually using Paul's letters, his narrative is in essential agreement with the main points and many incidental details of his epistles (431). Zahn goes on to list and discuss many points of contact between the epistles and Acts, as well as between Acts and secular history. The examples are extended in his commentary, where Zahn attempts to answer the critics of the Lucan history by a minute examination of the text of Acts and its points of contact with both the epistles of Paul and secular history.

Perhaps it was due to his defense of unlikely theses — such as the Lucan authorship of both the "Western" and "Alexandrian" texts of Acts, and Luke's intention of a third volume. Or perhaps it was due to his identification with traditional, confessional Lutheran theology at a time when the representatives of "liberal" theology in the universities of Germany were not especially liberal in their attitude toward those who were unable to join them in their disdain for orthodoxy. For one reason or the other — perhaps for both — Zahn failed to make much of an impression on the representatives of *wissenschaftlich* exegesis in Germany[37]. Zahn was honored as a master of philological detail and theological erudition; but his views were generally rejected as *eigenwillig* and *strengkonservativ*.

---

dedicated to him indicates that Theophilus was favorably inclined toward the faith. The fact that Luke dedicated a second book to him is proof that the first had met with a kindly reception, while the absence of κράτιστε in Acts 1.1 may mean that he had ceased to be a man of distinction and had become ἀδελφός (362).

[37] On the other hand, his works were greatly appreciated in Britain and North America.

Like Zahn, Adolf Harnack[38] (1851—1930) was often individualistic in his opinions. Yet unlike Zahn, Harnack was *never* intentionally conservative in any of his conclusions. No one could accuse him of any prejudice whatsoever in favor of either orthodox theology or traditional views in the realm of biblical criticism. In spite of his natural inclinations, however, he came out as one of the strongest defenders of Luke's reputation as a historian.

Harnack is another imposing figure who, in company with de Wette, Baur, and Ritschl, has made a lasting impact on several theological disciplines in Germany. Of all German theologians it would probably be just to say that Harnack was the most widely influential and highly respected, both within and outside of Germany. He was perhaps most influential as an exponent of "liberal Christianity", his *Das Wesen des Christentums* (1900)[39] being the definitive statement of this particular credo, while his major and most lasting contributions were made in the areas of Church history and the history of doctrine[40]. His scholarly output was voluminous, being matched in breadth and length among his contemporaries only by Zahn.

It is customary to refer to the work of Harnack as the last important contribution to the source criticism of the Book of Acts[41]; however, his work is of much greater significance than this. (And, indeed, it was not the last important contribution to source criticism!) In fact, his suggestions for the source criticism of Acts[42] occupy only a part of his three books which are devoted to the study of the Book of Acts; none of the three monographs is concerned exclusively with source criticism. His discussions of the problems of authorship, the relationship between the Paul of Acts and the Paul of the epistles, the historical value, theology, and date — discussions which have been largely overlooked or ignored by much of subsequent scholarship — are far more important and, indeed, quite independent of any contribution he may have made, or failed to make, in the area of source criticism.

---

[38] On Harnack, see the brilliant study by G. W. Glick, *The Reality of Christianity: A Study of Adolf von Harack as Historian and Theologian* (New York, 1967); Mattill, *Luke as a Historian*, pp. 260—82, surveys his contribution to *Actaforschung*.

[39] E. T., *What is Christianity?* (London, 1901).

[40] Especially his *Lehrbuch der Dogmengeschichte*, 3 vols. (Leipzig, 1886—1890); and *Die Mission und Ausbreitung des Christentums in den ersten drei Jahrhunderten* (Leipzig, 1902).

[41] E. g., Haenchen, *Die Apostelgeschichte*, p. 29; Bieder, *Die Apostelgeschichte in der Historie*, p. 37; Dupont, *Sources*, p. 11.

[42] For a convenient summary of his views, cf. Dupont, *Sources*, pp. 35—38.

Between 1906 and 1911 Harnack wrote three important studies of the Lucan writings for his multi-volumed *Beiträge zur Einleitung in das Neue Testament* (vols. 1, 3 and 4). The first is entitled *Luke the Physician: The Author of the Third Gospel and Acts*[43]; it is, as its title indicates, concerned primarily with the problem of authorship. In particular, it is a careful examination of the often repeated opinion of orthodox German criticism that the Book of Acts could not have been written by Luke, the companion and fellow-worker of Paul — or, indeed, by any other friend of Paul.

The first chapter of Harnack's study (1—18) is concerned with the internal evidence of Acts which throws light on what has been the universally accepted tradition concerning the authorship of the Third Gospel and Acts since A. D. 140—50, i. e., that the author was the "Luke" mentioned in the Pauline epistles (Col. 4.14; Philm. 24; 2 Tim. 4.11) — (1) a Greek by birth, (2) a physician, (3) a sometime companion of Paul, and (4) a fellow missionary with Paul. Early tradition adds that he was a native of Antioch.

How did this tradition of the Lucan authorship arise, asks Harnack, if it is not based on fact? The Gospel, which begins with a prologue, of necessity must have contained in its title the name of its author (1)[44]. If Luke was not in fact the author, then the author's real name must have been suppressed and supplanted by another. If this had been the case, however, it would have been likely that the name of a more prominent person of the apostolic age would have been attached to it (2)[45].

In his introductory chapter Harnack draws attention to the following facts concerning the narrative of Acts as it relates to the problem of authorship. (1) "Luke" is never mentioned in Acts, which is exactly as it should be if he were the author[46]. (2) The Gospel and Acts, as all would agree, show abundant evidence of having been written by one who was a Greek by birth, rather than a Jew. (3) The literary standard of the whole work — the prologue, the

---

[43] *Lukas der Arzt: Der Verfasser des dritten Evangeliums und der Apostelgeschichte* (Leipzig, 1906).

[44] This is denied by some scholars, but it remains probable.

[45] Cf. "In the second century the bias was very strongly in the direction of attributing Apostolic authorship to documents accepted into the Canon. The burden, then, of proof lies with those who would assert the traditional authorship of Matthew and John, but on those who would deny it in the case of Mark and Luke" (B. H. Streeter, *The Four Gospels* (London, 1924), p. 530). Streeter goes on to suggest that if Luke-Acts were originally anonymous, it would have been attributed by later writers to Paul.

[46] On the other hand, Aristarchus, who is named with Luke in the epistles of Paul, is mentioned three times.

148

speeches of Paul in Acts, etc. — indicate that the author belonged to the middle or higher level of contemporary culture; and both the subject matter and style indicate that his profession was that of a physician[47]. (4) The author writes as an eye-witness in his narrative concerning Paul; this is the only really satisfactory explanation of the appearance of "we" in the narrative, and is also indicated by the disproportionate amount of space given to the history of Paul in the book. (5) The author was a missionary preacher with Paul (cf. 16.10 and 13)[48]. (6) The author shows a distinct affinity to Antioch in his narrative, especially in the earlier part of the book.

[68]   Bei der Lektüre des ersten Teils der Apg. atmet der prüfende Historiker an einigen Stellen frei auf und fühlt sicheren Boden unter den Füssen. *Fast jedesmal, wo das geschieht (c. 12 ausgenommen), sieht er sich in Antiochien oder in einer Geschichtserzählung, die auf diese Stadt hinweist (15)*[49].

Side by side with this must be placed the obvious fact that the author is quite clearly *not* a native of Palestine.

This examination of the tradition concerning the authorship of the Book of Acts is followed by a careful study of the so-called "we"-narratives (19—85). Even though Harnack is aware that the linguistic unity of Acts has been demonstrated many times — by scholars as diverse in their opinions as Zeller, Lekebusch, Klostermann, Vogel, and Hawkins — he lays out the evidence once again for the benefit of those critics who have either ignored the work of his predecessors, or who have refused to "see" the evidence. The

---

[47] Harnack draws from Hobart, although he recognizes that he went too far with the evidence and included much that was irrelevant. Cf. his detailed analysis (122—37), which, although it has to be revised somewhat in the light of Cadbury's criticisms, still remains of value.

[48] "Noch deutlicher geht das aus den in den Acta verstreuten grossen Reden hervor" (14n.).

[69]   [49] Important are (1) the account of the Seven in ch. 6, where only one is identified by his native city, Νικόλαος προσήλυτος Ἀντιοχεύς; (2) the account of Stephen and (3) the subsequent persecution and resulting mission in Antioch, which becomes a second Jerusalem (cf. 11.19—26); (4) the account of the church at Antioch in 13.1—2; (5) the connection of Paul's missionary journey with Antioch (ch. 13); (6) the crisis concerning circumcision in the church at Antioch; and (7) the mention of Antioch in 18.23. Cf. also 14.26; 15.23; and 15.35.

[70]   "Nach dem allen darf man wohl sagen, dass die Apostelgeschichte die Tradition, ihr Verfasser sei ein Antiochener von Geburt, nicht Lügen straft, sondern sich trefflich zu ihr fügt. Nicht dass der Verfasser ein Mitglied der antiochenischen Gemeinde gewesen ist, geht aus dem Buch hervor (aber das behauptet auch die Tradition nicht), wohl aber ein besonderes Interesse für diese Gemeinde und besondere Kenntnisse" (17).

linguistic analysis is preceded by a consideration of "wie sich die [71]
von dem Verfasser der Wirstücke erzählten Tatsachen und wie sich
seine Interessen zu denen des Verfassers des ganzen Werks verhalten" (20).

One of the striking facts which arises from the examination of the
content of the "we"-passages is that there is the same interest in the
miraculous — healings, manifestations of the Spirit, and appearances of angels — as in the rest of Acts and the Third Gospel (24).
Contrary to the statement of some, there is no evidence for the view
that the "we"-narratives are less miraculous in character. Further
points of similarity between the "we"-sections and the rest of the
Book of Acts include the following: Paul and his companions go
first to the synagogue or to the place of prayer; converts are baptised
"with their house"; Paul teaches "the way of salvation" or "the
way"; bread is broken in Christian assemblies; a college of elders
exists in the Jerusalem church; James appears as the leader of the
Jerusalem church; Christians use the expression, "the will of God
be done"; Paul is ready to die "for the name of the Lord Jesus";
Paul heals through the laying on of hands; and there is no strong
interest in the ecclesiastical[50]. In short, "wo nur immer eine Ver- [72]
gleichung möglich ist, da ist also auch eine vollkommene Übereinstim-
mung gegeben" (25–26).

From this Harnack proceeds to a careful — and, one would think,
exhaustive — study of the vocabulary, grammar, and style of the
"we"-sections and a comparison of this to that of the rest of Acts.
This leads him to the unquestionable verdict: "Die Wirstücke und [73]
die Apostelgeschichte haben einen und denselben Verfasser" (56).
The constant "undesigned coincidences" of language cannot be explained as due to accident; nor is the theory tenable that some
source has been reworked by a later hand, for this would have involved a revision which was so thorough that only the "we" was
left to stand[51].

---

[50] It is remarkable that the word "church" never occurs in the "we"-
sections. "Die Christen in Tyrus, Ptolemais, Cäsarea, Jerusalem, Sidon und [74]
Puteoli individualisiert er und nennt sie 'die Jünger', 'die Brüder', 'die Freunde'
... Im Luk.-Ev. findet sich bekanntlich ἐκκλησία nie, in der Apostelgeschichte
dagegen allerdings 23mal; allein 1. die Apg. braucht das Wort auch für die
jüdische und heidnische Gemeinde (7.38; 19.32. 39, 41) und zeigt schon dadurch, dass ihr das Wort noch nicht sakral ist, 2. von den übrigen 19 Stellen
beziehen sich 15 auf die Gesamtkirche und die Gemeinden von Jerusalem und
Antiochien. Sonst wird (für Asien und Europa) 3mal pluralisch von den Kir-
chen gesprochen (14.23; 15.41; 16.5) und 1mal von der Kirche in Ephesus"
(25–26n).

[51] Harnack points out that many of the *hapaxlegomena* which are noted as

150

Following a discussion of the implication of the linguistic data of Acts for the question of sources[52], Harnack turns to the objection that, in spite of the evidence of tradition and linguistics, it is still impossible to ascribe the Third Gospel and Acts to a companion and fellow-worker of Paul (86—103). The evidence brought forward by the exponents of this view — which he judges to be due to a false critical methodology, based on the theories of F. C. Baur, which have been refuted long ago but which manage to continue to exert an influence over New Testament criticism[53] — is put to the test by Harnack and found to be the result of hyper-criticism, rather than fact.

In answer to the critics of Luke, Harnack brings forward the following: (1) It was just as possible for Luke, a disciple of Paul, to make historical mistakes — such as the *hysteron-proteron* in regard to Theudas (5.36)[54] — as it was for anyone else. He certainly believes himself to be a historian (cf. his prologue), but his abilities are limited. (2) Even though the picture of the Jerusalem church in the early chapters leaves much to be desired (though not nearly so much as some critics allege!), the main features — the thoroughly Jewish character of the *Urgemeinde*, its relationship to the Jewish population up to the appearance of Stephen, and the motive of the first great persecution — all stand the test of historical criticism[55]. Indeed, in his veneration of the Jerusalem church Luke agrees with the historical Paul. (3) In his understanding of the historical development of Gentile Christianity, Luke is much more trustworthy than the later conceptions which were to replace his views only a few decades later.

What, then, of the alleged misrepresentation of Paul in Acts? What, specifically, about Paul's "Jewish" behaviour? Surely this cannot be reconciled with what we know of Paul from his epistles!

---

evidence for a different author in the "we"-sections are *termini technici* describing the voyage and shipwreck of chapter 27 (which comprises nearly half of the "we"-sections). When these *t. t.* are removed, there remains approximately the same proportion of *hapaxlegomena* as in the rest of the book (58—60).

[52] His tentative conclusion is this: "Es spricht Wichtiges dafür, dass Lukas in der ersten Hälfte der Acta eine aramäische Quelle übersetzt und benutzt hat, aber schlagend kann die Annahme nicht widerlegt werden, dass er lediglich auf mündlichen Mitteilungen fusst" (84).

[53] See especially the long note on pp. 86—87.

[54] However, the *hysteron-proteron* is not a proven fact; "auch bei Josephus ist ein Irrtum möglich" (88n.).

[55] "— so weit von einer solchen die Rede sein kann, wenn doch nur eine Quelle existiert" (88)! This fact is often overlooked by the critics of Luke's history.

If the author has here given to Paul less honor than appears from his letters to be due to him, and if in chapter 21 and following he makes him appear more Jewish than we, on the basis of these same letters, would assume, the question may be raised as to which is right — our assumption or the account given by the author of the Book of Acts? But even supposing this portrayal of Paul in Acts were incorrect, why could not the author, "der als geborener Hei- [78] denchrist die haarscharfe Linie, auf der Paulus als Jude und Christ wandelte, überhaupt nicht zu begreifen und wiederzugeben ver-möchte, ihn an einer Stelle jüdischer und an einer anderen Stelle freier darstellen, als er wirklich war" (90)? According to all we know and can conjecture about Paul in this connection, he must have more than once appeared quite incomprehensible to his Gen-tile Christian, as well as Jewish Christian, companions. However, it is by no means certain that Luke's account of Paul is unhistorical in its account of Paul's "Jewish" practices.

What about the "discrepancies" between the epistles and the Book of Acts? Harnack, admitting that there may be some (Luke was neither infallible, nor did he necessarily understand, or even agree with, Paul in every detail of theology), argues that these are greatly overstressed by the critics. When all is said and done, the agreements between Acts 15 and Galatians 2 — assuming that the reports refer to the same occasion — are greater than the disagree-ments (91). In fact, the agreements between the epistles and the Book of Acts are quite extensive[56]. Even in terms of theology the agreements are not a few. The author's reverence for Judaism, and especially the Old Testament, is certainly in agreement with the one who penned Romans 11 (91). The whole discourse to the Ephesian elders at Miletus calls to mind the epistles to the Thessalonians, in the same way the words of 13.38 and 39 remind us of Galatians and Romans (99). Furthermore, Luke's universalism, although not expressed in precisely the same way as in Paul's letters, is certainly essentially Pauline (99—100).

"Critical orthodoxy" is unimpressed by these facts, argues Har-nack, only because it expects too much of a disciple of Paul, and

---

[56] In an appendix to his second study of Acts, *Die Apostelgeschichte*, pp. 199 to 205, Harnack lists thirty-nine "undesigned coincidences" of agreement be-tween the early chapters of Acts and the Pauline letters. The list is by no means exhaustive and only hints at the points of contact between the later chapters of Acts and the epistles of Paul, but it is exceedingly important as an up-dating of Paley's argument (cf. *Supra*, pp. 17—19). These points of agreement between the letters of Paul and the narrative of Acts are consider-ably greater than any suggested contradictions and provide a telling argument against the view that Luke's narrative is to any large degree fictional.

because it has a warped conception of the history of early Christianity. Of course, the Book of Acts is not a mirror which allows us to gaze into the very soul of Paul. Are we, indeed, obliged to assume that a disciple of Paul must have been capable of looking into the heart of the author of Galatians, Romans and the Corinthian [79] epistles and writing down what he saw there? "Übrigens wissen wir nicht, ob Lukas ein Schüler des Paulus im eigentlichen (*sc.* German!) Sinn gewesen ist" (98n.). The way he places himself side by side with Paul in 16.13 is not in keeping with this view. Furthermore, it is totally unhistorical to think of these Gentile Christians who were Paul's companions and friends as Paulinists in the strict sense of [80] the word. If they were — "wie ist dann die Heidenkirche in Asien, Griechenland und Rom so ganz unpaulinisch geworden" (101)? In fine,

[81]   Man wird sich doch entschliessen müssen, sich nicht nur den Paulinismus elastischer zu denken, sondern vor allem sich eine andere Vorstellung davon zu machen, was Paulus in seiner nächsten Nähe ertragen hat. Wer Christus als den Kyrios bekannte, die Güter und die Laster der Welt floh, in dem A.T. die Gottesoffenbarung sah, die Auferstehung erwartete und den Griechen dies verkündete, ohne ihnen die Beschneidung und das Ceremonialgesetz aufzuerlegen, der war Pauliner (101).

The author was certainly a disciple of Paul in this sense, even though he may have fallen short of the standard which some German professors of theology expect from their students.

Harnack's first major contribution to *Actaforschung* contains much useful material, much of which must be passed over without mention because of the limitation of space. His development of the view which had been, and is, maintained by British scholars — that the sources of Acts were primarily personal — deserves mention. He considers it to be quite probable that Mark and Philip (and his daughters who were prophetesses) were two major sources for the Gospel and Acts (109—15). Evidence for the latter includes (1) the prominent place given to women in the Gospel, (2) considerable matter in Luke-Acts which is of special interest to women, (3) interest in prophecy and the Holy Spirit, and (4) interest in Samaritans. The information may have been received from Philip and his daughters during his stay in their home in Caesarea (21.8—9), or at a later date through conversation with Philip's prophesying daughters, who were famous personalities in the Church in Asia Minor. Mark's contribution in Acts would have been the traditions concerning Peter and the Jerusalem church. It is significant that the author is particularly well informed concerning the house of John

Mark's mother in Jerusalem, even to the point of knowing the name of one of her maid-servants (12.13).

In his second monograph on the Lucan writings, published two years later[57], Harnack gathers together all sort of data from Acts — chronological, geographical, ethnic, treatment of persons, handling of miracles, "Inkorrektheiten und Unstimmigkeiten"[58], and the like — which might be thought to throw light on the questions of authorship, sources, or point of view of the book. His study of the subject is probably the most exhaustive examination of these varying features which has ever been made, and it remains as a thesaurus of information for the student of the Book of Acts. In addition to his exercise in source criticism and his collation of a mass of linguistic material, the major significance of Harnack's second work is that it expresses an even stronger conviction concerning the Lucan authorship and the essential historical reliability of Acts. Two further years of close study of Acts had served to strengthen his conviction that it is not only in its major features a genuinely historical work, "sondern auch die Mehrzahl der Details, die es bringt, ist zuverlässig" (222). With the exception of a few idealizations of the *Urgemeinde,* the author follows no bias which leads him to distort the actual course of events. "Es ist fast von jedem möglichen Standpunkt geschichtlicher Kritik aus ein solides und respektables, in mancher Hinsicht aber ein ausserordentliches Werk" (222). Rather than demonstrating the unhistorical nature of the narrative of Acts, as some critics claim, the epistles of Paul provide a test of the accuracy for the larger part of the work which is as stringent as can be imagined[59].

[82]

[83]

[84]

Dass diese Schriftstücke Erzeugnisse des Augenblicks sind und von einem Manne ausgeprägtester Subjektivität stammen, erhöht noch die Schärfe der Prüfung. Dennoch können nur Skrupelsucht und Splitterrichterei verkennen, dass die Apg. an vielen Dutzend von wichtigen und unwichtigeren Stellen die Prüfung bestanden hat, welche die Paulusbriefe für sie bedeuten. Was nachbleibt, ist, von ein paar Kleinigkeiten abgesehen, die Schilderung des Apostelkonzils und die Schilderung der Selbstverteidigung des Paulus in den letzten Reden und überhaupt sein Verhalten den Juden gegenüber beim letzten Aufenthalt in Jerusalem (18).

[85]

---

[57] *Die Apostelgeschichte,* Beiträge zur Einleitung in das Neue Testament 3 (Leipzig, 1908).

[58] Under this heading (159—77) Harnack includes what are really stylistic peculiarities, alleged grammatical errors, ambiguities in the narrative, examples of looseness of expression, etc.

[59] *Supra,* n. 56. Cf. especially Harnack's conclusion concerning the evidence (204—5).

Even in reference to this latter point what Luke records may be harmonized with the character and theology of the Paul of the epistles, "wenn man diese nur nicht einseitig und starr nach dem Galaterbrief zeichnet, was freilich noch immer geschieht" (18). And in reference to the Jerusalem council of Acts 15 it has yet to be demonstrated "ob ... so schwere Irrtümer stehen, dass die Abfassung durch Lukas unmöglich ist" (18). Luke has his weaknesses as a historian, admits Harnack: his credulity in regard to the miraculous, carelessness due to attempt at brevity, and tendency to stylize important events. But in comparison to both the extravagancies of religious charlatans and the standards of historians of that age the author of Acts comes out near the top.

In commenting on Acts 21, Harnack has this to say concerning Paul and the Law:

Nach meinem Verständnis der Stellung des Paulus zu seinem Volk und dessen Gesetz, wie ich es seinen Briefen entnehme, war er nicht nur jeden Augenblick mit gutem Gewissen fähig, da er ein geborner Jude war, jüdische Kult- und verwandte Akte auf sich zu nehmen, sondern er wird sie selbst dort freiwillig und aus alter Pietät auf sich genommen haben, wo ein Missionsinteresse den Juden gegenüber gar nicht im Spiele war. Paulus "wurde" nicht nur den Juden ein Jude d. h. er brachte ihrer religiösen Art, auch wo er über sie hinausgewachsen war, Opfer, sondern *er war und blieb auch ein Jude*. Nichts spricht in seinen Briefen dagegen, dass er, wenn er die heilige Stadt betrat, nicht auch den Tempelkultus mitgemacht hat wie seine christlichen Brüder in Jerusalem. Galater- und Römerbrief können ... die Ansicht nahelegen, dass ihm das nicht mehr möglich war; sie brauchen aber nicht so verstanden zu werden ... (180—81)[60].

A further point overlooked by those who take a different view of the "historical Paul" is that the freedom of *all* Christians was never a source of debate between Paul and his opponents, whether one looks at Acts or the epistles, but rather the freedom of *Gentile* Christians from the Law (181).

Concerning the aim of the author, Harnack argues that Luke has grouped his material around a central idea. The book is not primarily a defense of Paul, except perhaps in a secondary sense[61]; nor is it intended as a political-apologetic of Christianity against its accusers[62]. Its aim, closely related to and regarded as a continuation

[86]

[87]

[88]

---

[60] Italics mine.

[61] Cf. *Die Apostelgeschichte*, pp. 7, 13—15.

[62] The dedication, in Harnack's view, indicates that it was addressed to a man who was an instructed Christian, rather than a pagan. Furthermore, Luke has not suppressed *all* instances of unfriendliness and hostility on the part of Romans and civic officials, nor has he kept silence concerning the friendly reception on the part of many Jews (12—13).

of his πρῶτος λόγος, is rather "die Kraft des Geistes Jesu in den [89] Aposteln geschichtlich darzustellen" (6). Here the term "apostle", not yet used by Luke in the strictly narrow sense, would include Philip, Barnabas, and Apollos, as well as Peter and Paul — the latter being selected by the author as the two great heroes of primitive Christian history[63]. Stated at length, the purpose of the author is to show how the power of the Spirit of Jesus in the apostles founded the *Urgemeinde*, called into being the Gentile mission, furthered the Gospel from Jerusalem to Rome, and set the Gentile world in the place of the Jewish people, who hardened their heart more and more against the Gospel (12)[64].

In *Lukas der Arzt*, Harnack indicated preference for a date of about A. D. 80 —

vor der domitianischen Verfolgung, vor der weiteren Verbreitung der [90] Paulusbriefe, vor der Einbürgerung des Namens "Christen" im christlichen Sprachgebrauch..., vor der Kanonisierung des Begriffs ἐκκλησία..., vor dem Gebrauch des Worts μάρτυς als Blutzeuge, aber einige Zeit nach der Zerstörung Jerusalems (18)[65].

Two years later, in an excursus to his *Die Apostelgeschichte*, he listed six strong arguments in favor of the early date, but concluded: "Also muss zur Zeit das Urteil gelten: Lukas schrieb zur Zeit des [91] Titus oder in der früheren Zeit Domitians, vielleicht aber schon am Anfang der sechziger Jahre" (221). However, in the final of his three monumental monographs on the Book of Acts[66], Harnack came down decisively in favor of about A. D. 62 as the *Abfassungszeit* of the book, thus adding the weight of his scholarship as a further testimony to the strength of the evidence favoring this conclusion[67].

---

[63] "Diese Zusammenstellung (of Peter and Paul) ... ist gewiss nicht von [92] Lukas geschaffen worden; die Geschichte selbst hat sie geschaffen" (5).

[64] Cf. B. Reicke, "The Risen Lord and His Church: The Theology of Acts", *Interp.* 13 (1959), pp. 157—69, for a careful working out of an almost identical understanding of the theological motif of Acts.

[65] He was tempted by the theory that Acts was written soon after the arrival of Paul in Rome, but thought that Luke 21 and Acts 20.25 precluded a pre-A. D. 70 date (47n.).

[66] *Neue Untersuchungen zur Apostelgeschichte und zur Abfassungszeit der Synoptischen Evangelien*, Beiträge zur Einleitung in das Neue Testament 4 (Leipzig, 1911).

[67] An important part of this third work is devoted once again to an examina- [93] tion and rebuttal of the chief argument against the Lucan authorship of Acts, i. e., Paul's attitude toward Judaism and Jewish Christianity (21—62). (He quotes someone as writing: "Eher sei glaublich, dass Calvin auf dem Todbette der Mutter Gottes einen goldenen Rock gelobt, als dass Paulus solche Wege

The first and only complete, systematic examination of the problem of the historical value of the Book of Acts was made by Alfred Wikenhauser (1883—1960), who was to become one of the leading Roman Catholic New Testament scholars in Germany. Lightfoot, Ramsay, and Harnack were content to discuss individual points which touched on the subject and drew general conclusions from their investigations. Their observations were careful and accurate; and their contributions, lasting. But they did not offer a comprehensive discussion of all aspects of the subject. Zahn was more comprehensive in his discussion, but it was done in the context of a commentary and mixed with other ideas which few critics were willing to take very seriously. Wikenhauser stepped in to fill the gap with a careful and definitive study entitled, *Die Apostelgeschichte und ihr Geschichtswert*[68].

Wikenhauser's work has never received the attention it deserves — at least, among protestant scholars. Perhaps the neglect is due to the fact that it was published in a very limited edition and has not been readily available to scholars. It is certainly very difficult to locate outside of Germany! However, a more likely explanation of its neglect is that it was written by a Roman Catholic scholar in a pre-ecumenical age, and in those days Protestants had no dealings with the Catholics[69]. Whatever the reason for the original neglect, there is no excuse for this neglect today (if ever there was one), since it is the only study of its kind — and an excellent one at that.

Wikenhauser's monograph is a model of careful, systematic, critical investigation. It is thorough (every conceivable aspect of the problem is covered, and every relevant fact is brought into the discussion), yet concise (in spite of its length, no words are wasted). Its four hundred and twenty-odd pages are filled with historical data and careful exegesis. Even those who disagree with his major conclusion must go over the same ground and provide alternative explanations of the same phenomena.

---

beschritten habe (24—25)!). My own opinion is that Harnack's position is unassailable. It is difficult to understand how one could fail to be convinced by the force of his argument.

[68] *Neutestamentliche Abhandlungen*, VIII. Band, 3.—5. Heft (Münster i. W., 1921). The work was essentially complete in 1918.

[69] Another valuable work on Acts, though not quite of the same standard of Wikenhauser, which has been either overlooked or dismissed as "dogmatic" or "uncritical" by many Protestant scholars is E. Jacquier, *Les actes des apôtres* (Paris, 1926).

It is worthy of note that both Wikenhauser and Jacquier are as thoroughly conversant with Protestant criticism as with Roman Catholic. The same cannot be said for any Protestant *Neutestamentler* of the time.

Wikenhauser argues that if one takes into consideration the practical and religious purpose of Acts[70], which causes the author to concentrate on the light, yet without ignoring the shadows (26—30), the reliability of the narrative of Acts can be verified in various ways. Two methods present themselves as ways of testing the historical value of the narrative:

1. Man untersucht die Verhältnisse, in denen der Vf lebte, seinen Bildungsgrad, seine direkten oder indirekten Beziehungen zu den Begebenheiten, die den Inhalt seines Werkes ausmachen, um dadurch ein Urteil zu gewinnen, inwieweit er befähigt und willens war, zuverlässige Berichte zu geben (= innere Kriterien). 2. Man erforscht die übrigen Geschichtsquellen für jene Ereignisse, soweit solche vorhanden sind, und prüft mit ihrer Hilfe die einzelnen Angaben der Apg. Punkt für Punkt (= äussere Kriterien) (3—4). [94]

For a large part of the narrative of Acts there are points of contact between it and the "external criteria"; for this the second method is sufficient. However, other parts of the narrative provide data which is unique to Acts, thereby necessitating the dual approach to the problem of historicity.

The first main section of the book ("Die Prüfung des Geschichtswertes der Apostelgeschichte auf Grund der inneren Kriterien") contains, among other things, valuable discussions of ancient historical writing (87—94), the literary genre to which the Book of Acts belongs (94—112), and the formulae used by the author which are typical of ancient historical writers (133—45). The other major section discusses the points of contact between the Book of Acts and the epistles of Paul (169—298), greatly expanding Harnack's list of agreements between the two[71], and those between Acts and the extra-canonical evidence concerning people, events, geographical details, political and religious organizations, and the like (298—421). [95]

Although the Book of Acts has its weaknesses — e. g., the first half of the book is less graphic and exact than the second, it is difficult to reconcile completely Galatians 2 and Acts 15, and in a few places it is difficult to harmonize the data provided by extra-biblical

---

[70] In this way the author of Acts is different from the great Greek historians. The main purpose of Acts, according to Wikenhauser, is to give an account of the spread of Christianity in fulfillment of Jesus' program for his disciples (Luke 24.47—49; Acts 1.8). In this context the author selects material from the tradition to emphasize the power of the Holy Spirit in enabling the spread of the Gospel, which resulted in the rise of the Gentile mission, and the rejection of the message by the Jews (12—24). Wikenhauser sees a secondary apologetic purpose in the desire to influence important Romans concerning the innocence of Paul (30—34). [71] *Supra*, p. 151.

sources with the narrative of Acts[72] — generally speaking, its historicity is confirmed magnificently by both internal and external criteria. In the face of so many "undesigned coincidences" between Acts and the epistles of Paul, on the one hand, and the facts which are known concerning the historical, geographical, and cultural environment of the events narrated, on the other, it is extremely difficult to suppose that the narrative of Acts is to any significant degree unhistorical.

Wikenhauser's study of the historical value of Acts contains little that is entirely new. Its significance is that he gathered together *all* the available data relevant to an evaluation of the historicity of the Book of Acts, whereas Ramsay and others had dealt with only individual points of the narrative. Wikenhauser's careful *Prüfung* demonstrated in detail Ramsay's conviction that "you may press the words of Luke ... and they stand the keenest scrutiny and the hardest treatment", provided that the critic has a thorough grasp of the historical material and is fair in what he expects of Luke[73]. One who advocates a different opinion of Luke's history is obliged to give another, more satisfactory explanation of the facts which are collected in Wikenhauser's monograph and set out for all who have eyes to see. Up to the present no one has been able, or even attempted, to do so[74].

Another very important contribution to the history of Acts-criticism from the historical point of view is contained in the three-volumed study of Christian origins by Eduard Meyer[75] (1855—1930), who was for many years professor of ancient history in Berlin.

Meyer is recognized by all historians as one of the greatest masters of the whole range of ancient history which the world of scholarship has ever produced[76]. His work as a historian was epoch-making, covering a wide range of historical subjects. He wrote two

---

[72] Cf. the list of nine differences listed by Wikenhauser (421); however, only one or two of these present any real difficulties.

[73] *Bearing of Recent Discovery*, p. 89; *supra*, pp. 137—38.

[74] Wikenhauser's mature conclusions concerning the Book of Acts are available in a more readily accessible, if less erudite, form in his commentary on Acts for the *Regensburger Neues Testament 5. Die Apostelgeschichte*, 4th ed. (Regensburg, 1961).

[75] *Ursprung und Anfänge des Christentums*, 3 vols. (Stuttgart and Berlin, 1921—23).

[76] "For the historian, the results of the last generation are summed up in the works of Eduard Meyer. His writings mark a striking advance: Meyer is as much at home in the ancient Near East as he is in the world of Greece and Rome. At his hands, for the first time in the history of history, that Near East has come into its own" (A. T. Olmstead, in *JNES* 2 (1943), p. 26).

major works on religious subjects from a strictly historical point of view. The first was his important study, *Die Entstehung des Judentums* (1896); the second was his *Ursprung und Anfänge des Christentums*, a masterly analysis of the early Christian writings as historical documents, perhaps the most important study of its kind ever written. The work was highly praised by historians as soon as it appeared, as indeed it is still highly praised by historians today[77]. Yet it has been sadly neglected by New Testament critics[78].

The first volume is devoted to a study of the Gospels, with a strong emphasis on Luke, which he regards as "eine wissenschaftliche Bearbeitung der Überlieferung" (I, 1) — the tradition being Mark, "Q", and possibly other sources. He emphasizes that the Third Gospel and the Book of Acts are in reality one Book. The prologue (Luke 1.1—4) is intended to be an introduction to both volumes and indicates by its very form that it was intended to be a *Literaturwerk* from the beginning. Contrary to the view of Zahn, Luke-Acts is not a *Privatschrift* for Theophilus, but rather a work intended to be read by a much larger audience (primarily Christians)[79]. The inclusion of Theophilus' name in the introduction to each volume simply indicates that Theophilus, probably a Christian, is Luke's patron — a custom which was quite common in antiquity[80].

[96]

The third volume of Meyer's great work is devoted largely to a study of the Book of Acts (and other writings bearing on the narrative of Acts). In it Meyer demonstrates a mastery of the historical materials, bringing light to bear on the Book of Acts and its prob-

---

[77] Cf. the words of A. T. Olmstead: "Today we realize that it was the product of his old age, a series of studies to record what he knew before he passed away, rather than a rounded history. Even with failing powers, so vast was his knowledge, so deep his understanding of the background, so keen his insight, that every page is a valued contribution to the study of the New Testament. Rarely indeed does Meyer discuss any problem when we do not feel that if he has not completely solved it, he is at least on the right track to the solution" (*JNES* 2, p. 27).

[78] Meyers's repudiation of his ties with the academic communities of Britain and America and strong identification with the cause of Germany in World War I may have been partly responsible for this neglect in the English-speaking world, in addition to the fact that his valuable study has never been translated into English. However, in Germany it was probably due to the influence of the representatives of "critical orthodoxy", like Jülicher, who protested against the historian's trespassing in their sacred realm of New Testament criticism; cf. Jülicher's reviews in *TLZ* 47 (1922), pp. 514—19; 49 (1924), pp. 337—45.

[79] See Meyer's important discussion of the prologue (I, 5—11).

[80] The twofold address of his patron, Epaphroditus, by Josephus in both parts of his work. *Against Apion* (Ap. i.1; ii.1), provides an almost exact parallel to Luke-Acts.

lems from the broader environment of historical research, Greek literature, the papyri, philology, and related fields of historical research. In reading Meyer's work one is strongly impressed, on the one hand, by the value of this approach to the study of the New Testament writings, and on the other, by the limited perspective of a large quantity of writing in the area of New Testament research. Meyer emphasizes, and that quite rightly, that the New Testament is only a small part, though very important part, of the documents and history of the Eastern Mediterranean world.

Meyer's perspective and conclusions are similar to those of Ramsay[81], although Meyer is more systematic and thorough in the way he goes about his analysis. With Harnack and Ramsay he is skeptical of the skepticism of the "hypercritics" (a term all three are fond of) concerning the historical value of Acts. The Lucan writings, he argues, should be treated as historical documents in the same manner as any other historical documents. But there's the rub! This is exactly what the New Testament critics in the Baur-Overbeck tradition have failed to do; they have treated the Book of Acts with a severity, indeed, with something akin to maliciousness with which no historian treats other historical documents (III, *passim*).

In the tradition of the historians Meyer judges Luke's historical work to be, in general, reliable, though not infallible. The author — who is most certainly the traditional "Luke" (III, 23—27 *et passim*) — is in the best tradition of the Greek historians (III, 7, 15, *et passim*). His careful selection of the material to suit his own point of view, which has given the critics so much trouble and has caused them to disparage him as a historical writer, is, in fact, one of the strongest proofs that he conceived of his own task in terms of that of a historian (III, 15n. *et passim*). In spite of his weaknesses, of all the biblical writers Luke deserves the title of "the historian" *par excellence*. This, argues Meyer, is a judgment with which any historian would agree[82].

The work of the scholars discussed in the present chapter serve to emphasize the importance of the materials of historical research for the study of the New Testament writings. The New Testament documents cannot — or, at least, *should not* — be studied in isola-

---

[81] N. B. He argues for the so-called South Galatian hypothesis for basically the same reasons as Ramsay (III, 196—205).

[82] There are only two notable exceptions: Theodor Mommsen, who was inclined to take a more negative view toward Luke-Acts, and Eduard Norden. There is, however, evidence that Meyer made some impression on the latter (see, for example, Meyer's note in vol. 3, p. 92).

tion from other documents of the same historical period, nor can New Testament critics ignore the significance of the contribution of classical scholarship and archaeology to New Testament research. To ignore the work of the "secular" historians by going about the work of New Testament criticism as if it were a discipline totally isolated from all others is to forfeit the right to the claim to be doing *historical* criticism. One would think that this is self-evident, an axiom which scarcely needs repetition — and to some it is. But in the face of the epochal contributions to *Actaforschung* by Ramsay, Zahn, Harnack, Wikenhauser, and Meyer, there remained scholars who continued to ignore, or to dismiss, work which was of great significance for New Testament research but which lay outside the sacred walls of *Bibelwissenschaft*. The harsh words of A. T. Olmstead, himself one of the leading historians of antiquity of his day, are not altogether unfair:

> The fundamental vice of these New Testament critics was obvious to all but themselves; they stubbornly refused to admit that the New Testament documents formed only a small part of the literature of antiquity, as New Testament times formed a small though important segment of one single period in ancient history. They refused to accept data at the hands of the outstanding authorities in the classical world if they did not possess theological credentials, and when their own pretensions to scholarship were challenged, they set the rules according to which the debate should be conducted. They had no reason for surprise when Ramsay and his fellows abandoned the hopeless task of converting these determined controversialists and henceforth submitted their studies to the more courteous criticism of those who knew the ancient world, and their discoveries to an educated public already distrustful of the "liberal" critic[83].

In spite of the weight of the evidence brought forward by Ramsay and his successors in favor of a more positive view of the historical value of Acts and its authorship by a sometime companion of Paul (i. e. Luke), the representatives of critical orthodoxy continued their research as if nothing new on the subject had been written. Ramsay was virtually ignored in Germany. Zahn was, of course, theologically conservative and therefore regarded as "uncritical"[84]. Har-

---

[83] *JNES* 2, p. 24. The whole of Olmstead's essay, entitled "History, Ancient World, and the Bible: Problems of Attitude and Method" (pp. 1–34), is very important and should be required reading for every aspiring New Testament scholar. If then he chose to disagree with Olmstead and take a different approach to New Testament research, he would at least have a clear understanding of the historian's point of view.

[84] It must be admitted, however, that his extremely idiosyncratic views did not help his cause any.

nack's work on Acts was, for some reason or other, written off as
superficial. Wikenhauser was a Roman Catholic *Neutestamentler*
and, therefore, could easily be dismissed because of his dogmatic
bias. The work of Eduard Meyer was regarded as invalid, because
he came to study the Book of Acts "with the presuppositions of a
historian of antiquity", thus misunderstanding "the nature of its accounts and the way in which they are connected"[85]. In this way the
most important contributions to *Actaforschung* in the early twentieth century were dismissed by orthodox criticism.

However, the work of these scholars was not entirely ignored. In
fact, if one were to "count heads" it would be accurate to say that
the majority of scholars were impressed by the defence put forward
for the historical reliability of the Book of Acts by these men. In
Britain, New Testament scholars, almost without exception — prin-
cipally through the influence of Ramsay, though Harnack's work
was also an influence — came down on the side of "Luke the historian"[86]. The same was true in the case of American scholars, with
only a few more exceptions. Even in Germany the majority of scholars took a more positive view of Acts than did the representatives
of critical orthodoxy, though the views of the "dissenters" have
tended to be overlooked by those concerned with the history of
critical research.

Thus the division of opinion in regard to the historical value of
Acts which was underlined a century earlier by the debate centering
around the views of the Tübingen critics continued into the twentieth century with little likelihood of the issues being resolved. The
two points of view were restated, modified to some degree, with a
vast amount of additional evidence in favor of the historical approach. Unable to convert the representatives of the opposing viewpoints, both seemed to give up in their attempts to convince the
opposition and went on their own separate ways. A reconciliation
of sorts was attempted in the great American work, *The Beginnings
of Christianity*, which will be discussed in the following chapter; but
the attempt was unsuccessful. Without wishing to be unduly pessimistic one must confess that it seems quite unlikely that there will
be a *rapprochement* of the two viewpoints at any time in the near

---

[85] P. Vielhauer, "On the 'Paulinism' of Acts", E. T. in *Studies in Luke-Acts*,
ed. by L. E. Keck and J. L. Martyn (New York and Nashville, 1966), p. 50,
n. 37.
[86] The same would be true in Britain today; cf. the recent commentaries by
F. F. Bruce, C. S. C. Williams, and R. P. C. Hanson. J. C. O'Neill is the only
notable exception.

future. A Hegelian might expect the conflict between the thesis (the "conservative" view) and the antithesis (the "critical" view) to produce a synthesis (?). But orthodox Hegelianism has very few representatives these days.

Chapter VIII

THE AMERICAN CONTRIBUTION

The modern critical study of the Book of Acts got off to a slow start in North America. The nineteenth century saw the appearance of very few commentaries or monographs on this part of the New Testament which were really significant or of lasting value. The commentary by Joseph Addison Alexander[1] (1809—1860) of Princeton was immensely popular and has managed to stay in print right up to the present day; however, in spite of its display of both learning and devotion, it belongs strictly to the pre-critical era.

Perhaps the most outstanding contribution to *Actaforschung* in North America in the nineteenth century was *A History of Christianity in the Apostolic Age* by Arthur Cushman McGiffert[2] (1861 —1923), professor of church history at Union Theological Seminary of New York. McGiffert, who was later to write the influential essay on the history of Acts criticism in Germany to be included in the second volume of *The Beginnings of Christianity*[3], had been a student of Harnack in Berlin and was thoroughly versed in German, British, and American theological literature. He is plainly attracted by the extreme criticism of F. C. Baur and Franz Overbeck, but the steadying influence of his own mentor, Harnack, caused him to have a much more positive view of the Book of Acts. His own view is that Acts presents a generally trustworthy account of the history of apostolic Christianity; what defects there are are due to lack of information, rather than to some underlying purpose of the author (437)[4]. He emphasizes the authentically primitive character of the speeches contained in the early chapters, as representing the actual theology of the Jerusalem church (53—64), and sides with Ramsay in advocating the "South Galatian" hypothesis (177—92). In spite of the general accuracy of the narrative, however, there are enough

---

[1] *The Acts of the Apostles*, 2 vols. (New York, 1857).

[2] (New York and Edinburgh, 1897); repr. many times.

[3] *BC* 2, pp. 363—95.

[4] See pp. 237—38, n. 2, for a list of what he regards as the major inaccuracies.

defects to suggest that the final redactor was not a companion of
Paul, but rather that he made use of a document containing the
"we"-passages. This latter document was undoubtedly written by a
companion of Paul, possibly even Luke[5]. However, the final form
of the book as we have it was probably produced sometime during
the reign of Domitian (437—38).

The only studies which appeared during the first decade of the
twentieth century in America which are worthy of mention are a
semi-popular comparative study of the Pauline section of the Book
of Acts and the epistles of Paul by Benjamin Wisner Bacon[6] (1860
—1932) of Yale and a history of the apostolic age in the light of
modern criticism by James Hardy Ropes[7] (1866—1933), one of the
most outstanding of the native-born American New Testament
scholars of the century. Bacon takes a similar (though slightly more
negative) position to that of McGiffert; his work lacks, however,
both the brilliance and critical acumen characteristic of McGiffert.
On the other hand, Ropes' monograph is much more solid, though
it pales into insignificance in comparison to his important commentary on the Epistle of James for the *International Critical Commentary* and his great work on the text of the Book of Acts[8], which
were to secure a place for him in the Hall of Fame of New Testament scholarship.

The first of a series of important American contributions to *Actaforschung* between 1916 and 1936 was a study of *The Composition
and Date of Acts* by Charles Cutler Torrey[9] (1863—1956), professor of Semitic languages at Yale University. Torrey had earlier argued that the redactor of the Third Gospel was an accomplished
translator of both Hebrew and Aramaic[10]. In this brief monograph
he defends the thesis that the very noticeable Semitic coloring of
the language of the earlier part of the Book of Acts, which all commentators have observed, is due to the fact that Acts 1.1—15.35 is
a translation from an Aramaic original.

---

[5] This may be the reason for the author's being identified as Luke; or
perhaps the Third Gospel and Acts were actually written by a man named
Luke who was mistakenly identified with the "beloved physician" of Colossians 4.14 (433—34).

[6] *The Story of St. Paul* (New York and London, 1905).

[7] *The Apostolic Age in the Light of Modern Criticism* (New York and London, 1906).

[8] See below, pp. 180—81.

[9] *Harvard Theological Studies* 1 (Cambridge, Mass., 1916).

[10] "The Translations made from the Original Aramaic Gospels", in *Studies
in the History of Religion presented to C. H. Toy*, ed. by D. G. Lyon and G. F.
Moore (New York, 1912), pp. 269—317.

He states his position in this way:

For the first fifteen chapters, the language is distinctly translation-Greek; in the remaining chapters, on the contrary, the idiom is not Semitic, and there is no evidence that we are dealing with a version. The whole book, however, shows unmistakable uniformity of vocabulary and phraseology, so that it is obvious (to him who recognizes the Semitic source) that the author of 16—28 was the translator of 1—15 (5).

The Semitisms represent, argues Torrey, Aramaic (rather than Hebrew) idioms; and "it is not enough to speak of frequent Semitisms; the truth is that the language of all these chapters is translation-Greek through and through, generally preserving the order of the words" (7).

What about the frequent suggestion that these Semitisms are due to the influence of the Septuagint on Luke's style? The style of the Septuagint, answers Torrey, is "simply the style of literal translations from Semitic originals, the clumsy result of putting Hebrew writings into a too closely fitting Greek dress" (8). Moreover, Luke's style in Acts 16—28 is *not* like that of the Greek Old Testament! On the other hand, the similarities between the Septuagint and Acts 1—15 can be best explained by the fact that both are translations of Hebrew or Aramaic originals.

Having stated his conclusion, Torrey then attempts to prove it by a detailed examination of alleged mistranslations and other awkward Greek phrases (10—41), as well as what he discerns to be a difference of point of view of the authors of the two parts of Acts. The final author, it seems, has translated his Aramaic document with such literalness that he renders in incomprehensible Greek that which is perfectly simple when put back into the "original" Aramaic.

The first historian of the Church was not the final author of Luke-Acts as we know it, but rather an unknown Judean who attempted to set forth the main facts concerning the growth of the Christian community from the original group of Jerusalem disciples to the large and rapidly growing, predominantly Gentile, body, as it began to spread into all the world.

He was a man of catholic spirit and excellent literary ability. He wrote in Aramaic, and with great loyalty to the Holy City and the Twelve Apostles, and yet at the same time with genuine enthusiasm for the mission to the Gentiles and its foremost representatives, especially Paul (64).

The work of this early historian (who wrote about A. D. 49 or 50) came into the hands of "Luke"[11], possibly when Paul was in prison

---

[11] "There seems to be no good reason why the church tradition, that the

at Caesarea or after he arrived in Rome in the year 62 (67). Luke combined this document with his own account of the subsequent missionary work of Paul and published it as an afterthought to the Third Gospel (68). Torrey dates the Gospel about A. D. 60—61 and Acts "*after* Paul had been transferred from his 'hired dwelling' to a veritable prison, and *before* Luke had received news of his death" (66). He finds no objection to this date in the argument that Luke 21.20—24 demands a date subsequent to the destruction of Jerusalem since "*every particle* of Luke's prediction not provided by Mark was furnished by familiar and oft quoted Old Testament passages" (70)[12].

Torrey's hypothesis of an Aramaic source for the first fifteen chapters of Acts caused a stir in the world of biblical scholarship in America and gave rise to much discussion[13]. Yet he won no more disciples for this theory than for his theory that all four Gospels represent translations of Semitic originals; nevertheless, he did succeed in bringing the fact of the Semitism of the early chapters of Acts to the attention of the scholarly public, and he showed up the inadequacies of the view that these Semitisms are due simply to Luke's deliberate attempt to imitate the translation-idiom of the Septuagint in those parts of the book which are especially "Jewish"[14]. This being said, however, all would be agreed that although Torrey's monograph was certainly the most important of the early studies of the Semitism of the Book of Acts, he cannot be said to have solved the problem[15].

---

writer was Luke, should not be retained, as certainly possible and perhaps well founded" (66 n.).

[12] Emphasis Torrey's; see his evidence, pp. 69—70.

[13] See bibliographical references in Dupont, *Sources*, p. 30 n.

[14] In 22.1—21, where Paul addresses Jews in Jerusalem "in the Hebrew language", at a time when he was especially keen to show himself a Hebrew of the Hebrews, there are no Semitisms, no Biblical language, no allusions to the Old Testament (55).

[15] The recent study by Max Wilcox, *The Semitisms of Acts* (Oxford, 1965), has demonstrated that both Torrey's hypothesis of a single Aramaic original lying behind Acts 1—15 and the explanation of the Semitisms as "septuagintalisms" (Cadbury, Sparks, Haenchen, Conzelmann, etc.) are over-simplifications. His conclusion is that "the Semitisms of Acts cannot be ascribed to the operation of one factor alone" (180). Wilcox agrees with Torrey that the so-called "hard-core" Semitisms are all but confined to the first fifteen chapters, but they are not numerous enough to indicate a translation from one Aramaic original. There are septuagintalisms, but there are other Semitisms which cannot be explained in this way. Wilcox inclines toward the view that Luke used sources for some of the material of the early chapters of Acts, for the speeches at least — especially those of Stephen and Paul's at Pisidian Antioch; but these traditions may have been already translated into Greek. Luke has re-

The most important name in the history of Lucan research in America belongs without doubt to Henry Joel Cadbury (1883–1974). His contributions to the study of Luke-Acts (to use a term which he seems to have invented) have been both numerous and continuous over a period of more than forty-five years. The first of his many important studies to appear in print was the revised edition of his doctoral dissertation which was published in two parts in 1919 and 1920[16].

Cadbury's monograph is, as the title indicates, a study of the language of the Third Gospel and Acts. Part I is the only part that is of special relevance to the study of the Book of Acts, though Part II is certainly by implication important as giving an indication of how Luke would have treated any sources he might have used in writing Acts. Cadbury turns first to a study of Luke's vocabulary, listing tables of statistical comparisons between Luke and the other New Testament writings, between Luke and various parts of the Greek Old Testament, and between Luke and secular Greek authors (1–39). He is very cautious in his use of statistics, calling attention to the pitfalls and *non sequitur* arguments of many who have used a statistical approach in literary criticism. His conclusion is that "the vocabulary of Luke, while it has its natural affiliations with the Greek of the Bible, is not so far removed from the literary style of the Atticists as to be beyond comparison with them" (38). This, of course, has always been the impression which classical scholars have had of Luke's writings; but Cadbury lays out the evidence for this conclusion[17].

worded the traditions, but he did not create them "out of nothing". Cf. his survey of research on the problem (1–19), especially his evaluation of the work of C. C. Torrey (6–10). See also D. F. Payne, "Semitisms in the Book of Acts", in *Apostolic History and the Gospel*, pp. 134–50.

[16] *Harvard Theological Studies 6, The Style and Literary Method of Luke I. The Diction of Luke and Acts* and *II. The Treatment of Sources in the Gospel* (Cambridge, Mass., 1919–20).

[17] His further comments illustrate the careful avoidance of extremes which marks all of Cadbury's writings: "The question may be pertinently asked whether the gulf between New Testament Greek in general and Attic or Atticistic Greek is not being exaggerated in our day owing to our fresh knowledge of the vernacular Greek through the papyri. If so, the exaggeration is probably due to two factors, namely, the overrating of the purely imitative and classical element in the so-called Atticists, and the underrating of the literary element in the vocabulary of the New Testament writers. I am inclined to revolt slightly also from the extreme view of Deissmann and Moulton, who minimize the Semitic or Biblical or Jewish element in the New Testament and ascribe such phenomena to the vernacular Greek of the time" (38–39). This sounds strikingly up-to-date, especially the last sentence, even though it was written some fifty years ago. Cf. N. Turner, "The Language of the New

The rest of Part I of Cadbury's monograph is devoted to a careful examination of "the alleged medical language of Luke" (39—72). Here he calls into question not only the "evidence" of Hobart[18], but also the most striking examples of Zahn and Harnack. Cadbury shows that most of the examples claimed to demonstrate the medical profession of the author are found not only in the writings of Greek physicians, but also in the Septuagint, Josephus, Plutarch, and Lucian. In an excursus he examines the "medical terms" in Lucian (65—72), showing that one could use the same method to "prove" that Lucian was a physician! His conclusion is that the alleged medical terms used to demonstrate that the author of Luke-Acts was a medical doctor are not really examples of a specialized medical vocabulary at all. "The style of Luke bears no more evidence of medical training and interest than does the language of other writers who were not physicians" (50)[19]. This does not mean of course, that a physician *could not* have written Luke-Acts. Luke "the beloved physician" and companion of Paul may have written the two books assigned to him; "but the so-called medical language of these books cannot be used as a proof that Luke was the author, nor even as an argument confirming the tradition of his authorship" (51)[20].

The five encyclopaedic volumes on the Book of Acts, entitled *The Beginnings of Christianity. Part I. The Acts of the Apostles*[21] were not, strictly speaking, an American enterprise. The two editors, Frederick John Foakes-Jackson (1855—1941) and Kirsopp

Testament", in *Peake's Commentary on the Bible*, rev. ed. (London, 1962), pp. 659—62; and M. Black, "Second Thoughts: IX. The Semitic Element in the New Testament", *ExpT* 77 (1965), pp. 20—23.

[18] See above, pp. 124—25.

[19] "The argument from language for Luke's medical language ... rests on the same fallacy as has led modern scholars to argue the Baconian authorship of Shakespeare's plays from alleged legal terminology in them. In neither case are the words cited technical, as their widespread use in contemporary literature plainly shows" (Cadbury, *The Making of Luke-Acts*, p. 118).

[20] Many scholars, however, continue to assume that a residue of medical terms remains, even after Cadbury's sifting, which confirms the traditional view; see especially the penetrating criticism of James Moffatt in *Expos.*, 8th series, 24 (1922), pp. 1—18, which at least raises a question-mark over against some of Cadbury's conclusions. See also A. T. Robertson, *Luke the Historian in the Light of Research* (New York and Edinburgh, 1920), pp. 9—12, 90—102.

[21] Edited by F. J. Foakes-Jackson and K. Lake (London, 1920—33); vols. 4 and 5 have recently been reprinted (Grand Rapids, 1966). Part I, vols. 1—5, is the only part which appeared of what was originally intended to be a study of the whole of the early Christian literature; for this reason Part I is usually referred to simply as *The Beginnings of Christianity*, vols. 1—5.

Lake (1872–1946), were both British born and educated. However, both were professors in America when these volumes were published (Foakes-Jackson at Union Theological Seminary of New York and Lake at Harvard University) and many, though by no means all, of their fellow contributors were Americans. The American contributions to the volume, above all those of H. J. Cadbury, represent the very best of all the contributions by Americans to the history of the study of the Book of Acts. Therefore, it would seem justified to discuss the whole work in the present chapter.

Volume one, *Prolegomena I. The Jewish, Gentile and Christian Backgrounds,* is probably the least valuable and most dated of the five volumes. It contains a number of important essays, particularly those by C. G. Montefiore ("The Spirit of Judaism", 35–81), H. T. F. Duckworth ("The Roman Provincial System", 171–217), and C. H. Moore ("Life in the Roman Empire at the Beginning of the Christian Era", 218–62). The essays on "Primitive Christianity" (265–418) — one would think that Lake had the greater responsibility in these[22] — are, however, mainly of historical interest in that they reflect an influential, but now generally dead, theological point of view, which included a multitude of unproven historical assumptions[23]. But taken in the light of the author's concern "to state problems (rather) than to advocate theories" (418) one may accept the unqualified statement of the opinions expressed as a basis for the discussion of the questions raised.

The second volume[24], which appeared in 1922, is a much more significant volume. It contains a collection of extremely valuable essays under three headings: (1) the Composition and Purpose of Acts, (2) the Identity of the Editor of Luke and Acts, and (3) the History of Criticism.

In the first part H. J. Cadbury and the editors write on the Greek and Jewish traditions of writing history (7–29)[25]. Here it is argued that although the purpose of Greek historians varied — sometimes the aim was apologetic, sometimes simply practical or moral, sometimes to glorify the deeds of man and nations, etc. — a predominant aim was generally to entertain or to interest the reader (10). This meant that the main emphasis was not necessarily on accuracy of

---

[22] See below, p. 179, n. 44. My guess would be that Foakes-Jackson was chiefly responsible for chapters 1, 3 and 4 on "The Jewish World".

[23] See K. Lake's essay, "The Problem of Christian Origins", *HTR* 15 (1922), pp. 97–114.

[24] *Prolegomena II. Criticism.*

[25] Cadbury, it would seem, is responsible only for the part which concerns Greek historical writing.

historical fact (although claim to this was sometimes made), but rather on form (11). History was regarded "as an art rather than as a science" (11). Thus the materials which the Greek historian had at his disposal (the ὑπομνήματα) would have been regarded as unfit for publication until they had been filled out in a rhetorical manner (12—13). Even where the historian was using real documents and memoranda, or even the finished work of a predecessor, he would recast the whole by means of paraphrase. The speeches which would be added belonged to the final literary stage, being inserted into the narrative at appropriate points, and would be the imaginative compositions of the historian (13—14)[26]. The suggestion is made that the author of Acts would have followed the general method of these Hellenistic historians, as one can observe from his paraphrasing, correcting, and recasting of the unpolished ὑπομνήματα which he had derived from Mark and incorporates into the first part of his work (i. e., the Gospel).

In Acts the elaborate, homogeneous and schematic speeches suggest, if not rhetoric, at least the free composition of the speeches in Greek and Roman histories[27], while the "we-passages" raise the insoluble problem of the use, imitation, or incorporation of autoptic records or the participation of the author in the events which he records (15).

The editors are a little less certain of the implications of a study of the Jewish tradition of historical writing for the methodology of the author of Acts. He seems to have closest affinities to Josephus, in whom the two streams of tradition merge; but it is uncertain exactly how much he was influenced by the one tradition or the other (29).

Building on the earlier work of Cadbury[28], J. de Zwaan contributes a masterly survey of the use of the Greek language in Acts (30—65). He is in essential agreement with Cadbury concerning Luke's alleged "medical" language as well as in regard to other details. At the same time, however, he is appreciative of Torrey's work on the Aramaic background of Acts[29], though he recognizes that Torrey pushed the evidence too hard. First, de Zwaan points out that Torrey's statement that there are few or no Semitisms in Acts 16—28 is not entirely accurate. There are, in fact, quite a few, especially in chapters 18—22 (45—46), although it is true that the

---

[26] This point, however, is debated by scholars. See below, pp. 225—28.

[27] Cadbury offers a fuller discussion of the problem of the speeches in *BC* 5, pp. 402—27, and *The Making of Luke-Acts*, pp. 184—90.

[28] *Supra*, pp. 168—69.   [29] *Supra*, pp. 165—67.

Semitic element is not nearly so evident as in the earlier chapters. Moreover, Torrey's method of re-translating awkward Greek into Aramaic overlooks the fact that "strange-sounding" Greek may be due to the influence of translation-Greek on the original composition (46—47). That is, it may be translation-Greek (as Torrey argued) or "sacred prose" (i. e., a Semitic style of Greek patterned after the Old Testament and other Jewish writings). However, to distinguish between the two types of Greek is not alway easy.

In distinguishing between translation-Greek and Semitizing prose, de Zwaan lays down the following rules: (1) Current septuagintalisms are to be eliminated. (2) Cases which can be closely paralleled from the papyri should be ruled out. (3) Semitisms which are possible in either Hebrew *or* Aramaic lying side by side with Semitisms which are explainable only in terms of the other are evidence of "sacred prose", since translation-Greek presupposes an underlying Hebrew *or* Aramaic document. (4) The frequency and clearness of cases of Semitisms should be tabulated, so that the relationship of the weak cases to the strong cases can be seen. (5) Expressions found in Acts 1—15 which also occur in Acts 16—28 should be acceptable as evidence only if they occur in the midst of a group of strong cases. Applying these rules de Zwaan modifies Torrey's hypothesis and suggests that the case for a Semitic document lying behind 1.1—5.16 and 9.31—11.18 is strong; for chapter 7, possible but uncertain (due to the difficulty of estimating the value of the examples which are among the large number of quotations and allusions to the Old Testament); and for chapter 15, also possible but uncertain (48). Beyond this de Zwaan calls attention to the Semitic (or perhaps "Christian") flavor of Luke's Greek, even in parts which are obviously his free compositions.

A third important essay in the second volume of *The Beginnings of Christianity* is on the use of the Septuagint in Acts and is by W. K. L. Clarke (66—105). The author collects a massive amount of data bearing on the subject, but comes to few very definite conclusions. He argues that there is no doubt that the author's vocabulary and style are influenced by his familiarity with the Greek Old Testament; and he finds that the language of Acts seems to have many affinities with that of the apocryphal books, especially 2 and 3 Maccabees, Tobit, Judith, Wisdom, and some of the Pseudepigrapha. But he is extremely cautious in drawing inferences from these facts. Clarke recognizes the force of Cadbury's criticism of Hobart's case for the medical vocabulary of Luke-Acts, but he expresses the conviction that a residue of "medical terms" remains unexplained (84).

Following these general observations, Clarke classifies the direct quotations of the Old Testament in Acts according to their agreement or disagreement with the Septuagint. The majority of the divergencies with the Septuagint he ascribes to free citation, "natural in an age when modern aids to study were not available" (93). A second major cause of difference is, in his view, the result of a conflation of two or more quotations (94). In one instance alone (Acts 3.25 = Gen. 22.18) does he suggest that the difference from the Septuagint might conceivably be due to an acquaintance with a Hebrew or Aramaic translation, but even here he thinks it best to suppose that other Old Testament passages (Gen. 12.3 or Ps. 21.28) have influenced the change in the text (95)[30]. He makes the significant observation, however, that most of the "loose" citations occur (a) in speeches and (b) in the first half of the book (93). Clarke is a little more favorable to the view that three allusions to the Old Testament in the Petrine speeches (2.24; 2.30; and 4.11) may be due to independent translation (97—98); if so, it is possible that the speeches in question are not the free compositions of the writer. However, even these can be explained as conflations or free quotations from memory. Possible influences of the language of the Septuagint on the narrative of Acts are also considered by Clarke, but he concludes that these influences, if they are indeed influences, are slight, except in matters of general style.

In a study of Luke's use of the Gospel according to Mark, F. C. Burkitt challenges the view which assumes, on the basis of the fact that it is impossible to isolate and determine the exact extent of definite sources in Acts, that the author of Acts used no sources in his composition of the early chapters (106—120). It would be impossible to reconstruct the narrative of Mark, or even the speeches of Jesus recorded in Mark, from an independent study of the Third Gospel alone; nevertheless, argues Burkitt, we know that Luke used Mark. Therefore, it is to be regarded as very probable that he worked in a similar manner insofar as the Book of Acts is concerned; that is, he probably re-phrased speeches, re-arranged the narrative, and created new settings for the speeches and events, but it is doubtful that he actually invented any of these[31].

---

[30] Clarke fails to consider the possibility of other Greek translations which follow a different textual tradition from that of the Septuagint; and he dismisses the probability of Aramaic or Hebrew sources. Here the monograph of M. Wilcox, which has been cited above (n. 15), marks a definite advance over Clarke's study.

[31] In his book, *The Earliest Sources for the Life of Jesus* (Boston and New York, 1910), pp. 79—80, Burkitt had suggested that Acts 1—12 was based on

In the final chapter to part one of volume two, the editors sum up what they regard to be the conclusion of the researches of Cadbury, de Zwaan, Clarke, and Burkitt:

> It is clear that the writer was thoroughly impregnated with the Greek Old Testament; there is no good evidence that he was acquainted with the Hebrew original. He is able to use Greek like a Greek, and in this respect he is more Greek than Josephus, but he does not always write thus; sometimes, perhaps, owing to the influence of Aramaic originals which he translated, sometimes owing to his imitation of the Septuagint. But it is also obvious ... that, at least in the Gospel, he was nearer to the old Jewish literary tradition than was Josephus. He does not, indeed, copy his sources with quite the same verbal fidelity as does the Chronicler, but he paraphrases and polishes far less than Greek custom would have demanded. Above all, in the Gospel he does not invent speeches. Luke, on the contrary, respects the sayings of Jesus more than the narrative of events which lay before him. That is Jewish: to give teaching and law rather than the accurate and full narration of events is the ideal (121).

The question which naturally follows is, is this equally true of the Book of Acts? The editors are somewhat uncertain in their answer, since they regard it as probably that Luke would have given a sense of authority to the words of Jesus which he would not have given to the words of the apostles (122).

The editors, after surveying the major contributions to the source criticism of Acts (122–30), conclude that although "there is a *prima facie* probability for the use of written sources in Acts, and especially for Aramaic sources in the early chapters[32], the writer wrote too well to allow us to distinguish with certainty either the boundaries of his sources or the extent of his own editorial work" (133). Moving from this basic assumption they attempt to solve the problem of the sources and traditions lying behind the Book of Acts by a consideration of the implications of the preface to the Gospel[33] and the internal evidence of linguistic peculiarities and "seams" which may indicate oral or written sources. Combining the insights of Harnack and Torrey, and adding a few points of their own, the editors suggest that there is a strong probability for the existence of at least two (Aramaic) sources lying behind the early chapters (139–57); these sources, they suggest, have been inter-

the original continuation (now lost) of the Gospel according to Mark. See Dupont, *Sources*, p. 29, n. 33, for the pedigree of this view.

[32] They are favorable to Torrey's work, arguing that he has not been successfully answered by his critics, even though he tried to press his evidence too far (129).

[33] This is discussed fully by Cadbury in an appendix to vol. 1 (489–510); see below, pp. 186–87.

woven skillfully in the same manner that the author has intertwined the material derived from Mark and his other source in the passion narrative in the Gospel. And as far as the latter chapters of Acts are concerned, the editors argue that the linguistic evidence is indecisive in solving the problem of whether the author of Acts and the author of the "we"- narratives are one and the same person (158—67). The evidence of Hawkins and Harnack only proves that, if he used sources for Acts 16—28, the author rephrased them in his own words (in much the same way he has rewritten Mark). The identity of the author of the "we"-narratives must be decided on other grounds[34].

The chapter is concluded with a valuable discussion of the plan and purpose of Acts (175—200). The plan of the author, in the sense of merely literary composition, is "to describe the spread of the Church from Jerusalem to Rome" (175). The author arranges his material in a natural and orderly manner to this end, and, as C. H. Turner has noted[35], he divides his narrative by short summaries of the progress made (176—77).

The question of purpose, as distinct from plan of composition, is more difficult and can hardly be described in terms of a single, all-pervasive purpose. "Few books are ever written with a single purpose" in view (177)[36]! It is obvious that the author is not concerned with "pure history". Rather, his fundamental aim was to give religious instruction. Another aim was undoubtedly to offer an *apologia* for Christianity to the heathen.

Taking the second suggested purpose first, the editors argue that Theophilus was "a Roman official concerned with the public safety and legal procedure" who "had heard stories damaging to Christions, perhaps especially to Pauline Christians" (179). The purpose of the author was to persuade him concerning the slanderous nature of these stories by putting before him the exact facts. Specifically, he wished to prove that Christianity is a "lawful religion" and that Christians were guilty of nothing which would call for official action

---

[34] This, it seems to me, is the weakest part of their discussion. On the analogy of Luke's handling of Mark, the retention of the ἡμεῖς is left unexplained: it will not do to argue that the author "desired to indicate that here at least he was using the narration of an αὐτόπτης" (137), since he has not used this or a similar device in the Gospel or in the early chapters of Acts, where (on the testimony of the editors) he is definitely using sources. In the final analysis, Harnack was right when he said that if the author is using a source in chapters 16—28 the ἡμεῖς is all that has not been assimilated by the author to his own style.   [35] *Supra*, pp. 127—28.

[36] This statement should be written in bold letters and placed in a prominent position on the desk of any scholar who seeks to write anything on the purpose of Acts.

on his part. This the author does by arguing that "Christianity is the true religion of Israel" (180), and therefore an established (not a new) religion. In the Gospel and in Acts "he is anxious to show the unity between Israel and Jesus, Jesus and the Twelve, the Twelve and Paul in order to establish the legitimacy of Christianity as the religion of the Chosen People" (182). Moreover, he attempts to make it equally clear that there could be no just charge of sedition against the Church (184). As evidence for the apologetic purpose of Luke-Acts the editors cite the same data which had been emphasized from Schneckenburger onward and which is generally recognized by most scholars even today (in spite of the variety of interpretations given to it), adding nothing especially new to the discussion. The analysis of the practical didactic purpose of Acts in terms of the doctrine of the Church, God, Jesus, the Holy Spirit, and the Resurrection (187—96) is even weaker and serves simply to date the editors theologically.

One hundred and fifty-odd pages of volume two are devoted to a discussion of authorship. Cadbury lists the relevant passages from the post-apostolic age which have a bearing on the subject, from the Canon of Muratori (which he dates about 170) onward, in Latin or Greek with English translations (209—45). This is followed by a brief account of the later tradition (146—50). In a discussion of the value of the tradition (250—64), Cadbury suggests his well-known thesis that the so-called "external" tradition for the authorship of most New Testament books is not really "external", but rather consists in more or less fanciful speculations about the occasion, date, purpose, and authorship of a given book (as is obvious in the case of the later writers), or simply educated guesses based on a study of the New Testament writings themselves. Above all, he insists, one must bear in mind that the early Christian writers were influenced in their opinions by a desire to identify the New Testament writings with apostles or disciples of apostles, which would give each writing the necessary credentials for inclusion in the Canon. Cadbury's view is that the Lucan tradition could have been the result of this concern, or, more probably, simply the result of a conjecture by some early Christian(s) on the basis of a comparison of the "we"-passages of Acts with the names of Paul's companions in Philemon 23—24, Colossians 4.10—14, and 2 Timothy 4.9—12. The early Fathers may not have had access to any more information on the subject than we have[37]. The tradition, therefore, is of little value in and of itself.

---

[37] Cadbury has stood steadfastly by this opinion over the years; see for example, his essay on Acts in *IDB* 1, pp. 40—41.

If the internal evidence unmistakably proves or disproves Lucan authorship, its testimony is worth more than tradition; if it is inconclusive, the tradition may be right, but it is not adequate proof, and we must be content, as in the case of many others of the greatest books, to be ignorant of the author (264)[38].

C. W. Emmet puts forward the case for the traditional view on the question of authorship (265—97). Rather than deal with the problem in general, he attempts specifically to answer the objection that the "Paul of Acts" and the "Paul of the epistles" are so different that it is impossible to believe that the author of Acts was actually a former travelling companion of Paul. Although his essay is by no means brilliant — it is certainly not the best case which could be given for the traditional position — he does make some good points.

At the beginning of his essay Emmet points out that those writers who challenge the Lucan authorship often seem to require *absolute agreement* between the Book of Acts and the letters of Paul in order to be convinced that the former could have been from the pen of a companion of Paul. This is very unfair. The real question is whether the differences between the two are so great that Acts must be regarded as such an unreliable witness that it is impossible to conceive of its having been written by one who was close enough to the historical Paul to have gotten the facts more accurately[39]. Emmet then proceeds to treat three basic problems: the relationship between Galatians 1—2 and the narrative of Acts (266—86), the indirect coincidences and discrepancies between Acts and the epistles of Paul (286—91), and the general presentation of Paul by the author of Acts (291—97).

Emmet's summary of the problem of harmonizing the words of Paul in Galatians 1 and 2 with the narrative of Acts is probably the best and most detailed discussion in English of the issues involved. The psychological impression given is that he is struggling hard to defend a difficult position; but this is due to the fact that he is willing to take *all* the arguments of the opposition with equal seriousness and seeks to give an adequate answer to each objection. The fact of the matter is that the *onus probandi* lies on the shoulders of the critic who argues that the narrative of Acts is unhistorical; the mere difficulty of our understanding the exact relationship between

---

[38] Cf. *infra*, p. 188, n. 80.

[39] It does not follow, of course, that a companion of Paul, or even Paul himself, would have been necessarily the best qualified to write an objective and accurate narrative of events.

the events narrated by the author of Acts and those mentioned by Paul in Galations 1 and 2 does not prove the point[40]. If, as Emmet argues, the visits of Paul to Jerusalem recorded in Acts 11 and Galatians 2 are to be identified; if the Epistle to the Galatians was written to the churches of South Galatia; and if the same epistle was written *before* the council of Acts 15, the "contradictions" between Acts and Galatians all but disappear. And Emmet gives a good case for the acceptance of these three basic conclusions.

In the manner of Harnack, though independently of him, Emmet lists dozens of "undesigned coincidences" between the narrative of Acts and the epistles of Paul which make it impossible (for him) to believe that Acts is to any significant degree unhistorical. There are one or two seeming discrepancies — such as the movements of Timothy and Silas according to Acts (17.14 and 18.5) and 1 Thessalonians (3.1—6)[41] — but these are insignificant in contrast to the multitude of agreements.

In the final section of his essay Emmet argues that the view that Paul's conduct in Acts — that is, his "Jewish" behavior — is inconsistent with the epistles is based on a false inference and a misunderstanding of his teaching. Paul never forgot that he was a Jew.

The wider the breach between his nation and Christianity, the more burning was his patriotic love, and the stronger the stress laid on the real privileges of the Jew (Rom. ix, x) . . . He never drew the conclusion that the Jewish Christian should cease to be a Jew or hold himself exempt from the Law. This conclusion was drawn by a later generation. . . (291—92).

Modern critics may think that Paul would have been acting inconsistently, but it is doubtful whether Paul would have understood or appreciated their objections.

The impression given by Emmet's essay is that the only major problem of harmonizing the narrative of Acts with the epistles is in connection with Acts 15 and Galatians 2, and only then on the as-

---

[40] The difficulty is caused, it seems to me, by two facts: (1) the extreme brevity of the two accounts and (2) their independence of each other. Whereas such difficulties may be rare to the New Testament scholar (only here and in the Synoptic Gospels), they are a very familiar phenomenon to the classical scholar and historian, who is less likely to be disturbed by such apparent contradictions. Cf. the comments of A. N. Sherwin-White (*Roman Society and Roman Law in the New Testament*, pp. 186—89), which, although made in connection with the Gospels, are apropos in this connection.

[41] The accounts are not necessarily contradictory, if one takes into consideration the fact that the account in Acts does not necessarily include the whole sequence of events. See the reconstruction of the movement of Paul and his companions in Bruce, *Acts*, p. 330 (based on K. Lake, *The Earlier Epistles of Paul* (London, 1911), p. 74).

sumption that both refer to the same event. This impression is confirmed by Hans Windisch's case against the traditional view (298 —348)[42]. Windisch categorically asserts the identification of the visits of Paul to Jerusalem in Acts (322); he gives no strong reasons for doing so. Thus assuming the identification he presses a number of real and imagined difficulties in harmonizing the two accounts. Conclusion: Acts 15 is clearly unhistorical; *ergo*, Luke clearly could not be the author of Acts, since he would have known better (327). The other arguments of Windisch are decidedly incidental to this and, one may add, so arbitrary as to call into question the whole of his methodology[43]. If there is really so little to be said for the authorship of Acts by a companion of Paul as Windisch believes, it becomes difficult to understand how even the early Fathers were deceived, much less such a large number of modern critics!

In an appendix to the discussion of authorship, the question of "medical" language, the relationship of Acts to Josephus, and the date of the Lucan writings are discussed. Cadbury reiterates his reasons for rejecting the arguments of Hobart and Harnack concerning Luke's medical vocabulary (349—55), while the editors point out that the evidence for Luke's use of Josephus is inconclusive (355—58). Concerning the date, "there is no decisive proof that Luke was not written before the fall of Jerusalem" or "that it was used by any writer before Marcion" (358). The editors are clearly torn between the points of view expressed by Emmet and Windisch, although they (Lake?) obviously lean in the direction of the latter; but at the same time it is admitted that the questions of authorship and date are not closed issues[44].

The remaining section of volume two of *The Beginnings of Chris-*

---

[42] "For the critical investigator the decisive point must always be the 'Lucan' presentation of the Council of Jerusalem" (321).

[43] His frequent positive references to the Tübingen critics (298—300, 306, 307, 317—19, 321, and 348), with whom he differs chiefly in his understanding of the author's *Tendenz*, does not boost our faith in his methodology. See especially his concluding paragraph (348).

[44] Earlier "the editors" had been of the opinion that Acts was actually written by Luke, the companion of Paul. Impressed by the weight of the argument derived from the comparisons between Acts and the epistles they came to incline toward the view that Luke was responsible only for the "we"-sections, and probably the narrative surrounding them, but that the whole of the Book of Acts and the Third Gospel was the composition of a later writer who wrote ca. A. D. 95 (358—59).

My opinion is that "the editors" in this instance means Kirsopp Lake. If Foakes-Jackson was of this opinion in 1922 he clearly changed his mind later. In his commentary on Acts in the Moffatt series (*The Acts of the Apostles* (London, 1931)) he favors the Lucan authorship (x—xi) and disfavors the

tianity deals with the history of the criticism of Acts. In the influential essay to which reference has been made a number of times in the course of our study, A. C. McGiffert surveys the work of critics in Germany from J. D. Michaelis to Harnack (363—95), whereas J. W. Hunkin casts his net rather wider by beginning his survey of British work on Acts with Pelagius and ending with Dean Inge (369—433). A comparison of the two essays emphasizes the differences between the two critical traditions[45]. Among the various appendices to the volume the commentary on the preface of Luke by Cadbury is the one item of lasting value (489—510)[46].

The third volume of *The Beginnings of Christianity*, regarded by many scholars to be the most valuable of the five volumes[47], is a study of *The Text of Acts* by James Hardy Ropes (1866—1933)[48]. This is strictly a specialist's volume, the most thorough study of the textual criticism of the Book of Acts which has ever been made. It begins with a two-hundred page essay discussing the various Greek manuscripts, ancient versions, and quotations in the Greek fathers which provide the textual critic with his material; this is followed by another hundred pages on the criticism and history of the text. Then follows the text of Acts, Codex Vaticanus and Codex Bezae being printed on opposite pages with a very full textual apparatus and notes. Five longer notes on Acts 1.2, 13.27—29, 13.33, 15.29, and 15.34 are placed at the end of this section (256—70). There are then five appendices by the author: on the papyrus Wessely 237 (= P[41]), the Vulgate, the Peshitto Syriac, the Sahidic, and the Bohairic versions, as well as a translation of fragments of the commentary of Ephraem by F. C. Conybeare[49].

Josephus' theory very strongly (xiii—xv). It would be an interesting study in *Redaktionsgeschichte* to seek to isolate "F-J" (Foakes-Jackson) and "C" (Cadbury) from "L" (Lake) in those parts of *BC* which are of composite authorship. It should not be too difficult a task, since both Foakes-Jackson and Cadbury have other books on the same subject. At various places in the present chapter I have indicated the results of my own preliminary study of the subject.

[45] It should be pointed out, however, that McGiffert treats only one stream of German criticism, as have most other writers on the subject. Side by side with the writers he lists as important were others, as we have had more than one occasion to observe, whose work was of equal significance with that of the more radical critics, who are referred to as if they were the sole legitimate representatives of German criticism. The manner of McGiffert's treatment has greatly influenced the subsequent surveys by Haenchen, Bieder, *et al.*

[46] See below, pp. 186—87.   [47] Cf. F. F. Bruce in *Interp.* 13 (1959), p. 132.

[48] It was published in 1926. Ropes had earlier given an account of his general conclusions concerning the Book of Acts and the apostolic age in his book, *The Apostolic Age in the Light of Modern Criticism (supra, p. 165).*

[49] With notes by F. C. Burkitt.

Ropes' tome on the text of Acts is clearly not a book for Everyman, or even for Every Theologian. It is a reference tool for experts, chiefly textual critics. Its significance lies in the fact that it is *the* major work to date on the textual criticism of the Book of Acts. It is the best case which has been given against the theory of the priority or superiority of the "Western" text of Acts and in favor of the general superiority of the Old Unical group of manuscripts (represented in greatest purity by Codices B, ℵ , A, C. and 81)[50]. The views of Ropes in this regard have been challenged by one or two scholars since 1926 — chiefly by A. C. Clark[51] — but most textual critics would agree with his major conclusions.

The long awaited commentary on the Book of Acts appeared in 1933 as volume four in the series. It was the work of Kirsopp Lake and H. J. Cadbury. In the preface Lake gives the impression that the work of the commentary was more or less equally divided between them, Cadbury's emphasis being on the linguistic and literary and his on the doctrinal and historical (vii). In fact, Lake had a much greater hand in the writing of both commentary and translation than did Cadbury[52]

The work was, and probably still is[53], the most important commentary to be written in English. A major feature which sets it apart from most other commentaries is that space is given to the discussion of *difficult* expressions and topics[54] — i. e., words and phrases

---

[50] Ropes' major conclusions are summarized on pages ccxc–cccii.

[51] *The Acts of the Apostles* (Oxford, 1933).

[52] From a study of the commentary in the light of Cadbury's other writings on the Book of Acts I came to this conclusion, and it was confirmed to me in a letter from Professor Cadbury (13 October 1967). Cadbury was given the opportunity to add notes on matters which were of special interest to him, as well as to criticize in detail Lake's notes and translation; although he made some changes, much of what Lake had written was left unchanged.

As I studied the writings of the two scholars, it seemed to me that Lake was probably more skeptical about the historicity of Acts than was Cadbury, and that he was chiefly responsible for this element in the commentary. Cadbury admits that this was probably so, although there was no conscious contrast of viewpoint between them.

[53] Its only rival would be F. F. Bruce's commentary on the Greek text.

[54] See, for example, the notes on συναλιζόμενος (Acts 1.4); ἐν τῷ συνπληροῦσθαι τήν ἡμέραν τῆς πεντηκοστῆς (2.1); the quotation of Joel 2.28–32 in Acts 2.17–21; the alleged medical language of 3.7; the meaning of συνέστειλαν in 5.6; the grammatical construction of 10.36–42; Elymas (13.8) and Σαῦλος ὁ καὶ Παῦλος (13.9); James' speech at the Jerusalem council (15.13–21); the setting of Paul's sermon at Athens (pp. 208–13); the meaning of σκηνοποιοί in 18.3; τῇ μιᾷ σαββάτων (20.7); ἀσπασάμενοι (25.13); the meaning of 26.28; and the ending of Acts (pp. 349–50). The longer notes were detached and expanded into a separate volume: *BC* 5.

which really need explaining, rather than those which are perfectly clear in and of themselves. This means that many items are passed over without mention or comment, but the resulting fullness of the discussion of historical, philological, and linguistic details completely justifies these omissions[55]. As a historical commentary it is in the best of the British (and German!) tradition. The breadth of the learning of both Lake and Cadbury is extremely impressive: there seems to be scarcely an area of historical or theological study of which they are not masters. Lake seems to have read nearly every important work related to the interpretation of Acts; he draws equally from the writings of the conservatives as well as from the radicals, from patristic commentators as well as from modern critics, from biblical scholars as well as from classical historians[56]. Cadbury, on the other hand, is a master of Greek literature and history; he knows the times as well as the writings, the non-literary papyri as well as the literary masterpieces, and, above all, the language of the New Testament. If, between the two of them, Lake and Cadbury do not solve all the problems touched upon, they will have helped the student of the Book of Acts to see the major problems more clearly; and they will have called his attention to both the relevant data bearing on each problem and the various alternative solutions possible.

Perhaps the major weakness of the commentary is in the area of theology. It is, indeed, intended to be a historical *and theological* commentary. Lake (presumably) comments frequently on this or that aspect of the theology of "Luke"; but his comments are often quite beside the point. The difficulty is that, in spite of his claim to a strictly objective and historical point of view, he fails to recognize that his understanding of early Christian origins and of the theology/ies of the early Christians is strongly influenced by his own liberal theology of the early twentieth century variety. His comments on Luke's theology, or on the theology of early Jewish and Gentile Christianity, often tell us as much about Lake's own per-

---

[55] In this connection one may question the value of the ultra-literalistic English translation which takes up so much space in the book. The "harsh" expressions and "clumsiness" of the Greek of the early chapters could be indicated in the notes (as indeed they are). The translation itself is of little or no value apart from the notes, which are necessary to explain its own difficult expressions. The translation of phrases which receive no comment is super-fluous.

[56] This seems to be the only major commentary to make full use of the material contained in A. Wikenhauser, *Die Apostelgeschichte und ihr Geschichtswert* (*supra*, pp. 156–58), and E. Meyer, *Ursprung und Anfänge des Christentums* (*supra*, pp. 158–61).

sonal theological convictions as about the theology of the early Christians[57].

Nevertheless, in spite of this minor shortcoming, the historian of New Testament criticism must pay tribute to the commentary by Lake and Cadbury as the *magnum opus* of British and American *Actaforschung*. This, with its companion volume (*BC* 5), will continue to be an indispensable tool for the scholarly study of the Book of Acts for many years to come[58].

In their view of the historical value of Acts, Lake and Cadbury would be a little to the left of mainstream British criticism but far to the right of radical German criticism[59]. In their view, the author of Acts has confused some things here (especially in the earlier chapters) and has arranged his material in a manner in keeping with his own editorial interests or motives there; but, on the whole, his account is generally reliable. Lake sees sources (possibly Aramaic) lying behind the early chapters, and some of these are very reliable[60]. The second half of the book is regarded to be generally quite reliable, due to the fact that the author has access to an excellent source, either a document by an actual companion of Paul (Lake's preference) or information obtained through a personal participation in the events narrated (Cadbury's preference). Their comments on the narrative concerning Paul's experiences in Athens illustrate their general outlook. "Taken as a whole" the account "commends itself at once as a generally historical narrative" (208); it is open to question, however, whether the speech of Paul represents the actual words of Paul or is due to the composition of the editor/author. Each point of the narrative must be considered on the basis of its own merits. Whereas Lake and Cadbury would regard Ramsay as being rather too enthusiastic in his support of the author's abilities as a historian, they would regard the radical German critics as being unnecessarily negative in their criticism of Luke's history.

The fifth volume of *The Beginnings of Christianity* consists of a collection of thirty-seven notes to the commentary by Lake and

---

[57] Cf. the commentary by Rackham, whose High Church Anglican theology led to a similar intermingling of first and nineteenth century theologies (*supra*, pp. 131–33.

[58] *The Beginnings of Christianity*, vols. 4 and 5, have been recently reprinted (Grand Rapids, 1966) — an event for which many students of the Book of Acts will be profoundly grateful.

[59] To describe their outlook — in spite of the language of composition — in terms of "conservative German criticism" would not be far beside the mark!

[60] His sources and judgment on the individual value of the sources are roughly those of Harnack.

Cadbury[61]. The strength of these essays, nearly half of them by Lake himself, is in the area of the historical. Many of them are classic statements of particular problems relating to the historical background of the New Testament, and all of them are monuments of exacting scholarship. Although some of them are now badly dated, and all of them are probably in need of some revision in the light of subsequent research, volume five of this encyclopaedic work continues to be one of the indispensable tools of the *Neutestamentler*. Because of the extended nature of the essays and the expertise

---

[61] It may be useful to have a list of the articles: (1) The Preface to Acts and the Composition of Acts (K. Lake); (2) The Command not to Leave Jerusalem and the "Galilean Tradition" (Lake); (3) The Ascension (Lake); (4) The Death of Judas (Lake); (5) Μάρτυς (R. P. Casey); (6) The Twelve and the Apostles (Lake); (7) The Hellenists (H. J. Cadbury); (8) Proselytes and God-fearers (Lake); (9) The Holy Spirit (Lake); (10) The Gift of the Spirit on the Day of Pentecost (Lake); (11) The Name, Baptism, and the Laying on of Hands (S. New); (12) The Communism of Acts 2 and 4–6 and the Appointment of the Seven (Lake); (13) Simon Magus (R. P. Casey); (14) Paul and the Magus (A. D. Nock); (15) The Conversion of Paul and the Events immediately following it (Lake); (16) The Apostolic Council of Jerusalem (Lake); (17) Paul's Controversies (Lake); (18) Paul's Route in Asia Minor (Lake); (19) The Unknown God (Lake); (20) "Your Own Poets" (Lake); (21) Artemis of Ephesus (L. R. Taylor); (22) The Asiarchs (L. R. Taylor); (23) The Michigan Papyrus Fragment 1571 (S. New); (24) Dust and Garments (Cadbury); (25) The Policy of the Early Roman Emperors towards Judaism (V. M. Scramuzza); (26) Roman Law and the Trial of Paul (Cadbury); (27) The Winds (Lake and Cadbury); (28) Ὑποζώματα (Cadbury); (29) The Titles of Jesus in Acts (Cadbury); (30) Names for Christians and Christianity in Acts (Cadbury); (31) The Summaries in Acts (Cadbury); (32) The Speeches in Acts (Cadbury); (33) The Roman Army (T. R. S. Broughton); (34) The Chronology of Acts (Lake); (35) Localities in and Near Jerusalem mentioned in Acts (Lake); (36) The Family Tree of the Herods (Cadbury); (37) Lucius of Cyrene (Cadbury).

It would be invidious to single out any of the essays as the "best" — all are of an extremely high quality. Lake's essays are notable for their comprehensiveness: all, or nearly all, of the data relevant to any given problem, together with the most important (and many unimportant!) suggested or possible solutions, are set out in a careful and systematic fashion. If there is a weakness in his writings, it is in the area of theological discussion, as has already been noted. Cadbury's essays are of a consistently high standard: although he is usually less speculative than Lake, and as a result a little less stimulating, he is no less thorough and always carefully accurate. If Cadbury often fails to come down hard on the side of one of two or more possible alternative interpretations, it is because he recognizes the reality of the complexity of the problem under discussion and feels under no compulsion to close an issue which must be left open. As far as the remaining essays are concerned, students of Graeco-Roman history will recognize by the names of the authors that in each case the author chosen was eminently qualified to write on the subject under his jurisdiction.

Both this volume and the commentary volume contain very full indices, which enhance their value for the student.

which the various contributors bring to their task, it is probably safe
to say that this final volume is at least of equal value for the scholar
in his work with the commentary volume. At any rate, it would
certainly be true to say that the two volumes together represent the
most extensive and carefully executed study of the historical and
critical problems related to any New Testament writing. And, although many points of interpretation contained in its pages have
been and will continue to be challenged, it will likely remain as one
of the most important commentaries on the Book of Acts for many
years to come.

It is difficult to do justice to the immense contribution of H. J.
Cadbury to the study of the Lucan writings. In addition to his *The
Style and Literary Method of Luke*, a study which set the tone for
the American contribution to Lucan research[62], and the large part
he had in the production of *The Beginnings of Christianity*, he also
penned two important essays on the preface of Luke-Acts[63], a number of significant lexical and grammatical notes[64], and two valuable
books[65].

A major emphasis in all of Cadbury's writings is on the importance of the unity of Luke-Acts[66]. Generally speaking, scholars have
been content to study the Gospel according to Luke, alongside the
other Synoptic Gospels perhaps, but in isolation from the Book of
Acts — and *vice versa*[67]. Yet the Third Gospel and the Book of

---

[62] *Supra*, pp. 168—69.

[63] Very important are "The Purpose Expressed in Luke's Preface", *Expos.*,
series 8, 21 (1921), pp. 431—41; and "The Knowledge Claimed in Luke's Preface", *Expos.*, series 8, 24 (1922), pp. 401—20; cf. his commentary on the
preface of Luke in *BC* 2, pp. 489—510.

[64] In addition to those contained in *BC* 4 and 5, important lexical and
grammatical notes by Cadbury were published over the years in *JBL* 42 (1923),
pp. 150—57; 44 (1925), pp. 214—27; 45 (1926), pp. 190—209, 305—22; 48
(1929), pp. 412—25; 52 (1933), pp. 55—65; 81 (1962), pp. 399—402; 82 (1963),
pp. 272—78; in *Amicitiae Corolla... presented to J. R. Harris* ed. by H. G.
Wood (London, 1933), pp. 45—56; in *Studies in Luke-Acts*, pp. 87—102; in
Festschrift to Honor F. W. Gingrich (Leiden, 1972), pp. 58—69; and in *Studies
in New Testament and Early Christian Literature*, ed. D. Aune (Leiden, 1972),
pp. 3—15.

[65] *The Making of Luke-Acts* (New York, 1928; repr. London, 1958 and 1961)
and *The Book of Acts in History* (London and New York, 1955). The former
of these is one of the most strikingly original studies of the Lucan writings
ever conceived; the latter, although lacking in the same degree of originality,
is a not less valuable complement to it.

[66] Cadbury seems to have coined the expression "Luke-Acts" to emphasize
the fact that they are not two books, but rather two volumes of one book; see
The Making of Luke-Acts, p. 11.

[67] Eduard Meyer and Harnack are notable exceptions to the rule. Ramsay,
on the other hand, with all his devotion to the Lucan writings, gave very

Acts are not two independent writings; they are two parts of a single and continuous work by the same author. "Acts is neither an appendix nor an afterthought" to the Third Gospel, but rather "an integral part of the author's original plan and purpose"[68].

Thus the translation of τὸν πρῶτον λόγον in Acts 1.1 is misleading when it is translated "former treatise"; the meaning is rather "volume one". By dividing his work into two volumes Luke[69] is simply following the custom of ancient writers of dividing long works into a number of rolls as a matter of physical convenience[70].

In his discussion of the preface of Acts[71], Cadbury challenges a number of critical assumptions. First, it is argued, quite convincingly, that Luke 1.1—4 is "the real preface to Acts as well as to the Gospel, written by the author when he contemplated not merely one but both volumes"[72]. It may have been written when the second volume was completed, as seems to have been the custom of Hellenistic writers[73], and therefore would apply especially to that which had been most recently in the mind of the author. Moreover, since the preface is of prime importance as the one place where we clearly have an expression of the author's own self-consciousness[74], a correct understanding of what Luke actually says and implies is highly desirable — indeed, essential.

In his paper on the purpose expressed in Luke's preface[75], Cadbury challenged the usual understanding of the phrase ἵνα ἐπιγνῷς περὶ ὧν κατηχήθης λόγων τὴν ἀσφάλειαν (Luke 1.4), whereby it is understood as implying that Theophilus had already received instruction about Christianity and that the author's purpose is to confirm this knowledge by supplying a full, orderly and reliable record of what had taken place. He argues that κατηχέω here is simply neutral and does not imply that Theophilus was a present or probable convert; that ἡ ἀσφάλεια means "the facts" rather than "the

---

little attention to the narrative of the Gospel (with the exceptions of Luke 2.1—2 and 3.1).

[68] *The Making of Luke-Acts*, p. 9.

[69] Cadbury uses the traditional name of the author; although he believes Luke-Acts is probably the work of a companion of Paul, he is unwilling to admit that it has been demonstrated that he is the traditional Luke (though he might be).

[70] As has already been noted (*supra*, p. 159n.), Josephus' work, *Against Apion*, is an almost exact parallel to Luke-Acts.

[71] See n. 63, above.   [72] *BC* 2, p. 492.

[73] Cf. *Luke-Acts*, pp. 194—98.

[74] "Only in the preface does the composer step in front of the curtain. Except in this quite usual way the author nowhere explicitly discloses his self-consciousness" (*Luke-Acts*, p. 347).

[75] See n. 63, above.

certainty or trustworthiness"; and that ἐπιγινώσκω is to be interpreted in the sense of "to recognize a fact in its significance" or
"realize"[76]. According to Cadbury's interpretation, the author's
statement is to be understood as implying that his purpose is apologetic: his aim is to defend the Christian movement against unfavor-
able reports which have come to the ears of Theophilus, "a man of
influence liable to entertain a hostile view towards Christianity unless by a clear statement of the facts his neutrality and fairness are
guaranteed" (432)[77]. Thus the author's purpose is to correct mis-
information about Christianity rather than to confirm the historical
basis of Theophilus' religious faith.

In his essay on the knowledge claimed in Luke's preface[78], Cadbury challenged the general understanding of the participle παρηκολουθηκότι (Luke 1.3). Rather than research, παρηκολουθηκότι implies
that the author has been in intimate touch with, or even an eye-
witness of, the facts he narrates; he has a first-hand or contemporary
knowledge ἄνωθεν, that is, from the beginning of his own association (a considerable time ago) with the movement he is describing[79]. The author's mind, therefore, is on the second volume of his
work as he pens the preface to the whole work.

In his two books, Cadbury attempts to place Luke-Acts in its
proper historical setting. *The Making of Luke-Acts* is an attempt to
understand the author's method of writing in the milieu of first
century historical writing. By a study of the author's finished product and what is known of the literary methods of ancient writers,
Cadbury seeks to understand what must have been the manner in
which Luke went about his work, the materials he used, how he was
influenced in his task by prevailing literary customs of the time, the
author's personality as it affected his work, and finally his purpose

---

[76] In addition to the articles cited, see his notes on these words in *BC* 2.

[77] An objection to this view which is often regarded as fatal is that much of
the religious matter would be of interest only to Christian believers and would
have been incidental to an apologetic purpose. But, as Cadbury comments,
"we cannot be sure that Theophilus would be more interested in 'all that Jesus
began both to do and to teach' than the second-century emperors were in the
works dedicated to them on Greek word accent (twenty volumes by Herodian),
on military strategy (by Aelian and Polyaenus), on the sayings of kings and
generals (by Plutarch), on geography (e. g., Arrian's Periplus of the Euxine
Sea), not to mention dictionaries (e. g., Pollux) and many defences of Christianity by the apologists (Quadratus, Aristides, Justin, Melito, Apollinarius,
Miltiades, Athenagoras and probably others)" (*Luke-Acts*, pp. 203—4).

[78] See n. 63, above.

[79] Cadbury finds no evidence for the interpretation of Παρηκολουθηκότι
as meaning "to look closely into, to investigate, to do research" — in spite of
the references which are generally cited in support of this interpretation.

or purposes in writing in the first place. Only after he has gone through all of these details does he turn to the traditional concerns of New Testament introduction with questions of authorship, date, provenance — which he regards to be more or less irrelevant to an understanding of the Lucan writings[80].

It would be anachronistic to refer to Cadbury's study as an exercise in the *redaktionsgeschichtliche Methode (*"editorial criticism"), but it would not be misleading to describe it in this manner[81]. In fact, it might be justly claimed to be a model of this approach, insofar as it is a legitimate task of criticism[82]. Some will no doubt be impatient with what they regard as the exercise of undue caution on the part of Cadbury[83]; but no one can deny that he has made a most valuable contribution toward an understanding of the author's personality and literary methodology in the context of history.

[80] "It is far more important to know the personality of the author than his name, to know his purpose in writing than his profession, to know the technique of his age than the exact year, to know his position in the transmission of history than his habitat. Even Paul's very personal letters are not much illumined by our knowledge of such questions — that he wrote in the sixth decade of the first century and that he was born in Tarsus and wrote from Ephesus or Corinth. Much less significant are such personalia in the writers of history" (353). Cf. *The Book of Acts in History*, pp. 136—37.

[81] See the comments of R. M. Grant in *JBL* 87 (1968), p. 46.

[82] One would think that the more recent *redaktionsgeschichtlich* studies of Luke-Acts might have been less extravagant in their individualistic conclusions if they had had the benefit of Cadbury's historical perspective and careful methodology. It is in fact surprising how Cadbury's work — certainly the most important study of this type before H. Conzelmann's *Die Mitte der Zeit* (see below, pp. 291—96) — has been neglected by recent writers. Conzelmann, for example, makes only one passing reference to *The Making of Luke-Acts* (3rd. ed., p. 187; he refers elsewhere to two of Cadbury's notes in *BC* 2 and 5). Once again critical orthodoxy begins a new phase of New Testament criticism *de novo* and *in vacuo* — ignoring completely the most significant study on the subject under discussion!

[83] Although I feel that Cadbury may be over-cautious in a few places, as, for example, concerning the question of authorship, in general I regard his caution as a virtue rather than a vice. Here are a few examples of the wisdom of a careful critic:

"To discover the exact interests and uses of the material now in our gospels is a difficult and sometimes dangerous task. Those who have sought a single clue have mostly gone wrong. Above all things the multiplicity of interests must be emphasized" (38—39).

Concerning the style of Luke's Greek: "Exact classification must be a delicate if not impossible task for late-born barbarians like ourselves, unable to acquire for Greek that spontaneous sensing of difference of style that we feel for a native tongue" (114).

"The uniqueness of a word in Luke's writings is not proved by its absence elsewhere from the New Testament, for the New Testament is linguistically a purely accidental collection; nor is it proved by its rarity in secular Greek

In the first section of *The Making of Luke-Acts* (21—110), Cadbury discusses the various stages in the history of Luke's materials, the motives lying behind the preservation and transmission of these materials, the forms in which the traditions were probably (according to the principles of form criticism) transmitted before they reached the author, and the author's use of sources (specifically Mark and "Q"). In part two (113—209) he considers the literary habits which Luke would have shared with his Hellenistic contemporaries. In failing to mention his sources by name, in his preference for paraphrase rather than verbatim quotation, and in the use of one source at a time, Luke is following the general custom of Greek historical writers. Although the author faithfully reproduces the speeches of Jesus in the Gospels (although by means of paraphrase), Cadbury argues that in Acts he probably followed the general custom which prevailed among ancient historians whereby speeches which had no other foundation than the author's own sense of what was appropriate were put into the mouths of the leading characters of the narrative[84]. Although he admits that there were probably variations in what is regarded as the general custom of ancient writers (188) and that it cannot be definitely demonstrated that Luke did in fact compose the speeches himself[85], Cadbury argues that it remains probable that the speeches of Acts are the author's own compositions[86].

---

literature which we possess, a still more accidental limitation" (117). Cf. the similar warnings on pp. 214—15 and in *The Book of Acts in History*, pp. 35 to 37.

"Essential for any judgment of Luke's work is the perspective that compares him with his own time rather than our own. ... In the matter of accuracy, for example, we ought not to judge Luke more severely than we judge the Greek historians" (349—50).

[84] "The speeches offered the writer an opportunity for variety and for the display of his rhetorical powers. Like the chorus in a Greek play they served to review the situation for the reader, and they brought out the inner thoughts and feelings of important persons. ... They were the objects of special care and pride on the part of historians interested in style, and were the parts of history most appreciated by literary connoisseurs" (184).

[85] "One cannot speak more positively than in terms of impression, or more inclusively than so as to leave the possibility that some of the speeches are closely dependent on written sources or oral information. ...

"That the style of [the speeches] is that of the evangelist no one can deny. How much if any of their contents has an earlier tradition, oral or written, Greek or Aramaic, is a question often debated, and in the absence of external evidence not settled with finality in the case of a single one of them. The supposition of some authentic written or oral information is most attractive in the case of Stephen's speech and of the speeches of Paul at Athens and Miletus" (189).

[86] See his essay on the subject in *BC* 5, pp. 402—427. Cadbury's views

In the third part of his study of Luke's literary method (213—96), Cadbury considers the factor of the author's individuality, the distinctive features of his writings which reveal something of his own personality: his language and style, "secular" interests (which indicate that he is a man of some contacts with culture), his social and religious attitudes, and his theological concerns. In the chapter on Luke's "secular" interests Cadbury introduces a subject to which he is to return nearly thirty years hence[87]. He sees indications of the author's cosmopolitan outlook in his understanding of both Greek political organization and Roman law, his knowledge of the existing friction between Jews and Romans and the difficult middle position of the Herods, and his accurate portrayal of local color by his casual notations concerning points of detail[88]. In contrast to the narrative of the Synoptic Gospels which has as its background the country, the author of Luke-Acts, even more than Paul, writes from an urban point of view. As Paul thinks in terms of Roman provinces (Galatia, Asia, Macedonia, Achaia, and even Illyricum and Spain), Luke thinks in terms of cities or city-states (which is the Greek point of view). Thus it is that the Book of Acts deals almost entirely with cities, and that the Third Gospel, when compared with the others, gives an urban flavor to the ministry of Jesus by frequent reference to cities.

Under the heading of the social and religious attitudes of the author are listed the familiar emphases on universalism[89], Jesus' concern (in the Gospel) for the outcasts of religious society[90], the prob-

---

represent a development upon the views expressed by P. Gardner, "The Speeches of St. Paul in Acts", in *Cambridge Biblical Essays*, ed. by H. B. Swete (Cambridge, 1909), pp. 379—419, and together they represent the major attempts to argue the case against the authenticity of the speeches in English (though Gardner accepted the speech at Miletus as essentially Pauline). They have not, however, convinced the majority of British critics. F. F. Bruce, *The Speeches of Acts* (London, 1944) is the major attempt to argue the opposing view that the speeches of Acts are *not* the invention of the author, but may be summaries giving at least the gist of what was actually said on the various occasions. Others would not go quite so far, but would insist upon the likelihood that the speeches have at least sources or traditions of some sort lying behind them. See below, pp. 228—33.   [87] See below, pp. 192—94.

[88] Cadbury admits that it is possible that the author was less familiar with Palestine than with other parts of the Mediterranean world, but suggests that even here the evidence is not all on one side (241—42, 244).

[89] However, in Cadbury's view Luke's emphasis is more on God's rejection of the Jews which has resulted in his acceptance of the Gentiles than on the more positive understanding of the doctrine (254—57).

[90] Here too Cadbury has an essentially negative understanding of this emphasis: Luke's purpose is not so much to stress God's love and forgiveness for the outcast as it is to show Jesus' rebuke of the self-righteous (258—59).

191

lems of poverty and wealth, the frequent references to women, salvation for the lost, joy, prayer, and the Holy Spirit[91]. Cadbury sees
little evidence to indicate that the author of Luke-Acts is to be regarded as a creative theologian. On the one hand, he seems to take
for granted the Christian teaching of his own day (though this does
not have a great influence on his narrative); on the other hand, he
seems accurately to represent the primitive Christian theology,
whether by the use of historical imagination or by actual personal
knowledge.

The fourth part of *The Making of Luke-Acts* (199—350) is concerned with the purpose, or better, the multiplicity of purposes of
the author. A primary motive was certainly historical.

The form of his work is narrative, and narrative carries with it the
intention of supplying information. No matter how much Luke differs
from the rhetorical historians of Israel, his narrative shares with them the
common intention of informing the reader concerning the past. Even were
it plain that the story was intended to serve also as an argument, in any
analysis of the writer's purpose this purely didactic motive would have to
be accepted as significant (299).

Artist or advocate, the historian is still historian, even if not in our
modern sense. Luke's words about his own work and the work of his
predecessors, a "narrative of the things fulfilled among us", "a treatise
concerning all that Jesus began both to do and to teach", mean this, whatever else they may mean, or whatever motives he had which he does not
express (300).

Thus the material itself both suggested and provided his major motive in writing. The apologetic motive is possibly another motive,
though probably not the primary one: therefore, Luke marshals the
many evidences of divine guidance and control in establishing the
Christian movement (popular apologetic), the legitimacy of Christianity as the fulfillment of Judaism and the Old Testament (defence
before Judaism), and the legality of Christianity before the Roman
law (defence before the Romans).

In the final, brief chapter on the questions of authorship and accuracy (351—68), Cadbury minimizes the importance of the former
and is somewhat equivocal in the attitude he takes toward the latter. He rightly separates the two questions, observing that "authorship by a companion of Paul is in itself no guarantee of trustworthiness" (363), and that a second-hand account is not necessarily
less reliable than the first-hand impressions of any eyewitness (as
any reader of autobiographies or visitor to the lawcourts knows). He

[91] He also finds a special emphasis in the Gospel on Jesus' appeal to common
sense (271—72)!

is, however, skeptical concerning the Lucan tradition of authorship, but is unwilling to decide the question more definitely. Although he recognizes that the author is a child of his time, following the literary customs of the age (which include, in his opinion, the invention of speeches and a naïveté in regard to the miraculous), Cadbury is not to be classed with those who dismiss the narrative of Acts as largely unhistorical. The fact that in the Gospel "Luke evidently reproduced his sources faithfully, in general purport though not in wording" (365), that his outline of Paul's missionary career is confirmed time and time again by striking coincidences between Acts and the Pauline epistles, and that the geographical and political setting of Acts is generally confirmed by archaeological and geographical research lead him to regard the narrative generally, though not infallibly, trustworthy. In spite of his personal unwillingness to commit himself too strongly in favor of the historical reliability of the Lucan writings, his demonstration of the "verifiable fitness (of the narrative of Luke-Acts) to its historical setting" (368)[92] places him in the Lightfoot-Ramsay tradition, if only by implication.

In *The Making of Luke-Acts*, Cadbury sought to understand the Third Gospel and the Book of Acts in the context of ancient literary composition. In his book, *The Book of Acts in History*[93], published nearly thirty years later, he returned to his subject, this time concentrating on the second of Luke's two volumes. His concern here is the way in which the Book of Acts fits in with its wider contemporary environment, that is, the manner in which it conforms to what we know of the history and culture of the first century of the Christian era. Once again, he is not concerned to demonstrate the accuracy of the narrative, but rather to establish "the realism of the scenes and customs and mentality which it reflects" (V), that is, its general fitness to its time — though many will feel that he succeeds in doing both[94].

---

[92] Cadbury is only willing to say that this is achieved either by the author's exceptionally talented use of historical imagination *or* by an accurate knowledge of the historical facts. Although the former possibility cannot be proved to be impossible, most students of ancient literature will agree that the latter is the more probable.

[93] (London, 1955).

[94] Cf. F. F. Bruce, *The New Testament Documents: Are They Reliable?* (5th ed.; London, 1960), p. 91. Cadbury recognizes, however, that the evidence he cites is relevant evidence for the view that "the author of Acts is dealing with fact and reality" (4), even though he is obviously disinterested in apologetics. In the scope of 170 pages of his monograph he restates and updates most of the basic points brought forward by the defenders of Luke's history from Paley to Wikenhauser, and adds to them. The points where Luke has the

The work is divided into six chapters. The first five illustrate how a study of the writings of the author's contemporaries, the Greek papyri, archaeological research, inscriptions and coins illustrate five aspects of the cultural and historical background of Acts: (1) the "general" (i. e., non-Jewish oriental), (2) the Greek, (3) the Roman, (4) the Jewish, and (5) the Christian. A final chapter discusses what we know of the subsequent history of the Book of Acts in the early Church, including the problem of its divergent textual traditions.

Cadbury adds little that is startlingly new or original to the history of *Actaforschung*. Perhaps his discussion of the Greek point of view of the author (32—53), manifesting itself in the account of the βάρβαροι at Malta (28.2) and, more clearly, by his emphasis on cities throughout his narrative[95], is the most interesting, whereas his account of the implications of and questions raised by Paul's Roman citizenship (65—82) is also worthy of special mention as a comprehensive and generally accurate discussion of this fact as it relates to the narrative of Acts[96]. However, as in the case of his earlier work, it is primarily his unique approach to his subject which gives to his study its originality. Nevertheless, *The Book of Acts in*

---

facts confused seem to be few indeed and nearly all of them very minor. Although Cadbury sticks by his view that the speeches are Lucan compositions, he recognizes that they are entirely "in character" (130). In addition to the many incidental items which confirm Luke's history (points of contact with the Pauline epistles and what we know from other sources about the life and customs of the time), the author of Acts is certainly accurate in the main lines of his portrayal of early Christianity (see pp. 129—32).

Cadbury's statement on page 120, that Greek and Latin novels are often as full of accurate local and contemporary color as are trustworthy historical writings, is misleading in that it overlooks the fact that Acts does not make the historical *faux pas* which are so typical of ancient fictional works and (say) the apocryphal books of Acts. Whereas the author of Acts is carefully accurate in his representation of *the time and places of which he writes*, the local and contemporary color contained in the writers of fiction *is that of the time and places in which they write*. Writers of modern historical novels, who have access to reference libraries, may be capable of achieving this sort of accuracy; but it is questionable whether the authors of any ancient novels were capable of the accuracy which a statement like Cadbury's implies.

[95] Other possible indications of the author's "Greek" point of view: the account of Paul's dialogue with Claudius Lysias (Acts 21.37—39; see pp. 32—33); Luke's style of language, especially in the second part of Acts (cf. 1.19, where he refers to Aramaic as "*their* language"); his literary allusions; and his accurate portrayal of municipal institutions and local color of Thessalonica, Ephesus, and especially Athens.

[96] Cf. A. N. Sherwin-White, *Roman Society and Roman Law in the New Testament* (Oxford, 1963), pp. 144—62, 172—85, for an up-to-date discussion of the subject by one who is a recognized expert in his subject; the author corrects Cadbury on a few points.

History is a monograph which rightly deserves an honorable mention among the important American contributions to the study of Luke's second volume.

The major study of the purpose of Acts by an American scholar is a small monograph by Burton Scott Easton (1877—1950), published first in 1936[97]. Easton argues for a dual purpose for Acts, corresponding to two types of readers which the author has in mind. Luke was concerned to edify his fellow Christians, on the one hand, and to offer a defence of Christianity to Theophilus, "a Roman official of some standing" who was "not a Christian" (33), and hence (presumably) to other cultured non-Christians.

For the sake of his fellow-believers, who were mostly simple folk who were unfamiliar with formal literature, Luke makes a number of simplifications in his narrative. In the first place, he simplifies the story by "beginning with a city (Jerusalem) and ending with a city (Rome)" (34); the actual history of the expansion of the Church during the decades between A. D. 30 and 60 was, of course, much more complex. In addition to this geographical simplification there is a biographical one: the author tells the story in terms of two early leaders, Peter and Paul[98]. Thirdly, there is a chronological simplification: Luke is not overly concerned with time sequences; he includes a temporal reference in terms of months or years, all of them pertaining to the length of Paul's stay in various cities (18.11; 19.8, 10; 20.3; 24.27; 28.11; 28.30), but otherwise he simply refers to the happenings of individual days or indefinite periods of time[99]. Fourthly, the speeches are used to set forth the nature of Christianity as the author understands it in a way which can be easily grasped by the readers. Fifthly, the apostolic miracles[100] serve to impress upon the mind of the readers in a dramatic manner the fact

---

[97] *The Purpose of Acts* (London, 1936); repr. as a part of *Earliest Christianity: The Purpose of Acts and Other Papers* (London, 1955). The references which follow are to the latter volume.

[98] "The only other persons in Acts that are at all individualized are Stephen and Philip, who serve chiefly to link together the work of the two apostles" (34—35).

[99] Easton couples this with the form-critical observation that "the narrative is really made up by the juxtaposition of a great number of separate sections, each of which is substantially complete in itself. The references in any part of Acts to what precedes are few and unimportant" (935—36). Cf. S. E. Johnson, "A Proposed Form-Critical Treatment of Acts", *ATR* 21 (1939), pp. 22—31.

[100] In addition to the familiar miracles effected by or on behalf of the apostles — especially Peter and Paul (Easton notes the usual parallels) — there are miracles of revelation (tongues, prophecy, earthquake, dreams, visions, angelic mediation, a voice from heaven, and the opening of heaven itself) and miracles of conversion (cf. pp. 38—40, with references).

of divine approval of the teaching contained in the speeches. And, finally, "the definite teaching material is interspersed with narrative, whose design may be only to interest the reader and to refresh him after the exactions of the more serious passages" (41). In short, Luke's aim as far as his Christian readers are concerned is to encourage and to challenge them by an exciting and didactic account of the missionary expansion of the Church during the first three decades of its existence.

Wherever the missionary sets his foot, there a Church springs into being. Jews may be obstinately hostile, Athenian philosophers supercilious, idol-makers frenzied, vile fellows of the rabble ready for any mischief, but the work goes on triumphantly. ... Stephen may be martyred, Peter imprisoned, Paul stoned and left for dead, but the work goes on triumphantly. Countless souls have been stirred to their depths by Luke's story and made to ask: "Since God could do these marvels through the first believers, may He not do something today through me? His arm is not shortened!" And to give men this inspiration was one of the most potent reasons why Luke wrote Acts (40).

Edification of his fellow-believers was not, however, Luke's sole purpose. He also wishes to demonstrate (especially for Theophilus and his fellow Romans) "that Christianity is a religion that should be tolerated by the state" (42). This he seeks to do in a number of ways. First, he emphasizes Paul's positive relations with the representatives of the Roman authority. Sergius Paulus at Cyprus, the *praetors* of Philippi, the magistrates of Thessalonica, Gallio at Corinth, the γραμματεύς at Ephesus, Claudius Lysias, Felix, Festus, and Agrippa, all recognize Paul's innocence of any wrong-doing insofar as the Roman law is concerned[101]; and in the closing verses of the book, the author observes that Paul was permitted by the authorities to live two years in his own hired house in Rome, preaching and teaching ἀκωλύτως. Secondly, the author argues that Christianity has a legal right to toleration, since it "is no new and independent religion, about which the government still has to make up its mind", but rather "nothing more or less than Judaism", which "has been explicitly recognized by Rome as a *religio licita*" (43).

The emphasis on the Gentile mission in Acts, and the hostility of many Jews to the preaching of Paul has caused many to overlook this second aspect of Luke's argument. It should be remembered, however, that a Jewish mission to Gentiles was no novelty in the

---

[101] "To a very real degree chapters 13 to 28 may be regarded as a casebook in Roman law" (42). This first line of evidence (which has already been observed several times in the course of the present study) is certainly the strongest in favor of an apologetic motive of the author — at least, for chapters 13–28.

apostolic age[102], and that Judaism was a highly complex phenomenon. Pharisees, Sadducees, Zealots, and Essenes were only a few
of the many sects of Judaism. These different sects were marked by
acutely different beliefs and practices, but they were all nonetheless
Jews. As far as the Roman government was concerned, a Jew was a
Jew; the party distinctions, the reasons for which they were probably unable to comprehend anyway, were altogether disregarded.
And this point is precisely the one that Luke is concerned to emphasize. "From what he conceived the Roman theory ought to be,
the Christians were simply one more Jewish party" (46)[103].

Luke devotes a considerable part of the Book of Acts to this
theme. This, argues Easton, is the purpose of the lengthy openings
of the speeches in chapters 7 and 13, which are simply rhetorical
and have little to do with the arguments which follow: "the aim is
to convince the listeners of the speakers' (Jewish) orthodoxy" (47).
And this is the reason for the strong emphasis on the Old Testament in the sermons. Furthermore, Luke emphasizes the previous
decisions of Roman officials (e. g., Gallio (18.15), Claudius Lysias
(23.29), and Festus (25.19)) that the Christians were in fact a Jewish party. Jews themselves — Gamaliel (5.38—39), the Pharisees
(23.9), and the common people in Jerusalem (2.47; 5.13; 5.26; etc.)
— recognized this fact: even the opposition of the Sadducees, "a
group despised by most Jews as worldy rationalists" (49), was in
terms of Jewish sectarianism. Moreover, the Christians themselves
considered themselves to be Jews: Jerusalem Christianity remained

---

[102] Cf. Matthew 23.15 and the constant presence of Gentile proselytes and
semi-proselytes in the pages of Acts (see references in Easton, p. 44). In E.
Schürer's classic essay on the Diaspora in *HDB* 5 (1904), p. 91 he argues that
the millions of Jews outside of Palestine could not have been due simply to
migration and natural reproduction, but must have also been due to widespread
Gentile conversions.

[103] A major difficulty with Easton's statement of this point is that the author
of Acts' frequent use of the term οἱ Ἰουδαῖοι seems to indicate that he regards
them as a group distinct from both non-Christian Gentiles and Jewish and
Gentile Christians. It seems probable that Luke would have argued on theological grounds that the Church is in reality the "new Israel" (in a manner
similar to Paul in Romans 9—11, etc.); however, it is unlikely that he would
have regarded the Church as simply a *part* of Judaism. To him, the Church
would have been understood as the replacement of ethnic and national Israel
as the people of God. At any rate, it is unlikely that a Roman magistrate
would have interpreted the narrative of Acts as an attempt to argue that
Christianity should be recognized as a sect of Judaism. A further objection to
Easton's argument in this connection is that he treats the Book of Acts in
almost total isolation from the Third Gospel. Is there any evidence to be
found in volume one of the work dedicated to Theophilus of this defence of
Christianity as a sect within Judaism?

faithful to the temple and to the Law, and Gentile Christianity is everywhere depicted as under the supervision of Jerusalem Christianity[104].

The remainder of Easton's monograph is devoted to working out in detail the "proof" for this final point in terms of (1) Paul's supposed subordination to the Twelve, (2) Paul's "Jewish" practices, (3) the government of the Church as centered in Jerusalem[105], (4) the Jewish-primitive nature of the theology of Acts, and (5) the moralism of the author. As is so typical of studies of this type, the further the argument of the critic progresses the weaker is his case. There is no doubt that there is some basis to Easton's two major points: nearly all scholars have recognized the fact that the author is concerned to edify his Christian readers and to defend the Christian Church against its (Roman?) critics. But it is questionable whether these are the *only* important motives of the author, and it is doubtful in the extreme whether the author himself would have understood the subtlety of his own argument as Easton expounds it[106].

Nearly all of the really important works on the Book of Acts which have originated in North America were published between the years 1916 and 1936[107], *The Beginnings of Christianity* representing by far the most significant contribution of the era. One final volume should be mentioned, however, not for its intrinsic worth, but because of the influence it has exerted on the work of a number of younger American scholars in recent years.

John Knox (1900–), former student of E. J. Goodspeed and perhaps the most influential second-generation member of the so-called "Chicago School" of biblical criticism, first brought forward his suggestions for a radical reconstruction of the outline of Paul's life and ministry in two essays published in the '30s[108]. The material

---

[104] "Nowhere in Acts do we meet a Church like that at Colossae, founded by a Gentile, composed almost or quite entirely of Gentiles, and leading a practically autonomous life of its own. As Luke tells the story, there was nothing haphazard about the development of the Gentile mission" (52).

[105] "It is a thesis of Acts that the 'Way' has a centralized Jewish authority, fixed in Jerusalem" (56).

[106] Easton's case is impressive when taken as a whole. When one begins to examine the proof-texts cited as evidence for his theses, it becomes clear that his exegesis of many of the passages cited is highly eccentric and open to serious objection. His case becomes weak from page 57 and very weak from page 67 onward.

[107] H. J. Cadbury, *The Book of Acts in History* is the most important volume lying outside of these two decades of research.

[108] " 'Fourteen years later': A Note on the Pauline Chronology", *JR* 16 (1936), pp. 341–49; and "The Pauline Chronology", *JBL* 58 (1939), pp. 15–29.

of these essays was published in a revised form as a part of his well-known book, *Chapters in a Life of Paul*[109]. In his work Knox lays stress on the unanimously recognized fact that the epistles of Paul provide the critic with his primary source for the life of Paul, whereas the narrative of Acts is secondary (30—31)[110]. Although all scholars would recognize the truth of this fact, very few, argues Knox, have faithfully followed the implications of this fact in practice. Rather than attempting to reconstruct the external aspects of Paul's life first on the basis of the data provided by his letters, New Testament critics have continued to follow an outline which is almost totally dependent on the narrative of Acts.

Although Knox gives lip-service to the view that the data of Acts may be used "with proper caution ... to supplement the autobiographical data of the letters (of Paul)" (33), in practice he tends to limit his discussion of chronology and the facts of Paul's life to the scanty autobiographical references contained in the epistles and clearly regards Acts as grossly inaccurate (primarily, it would seem, as a result of the author's allowing his "tendencies" to influence his narrative of events (23—28))[111]. It is not simply that Knox uses the letters of Paul *first* and then turns to the Book of Acts to see what supplementary information can be found, but that the letters of Paul are used *almost exclusively*. If it were agreed that the narrative of Acts is extremely unreliable as a historical source, this exclusive use of the epistles might seem justified. However, in the light of all the evidence which has been provided by scholars of the most diverse backgrounds and theological points of view in favor of the reliability of the Lucan history[112], there seems to be little justification for this approach. All historians would agree that the per-

---

[109] (New York and Nashville, 1950; repr. 1954 (London), 1964 and 1965 (London)). References which follow are to this work, which is exactly the same in each edition.

[110] But it should not be overlooked that (as T. H. Campbell, "Paul's 'Missionary Journeys' as Reflected in His Letters", *JBL* 74 (1955), p. 81, has pointed out) the author of Acts is either himself an eyewitness or is using the journal of an eyewitness for part of his narrative.

[111] The attempt of J. C. Hurd, Jr. ("Pauline Chronology and the Pauline Theology", in *Christian History and Interpretation: Studies presented to John Knox*, ed. by W. R. Farmer, C. F. D. Moule, and R. R. Niebuhr (Cambridge, 1967), pp. 225—48) to deny that Knox fits into the category of those who assume the narrative of Acts to be almost entirely unreliable is wholly unconvincing to the critic who follows Knox's principle of examining the *primary* source first.

[112] There is no attempt to deal with *any* of the evidence brought forward by *any* of the defenders of the historical reliability of the Book of Acts. Indeed, as is the case with most of Knox's writings, *Chapters in a Life of Paul* is marked by a sovereign disregard of the views of nearly all other scholars.

sonal information noted by Paul in the course of his letters provides one with the primary material for an attempted reconstruction of the events of Paul's life; but very few indeed would agree that this material should be used to the exclusion of most of the data provided by the Book of Acts, especially in view of the fragmentary and often ambiguous nature of the data of the epistles, on the one hand, and the availability of a secondary source which is broader in scope and which has good claims to a high standard of historical trustworthiness, on the other hand. Although the views of Knox will probably continue to be of influence in North America among the spheres of influence of his former students and associates[113], the arbitrary nature of his conclusions will more than likely prevent their acceptance by very many scholars outside of this small circle[114].

The major contribution of American scholarship to the history of *Actaforschung* was, as we have seen, in the area of philology and historical research. Here, of course, the five-volumed work, *The Beginnings of Christianity*, dwarfs all other work in this area in terms of both quantity and quality. The views expressed in the course of the five volumes were mixed and even contradictory. The authors were often unwilling, or perhaps unable, to make up their minds regarding a number of differing options and to come to definite conclusions. It would not be amiss to say the *BC* provided not so much the *solutions* to the critical problems related to the scientific study of the Book of Acts, but rather the *raw materials* for a balanced consideration of the problems.

The major weakness of the work was, as has already been noted, in the area of theology. On the one hand, the work is generally lacking in a theological consideration of the Lucan writings; on the other hand, the places where the authors attempted to make theological comments and pass judgement on (say) the Lucan or primitive Christian theologies are marred by the superimposition of the theological standpoint of the commentators over that of the biblical writer. Thus the need of a theological study of the Book of Acts is underlined but left unfulfilled.

---

[113] J. C. Hurd (n. 111) lists a few of those who have accepted Knox's conclusions, to a greater or lesser degree. In addition, see Hurd's work, *The Origin of 1 Corinthians* (New York and London, 1965), and C. H. Buck, Jr., "The Date of Galatians", *JBL* 70 (1951), pp. 113–22.

[114] On Knox's conclusions, see G. Ogg, "A New Chronology of St. Paul's Life", *ExpT* 64(1953), pp. 120–23. Ogg's own study of the subject, *The Chronology of the Life of Paul* (London, 1968), is much more satisfactory than Knox's.

As far as the historical value of Acts is concerned, the contributors to *BC* were moderate in comparison to radical German criticism, but not as conservative as mainstream British criticism. Lake became more skeptical regarding the historicity of Acts as the years passed, but Foakes-Jackson and Cadbury seem to have come to regard Luke's narrative rather more highly as a historical source. Cadbury gave as good a case as can be given for the view that the speeches of Acts are wholly due to the author's historical imagination and succeeded in convincing many, though by no means all, of his compatriots. One feature of *BC* which is greatly to the credit of the authors is the fact that few, if any, significant opinions were overlooked. Thus, for example, the authors seriously attempted to come to terms with the contributions of Ramsay, Harnack, Zahn, E. Meyer, and Wikenhauser, as well as the more radical critics. Although many will feel that the attempted compromise between conservative and radical opinion was unsatisfactory, neither side can complain that its views were neglected.

Chapter IX

THE INFLUENCE OF MARTIN DIBELIUS

Formgeschichte — that formidable-looking German word which has been unhelpfully translated into English as "form criticism" — signifies the most important development in the study of the Gospels since the First World War[1]. As its name suggests, it is an approach which attempts to get behind the written forms to the oral stage in the transmission of the Gospel tradition by a study of the forms which it has assumed. The goal is to determine, insofar as this is possible, the *Sitz im Leben* ("life-setting") of the individual pericopae and sayings in the life of the early Church and/or the ministry of Jesus[2]. As the method has been used by many scholars — and here one thinks especially of the German pioneers of this approach to Gospel criticism: Karl Ludwig Schmidt, Rudolf Bultmann, and Martin Dibelius — it has often led to extremely skeptical conclusions regarding the historical foundations of the life and ministry of Jesus; but it need not necessarily do so[3].

Martin Dibelius (1883—1947), professor at the University of Heidelberg for many years and one of the leading figures in the development of the *formgeschichtliche Methode*, was the first to attempt to apply the insights of this approach to the study of the Book of Acts[4]. Although he never wrote a commentary on Acts, or even

---

[1] See S. Neill, *Interpretation of the New Testament*, pp. 236—62; G. Bornkamm in *RGG*[3] 2, cols. 749—53; and L. A. Schökel in *NewCathEnc* 5, pp. 1017 —23; with bibliographies.

[2] Many scholars have criticized the leading German form critics for what they regard as the unjustified assumption that the true *Sitz im Leben* of the pericopae and sayings is the post-Easter Church, rather than the life and ministry of Jesus.

[3] The writings of T. W. Manson, C. H. Dodd, V. Taylor, O. Cullmann, J. Jeremias, H. Schürmann, J. Dupont, and R. Schnackenburg — form critics all — to mention no more, are proof that negative historical conclusions are not the result of the use of the method of *Formgeschichte*, but rather of other philosophical and historical considerations on the part of some critics.

[4] More or less independently of Dibelius' specific work on Acts, S. E. Johnson, "A Proposed Form-Critical Treatment of Acts", *ATR* 21 (1939), pp. 22— 31, classified the material of Acts according to the categories suggested for the

a full-scaled monograph, Dibelius penned a number of important essays[5] between 1923 and 1947 which have exercised an immense influence on German *Actaforschung*, especially in the past two decades. In much the same way as the writings of F. C. Baur influenced critical thought a century earlier, the brief but suggestive essays of Martin Dibelius have served as the basic catalyst of scholarly debate concerning the Book of Acts from about 1950 to the present.

In the first of these essays, which was written for the 1923 *Festschrift* for Hermann Gunkel[6], Dibelius lays down the guiding prin-

---

Gospels by Dibelius' *Formgeschichte des Evangeliums* (E. T. *From Tradition to Gospel* (New York, 1935)) into (1) paradigms or pronouncement stories, (2) *Novellen* or *Wundergeschichten*, and (3) legends. He makes no reference to the essay by Dibelius on the *Stilkritik* of Acts (see below). Johnson would assign a much larger portion of the Book of Acts to tradition and a much smaller portion to Luke's literary *fiat* than would Dibelius. He does not seem to have followed up this essay by any further thoughts on the subject, at least not in print.

C. H. Dodd has taken a "form-critical" approach to the speeches of Acts. In his famous essay, "The Framework of the Gospel Narrative", *ExpT* 43 (1931/32), pp. 396—400, he pointed out (following a note in Dibelius' *Formgeschichte des Evangeliums*) the presence of "summary outlines of the life of Jesus embedded in the primitive preaching of the Church, appearing in various speeches in the Acts of the Apostles" (399). The fullest examples of such primitive *kerygma* he regards to be that contained in Acts 10.37—41 and Acts 13.23—31, both of which contain outlines which are more or less the same as the "framework" of the Gospels. This is, in his view, evidence for the fact that the primitive Church passed on in its tradition an outline of the Ministry of Jesus, an outline which is roughly that providing the framework of Mark. This Dodd developed in his *The Apostolic Preaching and Its Developments* (London, 1936), arguing that the speeches of Acts are not the free invention of the author, but rather derived from earlier sources. The speeches of Peter "are based upon material which proceeded from the Aramaic-speaking Church of Jerusalem" and stem from a substantially earlier period of the Church's history from the time in which the book of Acts was written (2nd ed., 1944, p. 20). They represent not "what Peter said upon this or that occasion, but the *kerygma* of the Church at Jerusalem at any early period" (21). Prof. Dodd's view has been very influential in the world of British scholarship (though it has been challenged by some — notably C. F. Evans, "The Kerygma", *JTS*, N. S. 7 (1956), pp. 25—41); it has not had much influence outside of the United Kingdom.

[5] Eleven of the most important of these are contained in his *Aufsätze zur Apostelgeschichte*, 4th ed. (Göttingen, 1961); E. T. *Studies in the Acts of the Apostles* (London, 1956). His essay, "Zur Formgeschichte des N. T.s (ausserhalb der Evangelien)", *TR*, N. F. 3 (1931), pp. 209—42, is also important; pages 233—41 are devoted to the Book of Acts.

[6] "Stilkritisches zur Apostelgeschichte", in *Eucharisterion für H. Gunkel* (Göttingen, 1923) 2, pp. 27—49; contained in his *Aufsätze*, pp. 9—28. The

ciples and, indeed, the basic conclusions of all his future work on Acts[7]. He begins by stressing the uniqueness of the Book of Acts among the New Testament writings. In spite of its connection with the Third Gospel — a fact which Dibelius believed had been over-emphasized by Eduard Meyer and Harnack — it belongs to a class all its own. "Vor allem hat sich Lukas in der Apostelgeschichte in viel höherem Grade schriftstellerisch betätigt als im Evangelium" (10). In the Gospel it was a question of framing and stringing to-gether fragments of the tradition; therefore, the writer was able to limit his literary activity to minor interpolations, chiefly those of an editorial nature. However, in Acts he has not only the "Überliefe-rungsstücke mosaikartig zusammengefügt, verbunden und gerahmt" (10) but also exercised a greater individuality as a *littérateur*. The speeches, which may be regarded essentially as due to the literary imagination of the author[8], are primary examples of the increased freedom of the author in his second work. A primary reason for this difference in technique between the two works lies in the fact that, whereas in writing the Gospel the author had predecessors whose example he followed, he had not such predecessors for the task of describing the progress of the Christian message from Jerusalem to Rome. This means, therefore, that the critic must use a slightly dif-ferent approach to the criticism of Acts than that which has been found fruitful in the case of the Gospels. Dibelius designates this new approach "Stilkritik".

As a starting point for the style-critical analysis of the Book of Acts, Dibelius takes the central portion of the book (13.1–14.28; 15.35–21.16) concerning the missionary travels of Paul. Here he thinks he can discern evidence for the existence of an itinerary-document which indicated the places where Paul stopped on his journeys and which probably originally included brief notes con-cerning the foundation of churches and the results of his evange-listic activity. This itinerary, he argues, provided the author with his framework for this part of his narrative[9]. To this series of notes Luke[10] made his own additions and possibly inserted other tradi-

[97]

[98]

references to the writings of Dibelius which follow are to the fourth German edition of these collected essays, unless indicated to the contrary.

[7] I see no evidence that Dibelius changed his mind on any point, major or minor, from the views put forward in this initial essay. In the subsequent essays he seeks to demonstrate his major theses at greater length, or is content simply to restate them. This results in a great deal of tedious repetition over the course of the essays.   [8] See below, pp. 214–24.

[9] He does not regard the presence of "we" in this and the latter part of Acts as in itself sufficient to determine a source or tradition.

[10] Although he does not commit himself in this first essay, Dibelius regards

tions. Among his own compositions are the speeches in particular, but also editorial observations (such as 14.22—23 and 19.20) and other items which cannot be determined with certainty, since it is impossible to determine the exact extent of the itinerary. Among the traditional elements which the author inserts into this framework are the stories which are complete in themselves and which, therefore, give evidence of having been handed down independently[11].

Dibelius finds little trace of similar frameworks for the other parts of the book. Concerning the remaining section of Acts, he writes:

[99] Reden und Redeszenen sind es, die diese Kapitel beherrschen: die grosse Rede an das Volk vor der Burg Antonia, die Streitszene im Synedrium, das Rededuell zwischen Tertullus und Paulus und die höchst ausführlich eingeleitete Rede vor Agrippa. Das alles lässt vermuten, dass hier der Schriftsteller gegenüber der Tradition die Oberhand hat. Diese Vermutung wird bestätigt durch die Beobachtung, dass einige dieser Reden ganz offenbar auf den Fortgang der Handlung keinen Einfluss ausüben, sondern lediglich epideiktischen Charakter haben (14).

Thus as soon as Paul desires to speak the raging crowd is silent, [100] but it renews its shouting as soon as "es die Regie des Schriftstellers zur Unterstreichung des pointierten Schlusses brauchen kann" (14). This makes it clear that the speeches are intended for the reader, rather than for the original audiences. The same judgment also applies to the narrative of the sea voyage in chapters 27 and 28: [101] "Trotzdem hier wieder die 1. Person Pluralis die Führung hat, steckt in der Schilderung des Schiffbruchs mit ihren technischen Einzelheiten weit mehr Literatur als Beobachtung" (14)[12]. Whether the author was an eyewitness of the journey or not, it is clear, argues Dibelius, that the account of Paul's voyage and shipwreck was elaborated by the author according to traditional literary models of similar exciting tales.

The situation in the early chapters of Acts is similar, suggests

---

the traditional ascription of the authorship to "Luke" as very probable. Cf. *Aufsätze*, pp. 79—80, 85 n., 92, 96, 108.

[11] See below, pp. 205—6.

[12] Here Dibelius refers to Eduard Norden, *Agnostos Theos: Untersuchungen zur Formgeschichte religiöser Rede* (Leipzig, 1913), upon whom he is dependent here and in his understanding of the speeches in Acts. J. Wellhausen (see Dibelius' note, p. 15) had made this suggestion as early as 1907. E. Haenchen and H. Conzelmann (see below) have followed up the suggestion of Dibelius with detailed argument in favor of a strictly "literary" understanding of the sea voyage to Rome. But see the criticism of A. D. Nock, *Gnomon* 25 (1953), p. 499.

Dibelius. Here, it seems, the author is writing without the benefit
of a unifying framework: there is no continuous account of the fortunes of the Jerusalem church, but rather a series of loosely connected stories, speeches, and trial scenes, linked together by the
author's general summaries. Tradition provided the author with no
connected description of the course of the inner development of the
Jerusalem church and by the nature of the case was unable to do
so[13]. The same is true for the section which runs from 6.1 to 12.25,
which contains a mixture of traditional material and the author's
own literary invention, thus underlining the fact,

dass es nicht angeht, das ganze Buch restlos aus ein paar Quellen abzu-
leiten oder auch den Anteil des Autors in allen Teilen des Werkes gleich-
mässig nach einem einheitlichen Rezept herauszuarbeiten. Die Frage, was
Tradition, was Komposition sei, muss bei verschiedenen Abschnitten, ja oft
auch bei den einzelnen Berichten gesondert gestellt werden (17).   [102]

Besides the itinerary-document, which forms the framework of
the central section of the Book of Acts, Dibelius considers the main
items of tradition to be a number of small units of tradition which
were handed down independently and which the author has inserted
into his narrative at various places, often embellishing them to some
degree. All who are familiar with his approach to the Gospels will
recognize in this Dibelius' application of the *formgeschichtliche
Methode* to the Book of Acts.

Thirteen of these small literary units, or independent stories, are
isolated by Dibelius on the basis of *Stilkritik* and apart from a
detailed examination of the narrative as a whole (18—28)[14]. They
are the story of the raising of Tabitha (9.36—42), the conversion of
Cornelius (10.1—11.18), the healing of the lame man at the gate
of the Temple (3.1—10), the conversion of the Ethiopian eunuch
(8.26—39), the sin and punishment of Ananias and Sapphira (5.1
—11), the contest between Elymas and Paul (13.8—12), the story
of Simon the magician (8.9—24), the resuscitation of Eutychus (20.
7—12), the misfortune of the sons of Sceva (19.14—16), the death
of Herod (12.20—23), the fortunes of Paul and Barnabas at Lystra
(14.8—18), Peter's escape from prison (12.5—17), and the miraculous experiences of Paul and Silas in prison at Philippi (16.25—34).

Dibelius concludes that, although they have their similarities, the
stories of Acts are generally different from the type to be found in

---

[13] "Wer bedenkt, wie wenig die Gedanken dieser ältesten Christen auf die   [103]
Bewahrung des Geschichtsverlaufs eingestellt waren, wird sich über den Mangel
einer Tradition nicht wundern" (15). This is one of a number of Dibelius' basic
assumptions which some scholars would question.
[14] Cf. his essay in *TR*, N. F. 3 (1931), pp. 233—41.

the Gospels. For example, the story of Tabitha is told in an edifying style like those of the Gospels which Dibelius calls *Paradigmen*; yet it is different, especially in the abundance of personal details —

[*104*] "Namensnennung, Charakterschilderung, Beweis ihrer Tugend durch die für die Witwen angefertigten Kleidungsstücke, vielleicht auch ihres Ansehens durch die ausdrückliche Erwähnung der Pflege des

[*105*] Leichnams" (18). This leads him to this conclusion: "Wir haben es mit einer an Petrus und Tabitha persönlich interessierten 'Legende' zu tun" (18). Similarly, the story of Cornelius is also a legend, but contrary to the situation in the case of the story of Tabitha and others which have been repeated with little or no embellishment[15], it has been greatly worked-up by the author, who uses it to argue a theological point (that the Gentiles have a right to be converted)[16]. Several conflicting traditions have been combined by the author in the story of Elymas, whereas part of the story of Simon has been omitted and new elements (concerning Peter and John) have been inserted into the narrative. Three "secular" anecdotes have been introduced into the narrative by the author, who modifies them only slightly or not at all. With the exception of the story of Cornelius, which has a large element of the author's own composition in it, these stories can be removed from their context in the Book of Acts without causing any real damage to the flow of the narrative.

With the exception of these few stories and a few additional notes scattered throughout the narrative, Dibelius regards the rest of Acts to be primarily due to the author's own composition, the result of his creative ability as a writer. He "solves" the problem of historicity by excluding the question from the realm of his present investigation. The following statement is typical of the opinion which

[*106*] he expresses many times in the course of his various essays: "Was an Geschichtlichem zugrunde liegt, lässt sich vom isolierten Einzelfall aus schwer ermitteln und soll auch nicht Gegenstand dieser Untersuchung sein" (18). Thus he closes his essay with the observation that his purpose has only been to classify and assess the author's work as literature and then to analyze the style of some of the important stories, not to judge the historical value of any part of the book.

---

[15] Others which belong to this category are the stories of the healing of the lame man, the conversion of the eunuch, the experiences of Paul and Barnabas at Lystra, Peter's prison break, and the Philippian jail experience of Paul and Silas.

[16] Dibelius thinks the original story was simply an example of the power of God in an independent conversion of a "God-fearing" Gentile. Its historical setting and interpretation as having theological significance is due to Luke. See especially *Aufsätze*, pp. 96–107, and below, pp. 208–9.

Nach der Geschichtlichkeit oder Ungeschichtlichkeit all dieser Erzählungen habe ich dabei absichtlich nicht gefragt; denn mit der Zuteilung zu
den Gattungen "Legende", "Novelle" oder "Anekdote" ist nur über den
Vortrag des Erzählers, nicht über die Wirklichkeit des Erzählten das Urteil
gesprochen. Aber wenigstens soviel darf als Ergebnis dieses analytischen
Versuchs gebucht werden: dass in der Apostelgeschichte die Frage der
historischen Zuverlässigkeit je nach den einzelnen Teilen verschieden zu
beurteilen ist, anders dort, wo der Autor das Itinerar benutzte, als dort, wo
er nur durch Sammelberichte verschiedene Traditionen verband, anders bei
den Legenden als bei den literarischen Reden, aber auch wieder verschie-
denartig bei den einzelnen Legenden im Vergleich miteinander. *Alle diese
Fragen können erst entschieden werden, nachdem die Stilkritik ihr Werk
getan hat;* wer jene Probleme vorzeitig lösen will, gefährdet noch mehr als
die Reinheit der stilkritischen Methode, er trübt sich das Verständnis der
Geschichten, die innerlich den Problemen der Geschichtswissenschaft so
weltenfern sind. Und nur wenn man erst einmal absieht von dem, was wir
als Fragen an diese Erzählungen heranbringen, lernt man lauschen auf
das, was die Erzähler zu sagen haben (28)[17].

Having read this and at the same time having discerned (quite
rightly) that Dibelius has assumed very negative conclusions concerning the historical value of the Book of Acts *before* he began his
"style-critical" study of the narrative, the reader has the suspicion
that he has had a great confidence trick played on him. Those who
have read the earlier chapters of this monograph will quite naturally
wish to know what Dibelius does with the writings of Ramsay, Harnack, Wikenhauser, and Meyer, and the evidence they had brought
forward in support of the high standard of historical accuracy on
the part of the author of the Book of Acts. The answer is: *Nothing!*
The contributions of these men and the problems with which they
were concerned are excluded *by definition* from   consideration[18].
Their approach was, so Dibelius would say, entirely wrong-headed.
They asked the wrong questions and were, therefore, led astray in
their investigations. However, in spite of his claim to a new approach to the problem and an attitude of aloofness toward the question of historicity, it is quite clear that Dibelius begins his work
with — indeed, his whole approach is presupposed by — a negative
judgment of the historical value of the Book of Acts which he has

---

[17] Italics mine.
[18] The *Aufsätze* contain two, quite incidental, references to the writings of
Ramsay (62n., 73), a few more to E. Meyer (10, 14n., 29, 39n., 60n., 91n.,
125n.) and still a few more to Harnack (12n., 29, 39n., 50n., 57n., 61n., 65n., 71,
80n., 93n., 119, 170). Harnack is the only one of the three with whom he seems
to be intimately familiar, and, consequently, it is he who has influenced Dibelius to some degree (particularly regarding his linguistic arguments and defence
of the Lucan authorship).

inherited from nineteenth century critical orthodoxy. And neither here nor elsewhere does he consider it worth his while to enter into dialogue with those critics who have given good reasons for a different opinion[19]!

The essay on the conversion of Cornelius (Acts 10.1—11.18)[20] provides one with a detailed illustration of the view of Dibelius concerning the interrelationship between tradition and composition in the Book of Acts. He regards this story as one of the small units of tradition which have been considerably embellished by the author. To the original story (which probably stems from the tradition of Hellenistic churches which had special interest in Caesarea and in the contents of the story) Luke has made a number of major additions. First he has added the speech in which Peter justifies himself before the apostles and brethren in Jerusalem (11.1—18).

[108]   In der Erzählung selbst spielt die Tischgemeinschaft gar keine wesentliche Rolle. Cornelius ist in der alten Überlieferung ein Heide, aber ein frommer und gottesfürchtiger, der um dieser Vorzüge willen von Gott einer besonderen, durch einen Engel überbrachten Botschaft gewürdigt wird. Die Überlieferung redet mit aller Sympathie von ihm und dürfte es kaum auf eine Selbstverteidigung des Petrus wegen seines Umgangs mit diesem Manne abgesehen haben. Diese Rechtfertigung hat jemand hinzugefügt, der der Geschichte prinzipielle Bedeutung geben wollte (96).

This "some one" was, of course, Luke[21].

The second addition by the author is Peter's speech of 10.34—43.
[109]   "In einer unter den Christen erzählten Legende von der Bekehrung eines Centurio kann eine solche verhältnismässig lange Rede nicht ihren Platz gehabt haben" 97). Furthermore, the analogy of the other speeches in Acts shows that the speeches are the literary com-

---

[19] One might think that his essay on "Die· Apostelgeschichte als Geschichtsquelle" (*Aufsätze*, pp. 91—95) would attempt to give some sort of an answer to those who defend a different view of Acts, but it does not. In it Dibelius simply spells out in detail the negative historical conclusions which can be read between the lines of his 1923 essay. His only argument is that the older
[110]   approach to the problem considered the question subjectively. By contrast, "Die 'formgeschichtliche' Betrachtung die aus Form und Stil der Überlieferung auf ihre Herkunft und ihre Entstehungsbedingungen schliesst, versucht, *auf ihre Weise mittels Beobachtungen von einer gewissen Allgemeingültigkeit zu minder subjektiven und jederzeit nachprüfbaren Massstäben der Geschichtlichkeit* zu gelangen" (91)! (emphasis mine) What can the critic say in reply?
[20] "Die Bekehrung des Cornelius", *CN* 11 (1947), pp. 50—65; = *Aufsätze* pp. 96—108.
[111]   [21] "Lukas handelt dabei als schriftstellernder Historiker, nur eben nicht als Historiker in unserem Sinn, der zeigen will, wie es wirklich gewesen ist, sondern als antiker Schriftsteller, der das Bedeutsame heraushebt und eventuell durch Reden unterstreicht" (97).

position of the author, intended for the readers, to show them the importance of an event or to impress upon them certain ideas pertaining to the faith[22].

Ob Lukas gewusst hat, dass bei dieser Gelegenheit eine Rede gehalten wurde und in welcher Art, wird sich nie mit Sicherheit ausmachen lassen. Es ist auch unwichtig, dergleichen Fragen nachzugehen, denn gebunden an diese Kenntnis wäre Lukas keinesfalls gewesen. Wir haben ja auch bereits festgestellt .... dass er selbst eine längere Rede mitgeteilt hat (97)[23]. [*112*]

Once again it is "eine literarisch-theologische, keine geschichtliche Aufgabe", which the author of Acts wishes to fulfill (98). [*113*]

Thirdly, it is probable that Luke is responsible for the vision of the clean and unclean animals in Acts 10.9—16. And from this it follows, fourthly, that 10.27—29 is also the composition of Luke, since it refers to the vision. In addition to these four items there are a number of other smaller points which were probably added to the narrative by Luke, such as the notes concerning the companions of Peter, who travelled to Caesarea with him as witnesses (10.23b; 10.45; 11.12b), and the concluding half-verse of chapter ten (10. 48b).

In this way a relatively brief and simple legend about a Roman centurion was greatly worked-up by Luke for a theological purpose. What was originally a straightforward legend of an individual conversion, "an einfacher Schönheit der Legende vom äthiopischen Eunuchen vergleichbar" (105), is elevated to the level of a theological principle. That is, what was at first simply an independent story, floating freely in the Church's tradition, of a single conversion with no great significance in itself is used by Luke as evidence for the view that it is God's will that Gentiles should be received into the Church apart from the obligation to keep the Law of Moses[24]. Here, as elsewhere in the Book of Acts, "Lukas ... auf die exakte Wiedergabe der Tradition verzichtet um einer höheren geschichtlichen Wahrheit willen" (107). [*114*] [*115*]

Perhaps the most influential and important of all Dibelius' essays are the two which are devoted to the problem of the speeches in Acts. The first of these, easily the most carefully argued and docu-

---

[22] See below, pp. 214—24.

[23] This statement is typical of Dibelius. He has not, of course, established anything; he has merely stated an opinion.

[24] Dibelius regards the allusion in Acts 15 to Peter's preaching to Gentiles ἀφ' ἡμερῶν ἀρχαίων (15.7) as further proof that the author alone is responsible for the theological significance the story of Cornelius has in the narrative of Acts (10.1—4). Cf. his essay, "Das Apostelkonzil", *TLZ* 72 (1947), pp. 193—98; = *Aufsätze*, pp. 84—90.

mented contribution from his pen, is on Paul's Areopagus address; it first appeared in 1939[25].

In his 1923 essay on the "style-criticism" of Acts, Dibelius expressed the conviction that the speeches were the part of Acts which could be most confidently regarded as the author's own contribution, because they "aus überlieferungsgeschichtlichen Gründen schwerlich tradiert sein können, literarisch ihre Parallelen bei den Historikern haben und in ihrem Inhalt oft genug einen späteren Standpunkt zum Ausdruck bringen (15,10.11.19—20; 20,25.29 f.)" (10)[26]. With this basic understanding of the nature of the speeches (which was essentially the same as that held in the nineteenth century by the Tübingen critics, Overbeck and the other radical critics, and by critical orthodoxy (for the most part) at the end of the century), Dibelius turns to a detailed consideration of Paul's speech at Athens (Acts 17.19—34), which, in his view, "bezeichnet und will bezeichnen einen Höhepunkt des Buches" (29). His main thesis is that the Areopagus address is "eine hellenistische Rede von der wahren Gotteserkenntnis" (54), "die Synthese von rationalem Hellenismus und christlicher Missionsbotschaft" (69). Its conceptual background is Greek philosophy rather than the Old Testament. In fact, the idea of the knowledge of, and man's natural kinship to, God contained in the speech are in stark contrast to the ideas of the Old Testament. It borrows not merely phrases and a few lines of poetry from Greek writers (as all commentators recognize), but it is Hellenistic throughout. Dibelius backs up these statements with extensive reference to what he regards to be parallels in Greek literature and thought, mainly Stoic[27].

[116]

[117]

[118]

[119]

[25] *Paulus auf dem Areopag, Sitzungsberichte der Heidelberger Akademie der Wissenschaften: Philosophisch-historische Klasse* (Heidelberg, 1939); = *Aufsätze*, pp. 29—70. "Paulus in Athen", *Forschungen und Fortschritte* 15 (1939), pp. 210—11; = *Aufsätze*, pp. 71—75, is a brief summary of the general conclusions arrived at in the longer essay.

[26] He makes the qualification that older formulae of a kerygmatic or liturgical nature may have been used by the author in his composition, however. In a footnote he comments: "Die Möglichkeit, dass auch Nachrichten über wirklich gehaltene Reden einzelner seiner Helden an Lukas gekommen sein können, ist natürlich nicht zu bestreiten. Nur verrät sich in den Reden der Apostelgeschichte das Bestreben zu typisieren, Beispiele und Vorbilder der christlichen Predigt zu geben viel mehr als die Erinnerung an bestimmte Personen und das bei bestimmten Gelegenheiten von ihnen Gesagte" (11n.).

[120]

[27] Dibelius is heavily dependent on the work of Eduard Norden (see n.12, above) in this connection. He differs from Norden, however, in a number of points, particularly in his rejection of Norden's view that the speech was an interpolation into the narrative of Acts. See B. Gärtner, *The Areopagus Speech and Natural Revelation* (Uppsala, 1955), pp. 38—41, for a brief summary of the views of Norden and the earlier discussion.

Not only are the ideas of the speech in clear contrast to the teaching of the Old Testament, but they are also foreign to the rest of the New Testament (with the possible exception of Acts 14.15—17) — and especially to the thought of Paul. Dibelius will not allow the harmonization of the ideas expressed here with those expressed in the Pauline epistles: the "natural theology" of Romans 1, which is often held to be parallel to the thought of Acts 17, is quite different from that of Acts 17.

Der Widerspruch zwischen Römerbrief und Areopagrede ist deutlich. Beide erwähnen zwar die Erkenntnis Gottes aus Schöpfung oder Ordnung der Welt; aber nach der Rede führt diese Erkenntnis zum ahnenden "Begreifen" und Verehren Gottes, nach dem Brief führt sie zwar zur Kenntnis Gottes, aber zugleich zur Verkennung seiner Herrschaft, zur Verweigerung des echten Gottesdienstes und zur Verstrickung in falschen Bilderdienst. Vom Irrtum des Bilderdienstes ist im Röm. 1,23.25 in empörtem Ton die Rede, Act. 17,29 korrigiert ihn in mahnendem und zurechtweisendem Ton (56—57). [121]

Perhaps the most important proof of this is in the speaker's reference to non-Christians as members of the family of God (17.28)[28]. "Paulus hätte so niemals geschrieben. Er ist zu tief durchdrungen von der Überzeugung, dass der Mensch Gott entfremdet ist (Röm. 1—3), und zwar wesenhaft, und nicht erst, nachdem jeder einzelne einmal gegen Gottes Forderung verstossen hat" (57)[29]. [122]

Dibelius finds even the setting of the sermon, which Ramsay, Harnack, Meyer, and a host of other classical scholars and historians have regarded as too full of accurate allusions to the historical situation in Athens to be unhistorical, to be largely the free literary creation of the author. The very items which these scholars would point to as evidence for the authentic nature of the narrative — the portrayal of the character of the Athenians, the Agora, the Areo-

---

[28] But surely, in spite of Dibelius' contentions, the phrase τοῦ γὰρ καὶ γένος εἰμέν is to be interpreted in the context of Paul's speech as a reference to the fact that man has been created by God, rather than to his natural kinship with the divine. Even Clement of Alexandria, who, with his philosophical bent, might have been tempted to understand it in a Hellenistic way, interprets this as a reference to God's creation of man (see Gärtner (n. 27), p. 194). Understood in this way there is no contradiction at all to the thought of Paul's epistles.

[29] Albert Schweitzer had expressed the conviction in two brief sentences in his *Geschichte der Paulinischen Forschung* (Tübingen, 1911), p. 74, that the author of Acts must take the complete responsibility for the Paul of the Areopagus address. In his *Die Mystik des Apostels Paulus* (Tübingen, 1930), pp. 6—10, he expands it to five pages. This seems to be the ultimate source of the view which Dibelius defends at length in his essay.

pagus[30], the Epicureans, and that typically Athenian catchword, σπερμολόγος — are considered by Dibelius to be evidence in favor of the view that the whole of the narrative is the author's literary composition (60—62)[31]. "Die Schilderung Athens und der Athener ist offenbar im Vorblick auf die Rede abgefasst" (61). Luke, finding a brief note in his itinerary-document which indicated that Paul paid a visit to Athens, possibly that he engaged in some evangelistic work with little success, possibly even mentioning the names of two willing listeners[32], takes this occasion to portray the hero of his story as preaching a "typical" sermon to Gentiles in the setting of the heart of Greek culture — Athens.

The Areopagus speech of Acts 17, then, is the composition of the author, who takes his cue from Greek philosophy rather than Old Testament revelation. It is intended to provide a model for Christian preaching to pagans in the author's own day, rather than to be understood as a sermon which Paul actually preached three decades or so earlier. In putting these words into the mouth of Paul the author, perhaps unwittingly, wholly misrepresented the message of the historical Paul and, indeed, paved the way for the future misunderstanding of him by the Church in the following centuries[33].

Dibelius' essay on the *Areopagitica* is, indeed, an impressive piece

[30] Dibelius insists on the interpretation of the Areopagus (17.19 and 22) as the hill, rather than the council, on "literary" (rather than topographical) grounds (62—64). He is followed in this view by E. Haenchen, *Die Apostelgeschichte*, KEK, 4th ed. (Göttingen, 1961), pp. 456—58; and H. Conzelmann, *Die Apostelgeschichte*, HNT 7 (Tübingen, 1963), p. 97. However, most scholars who accept the narrative as essentially historical understand "the Areopagus" to mean the council, rather than the hill (cf. Bruce, *Acts*, pp. 333, 335).

[31] Cf. A. D. Nock's comment: "Brilliant as is the picture of Athens, it makes on me the impression of being based on literature, which was easy to find..." (*Gnomon* 25 (1953), p. 506). But neither Nock nor any one else I have read who makes this point gives an example of a piece of Greek fiction which contains similar historical allusions to Athens which are based on the author's knowledge gained through reading. And it is quite unlikely that the author of Acts would have had access to a reference library!

[32] Acts 17.17 and 34 are probably remnants from the itinerary. "Vielleicht hat übrigens die Nennung des Areopagiten in dem Itinerar schon auf den Verfasser der Apostelgeschichte eine bestimmte Wirkung ausgeübt. Vielleicht hat sie ihn veranlasst, die Rede auf den Areopag zu verlegen und so der klassischen Heidenpredigt ... auch eine klassische Kanzel zu geben" (69).

[33] Cf. *Aufsätze*, pp. 59—60, 68—79. Dibelius' view that "der Areopagredner ist der Vorläufer der Apologeten" (59) of the second century and his negative attitude toward the common features of the Book of Acts and the writings of the Apologists are very important for the subsequent German criticism. What Dibelius says in regard to the Areopagus address in particular is later applied (by Haenchen and Conzelmann, among others) to the theology of Luke in general.

[123]

[124]

[125]

of work; and its arguments, when taken by themselves, are extremely hard to resist. However, "when taken by themselves" is the operative phrase. When one actually examines some of the alleged parallels to Greek literature and philosophy which Dibelius brings forward in support of his interpretation, grave questions are raised concerning the objectivity of his methodology[34]. But more important are the true parallels which he has altogether overlooked — parallels in the Old Testament and in Jewish-Hellenistic thought[35].

The work which has demonstrated the untenable nature of Dibelius' interpretation of Paul's speech is a study by the Scandinavian scholar, Bertil Gärtner[36]. Whereas Dibelius interprets the speeches as a collection of miscellaneous ideas, lacking essential homogeneity, based on Stoic philosophy, Gärtner attempts to demonstrate the homogeneity of its thought and that its background is the Old Testament and traditional Jewish apologetics. He argues his thesis in a most careful and minute manner, taking seriously the possibility that the background might be that suggested by Dibelius, but concluding quite the opposite. Rather than an exercise in Greek philosophical rhetoric with a Christian tinge, it is a Christian adaptation of Jewish-Diaspora preaching. The quotations and allusions to Greek literature and ideas are in this tradition, rather than the pagan-Hellenistic; words and phrases are borrowed from pagan writers inasmuch as they can be understood in a Jewish manner, but the *meaning* given to them is quite different from that of their original context[37]. The technique is that of any good preacher who

---

[34] Dibelius' methodology calls to mind the monograph of N. W. DeWitt, *St. Paul and Epicurus* (Minneapolis, 1954), in which he lists numerous "parallels" between the ethics of Paul and the followers of Epicurus in the attempt to prove that Paul was greatly influenced by the latter. One wonders whether or not DeWitt's views would have been more influential had he been a New Testament critic rather than a classicist.

[35] More recent German scholarship following in the Dibelius tradition, although accepting his view that the speech is a free creation of the author and that Paul could never have spoken in such a manner, has given due recognition to the fact that there is an Old Testament flavor (one specific quotation!) in the speech and that all the ideas expressed can be paralleled in Hellenistic Judaism. See especially H. Conzelmann, "Die Rede des Paulus auf dem Areopag", *Gymnasium Helveticum* 12 (1958), pp. 18–32; also his commentary, pp. 96–104. E. Haenichen, *Die Apostelgeschichte* (1961), pp. 453–68, recognizes this to a lesser degree. Although both writers list the study of Gärtner (n. 36) in their bibliographies, they give no evidence of having been at all impressed by his work.

[36] *The Areopagus Speech and Natural Revelation* (Uppsala, 1955) — nearly 250 pages of tightly packed argument!

[37] Two years prior to Gärtner's monograph, A. D. Nock (*Gnomon* 25, pp. 505–6) had pointed out Dibelius' neglect of the Jewish framework in

seeks points of contact with his audience in order to gain a hearing for his message.

Gärtner goes on to argue that Dibelius and others have too easily dismissed the Pauline character of the speech. The speech, when understood against its more probable Jewish background, contains no item which really contradicts what is known of Paul's theology (248–52). Although it is not possible to parallel every item of the speech to a similar idea or phrase in the epistles of Paul, it is possible to observe a number of important parallels. However, it is unreasonable to suppose that the few letters of Paul which are included in the canon of the New Testament contain everything which the Apostle could have said.

Gärtner does not defend the view that the speech is a verbatim report of an actual address by the Apostle (no one does this). The literary form is Luke's, as all recognize; but it is based on solid tradition. The actual contents may be Paul's — at least, this is not impossible. And although not all will be convinced by the arguments brought forward by Gärtner, he has presented a case which cannot (or, at least, *should* not) be ignored[38].

The second of Dibelius' important essays on the speeches in Acts is probably the best known and most celebrated of all his contributions to *Actaforschung*. "The Speeches of Acts and Ancient Historiography"[39] was read to the Heidelberg Academy of Sciences in 1944, but was only published in 1949, two years after the death of the author. As H. J. Cadbury[40] had provided the Anglo-Saxon world with the classic defence of the view that the speeches of Acts are the literary creations of the author, so Dibelius is responsible for the classic statement of this position in German.

Dibelius begins his essay by contrasting the differences in point of view between the historian of olden times and the historian of today. In writing history today, he contends, we would expect any quotation of speeches made by the historical personages to represent the actual words spoken by the persons involved. And even when these are included by the historian they do not normally have any
[126] great significance. Not so with the Greek or Roman historian. "Eine

which the Hellenistic phrases are embedded, and that some of the ideas have no true parallels in Greek thought.

[38] R. P. C. Hanson, *The Acts* (Oxford, 1967), pp. 177–83, gives an excellent (though brief) account of the main points brought forward by both Dibelius and Gärtner and decides in favor of the latter.

[39] *Die Reden der Apostelgeschichte und die antike Geschichtsschreibung, Sitzungsberichte der Heidelberger Akademie der Wissenschaften: Philosophisch-historische Klasse* (Heidelberg, 1949); = *Aufsätze*, pp. 120–62.

[40] "The Speeches of Acts", *BC* 5 (1933), pp. 402–27.

Verpflichtung, nur oder vorzugsweise den Wortlaut der wirklich ge-
haltenen Rede wiederzugeben, empfindet er gar nicht" (121)[41]. The
historian of antiquity incorporates speeches into narrative with a
view to the impression they will make on the reader. He may wish
to give the reader (1) an insight into the total solution, (2) an insight into the meaning which transcends the facts of history, (3) an
insight into the character of the speaker, or (4) an insight into ideas
which are introduced to explain the situation, or which are only
loosely connected with it. Another purpose of the introduction of
some speeches into the narrative was simply to further the action of
the narrative in order to maintain the interest of the reader.

Dibelius refers to passages in Thucydides[42], Dionysius of Hali-

---

[41] "Vielleicht weiss er nicht einmal, ob damals eine Rede gehalten wurde;   [127]
zuweilen weiss er es, kennt aber den Text nicht, kann ihn vielleicht gar nicht
kennen, wenn die Rede etwa auf der Feindseite in geschlossenem Kreise gehalten wurde. Und selbst wenn der Wortlaut bekannt war, so übernahm der
Historiker ihn nicht in sein Werk" (121). As proof of this last statement Dibelius offers the well-known speech of Claudius about the conferring of the *jus
honorum* upon the people of Gaul, which is preserved in *CIL* xiii, 1668, but in
a different form in Tacitus' *Annals* (xi. 24); the speeches which Josephus in the
Antiquities puts into the mouths of the patriarchs, and the fact that Josephus
reproduces a speech of Herod in two entirely different forms. Now, no one will
argue against the view that Josephus was wholly unscrupulous in his handling
of speeches; however, it is worthy of note that the example referred to from
Tacitus is *not* an example of a free literary *creation*, but rather of a free
revision (as Dibelius himself admits in the final footnote to the main body of
the essay [157n.]). See *Cornelii Taciti Annalium*, ed. with intro. and notes by
H. Furneaux, 2nd ed. rev. by H. F. Pelham and C. D. Fisher (Oxford, 1907) 2,
pp. 54—60, for the text of the surviving fragments of the published speech and
a brief comparison of the two versions. "On the whole, the substance of the
existing portions [of the inscribed speech] may be said to have been given
[by Tacitus], and the fact that they are represented by but a few sentences
would go to prove that the whole speech (as indeed the fragments themselves
suggest) was long and discursive, and could only be brought into a space pro-
portionate to the narrative of the Annals by much omission and abridgement"
(54—55). Thus the style and expression of the speech as found in the *Annals*
belong (with the exception of a few verbal parallels) to Tacitus. The matter of
the speech has been condensed, re-arranged, and adapted; but the historian has
remained true to the essential ideas or the original. This and other references
cited by Dibelius in support of his understanding of the handling of speeches
by ancient historical writers actually run counter to his argument.

[42] While admitting the ambiguity of the famous passage in Thucydides,
where he discusses his methodology in the handling of speeches (I.22.1),
Dibelius makes Thucydides say that his chief concern was to indicate the
character of the situation, rather than to give an accurate summary of what
was actually said. This seems to me to be a rather perverse interpretation of
the statement of Thucydides. It is perhaps noteworthy that he omits the classic
study of the speeches of Thucydides by A. W. Gomme ("The Speeches in
Thucydides", in his *Essays in Greek History and Literature* (Oxford, 1937),

carnassus, and Polybius[43] as evidence for this general agreement among the historians of ancient times:

> Die wichtigste Pflicht, vor die sich der Autor gestellt sieht, ist nicht die [l.
> für uns im Vordergrunde stehende Feststellung der tatsächlich gehaltenen
> Rede, sondern die sinnvolle Einfügung der Reden in den Organismus des
> ganzen Werkes. Auch wenn er den Wortlaut der gehaltenen Rede erin-
> nern, erkunden oder irgendwo lesen kann, wird der Autor sich nicht ver-
> pflichtet fühlen, ihn aufzunehmen. Er wird ihn höchstens benutzen bei der
> Komposition des grossen oder kleinen Redegebildes, mit dem er seine Dar-
> stellung ausstattet. Dieses Gebilde aber wird entweder das Ganze beleben
> — wenn direkte Rede den nüchternen Bericht ersetzt — oder es wird als
> Kunstmittel bestimmten Zwecken des Autors dienen (125).

Having said this, in the second section of the essay Dibelius moves on to consider whether the Book of Acts can really be considered to be a work of literature in the same way that the ancient Greek historians are (125—29). If not, then it is questionable whether one can expect the speeches to have been written in this tradition. At first glance, the Gospel of Luke would seem to tell against this theory. The four Gospels are obviously written with rather simple, believing communities in view — not for the eye of the educated public. The speeches of Jesus in the Synoptics, for examples, are compilations of sayings, not "speeches" in the sense of rhetoric. And the speeches of the Gospel of John belong to an Oriental setting and are quite different from the speeches in Acts. Nevertheless, Dibelius finds in the literary prologue of the Gospel (1.1—4), where the work is dedicated to a person of rank (κράτιστος Θεόφιλος) who would be thereby under an obligation to distribute the book to the general public[44], and in the literary form of the Book of Acts, where

---

pp. 156—89; cf. his *A Historical Commentary on Thucydides* (Oxford, 1945) 1, pp. 139—48) from his exclusively German bibliographical note on *Thukydides-Forschung* (122 n.). See below, pp. 224—26.

[43] The reference to Polybius XII.25.i is, again, misleading. Dibelius lists Polybius' criticism of Timaeus as *evidence for* the view that it was the accepted custom for historians to freely compose speeches. However, Polybius is, in fact, criticizing Timaeus for doing this very thing and makes a point of the necessity of the historian's being true to *what a speaker actually said* (XII.25.i.8)! Cf. F. W. Walbank, *A Historical Commentary on Polybius* 1 (Oxford, 1957), pp. 13—14; 2 (1967), pp. 397—99. Polybius steadfastly condemns the custom whereby historians put rhetorical compositions into the mouths of their characters (see references in Walbank). See also below, p. 226.

[44] Nock (in *Gnomon* 25, pp. 501—2) is of the opinion that Dibelius' suggestion involves a basic "misunderstanding of book-dedications and indeed of the nature of publication in antiquity". Books were generally dedicated to some individual on the basis of friendship, or to compliment, or to lend some added dignity to the work. In the case of works which were dedicated to emperors, as was often the case, it should not be imagined that the recipient would be under

the author practices the historian's technique in a much freer manner, evidence for the fact that the author has literary aspirations. In contrast to the Third Gospel, the Book of Acts was not written, in the first instance, with the Church in view; rather it was intended for the educated public who were accustomed to reading works of history[45]. On the other hand, the Gospel of Luke had from the beginning a two-fold audience in mind: the Church *and* the educated reading public. The fact that the Book of Acts had, at first, only the latter audience in view is the reason that it seems to have found its place in the Church's canon at a later date and independently of the Gospel[46].

Having established the fact of the author's literary aspirations, Dibelius turns to the actual speeches in Acts (129—42)[47]. His first conclusion from a brief survey of the material is that Luke makes no attempt to prepare the reader to make an independent judgment for himself by quoting both sides of a controversy — as some of the Greek historians did[48]. Normally, the reader hears only one side of the story. Even in the case of the verbal dual between Paul and Tertullus (24.2—21) the more detailed speech by Paul is destined to prevail. "Der Autor will gar nicht parteilos sein, er will ja   [129] für seine Sache werben; es wird sich zeigen, dass darin ein ganz wesentlicher Unterschied von der antiken Geschichtsschreibung liegt; Lukas erzählt, aber indem er berichtet, predigt er auch" (131)[49]

any obligation to distribute copies. "What dedication did mean is that the author had put his work into final shape and was addressing it to a wider circle ..." Nock refers the reader to Cadbury's, *The Making of Luke-Acts*, pp. 201—4, and H. I. Marrou, "La technique de l'édition à l'époque patristique", *VC* 3 (1949), pp. 208—24, for a more accurate understanding of the dedication and dissemination of books in antiquity.

[45] Contrast Easton, *Early Christianity*, pp. 33—41.

[46] The major proof for this view is the two-fold textual tradition of Acts. "Daran erkennt man, dass dieser Text noch lange 'frei' war, d. h. nicht der   [130] Zucht unterstand, wie sie für das Grosse und Ganze eines Buches der dauernde Gebrauch im öffentlichen Gottesdienst ausübt, der zwar mancherlei kleine Varianten hervorbringen mag, schwerere Eingriffe in den Text aber ausschliesst" (128n.). This view is developed in his essay, "The Text of Acts: An Urgent Critical Task", *JR* 21 (1941), pp. 421—31; = (in German) *Aufsätze*, pp. 76—83. But see the criticism of Nock, *Gnomon* 25, p. 502.

[47] Twenty-four are listed (130). The briefer comments, such as those by the risen Lord (1.4, 5, 7, 8), the apostles (6.2—4), Gallio (18.14—15), and Paul (27.33—34) are not classified as "speeches" by Dibelius.

[48] This statement by Dibelius (see references, p. 130) seems to tell against his understanding of the nature of speeches in the ancient historical writings. Were the two opposing views made up by the author out of his head? Or were they based on actually existing opinions — perhaps even to some degree on words actually spoken on certain occasions?

[49] Dibelius seems to attribute, in this instance, the objectivity of a positivistic

These observations are followed by a consideration of the major speeches in Acts one by one. For the reasons suggested in his earlier essay[50], the speech at Athens is regarded to be the creation of the author. Athens is chosen as the setting, not because of its importance in the missionary career of Paul, but because of its importance to the author.

[131]   Es entspricht der besten Überlieferung griechischer Geschichtsschreibung, wie sie von Thukydides begründet wurde, dass Lukas den Apostel hier, an berühmter Stätte, eine Rede halten lässt, die sich aufs engste mit den Gedanken hellenistischer Philosophie und nur in geringem Grad mit der Theologie des Paulus berührt (131—32).

Athen, nicht eben bedeutend in der Geschichte der Paulus-Mission, wird als Vorort hellenischer Frömmigkeit und als Hauptstadt griechischer Weisheit von Lukas zum Schauplatz dieser Auseinandersetzung des Christus-Apostels mit griechischen Gedanken erwählt (133)[51].

The speech of Paul in Miletus to the elders from the church at Ephesus (20.18—35), again, is important not for the actual sequence of historical events but for the narrative of Acts: it is the one speech made to a Christian church by Paul, the founder, and it is the last time that Paul speaks publicly before his imprisonment. The speech is something like a last will and testament, containing both retrospect (20.18—21, 33—35) and prospect (20.22—25, 29—30). Thus Luke seeks to honor the great apostle in the same way biographers

[132]   are accustomed to honor "ihren Helden mit ihren Enkomien" (134). Paul's references to his way of life in Ephesus are for the benefit of the readers rather than for the elders of Ephesus[52]. His purpose

philosophy of history to the ancient historians. It is, however, doubtful whether any ancient historian, even the best one, was concerned to be strictly impartial. The purpose of the historical writer in antiquity was fundamentally pragmatic. See Wikenhauser, *Die Apostelgeschichte und ihr Geschichtswert*, pp. 89—90; Wallbank, *Commentary on Polybius* 1, pp. 6—16. The latter gives an illuminating discussion of the historical point of view of one Greek historian.

[50] *Supra*, pp. 209—12.

[133]   [51] This is followed by these question-begging comments: "Alle Fragen, ob Paulus wirklich eine solche Rede gehalten und ob er sie in Athen gehalten habe, müssen zurücktreten, wenn man Lukas begreifen will. Ihm liegt nicht an der Darstellung eines einmaligen geschichtlichen Vorgangs, der keinerlei besonderen Erfolg gehabt hat; ihm liegt an der Typik dieser Auseinandersetzung, die im höheren Sinn geschichtlich ist und in seiner eigenen Zeit vielleicht noch mehr Aktualität hat als zur Zeit des Apostels" (133).

[52] The correspondence between 20.33—35 and an important emphasis of the historical Paul in his epistles (1 Cor. 9; 2 Cor. 11.7—11; 1 Thess. 2.5—12) is disallowed by Dibelius as evidence for the view that the speech reflects a

[134]   genuine historical situation: "Im Kreise der Ältesten von Ephesus wurde diese immer wiederkehrende Apologie doch verwunderlich — wenn wirklich bei alledem nur an diesen Hörerkreis gedacht wäre" (134—35). Two points could

is to inspire them by Paul's example and to warn them of the dangers of heretical teaching. The allusion to the death of Paul (20.23 —25)[53] is also important in indicating the literary significance of the speech in the plan of Luke.

The same holds true in regard to the other speeches. The speech Paul makes to the people before the fortress of Antonia (22.1—21) is included in the narrative because it is important to the author "den Apostel vor diesem Forum seinen Ausgang vom orthodoxen [135] Judentum bezeugen zu lassen" (137). In including new facts which were not mentioned in the account of Paul's conversion in 9.1—19 (where Luke reproduces with only slight revision a story which was not his specific creation), Luke desires to make up what was lacking in the original version of his conversion. Similarly, in the speech at the house of Cornelius[54] and at the council meeting of Acts 15[55] the speeches are literary devices by which the author underlines the significance of occasions which to him are extremely important in the Church's history (139—41).

Dibelius concludes this section of his essay with this summation:

Es hat sich gezeigt, dass Lukas an vier wichtigen Wendepunkten des [136] von ihm dargestellten Geschehens Reden in seinen Bericht einfügt, die die Bedeutung des Augenblicks erhellen: bei der ersten grundsätzlich wichtigen Heidenbekehrung, bei dem Vordringen des Apostels ins Zentrum griechischen Geisteslebens, bei seinem Abschied vom Missionsfeld und bei dem Konflikt mit den Juden in nächster Nähe des Tempels. Immer wieder macht man dabei die Beobachtung, dass die Reden der geschichtlichen Situation nicht eigentlich angepasst sind, sondern darüber hinausgreifen: man wundert sich, warum bei der Apostelberatung die Erfolge des Paulus und Barnabas nicht zur Sprache kommen, warum Paulus in Athen so wenig Christliches sagt, warum er vor den ihm vertrauten Ältesten von Ephesus sich selbst verteidigt und vor den Juden in Jerusalem den eigentlichen Streitpunkt, von dem der Konflikt den Ausgang nahm, überhaupt

---

be made in reply: (1) Paul's words are no more strange in the context of this speech than they are in letters to churches with which he is very intimate. (2) No one suggests that this or any other speech in the Book of Acts is intended *only* for the ears of the original hearers; the very fact that Luke includes any speech or event in the narrative of Acts indicates that he intends it to have an effect on the reader of his book — but this does not necessarily mean that he invented either the speech or the event.

[53] Must we pause to point out once again that it is not at all clear that these verses — and certainly not 21.10—14 (to which he also refers) — are a reference to the death of Paul? Possibly — yes. But Dibelius is generally unwilling to leave such questions in the realm of uncertainty.

[54] *Supra*, p. 208.

[55] See also his defence of this view in his essay, "Das Apostelkonzil", *TLZ* 72 (1947), pp. 193—98; = *Aufsätze*, pp. 84—90.

nicht erwähnt. Alles das erklärt sich, wenn wir die geschichtliche Frage ganz im Dunkeln lassen⁵⁶ und hier die Hand des gestaltenden Schriftstellers erkennen, der — trotz mancher Besonderheit sachlich im Sinne der grossen, von Thukydides begründeten Tradition — mit diesen Reden dem Augenblick erhöhte Bedeutung verleihen und die Kräfte sichtbar machen will, die hinter den Ereignissen wirksam sind (141—42).

In the fourth section of his paper (142—50) Dibelius begins by calling attention to the missionary sermons of Peter and Paul in chapters 2, 3, 5, 10, and 13, in which the author has employed a different literary device from those of the historians, *viz.* repetition. There is, he thinks, the same stereotyped outline behind these speeches.

[137]   Auf eine mit der jeweiligen Situation gegebenen Einleitung folgt regelmässig das Kerygma von Jesu Leben, Leiden und Auferstehen (2,22—24; 3,13—15; 5,30—31; 10,36—42; 13,23—25), meist unter Betonung der Zeugenschaft der Jünger (2,32; 3,15; 5,32; 10,39.41; 13,31); daran schliesst sich ein Schriftbeweis (2,25—31; 3,22—26; 10,43; 13,32—37) und eine Bussmahnung (2,38 f.; 3,17—20; 5,31; 10,42 f.; 13,38—41) (142).

The agreement of both outline and content is so striking that one must seek an explanation. The suggestion is made that these sermons were typical of the type of Christian sermons which were customary in the author's day ("um 90 n. Chr."). The similarity of the approach to the various audiences is considered to be proof of the fact that the sermons were not designed for specific occasions⁵⁷.

[138]   ⁵⁶ This admission is made in a footnote: "Ich würde sagen: 'wenn wir die Geschichtlichkeit dieser Reden verneinen' — aber so weit dürfen wir nicht gehen. Lukas kann von einzelnen Gelegenheiten gewusst haben, dass Paulus da geredet hat; er kann auch über die ξύμπασα γνώμη des Redenden oder der Rede in Einzelfällen und vielleicht sogar als Ohrenzeuge Bescheid wissen; aber wo und wann das der Fall war, können wir nicht bestimmen. Auch der Hinweis auf das Itinerar, das Act. 13 bis 21 zweifellos benutzt wird, hilft nicht weiter, denn wenn diese Quelle gehaltene Reden verzeichnete, so würden derartige Angaben öfter darin gestanden haben. Die Auswahl der Gelegenheit und die Ausarbeitung der Rede ist in jedem Fall ein Werk des Autors" (141n.—142n.). In spite of this significant qualification, the underlying assumption of Dibelius in the essay is that the speeches are *all* free inventions by the author. Cf. the concluding sentence of the appendix to the essay: "Zumal die Reden der Apostelgeschichte können in dem, was sie wollen, und in dem, was sie bringen, gar nicht verstanden werden, wenn man sie nicht als Werke des Schriftstellers würdigt" (162).

⁵⁷ Dibelius makes the observation that the agreement in matters of detail
[139]   and the presence of "altertümlicher Wendungen im Kerygma" (e. g., παῖς θεοῦ and ἀνὴρ ἀποδεδειγμένος ἀπὸ τοῦ θεοῦ εἰς ὑμᾶς) indicate the possibility for the use of older texts. "Aber die Frage lässt sich, soviel ich sehe, nur aufwerfen, nicht beantworten" (142). See note 26 above.

In these speeches the primary concern is not what the author wishes to convey to the reader about the historical situation or the significance of the development of the narrative. He is, rather, concerned to preach the Gospel to the readers in the same way the apostles once preached it to their hearers. In this way he invents a new category of speeches which has no real parallel among the ancient historians.

The speech of Peter at the house of Cornelius (10.34—43) seems to combine the approach of the historian and the evangelist. The purpose of this speech is to highlight and explain the importance of the historical moment to the reader; but it is also, in its contents, a missionary sermon designed to instruct the reader and to proclaim the message of salvation to him anew. Paul's address in the synagogue at Antioch (10.16—41) is simply a missionary sermon with an introductory survey of the history of Israel (13.16—22) added because of the synagogue setting. Thus with the single exception of the sermon to Cornelius and his family none of these missionary sermons has very deep roots in the narrative of Acts.

The longest speech of the Book of Acts, the speech of Stephen (7.2—53), is a missionary speech; but it is in some ways unique among the speeches of Acts. It is regarded by Dibelius as the composition of the author[58] which he inserted into the narrative as an addition to the story of the martyrdom of Stephen (which he had inherited by tradition), and as such it is considered to be wholly irrelevant to its immediate setting[59]. The lengthy recital of the history of Israel is not related to the occasion of the speech, but rather to the character of the speaker, who belongs to the world of Hellenistic Judaism. Thus the speech is a defence of Christianity over against the Hellenistic synagogue; but at the same time, in the tradition of the historical writers, Luke uses it to pave the way for the separation of the Church from the Jewish community which is to follow.

Sie eröffnet den Abschnitt der Acta (6—12), der den Übergang des Evangeliums an die heidnische Welt schildert. Sie zeigt die innere Entfernung des Redners vom Judentum, sie zeigt sie aber mit Mitteln, die selbst wieder [140]

---

[58] "Wie schon bei den Missionsreden möchte man auch hier die Abhängigkeit von einem älteren Text wenigstens für den reproduzierenden Teil nicht ausschliessen; dann würde sich dessen Neutralität am besten erklären. Die polemischen Stellen würden dem Lukas gehören, der natürlich das Ganze bearbeitet hätte" (145). Although Dibelius recognizes this as theoretically possible, he regards it as very improbable. [141]

[59] Contrast the recent study by M. Scharlemann, *Stephen: A Singular Saint* (Rome, 1968).

dem Judentum entlehnt sind. Auch das ist typisch für die Auseinandersetzung zwischen Christentum und Judentum, die durch diese Rede einge-
leitet wird (146).

In a similar manner the speeches of Paul in chapters 23, 24, and
26 are primarily apologetic. By the use of repetition Luke wishes to
impress upon his readers the importance of the resurrection (23.6;
24.15, 21; 26.6—8). The setting of the speech before the Sanhedrin
(ch. 23) abounds in improbabilities; the speeches before Felix (ch. 24)
and Festus (ch. 26) are marked by deliberate stylizations (for example, the introductory *captatio benevolentiae*, the use of "official"
language, and a few cultural additions such as the quotation from
Euripides in 26.14)[60], which are intended to give the reader a feeling for the varied settings. All of this is further proof that the
speeches are designed for the readers of the book rather than for
the original audiences to which they were ostensibly addressed.

In the final section of his essay on the speeches (150—58), Dibelius summarizes his conclusions concerning the relation of the
speeches in Acts to those in the ancient historical writings. The
fundamental point of comparison is found in the way Luke has inserted speeches which do not necessarily correspond to the situation
into his history in order to make certain points clear.

[142] Sie helfen an ihrem Teil mit, die Abkehr des Christentums vom Judentum verständlich zu machen (Stephanus) und verteidigen das Recht der
Heidenmission (Rede des Paulus vor dem Volk), sie zeigen, wie Gott selbst
die Heidenbekehrung herbeiführt (Cornelius), wie die christliche Predigt
Gedanken des griechischen Geistes aufgreift (Areopagrede), und deuten
die vergangenen wie die künftigen Schicksale der Gemeinden an (Milet)
(151).

---

[60] See the appendix to his essay, where he deals specifically with the literary
allusions in Acts (*Aufsätze*, pp. 160—62). Concerning Acts 26.14 he writes:
[143] "Das ist durchaus ein Bildungselement, denn die Neigung zu dergleichen Wendungen kann den Spruch an die Stelle gebracht haben, an die er eigentlich
nicht passt... Eine Himmelsstimme redet nicht in Sprichwörtern und erst recht
nicht, wenn sie aramäisch spricht, in griechischen Sprichwörtern. Und im Semi-
tischen ist das Wort nicht belegt. Auch begegnet es in den andern Wiedergaben
der gleichen Himmelsstimme 9,4 und 22.7 keineswegs. Es ist also in dieser am
meisten literarisch gepflegten Darstellung der Bekehrung im Sinne dieses Stils
vom Autor hinzugefügt. Es soll den Paulus in die Reihe derer stellen, die ver-
geblich gegen Gott angekämpft haben; es soll dem Leser aber auch die Freude
bereiten, die ein solcher literarischer Schmuck dem Belesenen gewährt" (160 bis
161). The references cited by Dibelius (not only Euripides, but also Pindar and
Aeschylus) only prove that this was an extremely common proverb. Although
it has not been found in an Aramaic source, it is, as Bruce points out (*Acts*,
p. 444), "the sort of saying that might be current in any agricultural community". The explanation of R. N. Longenecker, *Paul, Apostle of Liberty*
(New York, 1964), pp. 98—101, may, however, be correct. He suggests that

All of these speeches stand at significant places in the narrative and show themselves to be the conceptions of the author which he has inserted into his narrative, or rather into the narrative provided by his sources. In this he has followed the tradition of ancient historical writing.

The unique feature of the speeches of Acts in contrast to the speeches in the writings of the ancient historians is the fact "dass sie [144] mit dem erzählenden Text nicht in allen Punkten übereinstimmen, sondern ihn ergänzen, bisweilen nicht ohne eine gewisse Korrektur" (151). An example of this is the address at Athens. According to the narrative (17.16), Paul is disturbed over the idolatry of the city; but then he goes on to speak in praise of the Athenians for their well-known piety toward the gods! The explanation is not that Paul has changed his mind, or that he is speaking hypocritically, but rather that the speech is comparatively independent of the narrative[61]. And in the speech at Miletus the reader learns "dass Paulus [145] schon in anderen Städten die Prophezeiung künftiger Bedrängnis erhalten hat" and "dass er drei Jahre in Ephesus war und sich dort mit Handarbeit sein Brot verdient hat — alles Dinge, von denen vorher noch nicht die Rede war" (151)[62]. Another example of the way the author uses the speeches to supplement the reader's knowledge is the reference to the collection in 24.17.

Again, the missionary speeches of Peter and Paul, where the purpose for their presence in the text is the repetition and emphasis of certain themes, are also without exact analogy in the historical writings. Their purpose is kerygmatic; that is, they are intended not simply to narrate, but also to preach. Nevertheless, even here one

---

Paul may be simply "making explicit to Agrippa what was implicit in the words, 'Saul, Saul, why are you persecuting me?' " Thus he uses a common Greek proverb — which Agrippa will understand and appreciate. On the other hand, one may think that Luke is responsible for this translation of the words of Jesus into Greek idiom, without being convinced that he is entirely responsible for the whole of the speech.

[61] In his essay on the Areopagus speech (*supra*, pp. 209—12). Dibelius had emphasized quite the opposite, *viz.*, the close interrelationship between the narrative and speech, which he regarded as evidence that both narrative (with the exception of the brief note from the itinerary-document; 17.16—17, 34) and speech were the composition of the author.

[62] Waiving for the moment the question of the debatable interpretation Dibelius attaches to Acts 20.23, one would ask whether, if Paul's three years in Ephesus and the fact that he supported himself there by his own labor had been mentioned earlier in the narrative as well, Dibelius would not have regarded this too as evidence that the speech is the literary composition of the author. This is, in fact, his argument concerning the address of Peter at the Jerusalem council (84—90, 96—107).

can observe the use of typical literary devices, such as the sudden interruption and the indication that the speaker said more than what has been reported in the narrative (2.40).

Further differences between Luke's speeches and those of the ancient historians are listed. (1) Although it is certain that he has inherited the tradition of the literary historian, "durch Einschaltung eine Rede dem Augenblick Bedeutung zu verleihen", it is equally certain that his basic conception of the meaning of the speeches is different: "Er schreibt eine Geschichte, von der er glaubt, dass sie nach Gottes Willen so geschehen sei" (155). (2) The speeches of Acts are much shorter than those in the writings of the ancient historians[63]. (3) Although it seems at first that Luke, like the historians, invents speeches in order to illuminate important moments, it becomes clear that the speeches often are totally unrelated to their settings. Finally, (4) Luke, in contrast to the historians, does not aim at a uniformity of style; on the contrary, he displays a variety of styles in his speeches[64].

The author of Acts, then, is both similar to and different from the ancient historians in his use of speeches. He follows the historians in that he composes speeches freely, that he uses literary techniques designed with the readers in view, that the speeches are important in the development of the narrative, and that they are relatively independent of their immediate settings. On the other hand, there is a new element for which Luke himself is responsible: "Er wollte ... nicht nur die Situation erhellen, sondern auch die Wege Gottes; er wollte nicht die Fähigkeiten der Redner oder des Autors bezeugen, sondern das Evangelium" (157). In the final analysis Luke is "nicht Historiker, sondern Prediger" (157).

Many of the conclusions of Dibelius' essay on the speeches in

[146]
[147]
[148]
[149]
[150]

---

[63] "Zwar hat sich uns ergeben, dass die nur aus wenig Sätzen bestehenden Reden nicht ohne Analogie bei den Historikern sind. Aber gerade die grösseren Reden der Acta bleiben an Länge weit hinter ihren weltlichen Gegenbildern zurück. Denn ihnen fehlen mindestens zwei Elemente, die die Reden der Historiker füllen: das deliberative Element, die Erörterung des Für und Wider, und das epideiktische Element, die rhetorische Ausspinnung der behandelten Ideen" (156).

[64] This, as well as some of the other observations of Dibelius concerning the differences between the speeches of Acts and (his conception of) the speeches of the ancient historians, would seem to tell against his interpretation of the Lucan speeches as essentially the literary creations of the author. However, Dibelius regards *both* the Semitic flavor of the speeches in the early chapters and the more polished style of the speech at Athens to be further evidence of the author's literary creativity (154, 156). In this way both similarities and differences of language are regarded as evidence that the speeches are the creations of the author! I find this reasoning strange.

Acts in relation to ancient historiography are open to serious objections. Although this is not the place to offer a detailed reply, a few of these objections may be mentioned.

In the first place, it is not at all clear that it was the accepted practice for ancient historians to freely compose speeches and to introduce them into their narrative as expressions of their own ideas. Now, there is no doubt that *many* historians did just this. Josephus is a notable example[65], and he no doubt was following the pattern of many second-rate historians. The question is, however, whether this was the universal practice; that is, whether *all* historians freely invented speeches which had no basis in fact and put these into the mouths of the leading characters of their narratives, and whether this was universally recognised as an acceptable custom.

There are good reasons to think that some of the best of the ancient historians were more responsible in their use of speeches than the theory of Dibelius would suggest. A few notable exceptions to his conception of the principles of historiography in antiquity *disprove* the rule. Some of these exceptions are, indeed, referred to by him as illustrative of the acceptability of the invention of speeches, whereas, in fact, they point to the existence of higher standards on the part of some historians.

The celebrated passage from Thucydides, if taken at its face value, contradicts the thesis of Dibelius. In the section of his history where he spells out his historical methodology (1.22) he has this to say about his handling of the speeches contained in his narrative:

With reference to the speeches in this history, some were delivered before the war began, others while it was going on; it was hard to record the exact words spoken, both in cases where I was myself present, and where I used the reports of others. But I have used language in accordance with what I thought the speakers in each case would have been most likely to say, adhering as closely as possible to the general sense of what was actually spoken[66].

Although Dibelius admits that the interpretation of this passage is open to debate, he interprets it as an attempted justification by

---

[65] Cf. F. F. Bruce, *The Speeches in the Acts of the Apostles* (London, 1943), p. 7.

[66] Translation from T. F. Glasson, "The Speeches in Acts and Thucydides", *ExpT* 76 (1964/65), p. 165. The Greek reads: Καὶ ὅσα μὲν λόγῳ εἶπον ἕκαστοι ἢ μέλλοντες πολευμήσειν ἢ ἐν αὐτῷ ἤδη ὄντες, χαλεπὸν τὴν ἀκρίβειαν αὐτὴν τῶν λεχθέντων διαμνημονεῦσαι ἦν ἐμοί τε ὧν αὐτὸς ἤκουσα καὶ τοῖς ἄλλοθεν ποθεν ἐμοὶ ἀπαγγέλλουσιν· ὡς δ' ἂν ἐδόκουν μοι ἕκαστοι περὶ τῶν αἰεὶ παρόντων τὰ δέοντα μάλιστ' εἰπεῖν, ἐχομένῳ ὅτι ἐγγύτατα τῆς ξυμπάσης γνώμης τῶν ἀληθῶς λεχθέντων, οὕτως εἴρηται.

226

Thucydides of the practice of composing speeches with little or no
regard for what actually may have been said. In point of fact, the
natural interpretation of the passage would have Thucydides making the exact opposite claim, *viz.* that he did *not* invent speeches!
"For some of the speeches", he says, "I was present and heard what
was actually spoken. For others I am dependent on the report of
other people who heard them. It has been, of course, difficult to
recall verbatim what was said on each occasion; therefore, I have
made the speeches say what I thought was appropriate to the occasion, *keeping as closely as possible to the general idea of what
was actually spoken.*" Some scholars, it is true, have questioned
whether Thucydides really lived up to the high standard which he
claims. Others, however, have given a good case for the view that
he did[67]. At any rate, it is clear that the invention of speeches was
not an acceptable historiographical method insofar as Thucydides
was concerned — at least, in principle.

Polybius (ca. 201—120 B. C.), the second great Greek historian
after Thucydides, time and again explicitly condemns the custom of
the free invention of speeches by historians. In another passage referred to by Dibelius (xxi. 25.1) — once again to prove the opposite! — he roundly condemns a historian for inventing a speech and
makes the point that the historian, in his synopsis of a speech, must
be true to the actual words of the original. Elsewhere he accuses
another writer of trying to imagine the probable utterances of his
characters instead of "simply recording what was said, however
commonplace" (ii. 56.10). In his view there is the place for literary
embellishment in the speeches, calling attention to important stages
of development in the narrative; but even here the speeches must be
true to τὰ κατ' ἀλήθειαν λεχθέντα[68]. Once again, it is perhaps debatable whether Polybius always lived up to the high standard he
set for himself and his fellow historians. However, there seems to
be reason to expect that he often did — or he made the attempt to
do so. In the opinion of F. W. Walbank, "Any failure [for Polybius
to live up to the high standards set for himself in the recording of
speeches] is due to practical shortcomings rather than a deliberate
betrayal of principle" (I, 14).

The essay on "How to Write History" by Lucian of Samosata
(ca. A. D. 120—90) is very instructive in spelling out one educated

---

[67] See the works of Gomme, referred to in footnote 42. Cf. also F. E.
Adcock, *Thucydides and His History* (Cambridge, 1963), pp. 27—42; and the
essay by Glasson (cited above).

[68] See the references in the commentary on Polybius by F. W. Walbank
(cited in n. 43 above).

man's ideals of historical writing[69]. A careful study of this document will make it clear — to the surprise of many, no doubt — that his standards for writing history differ little from that of a modern historian who has any literary ambitions[70]. Lucian criticizes the rhetorical historians of his day, who "spend their time lauding rulers and generals, extolling their own to the skies and slandering the enemy's beyond all reserve" (7); such men, he says, do not realize that there is a great difference between history and encomium. In the case of the latter, a falsehood might be admitted in order to achieve one's aim; but history cannot admit the slightest falsehood. Lucian makes a clear distinction between poetry and rhetoric on the one hand and history on the other, and he condemns the aspiring historian who fails to maintain this distinction and who, therefore, includes the former in his professedly historical writing (8). The sole task of the historian is to tell the story as it happened, even if this means putting people he personally hates in a better light than those who are his friends (39). The emphasis of the historian is on facts, not imagination (41, 47), and it is this that makes his work quite different from that of the rhetorician (50). Although his work will be marked by artistic arrangement and an interesting and cultured literary style (since he desires his work to be read by others), the historian must not allow this in any way to distort the historical reality (43—48). Lucian criticizes one "historian" for composing a funeral oration to a fallen general which had no basis in fact (25—26); and, although he recognizes the fact that speeches have rhetorical value even in historical narrative, he argues that "what is said must be above all appropriate to the character and suitable to the occasion" (58)[71].

Reference to these three Greek writers[72] is sufficient to make it

---

[69] Πῶς δεῖ ἱστορίαν συγγράφειν, contained in the Loeb volume, *Lucian VI*, ed. by K. Kilburn (London, 1959), pp. 1—73. One should compare this with book xii of Polybius, where he sets down his own principles of historiography. See also A. W. Mosley, "Historical Reporting in the Ancient World", *NTS* 12 (1965/66), pp. 10—26. (R. P. C. Hanson's brief note (*The Acts*, pp. 36—37) brought the importance of the essay by Lucian to my attention).

[70] Those specialist-historians in the *Cambridge Ancient/Modern History* or the *Histoire Générale* tradition, who write to be read by other historians, may have rather different aims. I refer to those historians who desire their works to be read by the educated public, not merely by other scholars. The distinction is, I think, an important one.

[71] Hanson's translation. The Greek is: μάλιστα μὲν ἐοικότα τῷ προσώπῳ καὶ τῷ πράγματι οἰκεῖα λεγέσθω.

[72] Cf. the speech of Claudius contained in Tacitus (*supra*, n.41). See also the recent essay by S. Usher, "Xenophon, Critias and Theramenes", *JHS* 88 (1968), pp. 128—35, who argues on the basis of style and content that (1) the speech

clear that the free invention of speeches was not a universally accepted practice among historians in the Graeco-Roman world. It may have been the general practice; it was certainly a widespread practice. But Thucydides and Polybius, to name no others, were in principle opposed to the practice; and it is probable that they (and perhaps others as well) attempted to be more responsible in their handling of speeches.

As far as the speeches of Acts in particular are concerned, further objections may be made to Dibelius' general premise that they are, for the most part, the inventions of the author. First, there is the very evident contrast between the speeches of Acts and the obviously composed speeches of the second-rate Greek historians. Josephus (*Ant.* i. 13.3), for example, puts a lengthy speech into the mouth of Abraham as he is about to sacrifice Isaac[73]. Elsewhere he substitutes "several hundred words of dreary rhetoric, highly polished and unbearably insipid, whose frigidity is matched only by that of the answering speech" for the brief and moving words of Judah in Genesis 44[74]. By contrast, the speeches in the Book of Acts do not give obvious evidence of being simply the rhetorical compositions of the author. They are generally very brief, fitting to the occasion (in spite of Dibelius!), and not by any means the most literary part of the author's work. Furthermore, as A. Ehrhardt has pointed out[75], if the author has invented speeches as Dibelius suggests, he has missed a number of very good occasions on which a speech would be expected — for example, following 5.21 and 28.16. The best explanation of such omissions is that he knew of no speech on these occasions.

Dibelius quite dogmatically dismisses the speeches of the Third Gospel (where the author can be checked) as evidence for the author's methodology in regard to the speeches of the Book of Acts (where the author cannot be checked)[76]. In spite of his assertion to the contrary — based on the twin assumptions that the early Chris-

---

of Critias in Xenophon's account of the reign of terror of the Thirty at Athens (404—3 B. C.) is based on a complete copy of the original speech, which was condensed by Xenophon, and that (2) the speech of Theramenes was based on the report of an eyewitness who was careful enough to remember some actual phrases of the original, but which was revised by Xenophon to include Theramenes' statements of his political views which were made on other occasions. Although the literary technique is different in both cases, neither could justly be said to be "unhistorical" or in any real sense the literary compositions of the historical writer.

[73] Bruce, *Speeches*, p. 7.   [74] *Ibid.*
[75] *The Framework of the New Testament Stories* (Manchester, 1964), p. 88.
[76] *Aufsätze*, pp. 10—11, 126, 158.

tians had no interest in their own history[77] and that they would have been interested in remembering only the words of Jesus and not anything that the apostles had said — the fact that Luke does not invent speeches in the Gospel cannot be arbitrarily set aside when inquiring into Luke's historical methodology in the second volume of his work. Where we can compare Luke with Mark, presumably one of his sources for the Gospel, we find that he has re-arranged and re-worded the sayings and speeches to some degree (in the authentic tradition of the Greek historical writers)[78]; but he has not been unfaithful in his reproduction of their essential meaning. Thus the dictum of F. F. Bruce: "If this is the verdict on Luke in places where his fidelity to his source can be controlled, we should not without good reason suppose that he was not equally faithful where his sources are no longer available for comparison."[79] Luke's handling of the speech material in the Gospel is not *proof* that he must have used the same technique in the Book of Acts, but it would seem to demand a more serious consideration of this possibility than Dibelius would allow.

There is also the factor of the diversity of the speeches in Acts — both linguistically and theologically. Although Dibelius occasionally admits to differences in both language and theology among the various speeches, his emphasis is primarily on the unity of style and thought. Now, no one (as far as I know) denies that the *language* of all the speeches is, generally speaking, Luke's. This is true in the Gospel, even though the content stems from his sources. The real question is whether there is evidence to support the view that the author may have been dependent on sources of some kind, written or oral, for the *content* of the speeches.

In spite of all the similarities which exist among the speeches, the differences are also great. The layman who hears the suggestion that the speeches of Peter in the early chapters of Acts, the speech of Stephen, the Areopagus address of Paul at Athens, and Paul's farewell address to the Ephesian elders at Miletus are all the literary creations of a single mind may be tempted to scoff at the absurdity of the suggestion. This is not the impression which one has when one compares them. Although there is a basic unity of language and even of theology (as one would expect, if the picture the writer of Acts gives of the essential agreement of the early Church on basic issues[80] is accurate), there are also striking dif-

---

[77] *Aufsätze*, p. 15.

[78] See Cadbury, *The Making of Luke-Acts*, especially pp. 76—98, 158.

[79] *Acts*, p. 19.

[80] As has been noted many times in the course of this study, Paul himself

ferences. In spite of the rather artificial attempts of Eduard Schweizer[81] and Ulrich Wilckens[82] to demonstrate that they all contain
the same theology, it is clear that they do not. For example,
as C. F. D. Moule has demonstrated[83], the Christology of the
speeches in Acts is not uniform. If the older generation of scholars,
both conservative and radical, were agreed on anything, it was the
primitive nature of the theology of the speeches of the early chapters of Acts. Furthermore, Stephen's speech has no real theological
parallels in the rest of the Book of Acts[84]. Again, J. W. Doeve[85]

emphasizes his basic agreement with the other apostles concerning the gospel
message (e. g. 1 Cor. 15.3–11).

[81] "Zu den Reden der Apostelgeschichte", *TZ* 13 (1957), pp. 1–11; E. T.
"Concerning the Speeches in Acts", in *Studies in Luke-Acts*, pp. 208–16.
Schweizer has to juggle his materials considerably to fit them into his ready-
made mold, designed to demonstrate the essential uniformity of the speeches.
This is especially evident in his attempt to discern parallel features between
Paul's sermons at Lystra (14.15–17) and at Athens (17.22–31) and the six
speeches of the early chapters which form the foundation of his proof (2.14–
39; 3.12–26; 4.9–12; 5.29–32; 10.34–43; 13.16–41). Thus not only is the
stereotyped reference to "God who made the heaven and the earth and the
sea and all that is in them" (14.15) classified as a quotation from Scripture, but
both the similar reference in 17.24 and the quotations from pagan poets in
17.28 are also so classified! In addition, Paul's address to the Ephesian elders
(20.18–35), Paul's apologetic speeches of the latter part of the book (22.1–21;
24.10–21; 26.2–23), Stephen's speech (7.2–53), and all of the lesser speeches
are conveniently omitted from the discussion. If *all* of the speeches are carefully compared apart from the rearrangement of the component parts to fit a
preconceived mold, it is doubtful that they would in fact betray any greater
degree of uniformity in structure or detail than a random selection of Christian
sermons of today.

[82] *Die Missionsreden der Apostelgeschichte*, 2nd ed. (Neukirchen, 1963). Wilckens' monograph is much more complete than Schweizer's brief essay, but it
impresses one as none the less arbitrary. The author presupposes the conclusions of Dibelius' studies, virtually ignoring all objections to his methodology
and conclusions. He limits his study to the same six sermons from the early
chapters which form the basis of Schweizer's observations (see n. 81). He rules
out even the kerygmatic features which Dibelius thought Luke may have
drawn from tradition and attempts to demonstrate that they are entirely the
inventions of the author for his own theological purposes. His conclusion is
this: "Die Apostelreden der Acta aber sind in hervorragendem Sinne Summa-
rien dieser seiner theologischen Konzeption; sie sind nicht als Zeugnisse alter
oder gar ältester urchristlicher Theologie, sondern lukanischer Theologie des
ausgehenden ersten Jahrhunderts zu werten" (186). But see the penetrating
criticism of J. Dupont, "Les discours missionnaires des Actes des Apôtres",
RB 69 (1962), pp. 37–60; = *Études sur les Actes des Apôtres*, (Paris, 1967),
pp. 133–55.

[83] "The Christology of Acts", in *Studies in Luke Acts*, pp. 159–85.

[84] See Scharlemann (cited in n. 59).

[85] *Jewish Hermeneutics in the Synoptic Gospels and Acts* (Assen, 1953),
pp. 168–76.

[*151*]

has pointed out the different use of the same passage of Scripture (Psalm 16.10) in the speech attributed to Peter in Acts 2 and in the one ascribed to Paul in Acts 13. Both the structure and the argument in the two instances are different, the influence of Aramaic idiom being evident in the development of the argument of the former and the argument of a schooled rabbi being perceptible in that of the latter. Doeve's conclusion is this:

If the author of Acts composed the discourse in chap. XIII himself, then he must have had an excellent command of hermeneutics as practiced in rabbinic Judaism. If one assumes that he also composed the discourse in Acts II, this implies that he was capable of imitating different styles of exegesis (175)[86].

This author, it should be remembered, is recognized by the vast majority of scholars as a Gentile Christian and those who regard the speeches of Acts as his own compositions assign him to a time in history when the contacts between the Church and synagogue are all but non-existent. And this same author is considered to be responsible for the speeches of the latter part of the Book of Acts as well. To fulfill the requirements of a role like this the author must have been a remarkable *littérateur* indeed!

There are also many small phrases, often Semitic[87], which do not

---

[86] Doeve adds these further remarks: "Now the remarkable point is, that tradition ascribes the simpler discourse to Peter, and the more complicated one to Paul. The latter must have had a thorough rabbinic schooling. Moreover, tradition claims that the first speech was held in the street, addressed to all kinds of people, and the second in a meeting in the synagogue. Thus there is certainly no lack of harmony between the structure of the two passages and the information offered by tradtition as to the authors and the occasions when they delivered their discourses. In this position of affairs *it surely does not seem hazardous to assume that the author of Acts had good traditional material available here, speeches which really were made, or if preferred, teaching which really was given in this form, coming from two different authors.* And then it is not to be regarded as improbable that the two authors were Peter and Paul respectively. It is another question whether the historical location of the speech of Acts II was really at Whitsuntide in Jerusalem, and whether that of Acts XIII was pronounced in the synagogue of Antioch in Pisidia. This does not matter in the slightest. More important is, that by means of an analysis of this kind we may perhaps gain some access to the problem of the different ways in which Christianity was proclaimed. The two instances we have discussed have every appearance of having been transmitted by a reliable tradition, and from the use made of Aramaic in the first passage, this would certainly seem to be of Palestinian origin" (176). Cf. the similar comments of M. Black, *ExpT* 77, p. 22, concerning the conflation of the Septuagint and the Targum tradition in Acts 13.22.

[87] See especially J. de Zwaan, "The Use of the Greek Language in Acts", *BC* 2, pp. 30–65; Bruce, *Speeches*, pp. 8–9; *Acts*, pp. 18–20, and commentary

seem to be due to the author's own hand, presumably features which he has failed to edit out[88]. If Luke had simply invented the speeches for rhetorical and theological purposes, one would expect them to represent the high point of his literary achievement, comparable to (say) the prologue of the Gospel. But with the possible exception of the Areopagus speech of Acts 17 this is definitely not the case. In point of fact, the speeches of the early chapters are often extremely awkward in style. To suggest that his awkwardness is due to (or even evidence for!) Luke's literary ability, that he is deliberately patterning his style after that of the Septuagint to give an archaic flavor to the early part of his narrative, is scarcely plausible. Though it is theoretically possible that the author possessed the literary genius necessary to create speeches as different as Peter's Pentecostal address and Paul's speech before the Areopagus, to compose speeches in the style of the Greek Old Testament in the early chapters and in a semi-classical style in the latter, and to vary his theology according to speaker, it would seem that there is a higher degree of historical probability in favor of the view that some kind of sources (written or oral) lie behind the speeches.

Other points of criticism may be raised against Dibelius' conception of the speeches in Acts. For one thing, it is highly unlikely that the speeches are, as Dibelius suggests, intended to be regarded as actual sermons to be preached, or at least to be used as models in missionary preaching[89]. They are too short, and they are not all

---

on the individual speeches; R. A. Martin, "Syntactical Evidence of Aramaic Sources in Acts I—XV", *NTS* 11 (1964/65), pp. 38—59, and M. Wilcox, *The Semitisms of Acts* (Oxford, 1965), especially pp. 157—85. The monograph by Wilcox is the definitive study of the subject, at least for some years to come, and makes it extremely difficult to attribute all, or even most, of the Semitisms of Acts to the author's "septuagintalizing" style. (I am aware of the critisism of Wilcox by E. Haenchen (*TLZ* 91 (1966), pp. 355—57), but I find his objections singularly unconvincing). See the excellent survey and evaluation of recent research on the subject by D. F. Payne, "Semitisms in the Book of Acts", *Apostolic History and the Gospel*, pp. 134—50.

[88] Dibelius, of course, attributes this unevenness of Luke's style and Semitic flavor in the speeches of the early chapters to the author's literary ability; that is, he is seeking to give the reader the impression that the speeches correspond to their historical contexts — a long time ago when the Church was still "Jewish". Thus the diversity of the style of the speeches becomes "proof" that they are the literary creations of the author in much the same way that the local and historical color of the portrait of Athens (17.16—22) and the narrative of the sea-voyage and shipwreck (27.1—28.13) demonstrate the "fact" that they are literary rather than historical. Once again the one who seeks to criticize the views of Dibelius has the feeling that the deck has been stacked against him!

[89] *Aufsätze*, pp. 65, 72, 179—80.

that rhetorical. More probably — and this would be likely even in terms of the view that they are the author's own compositions — they are intended to be regarded as the author's synopses of actual addresses, although, admittedly, the author would probably consider them to be models of good preaching even in his own day. Finally, there is Dibelius' interpretation of the *Areopagitica*, which has been demonstrated to be extremely one-sided and essentially untenable by Gärtner's epochal monograph[90]. However, enough has been said to give some indication of the reason many New Testament critics take a very different view of the speeches in Acts from that advocated by Dibelius. The student of Acts must make up his own mind on the subject by making a careful study of the speeches for himself and then examining the arguments of Dibelius and those who follow him on one hand and their critics on the other.

In spite of his extremely negative attitude toward the historicity of the Book of Acts — the narrative as well as the speeches — Dibelius insists on retaining the term "historian" as an appropriate description of the author[91]. However, it must be clear to all who are familiar with his approach that he has a very different conception of "Luke the historian" than had Ramsay and Eduard Meyer, for example. As Dibelius himself comments,

Wir billigen ihm diesen (*sc.* "Historiker") zu, weil er mehr getan hat, als Traditionsgut zu sammeln. Er hat auf seine Weise versucht, das in der Gemeinde Überlieferte und das von ihm selbst noch in Erfahrung Gebrachte in einem bedeutungsvollen Zusammenhang zu verknüpfen. Und er hat zweitens versucht, den Richtungssinn der Ereignisse sichtbar zu machen (110). [152]

It is, however, just there "wo Lukas als Historiker arbeiten will und wo wir seine Leistung auf vollig unbebautem Felde bewundern" that he has departed from the earlier traditions and must be judged by the standards of historical criticism to be a second-rate authority (113). He is not so much concerned to tell his readers exactly what happened in the past (i. e., how the Christian Church came into being) as to help them to understand what it means in the present (i. e., the presence of the Christian Church in the midst of the Hellenistic world). Thus in the authentic tradition of the ancient historians, who had no desire to portray life with photographic accuracy, "sondern . . . das Typische darstellen und erhellen", [154]

---

[90] *Supra*, pp. 213—14.

[91] See especially his essay, "Der erste christliche Historiker", *Schriften der Universität* 3. Heft (Heidelberg, 1948), pp. 112—24; = *Aufsätze*, pp. 108—19. This was a *Universitätsvortrag*, delivered in the University of Heidelberg on 14 February 1947.

234

Luke partly omits, changes, and generalizes what actually occurred in history (119). "Und so wurde es möglich, dass er gerade mit den literarischen Mitteln des Historikers seiner anderen Pflicht genügen konnte, ein Prediger des Christusglaubens zu sein" (119).

What Dibelius admires in Luke is not so much his knowledge, arrangement, and interpretation of the facts of history, but his literary and artistic ability. Therefore, in his own terms of reference it is questionable whether Luke should be called a historian. A creative and interesting writer — yes. But not a historian. Even when judged by the standards of the ancient historians — which were often much higher than Dibelius cares to admit — the author of Acts (according to Dibelius' analysis) is a very poor historian, if a historian at all. At best he would be the type of historian condemned by Lucian in his essay on "How to Write History" and satirized in his *True History!* Furthermore, although it is true that authorship by a companion of Paul does not guarantee the historical veracity of the Book of Acts, it is questionable whether it is really compatible with Dibelius' extreme opinion of its historical worth[92]. It is therefore not surprising that most of those critics who have received their inspiration from Dibelius have taken a rather different view from his on these two points.

A great deal of space in this chapter has been given to the work of Martin Dibelius, because, although others have made more extensive contributions to *Actaforschung* in recent years, his occasional essays have actually set the tone of the recent discussion[93]. Many parallels could be drawn between the influence of Dibelius on the study of Acts (primarily in Germany) during the past two decades and the influence of Ferdinand Christian Baur a century earlier. Neither Baur nor Dibelius wrote a commentary or even a monograph on Acts; their opinions were put forward in the context of a series of essays. Yet the influence of both on the history of criticism has been enormous. The views of Baur were propagated and defended at length by Schrader, Schwegler, and Zeller; similarly, Dibelius has also had his disciples to expound and to develop the suggestions of his essays, and in this way his views have become well-known in the world of scholarship at large. Baur founded a small but influential school of biblical interpretation; Dibelius (with less direct intention, perhaps) did, in effect, the same. If one leaves

---

[92] Here, it seems, the older and more recent critics in the radical tradition are more consistent than Dibelius.

[93] Cf. J. Rohde, *Die Redaktionsgeschichtliche Methode* (Hamburg, 1966), pp. 124–25; R. H. Fuller, *The New Testament in Current Study* (London, 1963), pp. 104–7; W. C. van Unnik in *Studies in Luke-Acts*, p. 21; etc.

to one side Baur's special understanding of the *Tendenz* of the author, it is not difficult to note the striking correspondences which exist between the emphases of the two writers and their disciples on (a) the author as a creative writer, (b) the unhistorical nature of the allegedly historical narrative, (c) the invention of the speeches, (d) the post-apostolic perspective of the theology represented in the book, and so on.

To Professor Ernst Haenchen[94] (1894—) of Münster belongs the credit for having systematically applied the methodology of Dibelius to the interpretation of Acts as a whole. In addition to a number of important essays[95], he has authored a massive commentary on Acts[96] to replace the earlier commentary by H. H. Wendt in the Meyer series. His commentary is generally recognized as the definitive study of Acts from the point of view of the German critics who accept the general conclusions of Dibelius.

In the foreword to his commentary Haenchen indicated the *raison d'être* of his work to be the "Erkenntnis, dass die Apostelgeschichte in einem viel höheren Grade als Komposition gewürdigt werden muss, als dies bisher geschehen ist" (5*). His basic views on the subject were spelled out in his essay on tradition and composition in the Book of Acts[97], which appeared in 1955, the same year he completed the first edition of his commentary[98].

[156]

The dependence of Haenchen on the work of Dibelius is obvious from the start. According to Haenchen "neue Forschung" (in a foot-

---

[94] On Haenchen's contribution to the study of Acts, see Mattill, *Luke as a Historian*, pp. 297–314; C. K. Barrett, *Luke the Historian in Recent Study* (London, 1961), pp. 46–50; Dupont, *Sources*, pp. 126–32, 140–47; and Rohde (n. 93), pp. 157–64. His essay in *RGG*[3] (see n. 95) provides one with a convenient summary of his views.

[95] The following are the most important: "Tradition und Komposition in der Apostelgeschichte", *ZTK* 52 (1955), pp. 205–25; "Apostelgeschichte", *RGG*[3] 1 (1957), cols. 501–7; "Quellenanalyse und Kompositionsanalyse in Act. 15", in *Judentum, Urchristentum, Kirche. Festschrift für J. Jeremias*, ed. by W. Eltester (Berlin, 1960), pp. 153–64; "Das 'Wir' in der Apostelgeschichte und das Itinerar", *ZTK* 58 (1961), pp. 329–66, E. T. in *JTC* 1 (1965), pp. 65–99; "Judentum und Christentum in der Apostelgeschichte", *ZNW* 54 (1963), pp. 155–87; "Acta 27", in *Zeit und Geschichte. Dankesgabe an R. Bultmann zum 80. Geburtstag*, ed. by E. Dinkler (Tübingen, 1964), pp. 235–54; and "The Book of Acts as Source Material for the History of Early Christianity", in *Studies in Luke-Acts*, pp. 258–78.

[96] *Kritisch-exegetischer Kommentar über das Neue Testament. 3. Die Apostelgeschichte*, 10th ed. (Göttingen, 1956; 11th ed., 1957; 12th ed., 1959; 13th ed., 1961). The 1961 edition is cited below (and elsewhere in the text of the present study) unless indicated to the contrary.

[97] See footnote 95 above.

[98] The preface is dated 31 March 1955.

note he refers *only* to Dibelius!) has demonstrated the inadequacies of the older, source-critical understanding of the relation between tradition and composition in Acts (206). He begins his essay with an examination of the narrative concerning the election of Matthias in Acts 1.16—26. In Contrast to H. W. Beyer[99], who designated the account as a "gutes Stück" of tradition, Haenchen argues that the hand of the author can be seen, not only in 1.18—19, but also throughout the whole of the passage. In addition to the fact that Peter had no need to explain the circumstances of the death of Judas and the meaning of an Aramaic word to his audience (1.18 —19), he adduces the following points in support of his hypothesis: First, the Hebrew text (which Peter certainly would not have quoted in its septuagintal form) of Peter's two proof-texts (Psalm 69.25 (LXX: 68.26) and Psalm 109.8 (LXX: 108.8)) is quite different from the quotations in the narrative of Acts and is incapable of being applied to Judas' circumstances[100]. Secondly, the idea of an apostle (1.21—22) is quite different from what primitive Christianity understood by the term[101]. Thirdly, the prayer of 1.25 is obviously the author's own composition, as "auch ein so konservativer Forscher wie Bauernfeind"[102] recognizes. (Another illustration of the same sort of thing is found in the speech put into the mouth of James in Acts 15.14—21)[103].

[157]

Haenchen does not, however, wish to be misunderstood to imply that what "Luke" writes he writes without making any use of tradition. Certainly, the author must have had access to all sorts of traditions, stemming from different localities and of different dates.

---

[99] *Die Apostelgeschichte*, NTD 5 (Göttingen, 1933; 2nd ed., 1935; 3rd ed., 1938; 4th ed., 1947; 5th ed., 1947; 6th ed., 1951; 7th ed., 1955; 8th ed., 1957; 9th ed., 1959). Beyer's commentary has not been mentioned heretofore. It is a good piece of work in terms of its purpose (for the non-specialist); but it adds nothing in particular to the history of *Actaforschung* and is therefore omitted due to lack of space.

[100] Haenchen quips that even the text of the Septuagint had to be altered by the author to suit his purpose (207)! In fact, the second quotation is only slightly different from either the Masoretic text or Septuagint. The quotation from Psalm 69 is different enough from both to suggest that it stems for a version which does not conform to the Masoretic text or the Septuagint.

[101] The only "proof" of this statement which the reader is offered is a note referring to the fact that the idea stated here agrees with the conception of 10.39 and 13.31 and to two pages of an article by Ernst Käsemann (208n.).

[102] O. Bauernfeind, *Die Apostelgeschichte*, THK 5 (Leipzig, 1939); another commentary omitted in this study simply because of lack of space.

[103] See also his essay, "Quellenanalyse und Kompositionsanalyse in Act. 15" (n.95) and the appropriate passage in his commentary (381—414). This should be compared with the essay by Dibelius on the same subject: *Aufsätze*, pp. 84 to 90.

But it would be an error to assume that his traditions go back to the earliest days of Christianity; rather, they are to be regarded as the traditions of the Church in the author's own day, traditions which have been shaped by legendary accretions and theological developments (208–9). Furthermore, it is important to recognize the fact that the traditions which "Luke" incorporates into his work were independent, floating traditions; he alone is responsible for bringing them together into a connected narrative, thus giving them a unity which they did not originally possess.

In much the same way as in the case of the Synoptic Gospels, the author is regarded as being entirely responsible for the framework in which the elements stemming from the tradition are combined. The framework is an artificially constructed mold into which the traditions are fitted. With Acts, however, the literary work of the author in shaping the traditional materials themselves is much more extensive than is true in the case of the Gospels. Many items which were regarded by the source critics to be "Bestandteile einer Tradi- [158] tion" upon examination "erweisen sich als Erzeugnisse lukanischer Kompositionskunst" (209). "Luke" has not simply taken over written sources and connected them together, as the older critics thought; on the contrary, he has himself created entire scenes and sequences of scenes out of very different traditions. Thus Luke was not, and did not wish to be, a historian in the sense that we use the word today. The literary method he followed is, in fact, closer to that which we look upon as legitimate only in the case of historical novels (210).

Further proof for the fact that "Luke" did not work as a historian, but was a deliberately creative writer in his shaping of his narrative, is found by Haenchen in the varying accounts of Paul's conversion in Acts 9, 12, and 26 (210–18). The differences which the source critics regarded to be evidence of the use of different sources by the author are for Haenchen evidence that the author freely adapted his material to the occasion and did not feel under any obligation to be strictly historical. In fact, the author was acquainted with only a single tradition concerning Paul's conversion; but "durch Kürzung, Ergänzung und Änderung" he made the three [159] passages "zum Bestandteil einer grösseren Einheit" and thereby achieved his aim in writing (217).

The remaining part of Haenchen's essay is concerned to enumerate the various ways "Luke" has twisted the facts of history by arbitrarily altering or inventing material to suit his own purposes (218–25). The author is concerned to emphasize the unity of the Church under the leadership of the *twelve* apostles. Thus he arran-

ges for another person to be elected to take Judas' place, harmonizes the existing factions in the Church, "corrects" the tradition
concerning the origin of Gentile Christianity in Antioch, and makes
Paul into a Law-keeping Jew who is in complete agreement with,
and under the authority of, the leaders of the Jerusalem church. He
is also concerned to give an *apologia* for Christianity over against
the Roman state. Thus he makes Christianity a religion of the resurrection (in contrast to the Pauline emphasis on the cross) and in
essence simply a sect of Judaism (and therefore deserving of recognition by the state as a *religio licita*).

When one recognizes the true relationship between tradition and
composition in the Book of Acts, concludes Haenchen, two conclusions follow:

[*160*]
    (1) Man stellt dann nicht mehr an die Apg Forderungen, die sich nach
den Bedingungen ihres Entstehens unmöglich erfüllen kann. Man sucht in
ihr keinen Dokumentarbericht und kein Selbstporträt der Apostelzeit
mehr; dafür findet man in ihr das Bild, mit dem sich eine neue christliche
Epoche die eigene Vergangenheit gedeutet hat. Die Apg gibt nicht die
paulinische Welt- und Heilslehre wieder, sie ist ein neuer Entwurf aus
einer veränderten Zeit . . .

    (2) Damit hängt ein Zweites zusammen: auch dieser aus dem nach-
apostolischen Christentum stammende Entwurf der christlichen Lehre hat,
trotzdem er sich tief von der paulinischen Theologie unterscheidet[104], im
Kanon Aufnahme gefunden. Daraus ergibt sich für uns die Folgerung:
der neutestamentliche Kanon hat nicht den Sinn, das Bemühen der Chri-
stenheit um ein eigenes Verständnis der christlichen Botschaft in der jeweiligen Epoche auszuschliessen, er gibt dieses Bemühen vielmehr frei. Das
gilt für die Zeit der Apg ebenso wie für die der Reformation und für
unsere eigene Gegenwart (225).

Although Haenchen is clearly a disciple of Dibelius in the fullest
sense of that word, his views are different from those of Dibelius in
a number of points. In a brief note in the essay cited above (220–2,
especially n. 1 on p. 221) Haenchen enthusiastically supports the
hypothesis of an *Itinerar* as advanced by Dibelius[105]. The only ap-
preciable difference between the view which he expresses here and
that of Dibelius is that Haenchen argues that the author, for theological and literary purposes, re-wrote his source in such a thorough-
going manner that it is impossible to determine the exact extent of

[*161*]
    [104] "Man kann den tiefsten Unterschied vielleicht auf die kurze Formel brin-
gen: Für Paulus ist die Heilsgeschichte in der Geschichte verborgen (also nur
dem Glauben erkennbar: theologia crucis), für Lukas wird sie in der Geschichte gerade sichtbar" (225n.). This opinion is developed in the commentary
(99–103, *passim*).
    [105] *Supra*, pp. 203–4.

the itinerary-document. The same position is adopted in the earliest edition of his commentary on Acts (33, 97, *passim*). Haenchen disagrees with Dibelius, however, regarding the extent of the itinerary, excluding the geographical and historical data of chapters 13 and 14 concerning the so-called first missionary journey of Paul[106] and extending it to include Acts 21.15—26. The narrative of chapters 27—28 concerning Paul's journey to Rome is regarded as stemming from the travel diary belonging to a sometime companion of Paul; however, it is not certain that this is the same document as the one lying behind chapters 16—21.

From 1959 onward Haenchen completely parts company with Dibelius over the question of the itinerary. In response to the views of E. Trocmé[107], who gave the hypothesis of Dibelius a new twist[108], Haenchen came to reject the *Itinerar*-hypothesis altogether[109]. He now points out that the hypothesis of an itinerary-document (as understood by Dibelius and Trocmé) rests merely on the use of "we" in the latter part of Acts and the listing of the stopping places of Paul and his retinue, and that these two elements occur together in only a few places (16.11—12; 20.5—6, 13—16; 21.1—9, 15—16). He then raises two objections. First, it is unnecessary to have recourse to the supposition of a source in order to explain the use of "we" in the narrative. The older commentators understood it as evidence that the author wished to indicate his presence with Paul in the narrative. Even Dibelius understood it as an editorial device by which the author wished to indicate his personal participation in these parts of Paul's travels. Haenchen, however, suggests that the use of "we" is simply a literary technique of the author by which he aims at making his narrative more forceful; that is, the first person plural gives the reader the feeling that he is himself sharing in the events which are being narrated[110]. Secondly, it is also unneces-

---

[106] He regards this to be largely the composition of the author and, for the most part, unhistorical. It should be noted that it was this very section of Acts that first caused Ramsay to begin to take the historicity of the narrative of Acts seriously. See above, pp. 136—42, and Gasque, *Sir William M. Ramsay*, pp. 24—28. Even the most radical critics have seldom denied the essential historicity of Acts 13.13—14.28 (excluding the speeches). This is an illustration of Haenchen's methodology and underlines the difference of approach between the New Testament critic who has been schooled in a unique tradition of criticism and the classical scholar or historian who has been trained in a broader perspective of historical research.

[107] *Le 'Livre des Actes' et l'Histoire* (Paris, 1957). The work of Trocmé is to be discussed in the following chapter (*infra*, pp. 268—71).

[108] Dupont, *Sources*, pp. 133—36, gives a good summary of Trocmé's hypothesis. [109] Cf. 1959 and 1961 editions, pp. 76—78 *et passim*.

[110] Cf. his commentary, pp. 428—32 *et passim*, and especially the essay,

sary to seek to explain the information concerning the details of Paul's journeys in terms of a hypothetical travel diary. If some passages contain incidental details which are so specific that they are hard to assign to the author's literary imagination, others are extremely vague. At any rate, whatever actually factual information is contained in the narrative could have been obtained by "Luke" by other means than through the use of an itinerary-source[111]. Furthermore — and here Haenchen breaks decisively with Dibelius — the Book of Acts could not have been written by a person who was actually in close enough historical proximity to Paul to have entered into possession of a document of this nature[112].

This final point suggests the major difference between the views of Dibelius and Haenchen on Acts. In spite of the fact that Dibelius regarded the Book to be to a large degree unreliable in its portrayal of the history and theology of the apostolic age, he had steadfastly maintained the traditional Lucan authorship of the Third Gospel and Acts. Haenchen, however, regards the view that Acts was written by a companion of Paul to be wholly untenable. In his essay, "The 'We' in Acts and the Itinerary", he dismisses Dibelius' argument for the Lucan authorship by reference to A. D. Nock's criticism of his understanding of the nature of ancient book dedication and publication in antiquity (335–36 = E. T. 71; 365–66 = E. T. 98)[113]. However, his main reason for denying that Luke-Acts could have been written by a former travelling companion of Paul is theological.

"Das 'Wir' in der Apostelgeschichte und das Itinerar" (n.95 above). Dupont points out the crucial difficulty of this interpretation of the "we" phenomenon: "Is it really in this way that a reader of New Testament times would interpret the 'we' of these narratives? Would it not be natural that he should rather see in them an indication from the writer of his personal participation in the events?" (*Sources*, p. 131). All the evidence we have points to the fact that they were in fact understood in the way Dupont suggests.

[111] He lists three possible ways the author may have obtained information: (1) by personally visiting the cities which Paul had visited, (2) by acquiring information from others who had been in these places, or (3) by writing to the various churches to request information (77–78).

[112] There is little doubt that Haenchen has demonstrated the artificiality of the itinerary-hypothesis, even if one does not accept his explanation of the "we" phenomenon. Nowadays, the hypothesis has been generally abandoned. See Dupont, *Sources*, pp. 140–65, for a summary of Haenchen's views and the subsequent discussion. I have nothing to add to Dupont's penetrating criticism of Haenchen's views and would concur entirely with his objections to the artificial and arbitrary manner in which he deals with the text (cf. pp. 128–29, 131, 140–47) and, in general, with his summation of the problem.

[113] Surely there is more in favor of the Lucan authorship of Acts than simply Dibelius' arguments concerning the circumstances surrounding the pub-

According to Haenchen the author of Acts is too far removed, both theologically and historically, from the apostolic age to understand the theology of the *Urapostel* or of Paul. Assuming that the Church was always united in its teaching, the author has constantly read the theology of a later generation back into the earlier period of the Church's history, concerning which he has little authentic knowledge[114]. This is, in his view, especially true in the case of his presentation of Paul.

In his section entitled "Luke and Paul" in the introduction to the 1961 edition of his commentary (99—103), Haenchen lists three items which he considers to be proof that the author could not have been "ein Paulus Gefährte". First, the author solves the problem [162] of the Gentile mission and the controversy concerning the Law in a totally un-Pauline fashion[115]. Secondly, the portrait of Paul in

---

lication of the Book of Acts! Incidentally, Haenchen omits to mention the opinion which Nock expresses on the next page of the review to which he refers: "I must confess that for many years I have found it impossible to equate (the author of Acts) with Paul's friend, 'the physician, the beloved'. The objections remain formidable, but I am now inclined to agree with Cadbury and Dibelius that he was a companion of Paul and with Dibelius that the traditional name may be used" (*Gnomon* 12, p. 502). Nock goes on to assert that the only really satisfactory explanation of the presence of "we" in the narrative is the traditional explanation. In contrast to Haenchen's improbable suggestion as to what an ancient reader would understand by "we", Nock (who was no mean authority on the literature of ancient Greece and Rome) knows of "only one possible parallel for the emphatic use of a questionable 'we' in consecutive narrative outside literature which is palpably fictional" (503). Perhaps Haenchen's answer would be that the narrative of Acts is, in many places, "palpably fictional"; but few would agree with him in this judgment.

[114] "Das Paulusbild, aber auch das gesamte Bild der Missionslage in der [163] Apg zeigt, dass hier kein Mitarbeiter des Paulus zu Wort kommt, sondern dass ein Mann der späteren Generation sich Dinge auf seine Weise zurechtzulegen sucht, deren wirkliche Perspektive nicht mehr gegeben ist" (103).
"Man hat Lukas gelegentlich gelobt, weil er die primitive Theologie der christlichen Anfangszeiten so treu darzustellen vermocht habe. Aber es ist seine eigene schlichte Theologie (die er mit seiner Gemeinde teilte), welche er überall voraussetzt und die man aus den Predigten, Gebeten, liturgischen Wendungen und gelegentlichen Bemerkungen in der Apg entnehmen muss" (81—82). On Acts 10.35, Haenchen comments: "It is certainly not Pauline theology that appears here, nor is it anything ever thought by Peter. It is, rather, the theology of Gentile Christianity toward the end of the first century in which Luke lived not only outwardly but theologically..." (*Studies in Luke-Acts*, p. 266). He does not tell us his source for the theological *thoughts* of Peter.
[115] I think it would be safe to say that only a small band of Lutheran scholars would recognize Haenchen's summary of Paul's attitude toward the Law (99—100) as anything other than a gross oversimplification or, indeed, a perversion of the Pauline view. This simplistic understanding of Paul's relation to the Law, and therefore to Judaism, fails to take into consideration the many

242

Acts contradicts the epistles, in that Paul is made to be a miracle worker[116], a forceful speaker[117], and not an apostle of equal standing with the Twelve[118]. And, thirdly, he contradicts the Pauline epistles in his portrayal of Jewish and Christian relations. These theological objections are then allied with what he regards to be

---

passages where Paul has a positive view of the Law, e. g., Romans 3.31; 7.12; chs. 9–11; etc. German scholars in particular have failed to recognize that "Rom. 9–11 is not an appendix to chs. 1–8, but the climax of the letter" (K. Stendahl, "The Apostle Paul and the Introspective Conscience of the West", *HTR* 56 (1963), p. 205). A number of recent studies have shown that Paul's theology of the Law is much more complex than some others would allow. See especially the writings of Johannes Munck, *Paulus und die Heilsgeschichte* (Copenhagen, 1954), E. T. *Paul and the Salvation of Mankind* (London, 1959); *Christus und Israel: Eine Auslegung von Rom. 9–11* (Copenhagen, 1956), E. T. (Philadelphia, 1967); C. E. B. Cranfield, "St. Paul and the Law", *SJT* 17 (1964), pp. 43–68; D. E. H. Whiteley, *The Theology of St. Paul* (Oxford, 1964), pp. 73–88; R. N. Longenecker, *Paul, Apostle of Liberty* (New York, 1964; and R. L. Love, *A Reconsideration of the Relationship between the Law and the Gospel in the Teaching of St. Paul* (diss. Manchester University, 1964). Even the Jewish scholar, Leo Baeck ("The Faith of Paul", *JJS* 3 (1952), pp. 108–9), recognized the positive aspect of Paul's attitude toward the Law and the Jewish people; what separated Paul from the rest of the Jews of his time, Baeck rightly observes, was not so much his attitude toward the Law but his conviction that Jesus was the Messiah.

[164] 116 Haenchen must admit, however: "Der wirkliche Paulus hat zwar auch gelegentlich die 'Zeichen des Apostels' beansprucht" (2 Cor. 12.12), but "diese Wunder waren so wenig aussergewöhnlich, dass seine Gegner ihm die Fähigkeit zum Wundertum einfach abgesprochen haben" (101). As evidence for the second part of this statement Haenchen offers a reference to one page of an essay by Käsemann!

[165] 117 "Aber der wirkliche Paulus war — er gibt es selbst zu — alles andere als ein Meister der improvisierten Rede. Mochte er, wenn er seine Briefe diktierte, die Worte finden, welche durch die Jahrhunderte fortklangen — als Sprecher wirkte er schwach und machte keinen Eindruck (2 Cor. 10.10). Wenn Lukas ihn so anders schildert, dann ist keine verklärende Erinnerung am Werk, sondern die so naheliegende Voraussetzung der späteren Generation, dass Paulus, der grosse Missionar, auch der grosse Redner gewesen sein muss" (101). In addition to pointing out Haenchen's questionable use of 2 Cor. 10.10 — the only "proof" he offers for his assertion — one could ask whether it is probable that one who placed the emphasis Paul did on the *kerygma* and who, in fact, founded a number of churches in various cities could have been anything other than a forceful speaker.

118 His argument here seems especially weak, in spite of the wide influence this view has had in the past century or so of citicism. Once again it may be pointed out that although it is true that the word is applied to Paul twice only (Acts 14.4, 14 — which are disallowed by Haenchen as evidence), it is obvious that Paul is Luke's hero and church-planting missionary *par excellence*. It would seem that the author, if anything, would argue that Paul was not merely equal with the other apostles, but the greatest of the apostles, although he may have had a rather different theological conception of an apostle than did Paul.

numerous insuperable problems related to the history of the apostolic age as narrated in the Book of Acts[119].

The commentary itself (nearly 600 pages) is a brilliant attempt to demonstrate the theses set forth in the above-mentioned essays, and lengthy introduction (103 pages). It is in every way a magnificently impressive piece of scholarship — a treasury of bibliographical, philological, and exegetical detail. The technical arrangement of the material is excellent: a fresh translation of each paragraph of Acts into German is followed by a bibliography of most important literature, a phrase by phrase commentary annotated by footnotes, and finally a summary and theological interpretation of the passage as a whole. It would be difficult to imagine a more thorough discussion of the text of Acts and its problems. Even when one does not agree with the conclusions of the author (which will be, for most scholars, fairly often!) he must confess that Haenchen has made him look at the text and the problem raised by it from every possible angle[120]. Not least among the qualities of the commentary is the clarity and vigor of the language (insofar as this can be detected by one who does not read German as his native language). In short, it would be accurate to refer to Haenchen's commentary as the most elaborately conceived and carefully executed German commentary on the Book of Acts up to the present day.

When all is said and done, however, it must be noted with a sense of disappointment that it is probable that Haenchen's great commentary will be regarded by future generations of scholars more

---

[119] See his essay in *Studies in Luke-Acts*, pp. 258—78, for a convenient list of what he regards to be the major objections to a positive evaluation of the Book of Acts as a reliable historical source. It would take a commentary of the same length to answer all his objections; however, a few comments may be appropriate. First, it should be noted that much of the evidence he brings forward in support of his views is evidence only in terms of his own premises and presents nothing new to the student of *Actaforschung;* scholars who are intimately familiar with the narrative of Acts and the facts of historical research do not, for the most part, find his objections to the historicity of Acts very convincing. Furthermore, Haenchen seems to be over/eager to classify "difficulties" as "errors". These difficulties would cause the classical historian no loss of sleep; indeed, he would expect them by the nature of the case. As R. M. Grant has wisely observed, "Historical events are not always historically comprehensible; in their particularity they often resist general or logical classification" (*A Historical Introduction to the New Testament* (London, 1963), p. 146). Finally, Haenchen is often in error as to the actual facts of history when he seeks to correct Luke.

[120] Cf. the judgment of van Unnik (n.121): "One may have serious doubts and criticisms of various points in [the writings of Vielhauer, Haenchen, and Conzelmann], but one cannot deny that they forced New Testament scholarship to look at the problems of Luke-Acts afresh" (23).

244

as a historical phenomenon belonging to one era of the history of exegesis than as a lasting contribution to New Testament research. It will, no doubt, continue to have a wide influence on the present generation of New Testament scholars; and it seems likely that the issues raised in its pages will continue to be "a storm-center in contemporary scholarship" (to allude to the title of a recent essay)[121] for at least another decade or so. But when the storm has subsided and New Testament critics are in a position to look back over the past two or three decades of research from the perspective of history they will, I think, be able to see that the commentary of Haenchen is as tendentious and ultimately as unhistorical as he thinks the author of the Book of Acts was.

It may seem presumptuous for a younger scholar to pass judgment in this way on the work of a man who is many times his superior in scholarly experience. However, the judgment is passed with a full sense of awareness of the course of New Testament criticism in the past. If what has been written in the earlier chapters of this monograph has any validity, it must be concluded that Haenchen's work has been based on false critical and historical premises which can only lead down a dead-end street. If the Tübingen critics (chapter 2) were basically wrong in their understanding of the nature of early Christianity and the problems of the Book of Acts and the critics of the Tübingen scholars (chapter 3) were essentially right (as I have argued), then Haenchen is wrong. If the criticism of the radical descendants of the Tübingen critics (chapter 4) and the representatives of critical orthodoxy at the end of the century (chapter 5) was basically wrong-headed from the beginning and the approach of Lightfoot and the British scholars (chapter 6) ultimately more critical and historical, then Haenchen's approach stands condemned. If Ramsay and Harnack and E. Meyer and Wikenhauser (chapter 7) were, in the main, correct in their conclusions, then Haenchen is incorrect in his. Even if truth is to be found on the side of Foakes-Jackson, Cadbury, Lake and company (chapter 8), who refused to side wholeheartedly with the defenders of the historical reliability of the Book of Acts but took a much more positive view of the matter than have the radical critics, very little truth can possibly be found on the side of the theories of Haenchen which have been discussed in the present chapter. On the other hand, if Haenchen's basic understanding of the nature of the Book of Acts is correct in its major details, then all these other scholars stand condemned.

[121] W. C. van Unnik, "Luke-Acts, a Storm Center in Contemporary Scholarship", in *Studies in Luke-Acts*, pp. 15–32.

In the face of the massive scholarship of Haenchen's commentary the critic is placed in a position of psychological disadvantage. Can views which are argued at such great length and buttressed by such impressive erudition be so wrong? Is it possible to be so thoroughly conversant with the text of Acts and the critical research of the past century and still be so misled in one's conclusions? The answer is: Yes, if one's critical vision is impaired by the wrong kind of glasses — i. e., if one has followed a false critical methodology. The student of Acts who is tempted to be overly impressed by size and pedantry should be reminded that the commentaries of Overbeck[122] and Loisy[123] were no less massive in their bulk nor less erudite in their scholarship; but they have been recognized by the world of New Testament scholarship to have been dominated by false presuppositions and prejudices which have tended to vitiate

---

[122] *Supra*, pp. 80—86.

[123] The commentary of the Roman Catholic Modernist, A. Loisy, *Les Actes des Apôtres* (Paris, 1920), has not been included in this study, both because of lack of space and because of the difficulty of fitting it into a systematic outline. Yet, along with those by Overbeck and Conzelmann (see below), it is among the commentaries with which Haenchen's work could be most fruitfully compared. It is the only one-man commentary of this century which equals Haenchen's in both volume and ingenuity. For this reason a brief synopsis is included at this point.

The edition of the Book of Acts which was received into the canon was, in Loisy's view, the literary result of an unscrupulous *rédacteur* who re-wrote the work of the traditional Luke. The original work of Luke was a simple presentation of the historical facts (92—94). These facts were profoundly revised by the editor, who worked shortly after the beginning of the second century (108); his revision of Luke's original work was probably officially commissioned by the orthodox party of the Church of Rome (104—6). He re-wrote the history of the apostolic age in the way it was conceived in the Epistle of Clement, which was also a product of the same community (7, 106); he added miracles, speeches, and even many overtly "historical" details to suit his own purposes (55, *passim*). His primary aim was to demonstrate to all, especially to the Roman authorities, that Christianity was not a new sect, but rather the authentic form of the Jewish religion and the fulfillment of its hopes; therefore, the official tolerance that Judaism enjoyed should be given to the Christians (107). In character with his conception of the way Christianity had been transformed by self-seeking ecclesiastics from a simple religion into a system of dogma, Loisy is warm in his praise of the original author, whose work can be detected here and there peeking through the seams of the superimposed narrative; but he is equally harsh in his criticism of the redactor. The latter was neither a profound thinker nor a good historian, but rather "un rhéteur de second ordre" (124). Loisy differs profoundly from Haenchen in that he regards the Book of Acts to be very rough and extremely poorly arranged in its final form (51); the author is indeed a creative and imaginative writer, but he is much more of a dimwit than Haenchen's theories would allow.

whatever positive contributions they may have made to the on-going work of New Testament research.

One of the major blinders hindering Haenchen in his work is a scarcely concealed antipathy to the theology, or at least to his version of the theology, of the author of Luke-Acts. Does he think that the author has corrupted the primitive purity and simplicity of early Christianity? At times it seems so. Or is "Luke" a symbol for Haenchen of that type of theology in the Church of the present day for which he has an extreme aversion? Whatever the reason, Haenchen constantly seeks to place his understanding of the theology of Paul over against that of the author of the Book of Acts, and the latter seems always to come off second best[124]. The fact that many scholars regard his conceptions of the Pauline and the Lucan theologies to be caricatures of both does not seem to deter him in his steadfast maintainance of this position[125].

A similar blinder seems to be worn by Haenchen in his criticism of the author's handling of historical details. Following Dibelius — and taking his views to an even greater extreme — Haenchen regards the writer to be more of a creative author than historian. Over and over again he alleges that "Luke" is not concerned to be historically accurate, but rather is desirous of writing a work which will edify the Church[126]. (But are the two aims as mutually exclusive as Dibelius and Haenchen have supposed?)

It is typical for Haenchen to begin his discussion of a particular passage by stressing all of the problems which he sees as standing in the way of accepting the narrative as historically trustworthy. Then, following a lengthy attempt which seeks to prove that the passage as it stands is grossly inaccurate, the *coup de grâce* is delivered to the author by the observation that "Luke" would not have been interested in such questions anyway!

---

[124] Cf. P. Vielhauer, "Zum 'Paulinismus' der Apostelgeschichte", *EvTh* 10 (1950/51), pp. 1—15; E. T. "On the 'Paulinism' of Acts", in *Studies in Luke-Acts*, pp. 33—50. This essay is generally regarded as initiating the recent discussion of the theology of Luke-Acts in Germany (see, e. g., Haenchen's commentary, p. 45). See below, pp. 283—91.

[125] See U. Wilckens, "Interpreting Luke-Acts in a Period of Existentialist Theology", in *Studies in Luke-Acts*, pp. 60—83. Note Wilckens' conclusion: "It is Paul, interpreted existentially, who is so sharply set against Luke as the great but dangerous corrupter of the Pauline gospel. But the existentially interpreted Paul is not the historical Paul" (77).

[126] Cf. "The question of the historical reliability of the book of Acts does not touch the central concern of the book. By telling the history of apostolic times through many individual stories, the book primarily intends to edify the churches and thereby contribute its part in spreading the Word of God farther and farther, even to the ends of the earth" (*Studies in Luke-Acts*, p. 278).

While everyone must be impressed by the breadth of Haenchen's reading and the vitality of his imagination, few who come to the study of his commentary from the perspective of a less theologically oriented historical research will fail to be impressed by the arbitrary and unfair way he treats the narrative of Acts. It would be difficult, if not impossible, to find a scholar outside of the realm of New Testament (or perhaps Old Testament) criticism nowadays who would treat *any* ancient document in the manner in which Haenchen treats the Book of Acts. It would be doubtful whether even the histories of Thucydides or Polybius, much less those of lesser authorities, could stand up to such extreme and artificial criticism. If historians in general approached other historical texts with the methodology of Haenchen, the result would be a thoroughgoing historical skepticism. Fortunately, historical and literary critics who are not theologians have long since abandoned such methods.

It would involve too much space to go into further detail in criticism of the views of Haenchen. The only adequate answer would be to write a commentary on Acts which would be on the same grand scale as his work and would offer a more convincing and satisfying interpretation of the data which he discusses. In a sense this has already been done by Knowling and by Bruce[127], by Ramsay and by Wikenhauser, by Harnack and by Eduard Meyer; and a large body of New Testament scholars will undoubtedly continue to consider their writings as making a more lasting contribution to the illumination of the Book of Acts than the work of Haenchen and other like-minded colleagues. Nevertheless, the writings of Martin Dibelius and Ernst Haenchen do mark an epoch in the history of criticism and must be answered specifically, in their turn, by fresh researches on the part of the next generation of scholars.

One can hardly think of the name of Ernst Haenchen nowadays without thinking also of the name of Hans Conzelmann (1915 —). Conzelmann, professor at the University of Göttingen, is well-known as the author of a creative and stimulating monograph on the theology of Luke-Acts[128], a study which has probably had a wider influence than any other in the current resurgence of Lucan research. His conception of the literary method and theological point of view of the author is very similar to that of Haenchen, though he claims

---

[127] The work of F. F. Bruce, author of the major commentary in English since the *The Beginnings of Christianity* project, has been touched on only incidentally up to this point. His work is to be discussed in the following chapter (*infra*, pp. 257—64).

[128] *Die Mitte der Zeit* (Tübingen, 1954); E. T. *The Theology of St. Luke* (London, 1960). This work will be discussed in the following chapter (*infra*, pp. 291—95).

that they arrived at their basic conclusions independently of one another[129]. The slender commentary on the Book of Acts which he wrote for the newest edition of the *Handbuch zum Neuen Testament*[130] can be fruitfully compared to the larger commentary of Haenchen[131].

Conzelmann's commentary is hardly a commentary in the normal sense of the word. If the aim of the series of which it is a part is to include as much information as possible in a small number of pages, then Conzelmann outdoes himself in fulfilling this aim. The result is that the work is only barely intelligible to the expert, much less to the larger body of theological students and pastors for which it is ostensibly designed. With the exception of a few pages of introduction (1—10), outline (11—12), bibliography (13—14), and German translation of the Greek text of Acts (which occupies approximately one-half of every other page), the impression is that of a concordance-lexicon-dictionary combination (in a very abbreviated form) arranged in the order in which words, phrases, and concepts appear in the narrative of the Book of Acts. It is extremely valuable as a source-book for the exegesis of Acts[132], but its value as a commentary (if it is such) is much less.

Historical skepticism seems to have reached its peak in Conzelmann's treatment of Acts. Not even Bruno Bauer[133] could be more extreme, and Haenchen seems rather conservative by comparison. Conzelmann agrees with Haenchen in stressing the literary creativity of the author and in finding evidence of the hand of the author in composing events as well as speeches; but he goes further than Haenchen.

Did Haenchen argue that the account of the journey of Paul recorded in Acts 13—14 was largely the composition of the author (without denying that there was an actual journey)? Conzelmann argues that the whole idea of a missionary journey of Paul through the cities mentioned was invented by the author (72—81). Did Haenchen suggest that the use of "we" was merely a literary device to give a greater vividness to the narrative and to make the reader feel as if he were actually participating in the events personally (without denying a residue of historical fact)? Conzelmann rejects as unreliable nearly all the remaining items (admittedly few in num-

---

[129] See the foreword to his commentary.

[130] *Die Apostelgeschichte* (Tübingen, 1963).

[131] Conzelmann's review of Haenchen's commentary (*TLZ* 85 (1960), pp. 241—50) indicates some of the basic points of disagreement between the two authors; the differences are not, however, major.

[132] Its value would be enhanced by the inclusion of an index.

[133] *Supra*, pp. 73—77.

ber) which Haenchen had allowed to stand as accurate, or nearly accurate, portrayals of historical reality. Not only the *form* of the narrative of the voyage and shipwreck of Paul in Acts 27 is literary (as Haenchen), but he seems to imply that *every aspect* of the account is the result of the author's fictitious invention (140—47)[134]! With a very few exceptions the whole of the narrative of Acts seems to be attributed to *literarische und theologische Motive*. If the Book of Acts to Haenchen is something *close to* a historical novel, it *is* a historical novel to Conzelmann — and greatly lacking in the use of historical imagination at that.

As in the case of Haenchen, one can only confess to a great admiration of the erudition and creative scholarship manifested by Conzelmann in his commentary. Once more the student of Acts is made to look at the text of the Book of Acts from angles he did not even know existed and to re-examine all of his previous conceptions of the book and its problems. Nevertheless, the best which can be said of the commentary is that it is stimulating. Convincing, it is not. It is so extreme in its views and arbitrary in its criticism that, in the long run, it may even cause critics to have second thoughts about the *redaktionsgeschichtlich* approach altogether. At any rate, it brings out the grave weaknesses of this method of criticism (at least, in the hands of the more radical critics). Whatever one may say of Conzelmann's seminal work on the Lucan theology, it is doubtful whether the major conclusions of his commentary on Acts will ever command general acceptance in the world of scholarship[135].

As was true in the case of the Tübingen scholars near the beginning of the modern period of critical research and their second generation descendants at the end of the nineteenth century, so the writings of Martin Dibelius, Ernst Haenchen, and Hans Conzelmann illustrate the weaknesses of an inward-looking criticism. There is no question but that the ideas put forward by these three scholars have been creative and exceedingly stimulating. They have even

---

[134] Conzelmann's treatment of the narrative of the sea voyage and shipwreck might well be regarded as the *reductio ad absurdum* of the practice of unbridled *Redaktionsgeschichte*. R. P. C. Hanson, "The Journey of Paul and the Journey of Nikias: An Experiment in Comparative Historiography", *Studia Evangelica* 4, *TU* 102 (Berlin, 1968), pp. 315—18, has demonstrated the folly of Conzelmann's method by applying the same approach to an account of a sea voyage which every historian of the ancient world admits to be reliable, not only in substance but in detail. As Prof. Hanson remarks elsewhere: "No document in the world could stand up to criticism as captious as this" (*JTS* N. S. 15, p. 374).

[135] For the sake of space the reader is referred to the review of Conzelmann's commentary by R. P. C. Hanson in *JTS* N. S. 15 (1964), pp. 371—75, with which I am in essential agreement.

succeeded in founding something akin to a new school of thought in regard to the critical understanding of the Lucan writings. No serious scholar can afford to ignore their researches, nor will he fail to be grateful for their bringing the problems related to the study of the Third Gospel and the Book of Acts to his attention. All would be agreed that they have raised many questions which deserve careful consideration, but few will agree that they have said the last word or have given very satisfactory answers to the problems which they themselves have raised.

One thing which stands out clearly in the work of these scholars is their sovereign disregard for the work of other scholars outside of their own critical and theological circles. For a start, there is scarcely a mention of British and American scholars in the writings of Dibelius and Conzelmann. Haenchen, the only one of the three to give the slightest hint of being aware of non-German literature, does at least list a large number of British and American works in his bibliographical notes; but even in his case one does not have the impression that he really enters into dialogue with the writers listed. The contributions of the British and German scholars who, *for historical-critical reasons*, have been led to defend the essential reliability of the Book of Acts as a document of first century history have been, for the most part, ignored or by principle rejected. This in turn has resulted in the genesis of an allegedly new approach to the Book of Acts which has been built on exceedingly shaky foundations. Inasmuch as the Dibelius-Haenchen-Conzelmann point of view can be regarded as building on the past its foundations are the unquestioned assumptions of the older critical orthodoxy — which in turn were leftovers from the era of *Tendenzkritik* — combined with a few more modern ones derived from German existential theology. Neither source offers a very firm basis upon which to build critical hypotheses[136].

---

[136] There is no need (even if there were space) to list the detailed criticisms of the Dibelius-Haenchen-Conzelmann point of view at this point, as if it were an isolated phenomenon in the history of New Testament criticism. In addition to the specific criticisms which have been made in the context of the present chapter, the chapters which have preceded and the one to follow should be interpreted as implicit criticisms of this school of *Actaforschung*.

Chapter X

LUKE THE HISTORIAN AND THEOLOGIAN IN RECENT RESEARCH

Although the views of Martin Dibelius have exerted an immense influence on recent research in Germany, they have been much less influential in the world outside[1]. Generally speaking, non-German scholars (and not a few Germans in addition) have tended to regard the conclusions of Dibelius and the school of criticism which owes its allegiance to him as, at the least, unproven or even essentially erroneous. In contrast to what a few German critics suppose to have been "demonstrated" by the researches of Dibelius[2], a considerable number of scholars of varying theological and critical points of view persist in defending a radically different understanding of the literary and historical character of the Book of Acts. The principal difference of point of view is indicated by the fact that this latter group of critics continues to argue that Luke was concerned to be a historian, albeit an "ancient" one, and that he achieved some measure of success in the fulfillment of his conception of his task.

This difference of basic judgment concerning the Book of Acts as history is seen especially, though by no means exclusively, in the writings of British scholars. Their reasons for rejecting what some scholars assume to have been proven is not primarily theological, but historical. The dissenters would all view themselves as first and foremost exegetes and historians, rather than theologians; two of the major contributions to *Actaforschung* in the United Kingdom

---

[1] Contrary to the hope expressed by Haenchen (*Die Apostelgeschichte*, p. 39), the translation of Dibelius' *Aufsätze* into English has done little to alter this fact.

[2] One sometimes finds views being put forward as "the assured results of criticism" concerning the Book of Acts, which are, in fact, simply the personal opinion of a small minority of the international community of New Testament scholars. An especially notable example of this narrow outlook is the section on Luke-Acts in the recently-translated *Introduction to the New Testament* by Willi Marxsen (Oxford, 1968). Such a cavalier dismissal (or ignorance?) of the arguments of the opposition can only serve to raise questions concerning the integrity of the position which is being defended.

in recent years have been made by men who are, in fact, not theologians at all, but who have come to the study of Acts from the point of view of classical-historical research. Thus their views cannot be dismissed as though they were simply the expression of unreconstructed traditionalist opinion merely because they often defend traditionally held opinions. (Were students of the Bible *invariably* incorrect in their conclusions before the rise of modern criticism?). The view could be argued, with a degree of validity, that the scholars who have rejected the conclusions of Dibelius are, for the most part, freer from the influence of traditional views than are those who have followed in the footsteps of Dibelius — only the tradition from which they are free is a relatively modern one. Be that as it may, it is certain that critics who have been relatively independent of the influence of Dibelius have made lasting contributions to the history of the study of the Book of Acts. I would be prepared to defend the view that their contribution will ultimately be seen to have been much more lasting than that of those critics who have based their investigations on the foundation provided by the criticism of Dibelius. However, the reader will have to judge for himself whether this is true or not.

The purpose of the present chapter is to give a survey of a few of the most important of recent contributions to *Actaforschung*. An attempt has been made to include works which are representative of the whole spectrum of recent opinion. The underlying assumption of what follows is that the work of New Testament scholarship is an international enterprise, not the special perogative of one national group (whether German or British) or critical point of view (whether radical or conservative). The point of departure will be the research which has been carried on during the past two decades or so in Great Britain and on the Continent in relative independence of the influence of the work of Dibelius (though the work of these scholars has always been done with a full awareness of the views of Dibelius). This will be followed by a brief account of some of the more important contributions to the recent discussion concerning the theology of Luke-Acts. The survey will be of necessity very selective, since the bibliography of recent research is so vast[3].

---

[3] For bibliographical surveys of literature on the Book of Acts since 1940, see J. Dupont, *Les problèmes du Livre des Actes d'après les travaux récents, AnLov* 2, 17 (Louvain, 1950) = *Études sur les Actes des Apôtres* (Paris, 1967), pp. 11—124; W. G. Kümmel, "Das Urchristentum", *TR* N. F. 22 (1954), pp. 138—70, 191—211; E. Grässer, "Die Apostelgeschichte in der Forschung der Gegenwart", *TR* N. F. 26 (1960), pp. 93—167; and D. Guthrie, "Recent Literature on the Acts of the Apostles", in *Vox Evangelica II*, ed. by R. P. Martin (London, 1963), pp. 33—49. For an excellent and up-to-date account of recent

British scholarship has, for the most part, continued in the tradition of historically oriented criticism as pioneered by Lightfoot and Ramsay. In the study of the New Testament documents the emphasis has continued to be on the study of the primary sources in the context of the larger field of historical research — classical literature and history, archaeology, and the ancient world in general. This concern for an authentically historical understanding of the writings of the New Testament could be said to be the fundamental point of agreement of the British exegetes who are to be discussed in the present context. There is no evidence that they are members of a particular ecclesiastical tradition or school of theological interpretation; they are, rather, heirs of a common historical-critical method which they share with the world of classical and historical scholarship.

Between 1925 and 1948, W. L. Knox of Cambridge penned a number of strikingly original and generally helpful monographs on various aspects of the history of early Christianity[4]. The final of the four studies is a brief, but stimulating, book dealing with various problems related to the study of Acts[5], in which the author discusses the fundamental questions of authorship (1—15, 100—9), sources (16—39), the relation of the Epistle to the Galatians to the account of the council of Jerusalem in Acts (40—53), history (54—68), and theology (69—99). The book is not a comprehensive treatment of these topics, but rather a collection of thoughts suggesting the main line of Knox's approach to the solution of some of these problems.

In his treatment of the question of authorship Knox defends the view which is still the dominant view among British scholars, *viz.* that the author was Paul's friend, Luke. He writes:

We have ... evidence as good as can be expected both for the antiquity of the book and for the belief that the author was a companion of St. Paul, who also wrote the Gospel according to St. Luke. ... There seems no reason why Luke should have been selected out of the Pauline circle except on the basis of a good tradition; if the author were unknown, we should expect the second century to have identified the author with a more prominent figure (2).

Lucan research in general, see E. E. Ellis, *The Gospel of Luke* (London, 1966), pp. 1—60.

[4] *St. Paul and the Church of Jerusalem* (Cambridge, 1925); *St. Paul and the Church of the Gentiles* (Cambridge, 1939); *Some Hellenistic Elements in Primitve Christianity* (London, 1944); and *The Acts of the Apostles* (Cambridge, 1948). All four books contain data relevant for the exegesis of Acts.

[5] This volume is sometimes mistakenly described as a commentary, presumably by scholars who have never seen it.

The greater part of the chapter on authorship (in addition, there is an appendix on the subject at the end of the book) is, however, devoted to a linguistic examination of the data brought forward by A. C. Clark[6], in support of his view that the Third Gospel and Acts are the work of different authors. He demonstrates, to the satisfaction of all critics, the faulty nature of Clark's interpretation of the linguistic data.

Concerning the author's use of sources Knox suggests that there is good reason to favor the view that a written source lies behind chapters 1 through 5 (excluding the speeches, for the most part), but that otherwiese Luke's sources are probably oral (frequently having been taken down verbatim)[7]. He follows C. H. Dodd[8] in discerning in the speeches of the early chapters a more or less fixed pattern of preaching, which may or may not have existed in written form. Although he thinks he can see the hand of the author in adapting, sometimes altering to a degree, and often using his materials for theological purposes, Knox's general conception of the author's literary method is in stark contrast to that of critics who view Luke primarily as a creative writer. Except for the latter half of the book, where he was an eyewitness to many of the events he records, Luke is primarily a collector and editor of traditional materials.

Perhaps the most significant part of Knox's brief study is his discussion of "the central problem of Acts" (40), that is, the relation between the autobiographical statements of Paul in Galatians 1—2 and the narrative of Acts. Here he defends the view which has commended itself to many British exegetes since the investigations of Ramsay. He argues that the identification of Paul's visit recorded in Galatians 2.1—10 with that of Acts 15 has little to commend it outside of the fact that it is the traditional view. There is no internal evidence in either Galatians or Acts which compels one to identify the two visits. On the other hand, the historical events fit together much more easily if one identifies Galatians 2.1—10 with the famine visit of Acts 11.30 and dates Paul's letter to the Galatians prior to the council of Acts 15. The arguments of Knox are too detailed to

---

[6] *The Acts of the Apostles* (Oxford, 1933).

[7] He makes an important observation concerning Luke's possible use of oral and written sources: "I am not at all clear how one can be entirely certain in distinguishing between a written source and an oral source committed to memory in a fixed form for the purposes of liturgical usage. Nor is it clear whether information given by word of mouth can be distinguished from information given, for example, by letter: one is 'oral' and one is 'written', but it is hard to see what difference there is between them in reliability" (16n.—17n.).

[8] *Supra*, p. 202n.

be enumerated at this point[9]; it is sufficient to note that this interpretation of the historical data cannot be easily dismissed.

Knox also adds his voice to the almost unanimous opinion of British scholarship that there is no convincing reason for the view that Paul could not have consented to the agreement of the Jerusalem conference concerning dietary laws.

If he had gained his main point, that the Gentile converts need not be circumcised, there was no reason why he should not accept a rule with regard to food which was harmless in itself, and was at the moment rightly regarded as essential to the common life of the Church. It was circumcision that was the obstacle to any widespread conversion of Gentiles in view of the Greek dislike of mutilation of any kind. On the other hand sharing in the common meal and eucharist was the center of the life of the Church. If Jews would not eat with uncircumcised Gentiles at Antioch, it meant that Gentiles would be an inferior caste in the Church; but with the growth of Gentile Churches a refusal to recognize the Jewish law as to *kosher* meat would mean that the Jews would be in danger of becoming an inferior caste; and this would be equally undesirable (47)[10].

Again, Knox's conclusion concerning the historicity of the narrative of Acts is representative of British New Testament scholarship:

Thus there is no reason to doubt Luke's veracity within the limits which he sets himself; he is not a great historian or biographer by modern standards; but by the standards of his age he has given a fresh and interesting account of the vital part of Paul's missionary career, which has preserved on the whole an accurate account of the development of Christianity (61).

One must remember, however, the limits of the narrative. The Book of Acts is not a strictly arranged history of the early Church, but rather an account of "the advance of the Gospel from Jerusalem to Rome" (66). Therefore, the author dramatizes his materials, includes miracles in his narrative[11], and is sometimes careless in his

---

[9] But see above, pp. 141—42, 177—78; cf. also F. F. Bruce, "The Epistles of Paul", *Peake's Commentary on the Bible*, rev. ed., pp. 930—31; and "Galatian Problems: 1. Autobiographical Data", *BJRL* 51 (1968/69), pp. 292—305.

[10] Compare the view of Ritschl (*Supra*, pp. 62—63); F. V. Filson, *Three Crucial Decades* (London, 1963), pp. 109—14.

[11] Concerning the miracles of Acts, Knox makes these comments: "In considering the matter, we must bear two points in mind. The first is that Luke as a pious Christian believed that miracles were both possible and probable; so did all his contemporaries except those who were professedly Epicureans or Sceptics. Consequently we cannot expect that he would have been as strict in

compilation of his sources (but even here he is "no worse than (other writers) who set out to be serious historians" (67—68). He has chosen the form of a travel-story for his narrative, because this form was one which would probably appeal to the public taste (and probably to his own), but also because it suited the historical facts. When examined in terms of these limitations the author "appears to be a truthful recorder of the facts available to him" (68) .

Finally, in his chapter dealing with the theology of Acts, Knox gives special attention to the question of the speeches. Although they "are not historical in the sense that they are summaries of what was said" on the occasions indicated in the narrative (45), the speeches seem to be historically reliable in the sense that they portray in an accurate manner the theology of Paul and the primitive Palestinian church. Knox fails to find evidence for the claim that Luke has read the theology of the Church of his own day back into the early period (72—80), or that he has in any significant way misunderstood or misrepresented the theology of the historical Paul (69—71, 94—97)[12]. As far as the speeches of Paul in particular are concerned, Knox points out (a) the Hellenistic Jewish background of the theological ideas expressed in Acts 14.15—17 and 17.22—31 (and Paul was a Hellenistic Jew!) and (b) the authentically Pauline elements of the speeches. Moreover, although it would be inaccurate simply to equate the theologies of Paul and Luke, Knox detects allusions to characteristically Pauline doctrines even at various places in the historical narrative (e. g. 13.34, 48; 14.3).

Why then, one may ask, does Paul's characteristic emphases of "justification by faith", "grace", etc. fail to appear in the speeches attributed to him in Acts? Knox answers this with another question: Were these really *characteristic* emphases of the historical Paul, or simply aspects of his argument against those who argued that it was necessary for Gentiles to keep the Law in order to be saved? These emphases do not appear uniformly in the Pauline letters; for example, "justification by faith" is emphasized only in Galatians and Romans. In point of fact, neither the epistles of Paul nor the Book

---

demanding evidence for his miracles as we should have wished him to be. The second point is that 'miracles' actually occurred. No doubt there has been much exaggeration of the kind natural in an uncritical age; but Paul could not appeal to the miracles wrought by the Spirit of God among the Galatians (Gal. iii.5) as a desperate argument to prevent his readers from going over to Judaism, if he knew that the answer would be that his readers had never heard of any such miracles. Similarly he could hardly have spoken so 'boastfully' of what Christ had done through him in the way of signs and wonders, if in fact there had been none (Ro. xv. 18)" (62).

[12] See his discussion of Acts 13.38—39 (94—95).

of Acts provides one with a systematic exposition of Paul's theology. In brief,

it was not part of Luke's scheme to write a manual of dogmatic theology as expounded by his teacher, but to write an account of his travels, in which his expositions of the Gospel were introduced at appropriate points. ... Within his limits Lukes gives a good exposition of Paul's doctrinal position, all the better in that he does not over-emphasize that particular aspect of it which dominates Galatians and Romans and disappears from the rest of the Pauline Epistles (97).

Thus there is reason to conclude that even in the theological aspect of his task, Luke is a generally reliable historian.

The most important commentary to be written in English since *The Beginnings of Christianity* project, which was completed in 1933, is by F. F. Bruce, Rylands Professor of Biblical Criticism and Exegesis at Manchester University since 1959. Bruce is, in fact, the author of *two* commentaries on Acts[13], the only full-scale commentaries on the book to appear in Britain since those by Rackham and Knowling, which appeared at the turn of the century.

Bruce's conclusions would be classified as generally conservative, but they cannot be gainsaid for this reason. Both commentaries are thoroughly critical in the best sense of that word, and he never dismisses any serious point of view without stating his reasons. The chief value of Bruce's work lies in his strictly historical approach. Before turning to the New Testament he was a classicist, having been trained at the Universities of Aberdeen (where he studied under Alexander Souter, Ramsay's successor as Professor of Humanity), Cambridge, and Vienna. The commentary on the Greek text is a model of the best sort of commentary on any ancient historical document, religious or secular; the second is more theological,

[13] *The Acts of the Apostles* (London, 1951; 2nd ed., 1952); *Commentary on the Book of Acts*, NIC/NLC (Grand Rapids and London, 1952). It is not often recognized that these are two *different* commentaries. The first is a strictly critical commentary and limits itself to linguistic, textual, and historical matters; the second, although based on a careful exegesis of the Greek text, is an exposition of the English text of Acts (the American Standard Version of 1901). The second volume is not simply a re-hash of the material of the previous volume, but adds considerably to it. Those who have the patience to work through both volumes — a combined total of more than a thousand pages! — will be richly rewarded. The commentary cited below is the second edition of the commentary on the Greek text, unless indicated otherwise. A convenient summary of Bruce's mature conclusions will be found in *The New Bible Dictionary*, ed. J. D. Douglas (London, 1962), pp. 10—12. See also select bibliography of his writings in *Apostolic History and the Gospel: Biblical and Historical Essays presented to F. F. Bruce on his 60th Birthday*, ed. by W. W. Gasque and R. P. Martin (Exeter and Grand Rapids, 1970), pp. 21—34.

making up for what some would regard to be a deficiency in the earlier volume.

Bruce is perhaps the commentator on the Book of Acts who has been most strongly influenced by Ramsay. In the preface to the second edition of his Greek commentary, he makes this comment:

> My debt to the writings of Sir William Ramsay is evident throughout the book, and I am repeatedly amazed by modern writers who deal with areas of New Testament scholarship to which Ramsay made contributions of peculiar value, with hardly so much as a hint that such a person ever lived (viii).

But Bruce is by no means a blind follower of Ramsay. A careful examination of the eighty or so references to the writings of Ramsay in his Greek commentary will reveal that he feels free to call into question many of Ramsay's more speculative ideas and improbable suggestions. Nevertheless, Bruce and Ramsay are in essential agreement on two points — that the Book of Acts should be studied in the context of the larger world of historical research, and that from this perspective the Book of Acts has been demonstrated to be an essentially accurate piece of historical writing.

To go into great detail in discussing Bruce's reasons for the view that the Book of Acts, "viewed as a historical document, stands in the line of descent from Thucydides" (15) would demand the repetition of a great deal of what has been written earlier in our study (especially chapters 6 and 7). It should be emphasized, however, that, in company with Ramsay and Eduard Meyer, Bruce's reasons for this positive evaluation of Luke's history are (at least, overtly) historical, rather than theological. It is because he is thoroughly familiar with Greek historical literature in general that he judges the work of Luke in this fashion. Luke's method is that of the ancient historians (allowing for a difference of religious point of view, of course); and tested by the same standards whereby scholars test the historical accuracy of other ancient writings, his reputation as a historian comes through unscathed (15—18).

Perhaps the most valuable part of the lengthy introduction to Bruce's commentary on the Greek text is the section dealing with the problems raised by the attempt to relate the data of the Pauline epistles to the narrative of Acts (34—40)[14]. He regards the conflicts between the Book of Acts and the Pauline epistles, for the

---

[14] See his essay in *Peake's Commentary* (n. 9) and his *An Expanded Paraphrase of the Epistles of Paul* (Exeter, 1965) for further details of his views concerning the interrelation between the data of Acts and the data of the Epistles.

most part, to be apparent, rather than real. The contrasting "Paul of the Acts" and the "Paul of the Epistles", for example, are regarded as due more to the result of critical imagination than to historical exegesis. The theory that Peter and the *Urapostel* were rigid legalists who insisted on the continued observance of the Law by Gentile believers as well as Jews, and that Paul was (as some of his opponents said) an *antinomian* who advocated complete liberty from the Jewish Law for Jewish Christians, as well as for Gentiles, has little foundation in the epistles *or* in the Book of Acts. Although in Galatians Paul insists upon the fact that he received the Gospel and his commission to preach it directly from God, apart from human mediation (Gal. 1.1, 11—12), he says expressly in 1 Corinthians 15.11 that the Gospel he preached was essentially the same as that preached by the original apostles. The same is also implied in the Epistle to the Galatians, where Paul claims that Peter, John and James gave to him and Barnabas "the right hand of fellowship" (Gal. 2.9) in their ministry among Gentiles, without giving the slightest hint that there was any basic difference in the message to be preached to Gentiles and to Jews. Again, when "Paul pronounces a solemn and repeated anathema on any who should preach a different Gospel from that which he preached" (Gal. 1.8—9), "he says nothing to imply that the Jerusalem Apostles were liable to this anathema" (34). Furthermore, Paul emphasizes the fact that Peter's withdrawal from table-fellowship with the Gentile believers at Antioch was an act of ὑπόκρισις (Gal. 2.13), since, although he was in basic agreement with Paul, he was temporarily acting in a manner which did not, in fact, correspond to his own convictions in the matter[15].

The problem of relating Paul's actions in Acts (i. e., his acceptance of the decisions of the apostolic council, his circumcision of Timothy, his performance of a rite in the Temple to calm those who were alarmed by the rumour that he taught Jews to forsake the Law of Moses) to the anti-Judaizing emphasis of Galatians is essentially solved when one recognizes the one-sided nature of the latter, written in the white-hot heat of controversy, and when one recognizes Paul's positive emphasis on Christian liberty. Paul made a funda-

---

[15] For a discussion of the biblical data relevant to the problem of Paul's relation to the Jerusalem Church, see Bruce, "Paul and Jerusalem", *Tyndale Bulletin* 19 (1968), pp. 3—27. Cf. also J. Munck, *Paul and the Salvation of Mankind;* A. M. Hunter, *Paul and His Predecessors*, rev. ed. (London, 1961); P. Fannon, "The Influence of Tradition in St. Paul", *Studia Evangelica IV, TU* 102 (1968), pp. 292—307 (with extensive bibliography); and G. E. Ladd, "Revelation and Tradition in Paul", in *Apostolic History and the Gospel*, pp. 223—230.

mental distinction between keeping religious observances freely (Rom. 14.5–6) and keeping them with a view to securing divine favor (Galatians). The former would have been perfectly permissible to Paul (cf. 1 Cor. 7.18–19, where he indicates that converted Jews, like himself, need not cease to observe ancestral customs)[16]; but with the motive of self-justification in view, he would have regarded such as a denial of the grace of God. This attitude may seem inconsistent to some modern critics (as it was to Paul's Judaizing opponents), but it seems to represent the historical Paul fairly. Paul was not one to allow the principle of "freedom from the Law" to become, in effect, another yoke of bondage for the sake of consistency[17].

Whereas some critics would stress the difficulty of harmonizing the epistles with Acts (especially Galatians 1–2 with Acts 9–15), Bruce stresses the many points of obvious agreement which exist between the two. A few of these correspondences are listed. (1) The Paul of Acts is the Paul of the epistles in his attitude toward the Jews.

> It is the Paul who repeats in Rom., "To the Jew, first, and also to the Greek", who in Ac. visits the synagogues first in city after city, and who in Pisidian Antioch declares to the envious Jews: "It was necessary that the word of God should be spoken to you first." It is the Paul who suffers so much from Jewish hostility in Ac. who can speak of the Jews in I Th. ii.15 f. as those "who killed both the Lord Jesus and the prophets, and have persecuted us, and do not please God, and are contrary to all men, forbidding us to speak to the Gentiles, that they should be saved". It is also the Paul who in Ac. refuses to stop offering the Gospel to his brethren according to the flesh in spite of all his bitter experiences from their hands, who in Rom. ix. 2 f. tells of his great sorrow and unceasing anguish of heart at their refusal to receive the Gospel, and is willing himself to be accursed, if only his heart's desire and prayer to God for their salvation be accomplished (36–37).

(2) The Paul who works with his hands in Corinth and Ephesus (Acts 18.1–3; 20.33–35) and exhorts the Ephesian elders to learn a lesson from him in this respect (20.33–35) is the same Paul who shows the same example and teaches the same lesson to the Thessalonians and Corinthians in his letters (1 Thess. 2.3–10; 2 Thess. 3.7–9; 1 Cor. 4.12; 9.3–18; 2 Cor. 4.5; 11.7–9; 12.13). (3) The Paul who in Acts "can adapt himself so readily to Jew and Gentile, learned and unlearned, Areopagus and Sanhedrin, synagogue audi-

---

[16] Bruce points out that even in Galatians (5.6), Paul "insists that circumcision in itself is immaterial" (36n.).

[17] See above, pp. 66–67, 154, 178.

ence and city mob, Roman governor and King Agrippa" (37) is the
Paul who underlines his basic missionary strategy in 1 Corinthians
9.19—23. (4) The Paul who is, according to Acts, God's "chosen
vessel" to carry God's name before the Gentiles (Acts 9.15) is the
one who claims in his letters to have been divinely set apart, even
from birth, for this very purpose (Gal. 1.15—16; Rom. 1.1—6). And
so the list of agreements could be easily extended.

A further point is that the epistles of Paul and Acts throw considerable light on each other. The Book of Acts enables us to read
the epistles with greater understanding because of the historical
background it gives us (e. g., the founding of the Churches, the reference to Apollos in 1 Corinthians, the collection for the Jerusalem
believers, etc.), and the epistles do the same for the narrative of
Acts (by including various historical details which are omitted from
Acts). It is true that a comparison of the two raises a number of
difficulties of harmonization, but Bruce is of the opinion that these
difficulties are far from insuperable[18]. At any rate, the difficulties
are no greater than those which exist in the comparative study of
any other independently written documents from antiquity.

In company with nearly all British scholars, Bruce accepts the
traditional authorship of Luke-Acts (2—6). He is obviously sympathetic toward the view that Aramaic sources lie behind portions
of the early chapters of Acts (especially 1.1—5.16; 9.31—11.18; and
parts of chapters 12 and 15), but, with characteristic caution, he is
unwilling to make too many definite statements concerning their
exact extent and nature (22—23)[19]. For a large part of the book
the author is dependent on the knowledge gained through his personal participation in the events narrated and through conversation
with Paul himself (21). Even for the early chapters, however, one
must not rule out the possibility that most of his sources may have
been oral, i. e., that much of the information there recorded may
have been gained through personal conversation with members of
the primitive Christian community during his visit to Palestine in
A. D. 57—59 (22)[20].

As has been noted earlier in the present study[21], Bruce thinks

[18] Bruce identifies the visit of Paul to Jerusalem mentioned in Acts 11.30
with that of Gal. 2 and dates Galatians prior to the Jerusalem Council. See his
commentary on the Greek text, pp. 38—39, 241, 287—89; cf. also references
cited above (n. 9).

[19] He begins his section on the sources of Acts with this quotation from
Foakes-Jackson: "We should constantly remember that source-criticism in the
New Testament is largely guess-work" (from *The Acts of the Apostles*, p. xv).

[20] Cf. Knowling, *supra*, pp. 129—30.

[21] *Supra*, pp. 190n., 224—33. Cf. also his essay, "The Speeches of Acts —
Thirty Years After", in *Reconciliation and Hope*, ed. R. Banks (Exeter, 1974).

there are good reasons for the view that the speeches of Acts "are not Luke's inventions, but summaries giving at least the gist of what was really said on various occasions, and therefore valuable and independent sources for the life and thought of the primitive Church" (21).

Bruce discerns at least a dual purpose behind the plan of Acts: the first historical and the second apologetic (29—34). That Luke is concerned to write history is (or should be) clear from his own statement in his prologue (Luke 1.1—4), which should be taken as applying to the whole of his two-volumed work, as well as from the actual content of Luke-Acts. But Acts is not an ordinary historical work, but rather a theologically oriented and interpreted history. In the opening sentence of his second volume, Luke characterizes his πρῶτος λόγος as an account of "all that Jesus began both to do and teach"[22]. The second volume, therefore, might fittingly be called "The Acts of the Risen Christ" or ("since the Risen Christ acts through His Spirit in the Church") "The Acts of the Holy Spirit". Thus, as Luke intends to give an account of the earthly life and teachings of Jesus in the first volume of his work, in the second he wishes to tell of the continued ministry of Jesus in his Church through the Holy Spirit, who is seen active in every aspect of the Church's life[23].

"Equally clear", however, "is the writer's intention to defend Christianity and Paul against the accusations of various opponents" (30). Here Bruce refers to the familiar data of the testimony of Pilate, Herod Antipas, and the centurion at the cross that Jesus was innocent; Paul's good relations with the Asiarchs at Ephesus and the declaration of his innocence by the town clerk, the magistrates at Philippi, Gallio at Corinth and Felix, Festus and Herod Agrippa II in Palestine; and the fact of the steadfast Jewish opposition to the message of Paul, which is the root cause of most of the trouble wherever Paul has travelled[24]. Bruce rejects the suggestion (made by Aberle, Plooij, Duncan, etc.) that Acts, or even Luke-Acts, was written for the purpose of Paul's defense before the imperial tribunal in Rome, on the grounds that there is much in Acts (e. g., the

---

[22] He interpres ἤρξατο as "emphatic, implying that Luke is now about to tell us what Jesus *continued* to do after His Ascension" (29—30), rather than as simply a redundant auxiliary after the Aramaic idiom (so Haenchen, Conzelmann, *et al.*).

[23] Cf. B. Reicke, "The Risen Lord and His Church", *Interp.* 13 (1959), pp. 157—69; and below, pp. 296—97.

[24] Bruce notes (31), however, that Luke points out that the trouble on a few occasions was due to the fact that financial interests were threatened by the Gospel (Acts 16.19; 19.24—27).

theological matter) which would be quite irrelevant for this purpose, though he admits that this may have been a subordinate consideration[25]. The object of Luke's apologetic was probably much broader:

There was an intelligent reading public, or rather listening public, at Rome, and Luke may have availed himself of this opportunity to rebut in the Imperial City itself the popular charges brought against Christianity by insisting on its complete and acknowledged innocence before the law of the Empire (31).

Rome is the goal toward which the whole of the narrative of Acts aims.

The Gospel spread out from Palestine in every direction, but the direction in which Luke is interested is the road that leads to Rome. Hence he emphasizes the rise of Gentile evangelization, the Holy Spirit's choice of Paul and Barnabas for this work, the spread of the Gospel through Asia Minor to Europe, and at last the chain of events by which Paul achieves his long-conceived desire to see Rome. As Rome draws near, the interest quickens, and the climax is reached when Paul is established at the heart of the Empire, "proclaiming the kingdom of God and teaching the story of the Lord Jesus Christ, with all boldness, without let or hindrance" — the triumphant peroration ἀκωλύτως expressing Luke's exultation over the situation with which he concludes his work. Here is the final apologetic: not only do the provincial governors place no obstacle in the way of the Gospel, but in Rome itself the chief exponent of the Gospel is allowed to proclaim it unhindered (31).

Bruce follows this statement with the observation that such a joyful and optimistic note would have been unlikely after the Neronian persecution and the martyrdom of Paul.

This final observation indicates Bruces's preference for the early date of Acts (ca. A. D. 61). It is admitted, of course, that one cannot (or should not!) be dogmatic in his opinion of the matter; but he lists seven points which seem to favor the view that Acts was written in Rome toward the end of Paul's two years of detention there (11—13). (1) Acts betrays no use of the Pauline letters. (2) This is the best explanation of the abrupt ending of the book. (3) There is no certain reference to Paul's death (Acts 20.25, 38, notwithstanding). (4) The attitude toward the Roman authority and the confident optimism of the author makes it difficult to believe that it was written after the Neronian persecution. (5) There is no reference at all to the Jewish War of A. D. 66—70 or the fall of Jerusa-

---

[25] The view that Acts was written to provide information for Paul's legal defense at Rome has been argued once again in a recent doctoral dissertation by R. E. Cottle, *The Occasion and Purpose of the Final Drafting of Acts* (Ph. D. diss., Los Angeles, University of Southern California, 1967).

lem. (6) The author gives prominence to subjects which were important in the life of the Church *before* the fall of Jerusalem, but which soon afterwards lost their importance (e. g., the terms of Gentile admission into the Church, Jewish-Gentile relations in the churches, the food-regulations of the apostolic decree, etc.). And, possibly, (7) the primitive theology of Acts (though this may be due to the use of sources and is, in any case, an uncertain criterion)[26]. Whether or not Bruce's argument proves convincing to very many scholars, it is at least another testimony to the fact that what is to some scholars "obvious" (i. e., that Acts must have been written in the 80s or 90s or even later) is not at all obvious to others[27].

Much more could be said about Bruce's valuable commentary on Acts, but enough has been said already to indicate its essential point of view. Its chief value lies in the area of the historical, and it is unlikely that it will be superseded here in the near future. If it has any important deficiencies, these are in the area of theological comment (as the author himself would no doubt admit), though this is partially ·made up by the second work in *The New International/New London Commentary* series. The two commentaries together combine to offer the student the best all-round guide to the critical study of Acts which is available in English at the present time.

The commentary by C. S. C. Williams[28] in the *Black's/Harper's New Testament Commentaries* has beeen described as one which "comes to no conclusions of its own on the varied problems which Acts raises, but does make clear all the issues involved"[29]. This is not an altogether fair assessment of the work of Williams, but there is· a measure of truth in it.

The kinship of Williams's commentary to Bruce's (though the former gives little evidence of having been directly influenced by Bruce) is seen in the agreement of both on such matters as "the general trustworthiness of the author" (30), the equation of the visit

[26] See the full discussion in Bruce, and compare the arguments of Rackham (*supra*, pp. 131–33), Harnack (*supra*, p. 155), J. Munck, *The Acts of the Apostles* (Garden City, N. J., 1967), pp. XLVI–LIV, and D. Guthrie, *New Testament Introduction: The Gospels and Acts* (London, 1965), pp. 307–12.

[27] The early date of Acts has been defended in recent years by H. Sahlin (1945), N. Geldenhuys (1950), F. F. Bruce (1951, etc.), R. Koh (1953), B. Gärtner (1955), A. Hastings (1958), O. Michel (1959), E. M. Blaiklock (1959), B. Reicke (1962), D. Guthrie (1965), R. E. Cottle (1967), J. Munck (1967), and the majority of Roman Catholic scholars; others have argued for a slightly later, but pre-A. D. 70 date, e. g., T. W. Manson (1944), C. S. C. Williams (1967), and E. E. Ellis (1966).

[28] *A Commentary on the Acts of the Apostles* (London and New York, 1957).

[29] J. Munck, *Acts*, p. XC (the editors?).

of Galatians 2 with Acts 11.30 (24—27), the "South Galatian" destination of the Epistle to the Galatians (175—76), and preference
for a date prior to the Jerusalem council for the writing of Galatians
(26—27). Williams is somewhat more skeptical than Bruce in his
isolation of definite sources in Acts, though he would agree that the
author undoubtedly made use of sources (both written and oral).

Williams prefers an early date for Acts (pre-A. D. 70, though not
necessarily as early as 62 to 64), but he adds little to the argument
in favor of an early date. He makes the interesting suggestion, however, that Acts may have been written earlier than our canonical
Third Gospel (which he regards as possibly a revision, using Mark,
of Luke's πρῶτος λόγος)[30]. In answer to those who argue that Luke
21 reflects a post-A. D. 70 situation, he calls on the support of C.
H. Dodd[31], who has demonstrated that there is nothing in Luke 21
that could not have been derived from the Septuagint.

The speeches of Acts are regarded as (at least) samples of early
Christian preaching, in all probability authentically reflecting the
actual preaching of Peter, Stephen, and Paul, if only in outline
(36—48). At any rate, the speeches of Peter in the early chapters
reflect a clearly primitive theology; and the speeches of Paul, including the Areopagus address (so Gärtner contra Dibelius), contain nothing that Paul could not have said.

All in all, the commentary by Williams is an able piece of critical
scholarship, and it displays a wide-ranging familiarity with the contemporary literature on Luke-Acts. Nevertheless, it adds little to the
work of Bruce, other than a different scholar's slant on the various
problems of Acts and a fresh translation of the Greek text; in gen-

---

[30] It is sometimes mistakenly supposed that Williams' suggestion that Luke
wrote a first draft of the Gospel before he came into possession of Mark (cf.
"The Date of Luke-Acts", ExpT 64 (1952/53), pp. 283—84) is used to make it
possible for Acts to be dated before the writing of Mark, but this is incorrect.
Williams thinks that the Gospel according to Mark came into Luke's hands
before he wrote Acts (which he feels echoes some of the phrases of Mark) but
was only subsequently used in a revision of Proto-Luke (= the canonical
Third Gospel). Cf. also R. Koh, The Writings of St. Luke (Hong Kong, 1953),
pp. 23—35; and H. G. Russell, "Which Was Written First, Luke or Acts?"
HTR 48 (1955), pp. 167—74. B. Reicke, on the other hand, suggests that Luke
may have made use of a preliminary version of Mark in writing his first volume
(The Gospel of Luke, E. T. (Richmond, Va., 1964), pp. 26—35).

[31] "The Fall of Jerusalem and the 'Abomination of Desolation'", JRS 37
(1947), pp. 46—54; = More New Testament Studies (Manchester, 1968), pp. 69
—83. The same fact is pointed out (apparently independently of one another)
by R. B. Rackham (see above, p. 133) and C. C. Torrey (see above, p. 167).
I consider this point to be irrefutable by those who argue that Luke 21 reflects
a post-A. D. 70 situation.

eral, it does not come up to the high standard of careful scholarship maintained in Bruce's two volumes[32].

The critics who pass negative judgment on the historical worth of Luke-Acts often seem to work on the principle that what is artistic or literary in form cannot be historical. A more than casual acquaintance with the work of first-rate historians of the present day, or of the past, should give pause before accepting this assumption as valid. Are Professors Roland Bainton and Hugh Trever-Roper — or Thucydides and Polybius, for that matter — inferior historians because they take extra pains to insure that their writings are works of high literary quality as well as works of history? Yet all too often the observation that Luke's two-volumed work is a work of art has led critics to conclude that it has little to do with history; the fact that the author is concerned with matters of literary form and style has caused some to suppose that he pays little attention to the fundamental facts. The speeches of Acts, for example, are regarded to be literary inventions because of their obvious literary form; the account of the journey of Paul to Rome is considered to be fictitious because it has literary points of contact with other "travel narratives". This negative judgment does not, of course, follow from the initial observation. All that these observations prove is that in his literary method the author of Acts is heir to a tradition of Greek literature.

A work which seeks to do justice to both the literary/artistic and historical aspects of Luke-Acts is the study by the Swiss scholar, Robert Morgenthaler, entitled *Die lukanische Geschichtsschreibung als Zeugnis*[33]. It is a careful study of the form and content of the Third Gospel and Acts. The author emphasizes both the importance

---

[32] Three other commentaries which were written in the 1950s by British scholars (if one may include the Commonwealth under this term) are worthy of special mention. The commentary by G. H. C. Macgregor in *The Interpreter's Bible* 9 (Nashville and New York, 1954), pp. 3—352 (exegesis only), is a balanced, though generally undistinguished, work by a mature scholar and theologian. The lucidly written commentary by R. R. Williams in the *Torch Bible Commentaries* (London, 1953; rev. ed., 1965) lays stress on the theological message of the Book of Acts and is a model of its kind (i. e., for the general reader). *The Acts of the Apostles* by E. M. Blaiklock (London, 1959) in *The Tyndale New Testament Commentaries* is a very original work by the professor of classics at Auckland University, New Zealand; what it lacks in theological sophistication it makes up by its emphasis on the historical setting of the narrative of Acts in the context of the general culture and life of the Graeco-Roman world. All three accept the traditional authorship and take a very positive position regarding the historical value of Acts (though Macgregor is a little less conservative in his judgments than Williams or Blaiklock).

[33] *AbThANT* 14 and 15 (Zürich, 1949).

of studying the two Lucan writings as a unit and also the importance of taking seriously the author's statement in his preface that he is concerned to write history.

In brief, Morgenthaler finds the literary key to Luke's work to be the principle of "duality" *(Zweigliedrigkeit)*. He begins with the commonly recognized fact of Luke's fondness for parallels or doublets, both in his prose style and in his selection of narrative and discourse material. This principle of duality is not only illustrated by the fact that the author has written a two-volumed work, but also by the existence of intentional parallels between the two volumes, between various parts of each volume, and even between various words and phrases. Morgenthaler compiles long lists of words, phrases, sentences, and sections of narrative and speech material which illustrate the literary principle of *Zweigliedrigkeit* (vol. 1). The significance of all this, he argues, is that the author is concerned to bear *witness* to the facts he narrates. The requirement of Deuteronomy 19.15, which is echoed so often in the New Testament, is the ultimate reason for this emphasis. (Therefore, the double motif becomes occasionally a treble one, as in the case of the three-fold account of Paul's conversion in Acts). This witness motif is considered by Morgenthaler to be the central idea of the whole work (II, 7—24).

This duality is not, however, a sign that the author has simply invented his material in keeping with his literary and theological aims. On the contrary, if the story narrated were not in keeping with the historical facts, this would nullify completely the author's attempt to give an account which would stand up in a court of law. No, the parallels were not invented, but were historical "givens" which were selected by Luke for his purposes. The author does not distort the facts to fit his pattern, but he selects those facts which he has at his disposal which lend themselves to this presentation. The Lucan writings, then, relate real history. It is history which has been, to a degree, shaped by the literary method of the historian (as in the case of *all* written history) and which is theologically interpreted; but it is *history* just the same.

There is no doubt that Morgenthaler overstates his case. For one thing, he is much too zealous in his concern to find parallels; many of the "Doppelworte", "Doppelsätze", and "Doppelabschnitte" are not really convincing. And it is perhaps true that he has a little too high an estimation of Luke's artistry: certainly he fails to observe the fact that Luke's literary style is not uniform throughout, and at times there appear what look like unedited phrases which have been taken over from his sources and which do not reflect the best possible Greek style (for example, in the narratives of Luke 1 and 2, the early chapters of Acts, and some of the speeches). Nevertheless, enough of his examples remain to give a degree of plausibility to the main outline of his thesis; and Morgenthaler has made a valuable contribution to the recent study of Acts by calling attention to the importance of the idea of "witness" in Luke-Acts. He is certainly correct in stressing the fact that what is literary is not necessarily unhistorical[34].

The monograph by Étienne Trocmé, entitled *"Le Livre des Actes" et l'histoire*[35], calls into question many critical assumptions held by radical and conservative critics alike. For one thing, the largest part of the book is dedicated to the problem of sources — in a day when source-critical investigations are categorically declared to be out of date. Then, too, the author takes Luke-Acts seriously as a work of history. The author *ad Theophilum* was an *evangelist* as well a historian, but this does not negate the fact that he was a *historian*. The fact that he is a historian is betrayed by his use of sources, the geographical and chronological framework of the story he narrates, his display of knowledge concerning political and social institutions of the countries in which the action of his work takes place, and in his use of literary and even, sometimes, rhetorical language (77—113).

However, in all this the author remained an evangelist (113—21). This aspect of the author's own conception of his task as a writer is seen both in the form of his work (a Gospel) and in his conscious [166] imitation of the language of the Greek Old Testament. "Son motif essential a été, nous semble-t-il, le désir de suggérer à ses lecteurs un rapprochement entre son ouvrage et la Bible grecque. qui était pour eux le texte sacré par excellence" (114—15). By his use of the language of the Old Testament the author seeks to give to his work the dignity of a "holy" book.

---

[34] A work which bears some resemblance to Morgenthaler's study is M. D. Goulder's *Type and History in Acts* (London, 1964). Goulder applies the typological method of Austin Farrer (to whom the book is dedicated) to the study of Acts; he finds evidence of a cyclical pattern behind the development of the narrative of Acts, detailed parallelisms between the Third Gospel and Acts (as well as between various parts of Acts), and an all-pervasive influence of the Old Testament on the literary structure of Acts. Whereas Morgenthaler uses his discovery of the use of the literary device of *Zweigliedrigkeit* as a sign that Luke intended to write history, Goulder uses his discernment of various literary and typological motifs as an argument against the historicity of much of Acts. If one has the impression that Morgenthaler sometimes reads too much into his evidence, the same would be doubly true of the work of Goulder.

[35] (Paris, 1957).

Trocmé, following the suggestions of H. Sahlin[36] and P. H. Menoud[37], argues that Luke-Acts was originally one volume and that it was divided into two books (Luke 24.50—53 and Acts 1.1—5 being later additions) when the Gospel according to Luke came to be placed alongside the other three Gospels as a part of the Church's canon (30—34). To the objection that this combination of Luke-Acts into one volume would make the book too long, Trocmé answers that it would have been only slightly longer than the first book of Josephus' *Jewish War* (33). It would, indeed, have been more unusual for the author to have chosen to divide his work into two parts which correspond so closely to the size of the First Gospel[38].

Trocmé regards the work dedicated to Theophilus to be addressed primarily to the Christian public (48—50, *passim*), who would be the only people able to comprehend and appreciate the full meaning of the author's "Gospel". Whatever truth there may be in the idea that the work betrays a political-apologetic purpose, *viz.* that of demonstrating to the Roman authorities the inoffensive character of Christianity, this is certainly not the primary purpose (51). In Trocmé's opinion the fundamental aim is an ecclesiastical apologetic; it is an apologetic within the Church. Here Trocmé returns to a view similar to the Tübingen understanding of the purpose (though in the form expressed by Schneckenburger, rather than Baur). He regards Luke-Acts as primarily a defence of Paul against those Jewish Christians who still held an important place of influence in the Church of the author's day (ca. A. D. 80—85) and who recognized neither the universalistic teaching nor the apostolic status of the apostle to the Gentiles (53—70). It is Paul, therefore, who becomes the chief instrument in the hand of God for the fulfillment of the plan of God in proclaiming the Gospel in all the world (55), and it is he who is the unique continuator of the work begun by the Twelve (67).

Trocmé agrees with Schneckenburger against Baur and his disciples in his conclusion that the author's apologetic purpose does not cause him to pervert the historical data to any great degree (al-

---

[36] *Der Messias und das Gottesvolk* (Uppsala, 1945), pp. 1—62.

[37] "Remarques sur les textes de l'Ascension dans Luc-Actes", in *Neutestamentliche Studien für Rudolf Bultmann* (Berlin, 1954), pp. 148—56. Menoud is the author of a number of instructive, if sometimes eccentric, essays on Acts (see Mattill, *Bibliography*) and also of a commentary which has been announced for publication for nearly two decades but which has not yet (to my knowledge) appeared in print.

[38] This comment overlooks the fact that the length of Matthew, Luke, and Acts is about the maximum size which is convenient to handle in the form of a roll-book; cf. B. M. Metzger, *The Text of the New Testament* (New York and London, 1964), pp. 5—6.

though the author is by no means infallible). While it is true that he omits certain facts which might cast a negative shadow on his case (as, for example, his suppression of some of the conflicts in the early Church), there is no reason to suppose that he ever invented any of the episodes which he narrates or even composed the speeches out of his head (121). On the contrary, Trocmé finds reason to believe that the author makes extensive use of sources throughout the whole of his work.

Underlying chapters 16 through 28, Trocmé discerns two basic sources: the experiences of an "eye-witness" (i. e., the author) and a "diaire personnel" (121—53). The personal diary — roughly equivalent to Dibelius' itinerary-document — could have been from the hand of Paul himself, or possibly kept by another member of his missionary entourage, and would have been intended to serve Paul as an "aide-mémoire".

[167]   Il n'est pas impossible dans ce cas que l'auteur *ad Theophilum* ait occupé cette fonction à certaines époques. On pourrait même suggérer qu'il l'a fait pendant la dernière période de la vie de Paul et a conservé le journal après la mort de l'apôtre ou sa séparation d'avec lui (138).

In his discussion of the sources of chapter 1—15, Trocmé argues that the "diary" or collection of notes concerning the journeys of finds a number of different sources, some of them probably Aramaic, lying behind the narrative of the first twelve chapters (163—214); these stem no doubt from the tradition belonging to the churches of Jerusalem, Caesarea, and Antioch. Although the traditions have been linked together in a manner which is sometimes arbitrary, they are not Luke's creations; nor has he severely distorted the historical facts. Even the discourses of Peter and Stephen, although manifesting the literary workmanship of the author, are always based on the solid facts of traditional materials. All of these observations lead to the conclusion that, in spite of the difficulties and obvious gaps in Luke's narrative, it remains a work of great historical value.

Trocmé's monograph seems to have had very little influence in the world of New Testament scholarship. German critics have generally taken notice of it, but they do not seem to have been measurably affected by the author's argument and conclusions. Haenchen, in fact, abandoned the theory of an itinerary-document as a result of his interaction with the views of Trocmé! As far as I have been able to determine, Le *"Livre des Actes" et l'histoire* has received no major review in the English-speaking world, nor has it been used to any extent by any recent commentator (besides Haenchen).

It is unlikely that any of Trocmé's special theories will become generally accepted by scholars — whether that of the original one-

volumed character of Luke-Acts, his special understanding of the
apologetic aim of Acts, the existence of a personal diary which Paul
and his companions carried with them as an aid to memory, or the
isolation of various distinct sources lying behind the early chapters
of Acts. Nevertheless, his work serves to emphasize the historical
nature of the Lucan writings and the fact that to say that the author
has a special purpose in writing is not necessarily the same as saying
that he has distorted the actual facts of history or has made up incidents out of his head.

No man in recent years has done more to challenge New Testament exegetes to re-examine many of their critical assumptions than
the Danish scholar, the late Johannes Munck[39]. Quite apart from a
number of his more questionable theories (e. g., his interpretation
of 2 Thess. 2.6—7, following O. Cullmann; and his identification of
the "Judaizers" of Galatians with Gentile Christians), Munck did
the world of New Testament scholarship a valuable service in drawing attention to the fact of the continuing influence of the Tübingen
conception of early Christianity over many features of contemporary Pauline research. Although scholars have universally abandoned the literary theories of F. C. Baur and his followers, Munck
pointed out that they have continued to assume many of their historical conclusions, without realizing that these should have been
given up along with the faulty literary hypotheses upon which they
were based (69—86).

One of these assumptions which goes back to Baur is that there
was a broad cleavage of opinion between Paul and the primitive
apostles, between Gentile and Jewish Christianity[40]. This contrast between Gentile and Jewish Christianity is treated by many critics as
the leitmotiv of the history of early Christianity. Yet, in fact, there
is no evidence in the epistles of Paul or in the Book of Acts that
there was ever any fundamental disagreement between Paul and the
Urapostel on matters of basic Christian belief. The only difference
between the two was in spheres of ministry — as Paul himself emphasizes in Galatians 2.9. There was no difference concerning the
Gospel or even over the question of preaching the Gospel to the
Gentiles. The Tübingen theory that the Jerusalem Christians were
different from other Jews *only* in the fact that they believed that

---

[39] The most important of his essays are collected in his book, *Paulus und die
Heilsgeschichte* (Copenhagen, 1954), E. T. *Paul and the Salvation of Mankind*
(London, 1959). His commentary on Romans 9—11, *Christus und Israel* (Copenhagen, 1956), E. T. (Philadelphia, 1967) is also very important. The English
translation of his *Paulus* is cited below.
[40] See above, pp. 27—31, 41—42, 52—53, 105.

Jesus was the Messiah and would soon return cannot be supported on the basis of the New Testament data. On the contrary, the primitive Church was as universalistic in its theology as Paul; they differed only in that they conceived of their ministry as preaching to the Jews *first* as a means of the eventual conversion of the Gentiles, whereas Paul had been called by God to be *the apostle to the Gentiles*[41]. Munck makes the important point that it was the later "Catholic Church" that lost the original unversalism of Jesus, the early apostles, and Paul, when it no longer recognized the fact that the Gospel was for Gentiles *as well as Jews*, but turned its message to *Gentiles only* (71, *passim*).

Another important point emphasized by Munck is the important place held by Israel in the theology of Paul. Romans 9—11 has traditionally been regarded as something like a parenthesis in the epistle or an appendix to Paul's thought which is expressed in the first eight chapters, whereas it is a very important part of Paul's argument[42]. New Testament exegetes, possibly because of their own Gentile Christian, anti-law and anti-Jewish bias, have tended to overlook this and other non-controversial passages in the letters of Paul and have concentrated instead on Paul's polemic against the "Judaizers". This has led to the erroneous conclusion that "the apostle to the Gentiles" was anti-Jewish. The fact is that the epistles make it clear that Paul continued to regard himself as a Jew, Christianity as the true Judaism, and the Church as the true Israel (279). Only a warped and one-sided treatment of the Pauline epistles could lead to a denial of this fact[43].

The last of Munck's published writings on the New Testament was his commentary on Acts in *The Anchor Bible*, published posthumously in 1967[44]. In his final study he finds his views concerning

---

[41] See his commentary (n. 44), pp. LXII—LXX.

[42] Cf. Stendahl (*supra*, p. 242n.); also, F. F. Bruce, *The Epistle of Paul to the Romans* (London, 1963), pp. 181—182.

[43] A work which presents a more balanced and ultimately more satisfying account of the "historical Paul" and which throws much light on the exegesis of both the epistles and Acts is the monograph by R. N. Longenecker, *Paul, Apostle of Liberty* (New York, 1964). Longenecker's study has all the virtues of Munck's conception of Paul, quite apart from some of Munck's idiosyncratic exegetical conclusions. This is probably the best study on Paul which has appeared in English in many decades.

[44] *The Acts of the Apostles* (Garden City, N. Y., 1967). It is to be regretted that the volume is marred by a general lack of careful editing. The work abounds in inexact and often misleading translations, typographical errors, and in loose expressions. In addition, a number of appendices have been added by the editors (263—317), which are entirely independent of Prof. Munck's commentary. One may hope that the carelessness with which the work was produced will do nothing to detract from the reputation of a truly great scholar.

Acts becoming more and more conservative. Whereas in his *Paulus* he feels called upon to defend the narrative of Acts on only a few points, in his commentary he defends Acts at length — as the work of a companion of Paul (XXIX—XXXV), as written during Paul's two years' imprisonment in Rome (XLVI—LIV), and as essentially trustworthy in what it narrates concerning the course of early Christian history *(passim)*. He finds good reason to believe that the author did not invent either incidents or speeches, but rather made constant use of traditional material (XLI—XLIV).

In his discussion of the problem of reconciling the accounts of Galatians 2.1—10 with Acts 15, Munck makes this comment:

> In historical sources from other fields such discrepancies are no surprise to the scholar, nor do they make him doubt the historical reliability of the accounts except at a few points where they directly contradict each other. But many New Testament scholars adopt a very stringent attitude when no complete agreement exists among the different accounts, regardless of the fact that perfect agreement would be suspect or proof of artificial construction (XXXIII—XXXIV).

This observation will come as nothing new to the reader of the present study, but it is a true and important statement all the same.

Among the various points made by Munck in his commentary, only one need be mentioned. Following J. Jervell[45], he challenges the assumption of Dibelius, Haenchen, Conzelmann, and company, that the early Christian had no interest in their own history. An examination of the Pauline letters, argues Munck, shows that "accounts of the acts of the apostles and the faith of the Church [had] their place in the preaching and life of the church" (XXXIX). Thus in Romans 1.8, Paul gives thanks to God that the faith of the Roman church is proclaimed all over the world (cf. Rom. 16.19); in 1 Thessalonians 1.6—10 the example of the Thessalonian believers is known throughout the Church; the Corinthian church is said to constitute Paul's letter of recommendation (2 Cor. 3.1—3); in 2 Thessalonians 1.4 Paul says he gives an account of the experiences of the Thessalonian church "in the churches of God"; and in 2 Corinthians 8—9 Paul tells the Corinthians about the churches in Macedonia, where he formerly stressed the goodwill of the Corinthians[46].

Just as Paul speaks of the churches he established, so in the same way accounts must have been given about the church in Jerusalem. The church

---

[45] "Zur Frage der Traditionsgrundlage der Apostelgeschichte", *ST* 16 (1963), pp. 25—41. Cf. A. J. B. Higgins, "The Preface of Luke and the Kerygma in Acts", in *Apostolic History and the Gospel*, pp. 78—91.

[46] See the many references (XXXIX—XL).

in Thessalonica was undoubtedly an example to the churches in Macedonia and Achaia, but the church in Jerusalem was the original model
(I Thess ii 14). The Thessalonian church knows about the persecutions it
has suffered and about its relation to its Jewish countrymen (I Thess ii 14;
cf. I Cor xiv 36) and the Gentile Christians owe this church a debt of
gratitude for having shared its spiritual gifts (Rom xv 26—27) (XL).

It is also important to observe that the account of the appearances
of Jesus to Peter and the Twelve was a part of the original *kerygma*
(1 Cor. 15.3—5). Thus there are good reasons to believe that the
author of Luke-Acts would have had access to many reliable traditions about the early days of Christianity, as well as about Jesus.

Two important studies in the history of *Actaforschung* have been
written in recent years. The first is by a younger American scholar,
A. J. Mattill, Jr.[47] and is a study of the problem of the historical
value of Acts and the variety of ways this problem has been met by
critics since the days of the Tübingen critics. In spite of a number of
flaws in the author's presentation of his material[48], Mattill's monograph is an extremely valuable piece of work. It contains a wealth
of information concerning the views held by most of the important
critics of the Book of Acts during the last century and a half of
research; and, in general, the author's judgment on the issues under
discussion and concerning the value of the various attempted solutions of the critical problems facing the student of Acts is quite
sensible.

Mattill's position concerning the question of history in Acts
would be roughly equivalent to the view of the present author,
though he would be a little more hesitant than I have been to side
completely with the defenders of Luke as a historian. Nevertheless,
he comes down strongly against the tradition of radical criticism
concerning Acts — stemming from F. C. Baur (47—84), continued
by Overbeck (169—206), and culminating in Haenchen (297—314)
— as being based more on dogmatic prejudice and unbridled imagination than on careful exegesis. Although Mattill admits that
many issues must be held *sub judice*, because of the extreme disagreement among scholars, he has no hesitation in affirming the general historical reliability of the narrative of Acts in the picture it
gives of early Christian development; and he rightly emphasizes the
fact that when the Book of Acts is treated fairly, as one would treat
any other historical document, many of the difficulties disappear.

---

[47] *Luke as a Historian in Criticism since 1840* (Ph.D. diss., Vanderbilt
University, 1959).

[48] As in the case of most theses, the study suffers from a certain amount of
repetition and loose writing, together with a tendency to quote the opinions of

Some of the author's observations concerning the historical Paul are important. Perhaps the most important of these is one which is stressed throughout his study, *viz.* that it is important for the New Testament critic to give due consideration to the fact of the diversity of Paul's thought. The mistake of the Tübingen critics, as of many more recent critics, was to have a simplistic understanding of Paul. They grasped one strand of Paul's teaching, turned it into the fundamental feature of "Paulinism", and rejected anything said about or by Paul in Acts which did not coincide with their conception of Paul. But, in so doing, they missed the fact that "a personality so versatile as Paul's could combine many seemingly contradictory attitudes" (322). An adequate understanding of Paul must recognize the extreme breadth and versatility of Paul's mind, as all great minds, and not seek to fit it into a narrowly conceived mold.

The final chapter of Mattill's thesis offers some valuable suggestions concerning the manner in which this basic observation is applied to problems such as Paul's "Jewish" practices (322—25), his relation to the *Urapostel* (325—30), his alleged claim to be a Pharisee according to Acts 23 (339—41), the Pauline speeches in Acts (345—47), and the relationship between the narrative of Acts and the epistles of Paul (347—52).

Another important study of the history of Acts criticism is the monograph on the sources of Acts by Jacques Dupont[49], one of the leading Roman Catholic scholars of the present day. As I noted in the preface of the present study, Dupont's monograph is a model of careful, critical scholarship. He has failed to include no person or view of importance in his discussion, and he has dealt fairly and sympathetically with all the views he discusses. Because he has done his job so well and his work is readily available to the student, it has been unnecessary to stress the source-critical study of Acts in the present work.

Dupont's conclusions are very modest. (1) "Despite the most careful and detailed research, it has not been possible to define any of the sources used by the author of Acts in a way which will meet with widespread agreement among the critics" (166). Nevertheless, (2) all the varied attempts to analyze the sources of Acts have not been entirely wasted; in fact, they have given some credence to the view that the sources which have been used by the author have been

---

esteemed scholars on occasions when the author's own opinion in his own words would be sufficient.

[49] *Les Sources du Livre des Actes* (Bruges, 1960); E. T. *The Sources of Acts: The Present Position* (London, 1964). The English translation has been used in the present study.

276

edited and in a large measure re-written by the author. Dupont seems inclined toward the suggestion of P. Benoit[50], that Luke's written sources do not, for the most part, stem from the pen of another, but rather are Luke's own notes which he has combined, edited, and re-written. (3) Comparison with other ancient texts and a study of the "we"-narratives themselves leads one to the conclusion that "the author wishes it to be understood that he has personally taken part in the events he is recounting" (167). Dupont's study is concluded with a few brief, but carefully chosen, comments on critical methodology (167—68), which deserve a serious hearing among scholars of all persuasions.

Perhaps the most important of all the recent studies of the problem of history in the Book of Acts is the recent monograph by A. N. Sherwin-White, the Roman historian. In the published version of The Sarum Lectures for 1960—61[51], the author examines various aspects of the Synoptic Gospels and Acts in the light of the results of recent Roman historical research. Specifically, he looks at the trial of Jesus in the context of Roman law; the legal, administrative, and municipal background of the activities of Paul as portrayed in the Book of Acts; and the social and economic background of the synoptic narrative of Jesus in Galilee. The book is a very important one for the New Testament exegete, particularly in view of the fact that it presents a trained historian's careful appraisal of some of the most difficult problems of New Testament historical criticism.

In his study of the Pauline section of Acts, Sherwin-White argues that detail after detail of the account of Paul's varied experiences fit the historical conditions prevailing at the time of the dramatic date of the events (i. e., the middle of the first century A. D.) to a tee. He argues further that various legal practices, the meaning of Roman citizenship, etc. began to change toward the end of the century, and that the situation was very different in many important respects at a later date. He makes a careful examination of the narrative of Acts 16—28 and finds that the account of the preliminary trials before Felix and Festus; the details regarding the legal privileges and organization of the municipal governments in Philippi, Thessalonica, and Ephesus; the account of the hearing before Gallio at Corinth; the references to Roman legal problems; the use of names of Roman citizens and the meaning of Roman citizenship;

[50] "La deuxième visite de saint Paul à Jérusalem", *Biblica* 40 (1959), pp. 778—96.

[51] *Roman Society and Roman Law in the New Testament* (Oxford, 1963). This extremely important monograph seems to have attracted little attention outside of the United Kingdom.

and, above all, the details concerning Paul's Roman citizenship and his appeal to Caesar[52] — all correspond to what we know of the historical situation which existed during the last half of the first century, rather than at a later date. Sherwin-White concludes that the essential historicity of the narrative of Acts which pertains to Paul's adventures, when tested by the canons of historical criticism, is demonstrated beyond any serious doubt. This makes the suggestion that Acts was written by an author who was not very closely connected to the events which he narrates, or who lived at a time much later than the period about which he writes (say, in the second century), extremely implausible. It is historically improbable, if not impossible, for an author who lived much later than the time about which he writes to have been so minutely accurate concerning the actual historical setting of the period concerned. A later writer would certainly have been guilty of anachronisms of which the author of Acts is never guilty[53].

The only commentary to date which has made full use of the historical and exegetical data provided by Sherwin-White's important study is the admirable, but brief, commentary by R. P. C. Hanson in *The New Clarendon Bible*[54]. In his discussion of the date and authorship of Acts, Hanson begins by pointing out a number of facts which "suggest very strongly that Acts must have been written in the first century and could not have been written in the second ..." (2). The first item is the author's remarkable accuracy concerning the titles of both the municipal officials and the Roman imperial officials which he mentions in his narrative: the πολιτάρχαι of Thessalonica (17.6), the γραμματεύς and 'Ασιαρχοί of Ephesus (19.35, 31), the attribution of the title "proconsul" (ἀνθύπατος) to Sergius Paulus and Gallio (13.12; 18.12)[55]. The author of the third Gospel and Acts also mentions several emperors (Augustus, Tiberius, and Claudius) and three procurators of Judea (Pontus Pilate, Felix, and Festus) at the appropriate times. He also uses the correct terms to refer to the Roman soldiers he mentions: two centurions (Cornelius and Julius) with the names of their cohorts (Italian and

---

[52] Cf. also A. H. M. Jones, "I appeal unto Caesar", in his *Studies in Roman Government and Law* (Oxford, 1960), who comes independently to the same conclusion.

[53] Sherwin-White's monograph should not be misconstrued as the work of an apologist; it is simply the work of a historian who attempts to come to grips with the historical phenomena of the New Testament. In addition to the general observations mentioned, his study also contains many valuable exegetical insights concerning the interpretation of specific passages in Acts.

[54] *The Acts* (Oxford, 1967).

[55] *Supra*, pp. 119–20, 122.

Augustan) and one tribune (χιλίαρχος), Claudius Lysias by name (Acts 21.31–33, etc.). Moreover, the author seems to have detailed knowledge of the unique division of the province of Macedonia into (four) administratively separate parts (16.12). "Other examples of accuracy in referring to the details of the life and society of people in the Roman Empire could be adduced" (3), but it must be admitted that many of these details hold true for the second century as well.

Then there are many points of contact between the narrative of Acts and the epistles of Paul, such as the travelling companions of Paul which appear in both. Yet it must be admitted that there are also a few difficulties in harmonizing the narrative of Acts with the data of the epistles (especially Galatians 1 and 2 with Acts 9–15).

There is, however, the very important fact, which seems to be recognized by nearly all scholars, "that the author of Acts is anxious to present the Roman government as treating Christians fairly, no matter how others may treat them" (3). Yet "it is virtually impossible to reconcile this attitude to the Roman government with what we know about the relations between Church and State in the second century, even early in the second century" (4). The data of Pliny's letters to Trajan and the letters of Ignatius, both written about A. D. 115, and even the Book of Revelation, reflect a situation which is incompatible with the language of Acts about the Roman government. "To say of this situation that the Roman government is carefully neutral towards Christianity and, once it is apprised of the facts, regards it as harmless, would be grotesque" (5). Furthermore, in spite of the frequent claims to the contrary, the arguments of the Christian apologists of the second century are quite different from those of the author of Acts.

They remonstrate with the Roman authority for the attitude it takes to Christianity and for tolerating the legal situation under which Christians suffer; they refute the gross popular rumours which attributed to Christians such enormities as child-murder, cannibalism, and unnatural orgies. There is nothing whatever of this visible anywhere in Acts (5).

Thus the later we place Acts in the first century the more difficult it becomes to reconcile its language about the Roman Government with the contemporary situation; and ... if we place it in the second century (as late as 130), we cannot reconcile the two at all (6).

Further evidence for a first century date of Acts is adduced by A. H. M. Jones and A. N. Sherwin-White in their studies of Paul's appeal to Caesar, showing that the type of the appeal process reflected in Acts *(provocatio)* is an example of the process as it prevailed up to about the beginning of the last decade of the first century, rather than the modified practice of a slightly later date or the *appellatio* procedure of still later[56]. With this is connected Sherwin-White's observations concerning the activity of the town assemblies in Ephesus and Thessalonica (which became much rarer in the second century) and the attitude toward Roman citizenship reflected in Acts (i. e., it is still very rare in the Eastern provinces of the Empire and it is valued for the political rights it conferred).

Then there are the twin facts of (1) the absence of any reference or allusion to Gnosticism in Acts and (2) the existence of the "Western" text of Acts (which most scholars would date at the middle of the second century). Both these facts make it impossible to place Acts in the second century.

There are also "several small but significant points of historical detail incidentally retailed by Luke which suggest that he must have lived at a time not far removed from the events he was narrating" (8). The author has Paul encountering the high priest Ananias a short time before he meets the procurator Felix (23.2,33; 24.2,3); indicates that Felix was married to Drusilla at the time (24.24); says that Felix was superceded by Festus sometime afterwards, and that Festus shortly after his arrival in Palestine gave attention to Paul's case and gave him a hearing before King Agrippa II, who was living with his sister Bernice at the time (25.1–27).

This is a very remarkable piece of synchronization on the part of the author. . . . It would have taken a very considerable amount of research for a later historian to discover that Ananias must have been the high priest contemporary with Paul at that point, that this took place in the period when Felix was married to Drusilla (who had been born in 38 and had had one husband already before Felix), and that not long afterwards Bernice (who had already had two husbands) was living for a period (a limited period) with her brother, during the procuratorship of Festus (8).

There is also the further observation of Sherwin-White[57] concerning Felix's question to Paul asking him from what province he came and his decision to hear the case when he heard that he came from Cilicia (23.34–35). Ordinarily one would expect Paul to be sent back to his home province for trial. But, as Sherwin-White notes, Cilicia (at this particular time and *only* at this time) was merely a part of the larger province of Syria, and the legate of Syria would not wish to be bothered with a relatively minor case from an outlying part of his territory. The situation was different during the

[56] See ns. 51 and 52 above.
[57] *Roman Society and Roman Law*, pp. 55–56.

Flavian period (A. D. 69—96), when Cilicia was a province in its own right. Again, it would have been very difficult for the author to have discovered the fact that Gallio was proconsul of Achaia when Paul was in Corinth, if he were writing many years after the event and had no accurate knowledge of the actual facts. Another example of Luke's remarkable accuracy in his references to contemporary events is found in Acts 21.38, where the tribune refers to the Egyptian who recently stirred up a revolt and led the four thousand "ἄνδρας τῶν σικαρίων out into the wilderness" as if it were a recent occurrence. Josephus (*BJ* 1.261—3)[58] mentions the same minor incident as occurring during the procuratorship of Felix — a highly unlikely piece of historical accuracy on the part of a writer who is writing in the second century or even at the end of the first! Again, there is Claudius Lysias' statement (22.28) that he obtained his Roman citizenship by the payment of a large sum money (i. e., by a bribe), a practice which was common under Claudius but which was discovered and effectively ended in the time of Nero; both this incidental statement and his name fit the historical facts perfectly[59]. Finally, there is the accurate designation of the two Roman centurions mentioned in Acts — Cornelius (10.1) and Julius (21.1) — by their gentile *nomina* only. This was an old-fashioned type of name which was found only in the Roman army by the middle of the first century[60]. That Acts gives this type of Latin name to only two people, both soldiers, at the precise time in history when only soldiers are likely to be still using it, is surely no mere historical accident.

Hanson's conclusion is this:

This accumulation of facts, then, suggests very strongly that in the author of Acts we are dealing with somebody who lived during the first century, not the second; but more than this, that parts at least of his narrative correspond closely to a particular period of history, roughly from A. D. 41 to 70, which may be limited to the end of Claudius' reign and the beginning of Nero's. It seems likely that he has some close connexion with that period, either of sources or of personal experience; we are driven by the facts of the case to this conclusion. It should be noted that in reaching it we have not once referred to the "we" passages (11).

In spite of the detailed accuracy of chapters 16—28, Hanson finds a few examples of "confusion, inconsistency, and inaccuracy" in

---

[58] Hanson notes (9n.) that Josephus' account of thirty thousand men is probably an exaggeration, whereas Luke's number of four thousand is much more likely.

[59] Sherwin-White, *Roman Society and Roman Law*, pp. 154—56.

[60] *Ibid.*, pp. 160—61; the whole of Sherwin-White's discussion of the nomenclature of Acts is important.

the early chapters (11—20). Conzelmann and others have detected
in Acts 9.31 the author's ignorance of the geography of Palestine
(but cf. 15.3!). Then there are the possible confusions concerning
the location of Bethany (cf. Luke 24.50 with Acts 1.12), the layout
of the Temple (Acts 3.1—11), the miraculous release of the apostles from jail through the intervention of an angel (5.19), the order
and dates of the rebellions under Theudas and Judas of Galilee
(5.35—38), the exact nature of Stephen's ministry (ch. 6), the time
of the death of Herod Agrippa I (12.3), and the exact date and extent of the famine in Judea (11.27—30). These and other difficulties
lead Hanson to the conclusion that the author is working with very
scanty sources in the early chapters (in contrast to his access to
detailed and accurate knowledge concerning the events of chapters
16—28)[61]. Thus Hanson holds a view for the early chapters of Acts
which is similar to the view put forward by Dibelius in his 1923
essay on the style-criticism of Acts, *viz.* that the author has a limited
number of originally isolated, floating traditions and has molded
them into a unified whole, quite apart from any exact knowledge of
their original order or relationship to each other (14—15)[62].

The real problem, however, is the universally recognized difficulty
of relating Paul's accounts of his movements according to Galatians
to the data given by the Book of Acts. Hanson rejects the solution
of Knox, Bruce and others (i. e., that of dating Galatians prior to
the council of Acts 15) for two reasons: (1) there would have been
no reason for a consultation at such a late date if the meeting of
Galatians 2.1—10 had already taken place, and (2) the resemblance
of Galatians to Romans makes it difficult to accept the view that
Galatians could have been written such a long time before the latter
epistle. Hanson does, however, identify the second visit of Paul to
Jerusalem according to Galatians 2 with the famine relief visit of
Acts 11.30 and solves (?) the further problem of harmonization by
the suggestion that the account in Acts 15 is a "literary reconstruction" of the author on the basis of the "decree" (15.28—29), which

---

[61] It does not seem to me that any of these offers the historian serious
difficulty other than the account of Theudas and Judas (*if* Josephus is correct
and the rebels mentioned are the same ones referred to in Acts).

[62] This suggestion seems quite unlikely, if one is to accept Hanson's view
(21—28) that the author of Acts is also the author of the "we"-narratives. If
the author was actually in Palestine between the years A. D. 55 and 57 (even
if only for portions of this period), he would without doubt have had access to
more detailed information concerning the early days of the Church. In addition, it is quite unlikely that only isolated and floating traditions concerning the
Jerusalem chruch would have been known even outside of Palestine, if the
evidence of Munck and Jervell be allowed (*supra*, p. 273).

was issued at some unknown time "by the Jewish Christian Church in Jerusalem, to define the minimum conditions to be imposed on Gentile converts to Christianity, but not in the presence of Paul and Barnabas" (18)[63]. Thus, with the exception of the decree, the account of the apostolic council in Acts 15 is

> an imaginative reconstruction by Luke, designed to serve the purposes of his narrative and the lessons which he wished to convey, useful for effecting a transition between two missionary journeys about both of which he had some solid information. It is a carefully designed water-shed between a period of the Church's expansion about which Luke was often little informed; to reconstruct which he had usually little more than fragmentary material, and a period where his information, though neither complete nor exhaustive, was fuller, more detailed, and more reliable, because it was a period during which he himself had been a member of the Church and in some of whose events he had participated (155).

Although there is a basic historical core to the narrative of Acts 15 (i. e., the fact of the decree), Luke is chiefly responsible for the composition of the "ideal scene" as a whole[64].

In his discussion of the "we"-passages (21—28), Hanson argues that the best and most probable interpretation is that the author was a personal participant in the events narrated. He regards the objections to this conclusion on the ground that the author has misrepresented Paul as, in the final analysis, unconvincing[65]. In his discussion of the ending of Acts (28—35), Hanson presents a convincing case in favor of the view that Paul was released at the end of his two years' detention in Rome[66]; but he finds it extremely difficult to find a satisfactory explanation for the story's ending where it does, if it was written (as he suggests) in the 70s or 80s of

---

[63] See his discussion, pp. 153—59.

[64] It is doubtful whether very many will accept Hanson's reconstruction of the background of the narrative of Acts 15. It does not seem to me to answer as many questions as it raises, and one wonders whether the careful historian of Acts 16—28 would have been so free in his invention of overtly historical events in chapter 15.

[65] See his summary of the main points in answer to this objection, pp. 25 to 26.

[66] "It is admitted by everybody that Luke wants to represent the Roman government as neutral, and as just, towards Christianity. Is it conceivable that Luke knew, while he was writing to this effect, that Paul had been condemned by Caesar's court and executed, and that his audience knew? All Luke's protestations that Roman authorities do not regard Christianity as dangerous and subversive would be thus exposed as hollow, and it would not have been worth making the protestations. No, if anything is clear it is that the author of Acts believed that Paul was acquitted in Caesar's court. Such an event would not have been an extraordinary one" (31).

the first century. The best reason he can offer (and he admits that "even this does not quite satisfy") is that "the readers for whom the book was intended knew the rest of the story" (35)[67].

In spite of the fact that many scholars have been concerned with the problem of history in relation to the narrative of Luke-Acts, others have turned their attention almost exclusively to the question of the theology of the Lucan writings. This is generally recognized as due to the influence of the writings of Dibelius, who, although he recognized the author of Luke-Acts to be a historian of some sort, steadfastly excluded the question of historicity from the discussion and put forward a positive conception of Luke's literary methodology which is difficult to reconcile with any ordinary understanding of the work of a historian. Hence a large number of critics, mostly German and members of the so-called Bultmann school, have since abandoned the quest for history and have tended to emphasize the work of Luke as a creative theologian[68].

The commentaries by Ernst Haenchen and Hans Conzelmann, which represent this "new look" in Lucan research, were discussed in the previous chapter. Two further contributions which have set the tone of much of the recent discussion, but which have only been mentioned in passing up to this point, are Philipp Vielhauer's essay on the "Paulinism" of Acts[69] and the celebrated monograph by Hans Conzelmann on the theology of Luke[70]. The concluding section of this chapter will deal first with these two very important essays and then with a few of the responses to and criticisms of the major theses and premises of Vielhauer and Conzelmann. It need

---

[67] Hanson's commentary contains a good discussion of the theology of Acts (35—48), in which he concludes that Luke lived close enough to the primitive Church and Paul to be able to reflect some of the basic features of the earlier theologies fairly accurately ("He does not reflect the ideas, the interests and aims of the late first century ..." (48),), though he himself belongs to a slightly later age.

[68] This recent development in Lucan research is part of a larger movement, involving the application of the *redaktionsgeschichtliche Methode* to the Synoptic Gospels and Act. See Rohde, *Die redaktionsgeschichtliche Methode*, for a survey of the most important German contributions which have made use of this approach; pp. 124—83 surveys work on Luke-Acts. The New Testament introduction by W. Marxsen, who was one of the pioneers and is an enthusiastic supporter of the most extreme conclusions of recent German ciriticism, gives a convenient summary of the basic conclusions and point of view of some of the chief representatives of this approach.

[69] "Zum 'Paulinismus' der Apostelgeschichte", *EvTh* 10 (1950/51), pp. 1—15; E. T. "On the 'Paulinism' of Acts", in *Studies in Luke-Acts*, pp. 33—50. The English translation is cited below.

[70] *Die Mitte der Zeit* (Tübingen, 1954; 3rd ed., 1960); E. T. of 2nd ed., *The Theology of St. Luke* (London, 1960).

only be added that it would take a lengthy monograph to do full justice to the breadth and complexity of the recent discussion. Therefore, the reader should recognize that what follows is no more than a sketch of the highlights of recent research, rather than anything approaching an adequate survey of the work which has been done.

The influence of Dibelius is clearly discernible in the essay of Vielhauer. For example, in the third sentence he refers to the "speeches, which are *generally acknowledged*[71] to be compositions of the author and which, according to ancient literary custom, had deliberate and paradigmatic significance" (33). In fact, it is *not* "generally acknowledged" that the speeches are the author's composition; nor would all agree that this has the "ancient literary custom"[72]. If one were to "count heads", the opinion expressed by Vielhauer (following Dibelius) would probably be a minority opinion among scholars. Nevertheless, this statement by Vielhauer serves to emphasize the underlying assumption of a few influential German critics, *viz.* that many of the personal convictions which Dibelius affirmed in his various *Aufsätze* on the Book of Acts belong to the "assured results" of *Actaforschung*.

It is also important to recognize the influence of Franz Overbeck on the thought of Vielhauer[73]. This is seen both in the positive references to the work of Overbeck in the essay (42, 48) and in his carping attitude toward what he understands to be the theology of Luke. Thus Luke becomes, to Vielhauer, an early Christian theologian who is responsible for corrupting the original Gospel. Overbeck's stern reprimand is quoted with approval: "Luke took on his subject the one tactlessness of world historical dimensions, the supreme excess of a false viewpoint ... Luke treated historiographically what was not history and what was also not handed down as such" (48). It is not altogether clear exactly what this means, but it is clear that neither Overbeck nor Vielhauer cares very much for the ideas of Luke.

In his essay Vielhauer contrasts the theologies of the "Lucan Paul" (the Paul of Acts) and the "historical Paul" (the Paul of Romans, Galatians, and the Corinthian epistles) on four points: natural theology, the Law, Christology, and Eschatology.

His discussion of the "natural theology" of the Lucan Paul is

---

[71] Emphasis mine. Vielhauer refers in a footnote *only* to Dibelius' essay on "The Speeches in Acts and Ancient Historiography" in support of this statement! [72] See above, pp. 225–28.

[73] Vielhauer has come forward in a number of recent essays as a modern-day apologist for Overbeck. See, for example, his essay, "Franz Overbeck und die neutestamentliche Wissenschaft", *EvTh* 10 (1950/51), pp. 193–207.

totally dependent on Dibelius' essay on the Areopagus address of Acts 17[74]. It is argued that the ideas of the speech are essentially Hellenistic (based on Stoic philosophy), that the emphasis of the speech is on man's natural kinship with the divine, and that the thought expressed betrays a positive and definitely un-Pauline attitude toward pagan religion. By contrast, the "natural theology" of the real Paul (in Romans 1, for example) was connected with an emphasis on man's sin and God's wrath; it was the foundation for his scorching condemnation of the sinner. Moreover, the Areopagus address has no concept of "sin and grace" — and, above all, no "word of the cross". In both his positive emphasis and in his omissions the Paul of the Areopagus address is as far removed from Paul as he is near to the second-century Apologists (37).

According to Vielhauer, the historical Paul waged an anti-Jewish polemic against the Law, but the Lucan Paul is utterly loyal to the Law. (He lists eight points on page 38.) The Paul of the Book of Acts differs from other Jews *only* in the fact that he "believes in Jesus as the Messiah in contrast to the Jews" who have rejected him as such (38); he is the representative of the authentic Israel in contrast to the representatives of official Judaism. Although Vielhauer admits that it is a theoretical possibility that Paul could have kept some of the outward forms of Judaism merely as "an accommodation of practical attitude" (39)[75], he finds two points of the narrative of Acts impossible to believe.

The first of these impossibilities is Paul's participation, on the advice of James, in a Nazirite vow to disprove the accusations of the Jews and the Jewish Christians that he was teaching the Jews of the Dispersion to apostasize from the Law of Moses (21.18—28). In Vielhauer's opinion participation in such a vow would have been rank hypocrisy on the part of Paul, who was, in fact, guilty of teaching the Jews to forsake the Law! For Paul to have taken part in such a ceremony with the end in view attributed to him by the author of Acts would have meant a denial of "his actual practice and his gospel; that is, this would have been a denial that the cross of Christ alone was of saving significance for Gentiles *and* Jews" (40). The second impossibility concerns the account of the circumcision of Timothy (16.3). The Paul who wrote in Galatians 5.2, "if you receive circumcision, Christ will be of no advantage to you", could never have caused Timothy to be circumcised. "The state-

---

[74] See above, pp. 210—12.

[75] G. Bornkamm, "The Missionary Stance of Paul in 1 Corinthians 9 and Acts", in *Studies in Luke-Acts*, pp. 194—207, attempts to deny even this possibility.

ment about the circumcision of Timothy stands in direct contradiction to the theology of Paul, but it fits Luke's view that the Law retains its full validity for Jewish Christians and that Paul acknowledged this in a conciliatory concession to the Jews" (41).

A further contrast between the Lucan Paul and the historical Paul is found in Acts 13.38—39, the only reference to "justification" in any of Paul's speeches. Here, according to Vielhauer, justification is equated with the forgiveness of sins and thus is conceived entirely negatively, which Paul never does. Furthermore, the reference to "forgiveness of sins" does not occur in the major Pauline letters, but only in Colossians and Ephesians; on the other hand, it *does* occur in the speeches of Peter in Acts (2.38; 3.19; 5.31; 10.43). In addition, the forgiveness of sins is tied to the Messiahship of Jesus, which is based on the resurrection; as Overbeck comments, "nothing is said . . . about the particular significance of his death" (42). Finally, Luke, a Gentile Christian belonging to a later generation, never experienced the Law as a way of salvation and, therefore, was able to understand neither the antithesis between the Law and Christ in the thought of Paul nor the essential nature of the conflict over the Law in the early Church. Thus he "speaks of the inadequacy of the law, whereas Paul speaks of the end of the law, which is Christ (Rom. 10.4)" (42). In the theology of the author of Acts, "the 'word of the cross' has no place because in Acts it would make no sense" (43).

Thirdly, there is nothing at all of Paul's Christology in Acts. The Christology of the speeches is simply that of the undeveloped theology of the early Church (Dibelius). There is no reference to the pre-existence of Christ, which was so important for Paul. And there is not the slightest trace of the distinctively Pauline soteriology. Salvation rests solely on the resurrection of Jesus: the cross is not central in the preaching of the Lucan Paul, and it has no soteriological significance. "According to Acts . . . the crucifixion of Jesus is an error of justifice and a sin of the Jews, who despite knowledge of holy Scripture did not recognize Jesus' messiahship" (45).

Finally, Acts has no eschatology — at least, eschatology has little importance for the author. "Eschatology has been removed from the center of Pauline faith to the end and has become a 'section on the last things'" (45). Here Luke distinguishes himself "not only from Paul but also from the earliest Church, which expected the return of Christ, the resurrection of the dead, and the end of the world in the immediate future . . ." (45). Paul lived in the expectation of the imminent parousia; this fact motivated his mission and determined his relationship to the world. Luke, by contrast, has a theology of history[76]. His conception of history is that of "a continous redemptive historical process" (47). The *parousia* has been delayed and relegated to a place in the distant future; meanwhile, the Church digs its roots into history and prepares for a long period of existence and expansion.

This emphasis on redemptive history (in contrast to the eschatological emphasis of Paul and the earliest Christians) is seen by Vielhauer and other critics as being the fundamental feature of Lucan theology. "The fact of Acts" is considered to be a demonstration of the difference between the perspective of Luke and the first generation of Christians (including Paul). As long as the early Christians believed that the end of the world was at hand, they had no interest in writing about their own history!

The essay by Vielhauer is one of those all-too-frequent contributions to criticism which are difficult to criticize, not so much because the case which is argued is a strong one, but because there is so much that is questionable about the evidence which is allowed in the presentation of the case. It is full of unwarranted assumptions, question-begging exegesis, and false inferences. It would, in fact, be difficult to find a better example of allegedly critical research to illustrate the dangers of a false critical methodology and theological bias. Yet the amazing thing is the widespread influence that Vielhauer's brief, and one would think, ill-conceived essay has had in the world of New Testament scholarship! Haenchen dates the beginning of a new era of Acts criticism from the date of its publication[77], and many of the practitioners of the *redaktionsgeschichtliche Methode* accept the basic theses of Vielhauer as proven[78].

Vielhauer's essay will raise many questions in the mind of the student of the history of New Testament criticism. It is at once clear that the author stands in a specific critical tradition (Baur-Overbeck-Dibelius) which bases its understanding of Acts as much on a tradition of interpretation as on historical research and exegesis. To the impartial observer it seems quite evident that Vielhauer everywhere assumes what he is trying to prove. Moreover, it is doubtful whether his understanding of "the real Paul" is anything other than the product of the imagination of existentially dom-

---

[76] Eduard Lohse has dubbed Luke "the theologian of *Heilsgeschichte*"; see his essay, "Lukas als Theologe der Heilsgeschichte", *EvTh* 14 (1954), pp. 256 –275.

[77] *Die Apostelgeschichte*, p. 45.

[78] E. g., Haenchen, Conzelmann, G. Klein, Marxsen, Käsemann, Grässer and (in some respects) Kümmel. The only important feature of Vielhauer's essay that is rejected by some (though not all) of these scholars is his reference to Luke's thought as "early Catholic".

inated exegesis[79]. Some would regard both the "Lucan Paul" and the "historical Paul" of the present essay to be, in essence, Vielhauerian Pauls, rather than authentic representations of the Paul of Acts or the Paul of the epistles[80].

Many criticisms could be leveled at Vielhauer's conception of the main features of Pauline theology and his specific attempts at exegesis. For a start, his understanding of Paul's Areopagus speech is dependent on the interpretation offered by Dibelius and has been demonstrated by Gärtner to be essentially erroneous[81]. Then, his understanding of Paul's relation to the Law and Judaism is based more on a hyper-Lutheran understanding of the antithesis of Law and Gospel in Paul than on a careful exegesis of the letters of Paul[82]. There is not a shred of evidence in the Pauline epistles that Paul ever taught Jewish Christians to forsake the Law of Moses. Paul was not anti-Law (in the sense of Old Testament ceremonies and Jewish practices) but anti-legalism (i. e., the Law as a means of salvation)[83]. Vielhauer's conception of Paul's attitude fails to understand the practical problem of Paul's missionary career. If Paul was to engage in any evangelistic ministry among Jews — and the epistles bear witness to the fact that he did — it would have been essential for him to have done the sort of thing which the Book of Acts says he did. And, Vielhauer notwithstanding, no good reason has yet been brought forward in proof of the fact that he sould not have so acted.

Perhaps the basic criticisms to be leveled at Vielhauer are in the area of critical methodology. First, he is obviously concerned to defend a thesis, not primarily to understand a historical situation. He is as "apologetic" in his approach to the text of the New Testament as any of the older "apologists" were; it is just that he is concerned to defend a particular critical understanding of "Luke", rather than Luke himself. Secondly, his approach to the speeches is wrong, regardless of the view one takes concerning the nature of the speeches in Acts. Vielhauer's method is to take the teaching of

---

[79] Cf. "It is Paul, interpreted existentially, who is so sharply set against Luke as the great but dangerous corrupter of the Pauline gospel. But the existentially interpreted Paul is not the historical Paul" (U. Wilckens, "Interpreting Luke-Acts in a Period of Existentialist Theology", in *Studies in Luke-Acts*, p. 77; cf. I. H. Marshall, *Luke: Historian and Theologian* (Exeter, 1970), p. 220).

[80] Ellis comments that whereas Vielhauer has difficulty in recognizing Luke's Paul, he has "a similar difficulty in recognizing Vielhauer's Luke" (*The Gospel of Luke*, p. 47).

[81] See above, pp.. 213–14.

[82] *Supra*, pp. 241–43, 246n.

[83] See Cranfield, "St. Paul and the Law", *SJT* 17 (1964), pp. 43–68.

the speeches of Paul in Acts *as a whole* and to compare this with the teaching of the epistles *as a whole*. This approach overlooks the fact that one should not expect to find a full-blown and well-rounded theology of Paul in either the speeches of Acts or the epistles. It is not good criticism to expect a few representative sermons, even if they do represent the authentic thought of the speaker, and an accidental collection of four occasional letters to provide anything approaching an adequate account of Paul's theology — even if he were primarily a theologian, which he was not. What sort of picture would one have of the theology of Augustine or of Luther or of Calvin or even of Karl Barth if all that remained from the pen of each were four controversial letters and a half-dozen brief synopses of their sermons? No student of the history of thought will doubt for a moment that our understanding of them all would be quite different if this were all that remained of their thought, nor would he be surprised if it proved difficult to correlate the thought expressed in the sermons with that of the letters. (It is difficult enough as it is to harmonize the seemingly inconsistent strands in the theologies of these men, even when one limits oneself to their strictly theological writings!). But, narrowed by the limited perspective of concentration on a very small body of literature, the type of New Testament criticism represented by Vielhauer seems to have lost touch with the true nature of the documents with which it is working.

A few examples will be sufficient to illustrate the weakness of Vielhauer's method. Let us imagine that we had only Galatians from the pen of Paul. What then would we know of Paul's eschatology, which Vielhauer describes as "the center" of his faith? Nothing. One can conceive of scholars writing learned essays and monographs on Paul, arguing that eschatology had as little place in the theology of the historical Paul as in that of Vielhauer's Luke. But the fact is that Galatians gives us only a few of Paul's thoughts which were written with haste in the white heat of ecclesiastical controversy: it is by no means a reasoned theological treatise or a formal confesson of faith in the later sense of the term. Again, if Paul had not written 1 Corinthians, or if this letter had been among those which were lost to subsequent generations, we would not know that Paul ever heard of the eucharist. Nor would one know that the resurrection of Christ played a very significant role in his theology. Without the two Corinthian epistles (and assuming, as Vielhauer seems to do, that 1 Thessalonians is either inauthentic or unimportant), we would know very little about Paul's ideas concerning the final resurrection. One would have thought that it was a self-evident fact that *all* the epistles of Paul (i. e., the ones the critic considers to be authentic) as a group give only an indication of *some* of the aspects of the theology of Paul, rather than the whole spectrum of his thinking on the themes of Christian faith and practice; but Vielhauer's approach fails to give due recognition to this fact.

To ascertain whether the thought of the speeches in Acts is really compatible with the thought of the Paul of the epistles, the proper critical approach would be to see whether there are traces in the epistles of any of the ideas of the speeches. One should not expect to find *detailed* correspondences between the speeches and the letters. And there is certainly no obvious reason why a former associate of Paul should be expected to parrot Paul's theology in all its peculiarities outside of the speeches attributed to Paul[84]. On the other hand, assuming the independency of the Book of Acts and the letters of Paul, the fact of incidental agreements between the ideas expressed in the letters and in the speeches of Acts would at least indicate the possibility that the speeches could represent authentically Pauline thought, if not his actual words. When the problem is approached from this point of view, the impression is quite different from that given by Vielhauer's essay. There are, in fact, many "undesigned coincidences" between the speeches and the epistles. These are especially evident in Paul's speech before the Ephesian elders at Miletus (Acts 20.18—35), which contains the most detailed correspondences to the epistles[85]; but the same is also true of the Areopagus address (though to a lesser degree), as Bertil Gärtner has shown[86]. Thus when one frees the speeches from the critical strait jacket which requires them to contain a full-blown Pauline theology — and, it may be added, a theology which many would regard as a less than adequate representation of the theology of the historical Paul — they give some evidence of possible authenticity. This is, at any rate, the impression they have made on a considerable number of the most astute critics of Acts. Further questions could be raised regarding Vielhauer's assumption that Paul

---

[84] Cf. "It has sometimes been claimed that Luke cannot have been a companion of Paul because in neither the gospel nor the Acts is there any trace of the *specifically* Pauline doctrines to be found in the major epistles. This claim neglects the extent to which it is possible to associate and work with others without necessarily sharing all their concerns; in other words, it fails to do justice either to the variety to be found within the unity of modern Christianity or to that within the early church" (R. M. Grant, *A Historical Introduction to the New Testament*, p. 135).

[85] The evidence for this can be found in any good commentary; there is no need to repeat it here. Cf. also *supra*, pp. 61—62.

[86] *The Areopagus Speech and Natural Revelation*, pp. 248—52.

and the *Urgemeinde* "expected the return of Christ, the resurrection of the dead, and the end of the world in the immediate future" (45); but these will be best considered in response to the work of Conzelmann.

The monograph of Hans Conzelmann, *Die Mitte der Zeit,* is a much more substantial work than Vielhauer's essay, though some would view it as only slightly less tendentious[87]. It has been this book more than any other which has caused the attention of New Testament exegetes to be focussed on the Lucan writings for the past decade and a half. A large number of the several hundred scholarly essays and monographs which have been devoted to the study of Luke-Acts since 1954 have been written in response to some point made by Conzelmann.

Conzelmann's study is a combination of his doctoral dissertation (the section entitled, "Die geographischen Vorstellungen als Element der Komposition des Lukas-Evangeliums")[88] and his inaugural thesis. He is concerned to isolate the typical and characteristic features of the Lucan writings. The emphasis is placed on the Gospel, which can be compared to Mark and Matthew; he does not think that Luke's fundamental themes have been developed to quite the same extent in the Book of Acts[89].

He distinguishes his method from that of the traditional form-critical approach. Whereas the latter was concerned primarily with individual pericopae and their place in the tradition about Jesus, his intention is to study the special contribution of the author in his selection and editing of the traditional materials and in the formation of the literary end-product (1—4). Conzelmann stresses his own conception of the way Luke has used the Gospel of Mark. He

---

[87] His essay, "Zur Lukas-Analyse", *ZTK* 49 (1952), pp. 16—33, contains the main features of the view which he elaborates in his larger work.

[88] According to Conzelmann, Luke's geography is a part of his theology. Whatever geographical data he includes in his narrative he includes for the purpose of serving his general theological aims. Thus, when he refers to "the mountain", he does not mean a mountain which can be located on a map, but simply the place of prayer, the source of secret revelations and heavenly proclamation, where Jesus goes alone or with his disciples (38). This is why Luke (4.5—8) avoids all reference to the mountain in his account of the story of the temptation (23). In contrast to the mountain stands "the plain" (i. e., the place of meetings with the people) and "the lake" (i. e., the place of the manifestation of the Lord's power). Conzelmann argues that Luke is totally ignorant of the geography of Palestine: he thought that Judea and Galilee were immediately adjacent to each other and that both bordered on Samaria (61—62), that Capernaum lay in the middle of Galilee (33), and that it was possible to enter the Temple without going into the city of Jerusalem (68n.)!

[89] Conzelmann, *Die Apostelgeschichte*, p. 9.

argues that Luke has dealt in a very critical manner with the material he has taken over from Mark, retaining only those parts of the original which can be used to develop his own ideas[90]; and that, in so doing, Luke has written a completely original Gospel which is designed to replace Mark's story of Jesus.

Fundamental to Conzelmann's understanding of Luke's theology is his understanding of Luke's relation to the first generation of Christians. He is not a member of the earliest generation; in fact, he has never had any personal contact at all with any of the earliest disciples. He is certainly not the traditional Luke or any other former travelling companion of Paul. Rather, he is a member of the third generation of Christians, looking back on the ἀρχή of the Church as something unique and unrepeatable (5). The basic problem with which he is concerned is the fact of the delay of the *parousia* (6, *passim*).

In the view of Conzelmann, there was a tremendous crisis of conscience in the early Church when the return of Christ failed to materialize, as expected, within a few years after his death[91]. When the eschatological hopes of the earliest Christians began to wane, there was the danger of disillusionment among the rank and file members of the Church. It was in response to this crisis situation that Luke wrote his two-volumed work, to answer the question as [*168*] to why Jesus had not returned as had been expected. "Lukas stellt sich der Lage, in welche die Kirche durch das Ausbleiben der Parusie und die Entstehung einer innerweltlichen Geschichte gekommen ist. Er versucht sie zu bewältigen durch das Faktum seiner Geschichtsschreibung" (6).

Luke's theological solution to the problem of the *Parusieverzögerung* is in the form of a philosophy of history. According to Conzelmann, Luke is the first early Christian to think in terms of the history of the Church, to suggest that instead of expecting an im-

---

[*169*] [90] His comment on Luke 19.47 is representative of the general outlook of his study: "Nach Quellen für die Besonderheiten darf man an diesen redaktionellen Nahtstellen nicht fragen; noch weniger ist historisierende Reflexion über die Zuverlässigkeit der Lc-Form der Berichterstattung angebracht. Lc hat durchweg stilisiert, nicht auf Grund zusätzlicher Information, sondern auf Grund theologischer Reflexion" (70n.). Cf. Dibelius (*supra*, pp. 206—8) and Haenchen (*supra*, p. 246n.).

[91] E. Grässer, *Das Problem der Parusieverzögerung in den synoptischen Evangelien und in der Apostelgeschichte* (Berlin, 1957), offers a detailed defense of this understanding of the nature of the eschatological hope of the earliest Christians and the alleged influence of this problem on the first three Gospels and Acts. A. L. Moore, *The Parousia in the New Testament*, Suppl. *NovTest* 13 (Leiden, 1966), is the most recent and searching challenge to the correctness of this view.

minent *parousia* the Church should think in terms of a long period of time taking before the final *parousia* (that is, to concentrate on the time of the Church's life and witness in the world). Hence, while the hope of the *parousia* is maintained by Luke, it is consigned by him to the distant future. Rather than being simply a time of waiting (as in the earlier theology), the interval of time which passes before the *parousia* takes on a positive character in the thought of Luke: it is one of the stage's in God's unfolding plan of redemption, in which God is active in the world through the Church[92].

Conzelmann's Luke conceives of history in terms of three periods or epochs: (1) the time of Israel, which is concluded with the ministry of John the Baptist (Luke 16.16); (2) the time of Jesus' ministry (characterized by such passages as Luke 4.16—20 and Acts 10.38); and (3) the time of the Church, that is, the period between the ascension and the return of Christ. Thus the title of Conzelmann's book becomes clear: "the middle of time" is the period of Jesus' earthly life and corresponds to the subject of the Gospel according to Luke. In this way what had been originally *kerygma* becomes, for Luke, a part of history, a past event. The third period, the time of the Church, corresponds to the subject of the Book of Acts; and it is the basic idea of the Church as having a history of its own that sets the thought of Luke off from that of the authors of the synoptic Gospels and from Paul.

Conzelmann's monograph (and, in some ways, his commentary on Acts)[93] is an attempt to substantiate this basic conception of the Lucan point of view. Since his attention is directed primarily toward the Third Gospel rather than Acts, his work is only of indirect importance for the study of Acts. There is no question but that Conzelmann has made a real contribution to the study of Luke, not the least through his challenge to New Testament exegetes to offer more tenable solutions in the place of some of his own more improbable suggestions. However, it should be pointed out that nearly every major point made by Conzelmann has been challenged by some capable scholar, and that the majority of critics consider that his point of view has been anything but demonstrated. As I. H. Marshall[94] has suggested, it is probable that the most worthwhile contributions to Lucan research in the past decade of research have

---

[92] See especially his discussion, pp. 87—127.

[93] *Supra*, pp. 298—300.

[94] "Recent Study of the Gospel According to St. Luke", *ExpT* 80 (1968), p. 5. To these responses to Conzelmann has now been abded Marshall's own important monograph, *Luke: Historian and Theologian* (Exeter, 1970), certainly one of the more important of the recent contibutions to research.

been made by those works which have drawn attention to the debatable points in Conzelmann's exposition of the Lucan theology and so have attempted to place Lucan research on a firmer foundation.

In spite of the flashes of genuine exegetical insight which adorn the pages of Conzelmann's monograph, many of his basic conclusions are suspect. First, his negative evaluation of the way Luke handles the Marcan material would not be accepted by most critics. Many of the illustrations which he gives of changes which allegedly have been made because of the author's theological motifs are unconvincing and are often only stylistic variations. Moreover, Conzelmann seems to assume that Mark was Luke's only source (with the exception of a special source for chapters 1 and 2), and that where Luke differs from Mark this is due to Luke's editorial tampering with the Marcan material. The material that is peculiar to the Third Gospel, as well as a large part of the narrative of Acts, seems to have come out of Luke's head. This assumption has been challenged, with good reason, by a number of recent critics of Luke[95].

Secondly, the three-fold division of history into three distinct periods is far too artificial, and few would concede that this basic outline was really present in the mind of the author of Luke-Acts. It rests mainly on the interpretation of one verse of Luke (16.16)[96] plus the fact of Acts. The birth narratives of Luke 1—2 are significantly omitted from Conzelmann's discussion of the theology of Luke. As a number of scholars have pointed out[97], a consideration of the theological ideas expressed here (which emphasize the unity of the Old and New Testament, as well as the ministries of Jesus and John) does not support Conzelmann's thesis.

Also vulnerable is his hypothesis of the period of the ministry of Jesus as a "Satan-free" period[98]. And if one challenges the view that the time of Jesus and the time of the Church are to be regarded as two entirely separated historical epochs with the observation that Luke links the ministry of Jesus and the witness of the Church by

---

[95] See a few of the references in Marshall (n.94), p. 6.

[96] Conzelmann's arguments are not dissimilar to some of the older discussions of the biblical anthropology which argued, on the basis of 1 Thess. 5.23, that man was conceived by the biblical writers as a tripartite being. Cf. Minear (n.97): "Rarely has a scholar placed so much weight on so dubious an interpretation of so difficult a logion" (122).

[97] See especially P. S. Minear, "Luke's use of the Birth Stories", in *Studies in Luke-Acts*, pp. 111—130.

[98] "Conzelmann overlooks Lk 11[16] and gives a forced meaning to Lk 22[28]" (Marshall [n.94], p. 6n.).

the common fact of persecution[99], what becomes of Luke's three periods?

Just as serious is the inadequacy of Conzelmann's conception of the early Christian eschatology. The assumption, inherited by the Bultmann school from the "consistent eschatology" of A. Schweitzer and J. Weiss, that the *Urgemeinde* and Paul expected the return of Christ and the end of the world to take place very shortly is highly questionable. Conzelmann and those who take his view simply fail to do justice to the many passages of scripture, both in the teaching of Jesus and Paul, which imply an interval of indefinite length between the events surrounding the death and resurrection of Jesus and the future *parousia*. Contrary to Conzelmann's view, this idea of an interval of time is not exclusively the view of Luke. In addition, it is not correct to say that Luke has replaced the idea of the "nearness" of the *parousia* with the idea of a long, drawn-out period of time before the end. There are some passages in Luke-Acts which speak just as definitely of the nearness of the impending day of judgment and the kingdom of God as others in the Synoptic Gospels (e. g., Luke 3.9, 17; 10.9—12; 13.6—9; 18.7—8; 21.32), and it will not do (with Conzelmann and Grässer) to dismiss these as sayings which have been simply taken over by Luke without being integrated into his thought. It may be that Luke does not give the same emphasis to the possibility of the near return of Christ which one finds in Matthew, Mark, and Paul; but he has not (*contra* Conzelmann) removed this from the realm of possibility. Conversely, it is probably correct to say that he is more conscious than Mark (at least) of the place of the Church in redemptive history, but this is not to say that he invented the idea of *Heilsgeschichte*. A. L. Moore[100] has recently offered cogent argument for the view that, although the emphasis varies from writer to writer, the New Testament writings all agree in recognizing the nearness of the *parousia* (as one of the blessings of the Messianic age which has dawned with the coming of Christ) without the attempt to delimit the time; thus the two elements of the possible nearness of the end and the possible continuance of the Church for an indefinite period of time are held in tension[101]. Again, as W. G. Kümmel[102] has observed,

---

[99] Cf. G. Braumann, "Das Mittel der Zeit", *ZNW* 54 (1963), pp. 117—45.

[100] See n.91. Cf. especially pp. 108—90 of Moore's study.

[101] "The aspect of present fulfillment in the eschatology of Jesus, the possibility of an interim period between the passion and parousia in the thought of Jesus, and the tendency of apocalyptic to include both a hope for an imminent end of the age and the claim that the end is yet far away and will be preceded by signs, all argue against Conzelmann's reconstruction" (C. H. Talbert, *Luke*

Luke was by no means the first to introduce the idea of *Heilsgeschichte* into the Gospel tradition; it is present in the preaching of Jesus himself — and, we may add, certainly in Paul[103]. If Conzelmann were to speak in terms of Luke's emphasis, he might have a better case; but he is undoubtedly wrong to regard Luke's stress on the history of salvation as a quite different theological point of view from that of the other New Testament authors.

Since the publication of Conzelmann's study of the Lucan theology in 1954, a host of alternative interpretations of the Lucan theology and purpose have been advanced by other scholars. A few of these may be noted at this point.

Bo Reicke[104] understands the general theme of Acts to be the activity of the risen Lord in his Church[105].

According to the short introduction to Acts given in 1:1—2, this book was meant to be a direct continuation of the Gospel of Luke. In the Gospel, the acts of the Lord had been described. This is precisely what Luke intends to do in Acts also. It is a description of *what the risen Lord did* for his church through the apostles (157).

This theme is clear from the very beginning of the book — the risen Lord's commissioning of his disciples to be his witnesses and the promise of the Holy Spirit (1.3—8) and also in the Pentecost narratives — and in the central theological concerns of the author, *viz.* Christology and ecclesiology, Christ and his Church.

The Christology of Acts is seen both in the speeches and in the narrative. Reicke finds three different aspects of Christology represented by (a) the sermons of Peter (where "the emphasis is on

---

and the Gnostics (Nashville and New York, 1966), p. 106). Cf. also W. C. van Unnik in *NovTest* 4 (1960), pp. 45—46.

[102] *Introduction to the New Testament*, p. 102.

[103] In addition to the work of Munck and Cullmann, see U. Wilckens, "Interpreting Luke-Acts in a Period of Existentialist Theology", in *Studies in Luke-Acts*, pp. 60—83.

[104] "The Risen Lord and His Church: The Theology of Acts", *Interp.* 13 (1959), pp. 156—69. Reicke is also the author of a number of other worthwhile studies of Luke-Acts, among which are "Der geschichtliche Hintergrund des Apostelkonzils und der Antiochia-Episode (Gal. 2.1—14)", in *Studia Paulina*, ed. by J. N. Sevenster and W. C. van Unnik (Haarlem, 1953), pp. 172—87; "A Synopsis of Early Christian Preaching", in *The Root of the Vine*, by A. Fridrichsen *et al.* (London, 1953), especially pp. 138—43; "Die Verfassung der Urgemeinde im Lichte jüdischer Dokumente", *ThZ* 10 (1954), pp. 95—119, E. T. in *The Scrolls and the New Testament*, ed. by K. Stendahl (New York, 1957), pp. 143—56; *Glaube und Leben der Urgemeinde: Bemerkungen zu Apg. 1—7, AbThANT* 32 (Zürich, 1957); and *Lukasevangeliet* (Stockholm, 1962), E. T. *The Gospel of Luke* (Richmond, Va., 1964).

[105] Cf. especially the view of Harnack (*supra*, pp. 154—55).

Jewish ideals and God's specific revelation in the recent past, in the *historical* life of Jesus"), (b) the sermons of Stephen and Paul (both including the doctrine of general revelation), and (c) Luke's narrative (where the emphasis is on the present guidance of the steps of the early missionaries by the risen Lord). In his ecclesiology Luke stresses (a) the nature of the Church as the new Israel, the genuine people of God, (b) the Spirit, who is the power behind the expansion of the Church, (c) the constant expansion of the Church through the word which is preached by the apostles, and (d) the interpretation of history. The emphasis throughout is on the expansion of the Church: geographically and ethnically. Reicke concludes his essay with a positive evaluation of the theology of Acts, in contrast to those who fault Luke's "historicizing" and "early Catholic" point of view.

A. C. Winn[106] also discerns a theological purpose behind Acts. The problem which the author faces is not (as Conzelmann supposes) the delay of the return, but rather the fact of the rejection of the Gospel by the Jews, God's chosen people, and its acceptance by Gentiles. This theological motive of the author has determined both the form and the content of Acts. Thus, for example, the two foci of the book are Jerusalem and Rome: the Gospel which began to be preached in Jerusalem is now being preached in Rome. This transfer from Jerusalem to Rome is represented everywhere in Acts as the work of the Spirit. In all that he writes, Luke seeks to prove — by the use of the Old Testament, speeches, and incidents along the road to Rome — that the rejection of the Gospel by the Jews and its joyful acceptance by the Gentiles was not an unforseen catastrophe, but rather the fulfillment of God's plan and purpose.

The weakness of Winn's thesis is that, in the form in which he expresses it, it is based primarily on a consideration of Luke's second volume, the Book of Acts. It also suffers from a certain looseness of definition and a limited acquaintance with the work of the more important contributions to Lucan research, both ancient and modern. A work along similar lines, but which is much more carefully defined and executed, is J. Dupont's essay on "The Salvation of the Gentiles and the Theological Significance of the Book of Acts"[107].

---

[106] "Elusive Mystery: The Purpose of Acts", *Interp.* 13 (1959), pp. 144—56. Cf. also his commentary, *The Acts of the Apostles* (Richmond, Va., 1960).

[107] "Le salut des gentils et la signification théologique du Livre des Actes", *NTS* 6 (1959/60), pp. 132—55; = *Études sur les Actes des Apôtres* (Paris, 1967), pp. 394—419; the references which follow are to his collected studies. N. B. In addition to his study of the history of source criticism of Acts (*supra*, pp. 275—76), Dupont has written the commentary on Acts for the "Jerusalem

In contrast to Conzelmann, Winn, and many others, Dupont does not analyze Luke's thought as an attempt to answer any particular problem. Rather, he discovers a recurring theological theme at various important places in Luke-Acts: a concern to show how the message of salvation, in fulfillment of the Messianic prophecies and the divine plan, has been proclaimed to the Gentiles. He finds the theme of Acts in 1.8, which is not simply geographical (397). Ἕως ἐσχά- του τῆς γῆς, as we can see from a comparison with Acts 13.46—47, means "to the Gentiles" and is the equivalent of εἰς πάντα τὰ ἔθνη in Luke 24.47 (403—4, 418). Dupont makes a careful examination and comparison of the conclusion of Acts and the beginning of the Gospel (398—401), the conclusion of the Gospel and the introduction of Acts (401—4), the discourse of Jesus at Nazareth and that of Peter at Pentecost (404—9), the story of Peter's encounter with the Centurion at Caesarea (409—12), and the mission of Paul in Acts (413—19). In all these places he finds a dominant emphasis on the message of salvation and its proclamation, to Gentiles.

On the whole, Dupont gives a convincing case for the view that this theme is a major, if not *the* major, theological theme of Acts. His case is all the more impressive because he does not attempt to defend it by speculation concerning some imaginary occasion or crisis (concerning which we have no definite knowledge) which requires the author's response, and because he does not insist that this one theme is the *exclusive* theological concern of the author. If one is to isolate Luke's special theological motifs, Dupont has illustrated the manner in which this is to be done. His conclusions are based on careful exegesis and are free from the extreme speculation of some other critics; and he does not argue for more than the data seem to indicate. As in all his work as a New Testament scholar, Dupont's essay is a model of careful criticism and exegesis.

W. C. van Unnik[108] understands Acts as "the confirmation (βεβαίωσις) of what God did in Christ as told in the first book" (58) of Luke (i. e., the Gospel). The leading idea is salvation (cf. σωτηρία —σώζω word-group) and is stressed by Peter (Acts 2.21, 40; 5.31; 10.43; 11.14; 15.11) and by Paul (13.15, 26). At Philippi, Paul and Barnabas are called by the slave girl "servants of the most High God, who proclaim to you ὁδὸν σωτηρίας" (16.17); and the way is shown to the jailor, who cries: "What must I do to be saved?" (16.

Bible" (introduction by L. Cerfaux; Paris, 1962; 3rd rev. ed., 1964), a 407-page exposition of Paul's address to the Ephesian elders in Acts 20 (Paris, 1962), and many important essays on the Book of Acts (the most important are contained in his *Études*).

[108] "The 'Book of Acts' the Confirmation of the Gospel", *NovTest* 4 (1960), pp. 26—59.

ʻ30—31)[109]. Luke, therefore, sets forth God's eschatological plan of salvation which came into the world through Jesus Christ and explains how it was passed on to those who did not know him during his earthly life. Closely connected to the idea of salvation is the concept of the witness (μάρτυς)[110]. Then there are the further emphases of the author: that the witness has been substantiated by God himself, through "signs and wonders" and by the gift of the Spirit, and that men are called to make a decision for or against the message of God. Thus Acts *"is not a 'metabasis eis allo genos', but a legitimate sequel and complement to Luke's gospel because it formed its confirmation . . . (59).*

In *The Theology of Acts in Its Historical Setting* J. C. O'Neill[111] defends the view that the purpose of Acts (and the Gospel of Luke) is to preach the Gospel to unbelievers, "to persuade educated Romans to become Christians" (168). This is the sense in which it can be understood to be an "apology", rather than in a technical sense. Its design is not to gain official recognition for Christianity as some have suggested, but rather to bring men to the faith. The theme which the author adopts to give unity to his evangelistic treatise is the movement of the Gospel up to Jerusalem (in the Gospel) and from Jerusalem to Rome (in Acts). The emphasis of Acts is on the superintendence of God over the whole process: it is God who has fulfilled his promises to Israel in the Church, and it is God who has been with his messengers as they have gone forth preaching the Gospel. One of the primary functions of the speeches in Acts is to repeat "over and over again the framework of the Christian faith as understood by Luke and his Church" (171) — that is, to preach the Gospel.

There is little objection to some of the basic features of O'Neill's exposition of the theology of Acts, which are not, in any case, either new or startling. What spoils the whole of his work is his attempt to date Acts as late as A. D. 115—30 because of alleged similarities between "Luke's catholic theology of history" and the writings of Justin Martyr[112]. He even attempts to argue, against nearly all scholars, that Justin did not know the Third Gospel, but rather that Luke

---

[109] See the detailed discussion, pp. 50—53.

[110] See the detailed discussion, pp. 54—56. Both of these themes are important for the Gospel of Luke as well, as a glance at a concordance will indicate.

[111] (London, 1961).

[112] See the trenchant criticism of H. F. D. Sparks in *JTS* N. S. 14 (1963), pp. 457—66. O'Neill issued a revised edition in 1970 with a number of significant changes. Though his general conception of the data and purpose of Acts remains unaltered, he now believes that the author was using sources (being influenced by an essay by C. F. D. Moule in *Studies in Luke-Acts*, pp. 159—85).

and Justin both used the same source or sources (28—42). It is not surprising that few, if any, scholars have found his thesis concerning the date or the purpose of Acts convincing.

Two recent studies which were written with the express purpose of criticizing Conzelmann's conception of the theology of Luke are the doctoral dissertations of W. C. Robinson, Jr.[113], and H. Flender[114]. Both are focussed primarily on the Gospel, and therefore do not have too much to say about the Book of Acts. Robinson, who gives his dissertation the sub-title, "Ein Gespräch mit Hans Conzelmann", questions Conzelmann's thesis concerning the theological significance of Luke's geographical framework, his suggestion that Luke wishes to draw a rigid line of demarcation between the ministries of John and Jesus, and many other major and minor points of Conzelmann's conception of the theology of Luke. Positively, Robinson finds a constant emphasis in Luke-Acts on "the way of the Lord", beginning with the journeys of Jesus to Jerusalem and leading to the mission to the Gentiles (39—43). Flender challenges Conzelmann's unilinear interpretation of *Heilsgeschichte* in Luke, which he regards as superficial. He finds the theology of Luke to be much more complex than Conzelmann allows, and offers a dialectical understanding of Luke's theology in its place. He criticizes Conzelmann's threefold division of salvation history, his conception of the place of the *parousia* in Luke, and the negative judgment which Vielhauer, Conzelmann, and other members of the Bultmann school pass on Luke's theological point of view.

It is doubtful whether either Robinson or Flender have succeeded in offering a more viable option to Conzelmann — it is always easier to point out the weaknesses in the views of others than to replace them by better ones! — but their work has served to underline the unsatisfactory nature of Conzelmann's thesis.

In conclusion to what is basically a study in the history of theology, Daniel P. Fuller[115] turns his attention to Luke-Acts (188—261). Without defending the methodological correctness of his jump from the problems and approach of modern historians back to the first Christian century[116], one may recognize the importance of his analysis of Luke's approach to the problem of history.

---

[113] *Der Weg des Herrn: Studien zur Geschichte und Eschatologie im Lukas-Evangelium* (Hamburg-Bergstedt, 1964). This is the German translation of a thesis which was originally written in English and published privately. I have not seen the English version.

[114] *Heil und Geschichte in der Theologie des Lukas* (München, 1965); E. T. *St. Luke: Theologian of Redemptive History* (London, 1967).

[115] *Easter Faith and History* (Grand Rapids, 1965).

[116] Cf. the opening paragraph of his seventh chapter (188). Although I per-

Fuller emphasizes the importance of the author's own statement in his preface (Luke 1.1—4) in determining the purpose of the author. Here, Luke writes that he has written things down "in an orderly manner" (καθεξῆς) so that his reader, Theophilus, and others who read his work may have a sense of "certainty" (τὴν ἀσφάλειαν) regarding the oral instruction they have received. That is, by filling his readers in on the facts of the Gospel Luke seeks to provide verification of their faith.

Fuller recognizes a number of important themes in Acts (which is the part of Luke-Acts that he stresses): "(1) the spread of the Gospel, (2) the continuity between Christianity and the Old Testament, (3) the Jewish persecution of Christians, (4) Christianity's favor with the neutrals, and (5) the pre-eminence of Paul" (201). But the basic theme, indicated in Acts 1.1 and 8, is the spread of the Gospel through the Gentile mission. Fundamental to this is the resurrection of Christ, which is the only explanation of the faith of the apostles and of Paul, the presence of the Church in the world, and the success of the Gentile mission. And it is this fact of the resurrection of Jesus, confirmed both by the testimony of eye-witnesses and the presence of the risen Lord at work in his Church through the Holy Spirit, that is stressed by Luke as the chief means of giving to Theophilus and the other readers a sense of certainty concerning what they had heard.

R. R. Williams[117], in the manner appropriate to a bishop, considers the purpose of Luke to be primarily catechetical. At least, this is what the author seems to express in his preface (Luke 1.1—4).

He *says* that he wrote the Gospel so that Theophilus should know the sure foundation on which rested the teaching he had already received. As Acts was dedicated to the same person, it seems reasonable to assume that its main purpose was the same — instructional and edificatory (155).

Behind Theophilus, Luke could see many others with a similar need to be instructed in the faith. Thus, what he wrote for them was "not pure teaching, pure exhortation, but teaching given through the medium of history. To him, history *was* teaching" (156).

---

sonally would recognize Luke as both a historian and a theologian, I cannot make the historical jump over nineteen centuries of history with the ease with which Fuller does it. While Luke may provide the contemporary theologian with some of his basic materials for his attempt to solve the pressing problems of the present day, one cannot but recognize that there is a great difference between the issues which faced him and our own concerns.

[117] "Church History in Acts: Is It Reliable?", in *Historicity and Chronology in the New Testament* (London, 1965), pp. 155—56.

Charles H. Talbert[118] has recently defended the thesis that "Luke-Acts was written to serve as a defense against Gnosticism" (16). In an attempt to demonstrate his thesis, he stresses what he regards to be the basic theological themes of Luke: the witness motif (which is the dominant theme of Acts), an emphasis on the proper interpretation of the Old Testament (in keeping with the approach instituted by Jesus), and a succession of apostolic tradition (under the control of the Jerusalem apostles, through the early missionaries to the elders whom they appointed). In a manner reminiscent of O'Neill's comparison of the theology of Acts with Justin Martyr, Talbert compares Luke with John, the Pastorals, and 2 Peter ("three types of response to heresy") and finds confirmation of his view that Luke-Acts has an anti-Gnostic bias (57—70). Strangely enough, he finds *both* the silence of Acts concerning the Gentile controversies of Paul and the account of the conflict with the circumcision party to be further proof of Luke's apologetic against Gnosticism (83—97)!

The strongest point of Talbert's thesis is his first chapter (17—32), which discusses Luke's emphasis on the role of the eye-witness and the reality of the resurrection. There is little doubt that this is a fundamental concern of the author — few would dispute it. However, much of the rest of his discussion is clouded by his concern to prove an unlikely thesis, which often leads to extremely dubious exegesis. His work is further marred by his failure to give a precise and historical definition of "Gnosticism". It is obviously true that the message of Luke-Acts is contrary to what we know of Gnosticism, but Talbert fails to prove either that Gnosticism as a movement is as early as Luke-Acts or that Luke writes for the express purpose of defending orthodox Christianity against Gnostic teaching. If Talbert's study demonstrates anything, it is the danger of discovering a new idea and then going to the New Testament in order to "prove" it. Such an approach satisfies the requirement of originality pre-requisite for a Ph. D. dissertation, and it no doubt provides the aspiring scholar with many hours of worthwhile mental exercise; but it is to be questioned whether this speculative approach does much to further our understanding of the New Testament documents.

The variety of views which scholars have brought forward since Conzelmann — and we have mentioned only a few of them — to explain what they regard to be the purpose or the theological leitmotif of Luke-Acts is staggering. In the face of the extreme diver-

---

[118] *Luke and the Gnostics: An Examination of the Lucan Purpose* (Nashville and New York, 1966).

sity of opinion it is tempting to take refuge in extreme skepticism and to despair of ever knowing what the author of Luke-Acts was up to.

One conclusion which can be drawn from the past decade or so of discussion is that it is impossible, indeed, even misleading, to think of *one* exclusive purpose lying behind the writing of Luke-Acts, or *one* all-pervasive theological motif. It would be much more fruitful to think in terms of a variety of purposes and themes. It should also be clear by now that it is impossible for critics who are separated by nearly two thousand years from the publication of Luke-Acts to "imagine" the appropirate occasion which called forth this work. All we have to go on is the express statement of the author concerning his purpose in Luke 1.1—4 and his literary product as it now stands. It may be interesting to speculate concerning the hypothetical situation behind the author's writing and the possible purpose(s) which he has failed to express in his preface, but the student of Acts should be clear in his mind concerning the degree of uncertainty which is attached to such detective work. In its best form this type of investigation is interesting, stimulating, even profitable; at its worst it is not a complete waste of time, because it provides the scholar with a negative example of what to avoid in the way of critical methodology. In either case, it remains in the realm of critical speculation.

The malaise of contemporary Lucan research may be illustrated by reference to the recently-published *Festschrift* for Professor Paul Schubert of Yale University. *Studies in Luke-Acts*[119] is a collection of nineteen essays by European and American scholars. Three of these are translations of essays by German scholars which have appeared elsewhere: Vielhauer's essay on the "Paulinism" of Acts (33—50)[120], E. Schweizer's on the speeches in Acts (208—16)[121], and H. Conzelmann's on the Areopagus address (217—30)[122]. The other sixteen are original contributions concerned with general and specific issues of Lucan criticism and exegesis.

When the novice in critical research first turns to a book on New Testament introduction, he may receive the impression that there is general agreement among scholars on the basic issues of critical analysis. Even if a single author refers from time to time to those who differ with his conclusions, the impression often given is that his own point of view represents that of most reasonable-minded

[119] Ed. by L. E. Keck and J. L. Martyn (Nashville and New York, 1966).
[120] *Supra*, pp. 283—91.
[121] *Supra*, p. 230n.
[122] *Supra*, p. 213n.

critics and is identical with what is sometimes referred to as "the assured results of criticism". If the novice turns to a multi-authored volume like the Schubert *Festschrift*, which is truly representative of the variety of opinion among present-day critics, he may be in for a rude shock.

Let us suppose our novice turns to *Studies in Luke-Acts* in order to find out "the critical view" on the date of Acts. He is offered a variety of possibilities between the early 60s, "while Paul was still preaching in Rome" (E. R. Goodenough), and about A. D. 125 (John Knox). What is the author's purpose? According to Goodenough,

the author wrote Acts in the early sixties to assure Theophilus that, even though he might have heard disturbing rumors of Paul's teaching, Paul was actually a very great man who preached and lived for what he, like the author of the Letter to the Hebrews, considered the childish milk of the gospel . . . (58).

In the words of Ernst Haenchen: "By telling the history of apostolic times through many individual stories, the book primarily intends to edify the churches and thereby contribute its part in spreading the Word of God farther and farther, even to the ends of the earth" (278). Knox makes the novel suggestion that Acts was written as an apologia for orthodox Christianity against pre-Marcionite, or even Marcionite, Christians, probably in reaction to their schismatic use of Paul's letters (279—87).

What is the author's theological leitmotiv? According to Ulrich Wilckens, it is "that God's redemption is realized historically: that the histories of Jesus and of the church are in fact phenomena in world history" (71). Paul Minear refers to "the rich pluralism of Lucan motifs" (115). According to Haenchen, Luke's main theme concerns "the triumphal procession of the Word of God from Jerusalem to Rome" (278). Ernst Käsemann describes the theology of Luke-Acts as "early Catholic" (288—97), while Goodenough thinks the author deliberately rejected those features of early Christianity implied by the designation "early Catholic" (52—54). Van Unnik and Wilckens express generally favorable opinions concerning the value of Luke's theology, while Vielhauer, Käsemann, and Conzelmann clearly disapprove of what they understand to be the Lucan point of view.

Concerning the speeches in Acts, Eduard Schweizer is impressed with their uniformity, not only in outline "but also in a considerable number of details" (214); this leads him to support the view of Dibelius that they are, for the most part, the author's compositions.

By way of contrast, C. F. D. Moule's study of the Christology of Acts (especially of the speeches) leads him to the conclusion that "the Christology of Acts is not uniform, whatever may be said to the contrary" (181). He argues that

> it is flying in the teeth of the evidence to claim that Luke has uniformly imposed this mentality of his; on the contrary, the number of seemingly undesigned coincidences and subtle nuances that have emerged suggest strongly that Luke either dramatized, thoughtfully and with considerable versatility, in an attempt to impersonate various outlooks, or else used sources. If he did this, he no doubt adapted and arranged them with a free hand, but nevertheless retained their essential character (182).

Haenchen and Conzelmann defend their usual views of the historical value of Acts, while Nils A. Dahl (139–58), Moule (159 –85), and J. A. Fitzmyer (233–57), from their varied perspectives, give reasons for a more positive evaluation of Luke as a historian. Even concerning the textual criticism of Acts there seems to be no general agreement among scholars, as A. F. J. Klijn points out in his essay on the subject (103–110)[123].

Thus it seems clear that our novice, approaching a volume of essays like those contained in *Studies in Luke-Acts* in order to discover the results of contemporary New Testament criticism, would likely be confused. He would undoubtedly be impressed by at least one thing: there is no general agreement among scholars on even the most basic issues of Lucan research. It would be sad if this were to cause him to give up his study in despair. But if his initial encounter with critical research were to turn him to the pages of Luke-Acts, to compel him to study the basic document for himself and to test all the theories of the critics by his own first-hand evaluation of the data, he would have learned a great deal. And he would then be on the road to becoming an independently-minded New Testament critic himself.

---

[123] Klijn concludes his essay with the discouraging observation that "there has never been so little agreement about the nature of the original text as at the moment" (108).

Chapter XI

EPILOGUE

To spell out the conclusions reached in our study of the history of the criticism of the Book of Acts would demand much more space than that allotted to the present study, and it would necessitate the repetition of much of what has gone before. My own judgment on many matters has been indicated already in the above survey of the past century and a half of criticism. Where no judgment has been passed, an attempt has been made to summarize the important features of the problem and the alternate solutions in a manner which will allow the reader to draw his own conclusions. Here I offer only a few general impressions.

(1) F. W. Farrar has written: "The history of exegesis is, in a great measure, a history of errors."[1] Although he may have intended this to apply primarily to the history of biblical exegesis prior to the dawn of modern criticism, an investigation of the course of criticism since 1800 has not necessitated a drastic revision of Farrer's pessimistic statement. Harnack confessed as much when he commented, "Alle Fehler, die in der neutestamentlichen Kritik gemacht worden sind, haben sich in der Kritik der Apostelgeschichte wie in einem Brennpunkt gesammelt"[2]. Even allowing for a measure of exaggeration in this *obiter dictum,* one cannot easily deny that the study of the Bible from the point of view of modern criticism has not always led to a clearer or more historical understanding of the biblical writings. An inadequate critical methodology and/or theological or philosophical bias has vitiated the conclusions of modern biblical critics nearly as often as those of pre-critical exegetes. As a substitute for the older dogmatic approach to the problems of criticism and exegesis, the student of the New Testament has often been offered another "key" to guide him in his criticism; in many cases the point of reference has had little foundation in strictly historical study and exegesis, but rather has been based upon philosophical and theological prior judgments. To mention only one ex-

[170]

---

[1] *The Bible: Its Meaning and Supremacy* (London, 1901), p. 145.
[2] *Lukas der Arzt,* p. 87.

ample, the Tübingen conception of the nature of early Christianity and the Book of Acts was no great improvement over the older criticism which tended to maintain certain views simply because they were traditional ones; it meant only the acceptance of a new authority in the place of an older one, thought the new authority had an advantage over the older one in its claim to be "scientific". No one today would argue (I hope) that the contemporary biblical scholar should return to a pre-critical approach to exegesis; nevertheless, the modern-day exegete does well to remind himself that the mere profession of allegiance to the historical-critical method does not guarantee either objectivity or historical understanding.

(2) Our study of the history of the criticism of the Book of Acts has underlined the contribution which "secular" historical research has made to New Testament criticism. The danger of divorcing the New Testament writings from their broader historical setting, the history and literature of the Graeco-Roman world, should be evident to all. There appears to be no good reason why the discipline of New Testament criticism should be separated from the study of ancient history and literature in general, nor is there a unique critical method which belongs to the student of the New Testament alone. Indeed, it has been those theologians who have refused to learn from their fellow scholars who are experts in the history, literature, and archaeology of the ancient world who have gone farthest astray in their conclusions. By contrast, it has been, in general, those who have worked from a broader perspective of historical research who have made the positive and lasting contributions to an exact understanding of the Book of Acts. It is precisely this factor which is lacking in some of the contemporary studies of Luke-Acts, and it is in this area that we may expect some of the most important contributions of the future to lie.

(3) Another impression concerns the importance of exegesis, rather than speculation, as the means of solving critical problems. Speculation no doubt has some value, but only when it is recognized for what it is, *viz.* an attempt to theorize on the basis of conjecture when the evidence is insufficient to allow one to speak in terms of actualities. Yet how easily critics jump from the theoretical to the actual, from "it is possible that..." to "it is..."! All too often scholars have chanced upon a brilliant idea which has seemed to them to provide the key to a proper understanding of the Book of Acts and then have attempted to force all of the evidence into this mold of their own making; this attempt to substantiate a strictly speculative thesis has led to some very bizarre exegesis. Rather than trying to suggest new critical hypotheses which solve *all* of the prob-

lems, the student of Acts would be better advised to apply himself to careful exegesis in the endeavour to understand *some* of the problems. The need of the hour seems to be a careful and humble listening to the author of Luke-Acts, rather than the formulation of more (interesting, but wholly theoretical) hypotheses concerning historical situations of which we have no definite knowledge. The real test of all critical hypotheses is whether they can be sustained by careful exegesis, or better, whether they *are the result of* careful exegesis. The impression gained by my study has been that some of the most influential theories in the history of criticism have been due to the exercise of critical imagination as much as exegesis. Imagination has its proper place in critical study, but it is no substitute for facts.

(4) The number of New Testament scholars who are aware of the complexity of the problems which face them in their study appears to be few indeed. In spite of the fact that the modern critic is separated by language, culture, geography, and nearly two thousand years of time, from the historical background and thought of the New Testament writers, he often gives the impression that he thinks it is a very simple matter to step back over the years to a detailed and accurate understanding of not only what the author explicitly says, but also of the unspecified situation lying behind the author's writing which causes him to say what he says the way he says it. A knowledge of the history of criticism, if not of the principles of criticism, should tell him that it is difficult enough to understand the explicit statements of an ancient writer, much less to read his mind. Wikenhauser manifests true wisdom when he observes that a study [171] of the history of *Actaforschung* "hat nicht nur historischen Wert, sondern kann auch zeigen, dass es nicht so einfach ist, den Leitgedanken der Apg mit Sicherheit nachzuweisen"[3]. In spite of this, scores of critics have claimed moral certainty for their mutually exclusive conceptions of the purpose, occasion, or theological leitmotif of Luke-Acts. It should be self-evident that all simplistic approaches to the Lucan writings are erroneous. If anything has been learned from our study, it is that it is impossible to isolate one exclusive purpose or theological idea which is the key to the interpretation of the Third Gospel and Acts[4]. All books have a number of purposes, and few if any writings can be understood in terms of one basic concept; Acts is no exception. Even the question of his-

---

[3] *Die Apostelgeschichte und ihr Geschichtswert*, p. 8.

[4] Cf. "The large number of well-grounded proposals concerning the purpose of the book make it questionable whether an unequivocal answer to this question is possible..." (Kümmel, *Introduction to the New Testament*, p. 115).

toricity has no simple solution, although it would seem that there is no reason to doubt the essential reliability of the narrative of Acts.

(5) The primary gain of the recent criticism of Luke-Acts has been the recognition that the Gospel according to Luke and the Book of Acts are really two volumes of one work which must be considered together. Questions concerning purpose, theology, speeches, and historical value cannot be answered apart from a study of both volumes of Luke's two-volumed work. It is also to the credit of recent criticism that it has recognized that the author, whatever else he may be, is a theologian, even though no generally accepted understanding of the details of his theology has yet been reached. It seems likely that the debate which is taking place in the world of New Testament scholarship at the present day will continue to be centered around the idea of "Luke the theologian"; but it is doubtful whether an adequate understanding of the Lucan writings will be attained unless the author is also recognized as the historian he aspired to be[5].

---

[5] See I. H. Marshall, *Luke: Historian and Theologian.*

INDEX OF AUTHORS
(Italics indicates a major bibliographical entry.)

INDEX OF REFERENCES TO HOLY SCRIPTURE
AND TO OTHER ANCIENT WRITINGS

Old Testament

New Testament

Other Ancient Writings

TRANSLATION OF LATIN, FRENCH & GERMAN QUOTATIONS

1 Mention is made only incidentally of the others; and when Luke deals with Paul, he proceeds to speak about him alone. Concerning the other apostles' deeds, scarcely a report has come down to us.

2 It is not credible that he wrote at a later date; otherwise he would have carried his story further, at least mentioning the outcome of Paul's first imprisonment, concerning which his readers must have been curious.

3 (1) To record in a trustworthy manner the first outpouring of the Holy Spirit and with it the first miracles, which attested the truth of the Christian religion. It was absolutely essential that this account be trustworthy, because Christ had promised the Holy Spirit so often to his disciples. And if a pagan were to give credence to the Gospel, he must first raise this question: how is it that the Gospel first came to be confessed and believed in Jerusalem?

(2) To give the sort of information which would demonstrate the right of Gentiles to be admitted to the church of Christ, a right which was disputed especially by the Jews at the time Luke wrote. It was for this very reason that Paul, whose companion Luke cared to be, sat imprisoned in Rome: because he was accused by the Jews of receiving pagans into the church.

4 It called itself *tous kēpha*, because Peter had the primacy among the Jewish apostles; *tous christou*, because it made direct connection with Christ the chief mark of genuine apostolic authority, and therefore would not recognize Paul as a true apostle of equal rank with the others, since he made his debut as an apostle later and in an entirely different manner from the others; it believed that it was necessary to consider him far inferior to the least of the other apostles.

5 The definite connection which the Clementine literature had with Ebionite doctrine, and the well-known enmity which this sect manifested toward Paul, cannot but lead one to suppose that the doctrine of the Clementine literature, particularly in its main features, came

into existence in opposition to the teaching which Paul had given concerning the relation of the Mosaic Law to Christianity.

6 Indeed, whatever one may think of the historical trustworthiness of the Acts of the Apostles, it is, in its fundamental idea and innermost character, the apologetic attempt of a Paulinist to initiate and bring about the drawing together and uniting of two opposing parties by making Paul appear as Petrine as possible and, correspondingly, Peter appear as Pauline as possible, by throwing a veil of reconciliation over the differences which, according to the incontrovertible evidence of Paul's declaration in Galatians, actually existed between the two apostles; and by helping the Gentile Christians to forget their hostility toward Judaism and the Jewish Christians, their hostility toward Gentiles, and to concentrate on their common enmity toward the unbelieving Jews, who had made Paul the constant object of their implacable hatred. Just as the specific historical and critical questions which concern Acts can be solved satisfactorily only when they are seen from the vantage point of an attempt to make the careers of the two apostles appear parallel, for the purpose already indicated, so also we gain a new insight into the history of ecclesiastical relations, and we see by a new example how much these relations motivated and preoccupied that age, and how easily the need for unifying writings, like the ones which have been mentioned, came about, a need which was felt by the consciences of both parties.

7 but rather a new, amplified edition of Luke 24:50-53.

8 an entirely new introduction to what follows, a new prologue to an entirely new work, as it were, connecting it with the concluding event of the Gospel and alluding to the main features of the contents of Acts, just as the prologue to the Gospel alludes to its contents.

9 If a Paulinist and companion of Paul has written this book, then the special thought of the author, his specific tendency in writing, will appear especially in those places where he is not tied to an already fixed tradition but gives information on the basis of his own experiences or direct inquiries, information which has as its subject the man he sought to honor by being his disciple. This appears not to have been properly recognized until now. The earlier attempts to identify the purpose of the book made use primarily of the richer and more colorful first part. They began with the Gospel and then turned to Acts and thought the Pauline history was simply the factual account of an eyewitness, without much to take exception to. But the embarrassment one faces in turning to the epistles of Paul suggests a different opinion. Actually, recent scholars, such as Baur and Schrader, have generally started first with the epistles of Paul and then turned to Acts, and have devoted greater critical attention to the second part.

*10*No degree of heightened miraculous activity by Peter is related without a corresponding analogy by Paul.

*11*The decree was a charter of liberty for the Gentile Christians against the demands of the Judaizers, not something placing a new burden on them; for certainly they would have complied with this practice, as a general rule, before now, more or less according to these four points, for the sake of the Jews; according to Pauline principles they were expected to defer to the consciences of the weak.

*12*that presentation has the greater claim to historical reality which demonstrates itself to be impartial, and never betrays the interest to subordinate its historical material to a particular subjective purpose.

not an objective, but rather a presentation which has been altered by a subjective interest

deep into the second century

13 upon closer investigation it demonstrates itself to be a "tendency" writing of so free composition and so little historical reliability that we must at first leave it completely to the side.

*14*to the unhistorical and arbitrary methodology of the author of Acts which does not shrink from inventing fiction.

*15*In Acts we have neither the historical Paul nor the historical primitive apostles — certainly not the historical Peter. . . . Acts is . . . in the form of a history; however, even though older sources and reports may lie behind at least the first part, and possibly also the second, when we allow for the improbable, the impossible, the demonstrably unhistorical or that which is dependent upon the unhistorical, particularly the freely composed speeches and the numerous repetitions, there is really little left which is historically valid. The numerous tendentious omissions and silences speak against the thorough historical reliability of Acts. A writer who is intentionally silent concerning important occurrences and facts in order to put the subject matter of his description in a different light, and who deliberately omits characteristic features from the image which he presents in order to give it a different appearance, cannot be considered to be too upright and conscientious to allow positive distortions and unhistorical inventions as long as it is in his interest to do so. In assessment, we can say this much with certainty concerning our author: in using and arranging and transforming the materials given him by the tradition, he has gone about his work in a highly arbitrary and radical manner.

*16*The official mission of Paul on behalf of the church at Antioch, the position he assumes in Acts regarding the original apostles, the discussion of his affairs in a formal assembly of the church, the speeches which are put into the mouths of Peter and James, Paul and Barnabas, the resolutions of the assembly and their proclamation by an apostolic letter, the action which Paul is said to have undertaken on behalf of Timothy — all these features can only be explained as unhistorical.

17 a chain of improbabilities

18 as it actually was

19 In order to carry this out, he is willing to make all those concessions to Judaism with which we are already familiar: he sets aside the main features of Paul's doctrine, allows the Jewish Christians the practice of the Law and circumcision, makes Paul into a zealot for the Law, causes him to enter into his special ministry to the Gentiles only by compulsion, under the protection of Peter and with the permission of Jerusalem. Thus it is the author's chief aim to convince his readers concerning the validity of Gentile Christianity (to recognize this is to assume that these readers disputed its validity, i.e. that they gave allegiance to Judaistic particularism). From this point of view, our book appears to be an attempt to obtain the recognition of the independence of Gentile Christianity and its freedom from the Law, by means of concessions to the Judaistic party.

20 Our writing is the proposal of peace by a Paulinist who desires to purchase the recognition of Gentile Christianity on the part of Jewish Christians by concessions to Judaism and in this way to influence both parties.

21 not entering the scene before chapter 16, undertook to write his history only sometime after the death of the apostle, and who, when his personal knowledge was lacking, was dependent on oral and written tradition which had become partly legendary, because he had not *from the first* had the aim of writing a history and, therefore, had to content himself, for the most part, with the matter and form given to him by the tradition, in the atmosphere of which he himself lived.

22 But we have to take our view of what the *glōssais lalein* really was from the chief passage which speaks of the experience, 1 Cor. 12:14, according to which it . . . was an oral prayer, taking place in a state of extreme ecstasy and requiring an interpretation for understanding, and not simply speaking in a foreign language.

23 to confirm to Theophilus, by means of history, the Christian instruction he had received.

24 With this in mind he wrote this history; and the selection and limitation of its contents were determined partly by the need of Theophilus and partly by his own Pauline point of view, so that, following the pre-Pauline history in which *Peter* is the chief character, *Paul* and his work occupy the foreground almost exclusively right up to the end of the book, so that the history becomes and remains biographical. . . .

25 not *made up,* but rather historically *given.*

26 Failure to mention the event serves not as a proof that it had not yet taken place, but rather leads to the conclusion that it already belongs to the distant past.

27 absolute incompatibility of Judaism and Christianity, of Law and Gospel, of circumcision and faith in Christ.

28 With this sort of zeal for liberty, liberty itself is transformed once again into slavery.

29 According to this decisive declaration, liberty consists in not permitting ourselves to be controlled and restricted by external things but rather in being guided simply by inner discernment. If, therefore, all things are allowable, then circumcision is no exception; for such an exception would itself be a restriction of the principle of liberty.

30 Just as today, if I wished to preach the gospel among the Jews and saw that they were weak, I would be willing to have myself circumcised and to eat and to abstain from eating according to their custom. For in whatever respect I did not adapt myself to them, I would shut the door in my face and in the face of my gospel.

31 an original work from one pen, generally independent of written sources

32 Acts is not a *Tendenzschrift* written with an apologetic or conciliatory aim — still less with a Judaistic aim — but rather a purely historical work, just as it claims to be and, according to the admission even of recent criticism, appears to be at first glance. In it is set forth the gradual development of the church from its beginning in Jerusalem to the moment the great apostle reaches Rome, the hub of the Gentile world, by a continuous narrative and from the Pauline, universalistic — in a word, Christian — point of view. Acts is not a "party" document. But if one wishes to find traces of an interest in a particular party, one can only find it represented by an apologetic-Pauline point of view. . . . As the Third Gospel was identified in ancient times as the specifically Pauline gospel . . . and also today, so Acts too bears a genuinely Pauline character; this is made most clear by the fact that it was rejected by the enemies of this apostle and excluded from use in church.

33 On the contrary, we allow criticism its full right to test the trustworthiness of each item contained in Acts, without prejudice, and to explain this or that, as the case may be, as unhistorical or mythical. But we cherish the firm conviction that all the exceptions which might rightly be taken to the contents of this work are by no means serious enough to disprove the author's claim to have been a companion of Paul.

34 Acts is really the work of a disciple and companion of Paul, as the author himself indicates by the eye-witness type of narrative which manifests itself in a large part of his history and through use of *hēmin* in the introduction to his complete work.

35 in the case of the great difference between the parallel pictures of Paul, historical reality can be found only on one side or the other.

36 Is it not possible that both pictures have sprung from the same ground of purposeful reflection, and can one not maintain that this is the reason for the difference, indeed, for the first time make the full force of the difference felt?

37 The original of the Peter and the Paul of Acts is the Jesus of the synoptic gospels. The author of Acts had them . . . before his eyes as he borrowed features for the construction of his image of the two apostles.

38 When Acts was written, the tension between the parties had waned, the opposition had been veiled, the difference obscured, the peace had already been accomplished; Acts is not a proposal of peace but rather the expression and seal of peace and toleration.

39 It helped to secure the chains which bound the church to the Jewish world, and the church held on to Acts and recognized it as the canonical expression of its own consciousness, because it wished to have this link with Judaism and this marriage with the past and with Heaven.

40 The Judaism of which we speak is rather a power which has asserted its authority up to the most recent time, though in changing forms. . . .

We call this conservative, conciliatory, counter-revolutionary spirit which also preserves the spirit of the revolution, Judaism, because it received its classical expression in the Old Testament (in its inability to discern historical differences) and in the Jewish transformation of the historical product of a later period into a divinely effected tradition — in short, in Jewish theism, which condemns the historical creator to impotence and delivers to Heaven the prerogative of revelation. And, indeed, through this original heritage of the Old Testament which the young church possessed, this Judaism maintained its influence in the church and won for itself an even greater place.

41 On the one hand, the disproportion of the work, which devotes more than three-fifths of its space to Paul; on the other hand, the disproportion which may be observed even in the biography of Paul, whose first mission is narrated with great brevity, while certain parts of the second and third missions, and especially his last journey, are described in minute details. A man altogether a stranger to apostolic times would not have exhibited these inequalities. His work would have been better planned as a whole.

42 To write a celebrated name at the top of a document, as in the case of the second epistle of Peter and, in all probability, Paul's epistles to Timothy and Titus, was in no way contrary to the customs of the time.

43 sanctimoniously satisfied, determined to believe that everything goes on in the church in an evangelic fashion.

44 Too loyal to condemn his master Paul, too orthodox not to share the official opinion which prevailed, he smoothed over the differences of doctrine so that only the common end could be seen, an end which all these great founders pursued by paths so opposed and through rivalries so energetic.

45 Towards the end, in particular, the narrative assumes an astonishingly precise character. The last pages of Acts are the only completely historical pages which we possess concerning the origins of Christianity. The first, on the contrary, are those most open to criticism of the entire New Testament.

46 Acts is, in a word, a dogmatic history, arranged to support the orthodox doctrine of the time or to inculcate the ideas which seemed most agreeable to the piety of the author. Let us add that it could not be otherwise. The origin of every religion is known only by the accounts of the faithful. It is only skepticism which writes history *ad narrandum*.

47 The first twelve chapters of Acts are a tissue of miracles. Now it is an absolute rule of criticism to give no place in historical documents to miraculous events.

48 put forward as the draft of a proposal of peace with the Judaists from the Pauline side . . . [which] desires to purchase the recognition of Gentile Christianity by the Jewish Christians through concessions to Judaism and in this sense to influence both parties.

49 Nothing could be clearer than that Acts has abandoned Jewish Christianity as such and is written from the point of view which recognizes Gentile Christianity as the absolutely dominant element in the church.

50 Rather, the Judaistic element in Acts is already a component part of Gentile Christianity, which the book itself represents. . . .

51 a proposal of peace between those early Christian parties, but rather the attempt on the part of Gentile Christianity, which was itself already strongly influenced by the Judaism of early Christianity, to get in touch with its past, in particular its own origins and its founder, Paul.

52 In this presentation, one cannot . . . fail to recognize the aim of avert-

ing political suspicions from Christianity; and, in the form in which this is presented in Acts, it cannot have been intended for anyone other than Gentiles outside of the church.

53 A book which, like this one (especially in the first part), has been so strongly affected by the influences of legend, and in which the details of the events reported appear to be so contrary to the facts (especially in the second part), either must be an example of a completely meaningless fabrication, or presuppose a length of time between its date and the events it narrates sufficient to allow for the development, on the one hand, of purposeless legend, and on the other hand, of circumstances under which the past was reflected upon in a manner which led to its modification. In particular, the fact that Paul is the hero of Acts and that his image is so strongly distorted presupposes a history transcending the bounds of the apostolic age, for such results would be impossible otherwise.

54 a work of poetry and reflection, . . . free creation of the author.

55 Where he (sc. the author of Acts), according to the Tübingen criticism, would not see, according to recent interpretation he, for the most part, could not see.

56 an apology on behalf of the Christian religion for Gentiles in answer to the accusations of the Jews, showing how it happened that Christianity came to supersede Judaism in its mission to the world.

57 Where he (sc. the author of Acts) according to the Tübingen criticism would not see, according to recent interpretations he, for the most part, could not see.

58 lack of knowledge . . . the fragmentary character of the sources, and the inability of the author to think back to a former time.

59 Paul was not Judaized; nor Peter, Paulinized; but rather Peter and Paul were Lucanized, i.e. Catholicized.

60 One does Acts an injustice when, instead of recognizing the author's simple pleasure in telling a story, he continually seeks some hidden motive — not only where he adds freely to the tradition but also where he merely reproduces the tradition or where he omits certain events which we know from other sources.

61 the history (story) of God's power in the apostles.

62 its best knowledge of the first period of its history.

63 One cannot make a general judgment concerning the trustworthiness or untrustworthiness of Acts as a whole or even its major parts, for instance, the sections dealing with the primitive church or with Paul or the speakers of Acts.

64 exact intimacy with the works of Josephus and in the careful exploitation of his material, but rather in superficial remembrances of an earlier reading.

65 It is not conceivable that one who could write the stylistically polished sentences of Luke 1:1-4 should have made the mistake of writing *ton men prōton* in place of the more correct *ton men proteron logon* — in a passage where he is not following an older, hebraistic, or stylistically inferior source but is freely expressing his own thoughts at the beginning of a book — if he intended to say that the Gospel was the first of two books only rather than of a larger number of books.

66 A more awkward conclusion to the work than this would be difficult to imagine.

67 While the theologians have persistently charged Luke with ignorance of the historical conditions and personages with which he deals, first-rate historians and scholars who concern themselves with the study of ancient times, who have gone into the matter with great care, have judged Acts to be an important and predominantly trustworthy historical document throughout.

68 When reading the first part of Acts the careful historian breathes freely and feels firm ground under his feet in some passages. *Every time this happens* (ch. 12 excepted) *he finds himself in Antioch or concerned with a narrative which directs his attention to this city.*

69 This becomes still clearer from a consideration of the great discourses scattered throughout Acts.

70 All of this surely permits one to conclude that the evidence of Acts not only is not opposed to the tradition that its author was a native of Antioch but appropriately complies with it. The book does not suggest that its author was a member of the church of Antioch (but this is not asserted by the tradition) but rather that he took a special interest in and had special knowledge of this church.

71 how the facts related in the "we"-sections and the interests of their author relate to those of the author of the whole work.

72 wherever comparison is possible, there we find complete agreement.

73 The "we"-sections and Acts have one and the same author.

74 He individualizes the Christians in Tyre, Ptolemais, Caesarea, Jerusalem, Sidon, and Puteoli and calls them "the disciples", "the brethren", "the friends". . . . In the Third Gospel, as is well known, the word *ekklēsia* never occurs; on the other hand, it occurs 23 times in Acts. However, (1) Acts uses the word both for Jewish and pagan assemblies (7:38; 19:32, 39, 41) and by this shows that the word had not yet gained for its author a sacred significance; (2) of the other 19 instances, 15 refer to the church in general and to the churches of

Jerusalem and Antioch. Of the remaining four occurrences, the word is used 3 times in the plural for the churches of Asia and Europe (14:23; 15:41; 16:5) and once for the church at Ephesus.

75 There is much to be said for the view that in the first half of Acts Luke made use of and translated an Aramaic source, but it is impossible to disprove the hypothesis that he had access only to oral information.

76 an error is also possible in the case of Josephus.

77 in so far as we can speak of such a thing when only one authority exists.

78 as a Gentile by birth, be unable to understand or reproduce the fine line which Paul walked as a Jew and a Christian and thus represent him in one place more Jewish and in another place more free in his behavior than he actually was?

79 Moreover, we do not know whether Luke was a disciple of Paul in the strict sense of the word.

80 how is it then that the Gentile churches in Asia, Greece, and Rome became so entirely unpauline?

81 We must determine not only to think of Paulinism in more flexible terms but above all to form a different image of what Paul tolerated among his closest disciples. He who confessed Christ as the *Kyrios*, who forsook the riches and the vices of the world, who saw the revelation of God in the Old Testament, who expected the resurrection of the dead and preached this to the Greeks, without imposing on them the rite of circumcision and the ceremonial law — this man was a Paulinist.

82 inaccuracies and discrepancies.

83 but is trustworthy also in the majority of the details it contains.

84 From almost every possible angle of historical criticism it is a solid, respectable, and, in many respects, an extraordinary work.

85 That these writings were creations of the moment, the offspring of a man of the most definite subjectivity, further increases the stringency of the test. And yet it is only the superscrupulous and dividers of hairs who are unable to recognize that in dozens of important and insignificant passages Acts has passed the test imposed upon it by the letters of Paul. With the exception of a few minor details, only the account of the Jerusalem Council and Paul's defense in the last speeches and, in general, his attitude toward the Jews during his last visit to Jerusalem remain questionable.

86 if only one does not confine oneself narrowly and rigidly to the Epistle to the Galatians, which, of course, everyone still does.

87 whether . . . such serious errors occur as to render Lucan authorship impossible.

88 According to my understanding of Paul's position in regard to his people and the Law — as I derive it from his letters — he, born a Jew, would not only be capable of performing Jewish rituals and other functions at any moment but, where Jewish opposition to the interests of his mission did not come into question, he would even undertake such activities of his own volition and from deeply felt piety. Paul did not merely "become" a Jew to the Jews, i.e. he did not simply accommodate himself to them in matters of religious observance, even where he had outgrown them — *but he was and also remained a Jew.* Nothing in his letters prevents us from supposing that on his visits to the Holy City he, like his Jewish Christian brethren in Jerusalem, participated in the worship in the Temple. Galatians and Romans could be interpreted so as to imply that this was no longer possible, but they do not need to be interpreted in this way.

89 to present historically the power of the Spirit of Jesus in the apostles.

90 before the persecution under Domitian, before the epistles of Paul had been widely circulated, before the name "Christian" had established itself in Christian phraseology . . . , before the canonizing of the idea *ekklēsia* . . . , before the use of the word *martys* in the special sense of "martyr", but sometime subsequent to the destruction of Jerusalem.

91 Thus, concerning the date, this judgement must suffice: Luke wrote during the time of Titus or in the earlier period of the reign of Domitian, but perhaps as early as the beginning of the sixties.

92 This arrangement of Peter and Paul . . . was certainly not created by Luke; history itself had created it.

93 It would be easier to believe that Calvin on his deathbed should have vowed a golden dress to the Mother of God than that Paul would have acted in this fashion.

94 (1) One may examine the circumstances in which the author lived, his standard of education, his direct or indirect connections with the events which make up the content of his work, and by means of this seek to reach a judgment concerning how far he was able and willing to give trustworthy reports (= internal criteria). (2) One may investigate other historical sources for the same events, insofar as these are available, and with their help test the individual statements of Acts point by point (= external criteria).

95 The Testing of the Historical Value of the Acts of the Apostles on the Basis of Internal Criteria.

96 a critical reworking of the tradition.

97 Primarily, Luke has worked at a much higher standard literarily in Acts than in the Gospel.

98 fitted together, connected and framed fragments of tradition as in a mosaic

99 These chapters are characterized by speeches and by scenes involving speeches: namely, the great speech to the crowd before the castle of Antonia, the scene of the controversy in the Sanhedrin, the verbal duel between Tertullus and Paul, and the speech before Agrippa, which is reported in great detail. All this suggests that here the writer has mastery over the tradition. This supposition is confirmed when we note that several of these speeches quite obviously exercise no influence upon the progress of the action but are solely of an epideictic character.

100 the author's stage-managing can make use of it to emphasize the conclusion.

101 In spite of the fact that the first person plural has been used once again, there is more literature than observation in the description of the shipwreck, with all its technical details.

102 that the whole book cannot be traced entirely to a few sources, nor can the author's own contribution be worked out evenly and according to a uniform principle in all parts of the work. The question as to what is tradition and what is the author's own composition has to be repeated with reference to each section, often indeed to the individual accounts.

103 If we consider how little the thoughts of these earliest Christians were set upon preserving the course of history, we shall not be surprised by the lack of a tradition.

104 her name is given, her character is described, the clothing she made for widows is mentioned as evidence of her virtue, and perhaps some reference to her appearance is implied by the express mention of the care of the corpse.

105 We are dealing with a "legend" which has a personal interest in Peter and Tabitha.

106 It is difficult to ascertain how much historical fact underlies each isolated specific case, nor is this subject to enter into the present investigation.

107 I have deliberately not considered whether all these stories are authentic or not; for, in classifying the stories according to the different types, namely "legend", "tale", or "anecdote", we are assessing only the story-teller's method of writing, not the authenticity of what he relates. This, at least, we may record as the outcome of this attempt at analysis, that in the Acts of the Apostles historical reliability varies in the different sections. It is to be judged differently where the author has used the itinerary from where he has merely linked different traditions by means of summary passages; differently when dealing with legends from when dealing with literary speeches; and differently again when dealing with individual legends in comparison with one another. *All these questions can be resolved only after the style-criticism has been carried out*; any premature solution of the problems will do more than endanger the integrity of the style-critical method; it will obscure our understanding of the stories themselves. Intrinsically these stories are far removed from the problems of historiography, and it is only when we begin to look away from the questions which have been raised in connection with them that we learn to listen to what the story-tellers have to say to us.

108 In the story itself, table-fellowship does not play an essential part at all. In the older tradition, Cornelius is a Gentile, but a devout and God-fearing one who is honored by God with a special message through an angel on account of his piety. The tradition speaks of him most sympathetically, and it is unlikely that it would have perceived any necessity for Peter to defend himself for having associated with him. The defense was added by someone who wished to give major significance to the story.

109 A speech which is so long, relatively speaking, cannot have had any place in a legend which was told among Christians concerning the conversion of a Centurion.

110 The form-critical method uses the form and style of the tradition in order to draw conclusions about it concerning its origins and the conditions out of which it arose, and *in this way seeks to make observations which are universally valid in order to establish less subjective and continually verifiable criteria concerning the historicity of the tradition.*

111 Here Luke is acting as a literary historian; not as a historian in our sense of the word, one who wants to show what really happened, but rather as an ancient writer, who singles out what is significant and possibly gives it emphasis by means of speeches.

112 We shall never be able to discover for certain whether Luke knew either that a speech had been made on this occasion or what had been said. It is really unimportant to go into such questions, for, in any case, Luke would not have been bound by such knowledge. Indeed, we have already established . . . that he has, himself, given information concerning a longer speech.

113 a literary-theological, not a historical task.

114 a straightforward legend of a conversion, comparable in beauty with that of the Ethiopian eunuch.

115 Luke . . . wishes to abandon the exact reproduction of the tradition for the sake of a higher historical truth.

116 From the standpoint of the history of traditions, they could hardly have been handed down, and, from a literary point of view, they have their parallels in the historians and often express a later position theologically in their content.

117 shows and is intended to show a high point of the book.

118 a Hellenistic speech concerning the true knowledge of God

119 the synthesis of rational Hellenism and Christian missionary preaching

120 The possibility cannot, of course, be denied that records of actual speeches may have come down to Luke. There is evidence, however, in the speeches of Acts of an attempt to typify, give examples and models of Christian sermons, rather than to recall specific personalities and what was said by them on specific occasions.

121 The contradiction between Romans and the Areopagus speech is clear. Admittedly, both mention the knowledge of God on the ground of creation or the ordering of the world; but according to the Areopagus address this knowledge leads to an anticipatory "feeling after" and honoring God, whereas according to Romans it indeed leads to the knowledge of God, but at the same time to a misunderstanding of his power, to a refusal of the true worship of God, and to entanglement in the false worship of idols. Whereas Rom. 1:23, 25 speaks of the error of idolatry in an indignant voice, Acts 17:29 corrects idolatry in an admonishing and chiding tone.

122 Paul could never have written this way. He is too deeply influenced by the conviction that man is estranged from God (Rom. 1-3), and, indeed, really estranged, not merely in that every individual has once contravened God's claim.

123 The description of Athens and the Athenians was obviously composed with a view to the speech.

124 Perhaps also the mention of the Areopagite in the itinerary had a special effect on the author of Acts. Perhaps it led him to set the scene of the speech on Mars Hill, thus giving a classical pulpit to the classic Gentile sermon.

125 the one who speaks on Mars Hill is the forerunner of the Apologetes. . . .

126 The historian in antiquity did not feel under any obligation to reproduce only, or even preferably, the text of a speech which was actually given.

127 Perhaps he did not know whether a speech had been made on the occasion; sometimes he did know this, but he did not know the text of it — perhaps he could not have known it if, for example, the speech had been given to a limited audience in an enemy camp. Even if the exact words were known, the historian did not incorporate the text into his work.

128 What the ancient author sees as the most important obligation is not what seems most important to us — viz. the establishment of the actual words of the speech which was given — but rather the introduction of speeches in a meaningful way into the structure of his complete work. Even if he can remember, discover, or read somewhere the exact wording of a speech which was given, the author will not feel obliged to make use of it. He will use it, at most, in the composition of the large or small construction of·the speech which he introduces into his narrative. This construction will, however, either enliven the narrative as a whole (or when direct discourse replaces a prosaic report) or it will serve as an artistic device for the author's special purpose.

129 The author, by no means, wishes to be impartial — indeed, he wishes to make converts for his cause; it will be seen that this is essentially different from the approach of historical writing in antiquity. Luke narrates; but while he does this, he also preaches.

130 From this, one recognizes that this text was "free" for a long time, i.e. it was not subjected to the control which is exercised on a book when it is used for any length of time in public worship, in which case, though minor variations may arise, the occurrence of more serious alterations of the text is prevented.

131 It is in accordance with the best tradition of Greek historical writing, as established by Thucydides, that Luke lets the apostle make, in this famous place, a speech which is most closely connected with the ideas of Greek philosophy and only very slightly with the theology of Paul.

Athens, which is not actually significant in the history of Paul's mission, is chosen by Luke as the setting for a speech in which the Christian apostle makes use of Greek ideas because it is the center of Hellenistic piety and the chief city of Greek wisdom.

132 their heroes with their encomia

133 All questions as to whether Paul actually gave such a speech, and whether he gave it in Athens, must be avoided if one is to understand Luke. His concern is not to describe an event which one time happened in history, and which had no special success; rather, he is concerned to give a typical picture, which is in a higher sense historical and perhaps more real in his own day than in the time of the Apostle.

134 In the company of the elders of the church at Ephesus, this ever recurring apology would have seemed strange — if all this was really aimed only at that circle of hearers.

135 to allow the apostle the opportunity of testifying before this forum to his departure from orthodox Judaism.

136 We have seen that, at four important turning points in the events described by him, Luke adds speeches to his narrative to illuminate the significance of the occasion, viz. on the occasion of the first and fundamentally important conversion of a Gentile, on the occasion of the apostle's penetration into the heart of Greek spiritual life, on the occasion of his departure from the mission field, and on the occasion of his dispute with those Jews who were most closely concerned with the temple. We notice repeatedly that the speeches are not really related to the historical occasion but transcend it. We wonder why the successes of Paul and Barnabas are not mentioned in the apostolic council, why Paul says so little that is Christian in Athens, why he defends himself before the elders of Ephesus (with whom he was on intimate terms), and why, before the Jews in Jerusalem, he makes no mention at all of the real point at issue with which the conflict began. All this explains itself if we ignore completely the question of historicity and see here the author's hand fashioning the material. By employing much that is his own individual style, though still actually complying with the great tradition established by Thucydides, the author wishes to use these speeches to give greater significance to the moment and to reveal the forces active behind the events.

137 Regularly an introduction showing the specific situation is followed by the kerygma of Jesus' life, passion and resurrection (2:22-24; 3:13-15; 5:30, 31; 10:36-42; 13:23-25), usually with emphasis on the fact that the disciples were witnesses (2:32; 3:15; 5:32; 10:39, 41; 13:31); to this is added evidence from the scriptures (2:25-31; 3:22-26; 10:43; 13:32-37) and an exhortation to repentance (2:38f; 3:17-20; 5:31; 10:42f; 13:38-41).

138 I should like to say, "if we deny the historicity of these speeches", but we cannot go so far. Luke may have known of individual occasions when Paul spoke there. He may also have had information about the xumpasa gnōmē of the speaker or of the speech in individual instances; he may even have been an eye-witness, but we cannot say where or when this was the case. Nor are we able in this case to attribute the speeches to the itinerary, which was undoubtedly used in Acts 13-21; for if this source recorded any speeches that had been made, then they would have been found in the itinerary more often. The selecting of the occasion and the elaboration of the speech is in each case the work of the author.

139 antique expressions in the kerygma. . . . But the question can only be raised, insofar as I can see, not answered.

140 It opens that part of Acts (6-12) which describes the crossing of the gospel to the Gentile world. It shows how far removed spiritually the speaker is from Judaism, but it does so by the use of means which have been borrowed from Judaism. That too is typical of the controversy between Christianity and Judaism which is introduced by the speech.

141 As in the case of the missionary speeches, so here also one does not wish to exclude the possibility of dependence on an older text, at least for the part which consists of the recital of facts, for this would best explain its impartial tone. The polemical passages would have to be ascribed to Luke, who would, of course, have re-worked the whole.

142 They help to make the estrangement of Christianity from Judaism intelligible (Stephen) and defend the validity of the Gentile mission (Paul's speech before the Jewish people); they show how God himself brought about the conversion of the Gentiles (Cornelius) and how the Christian sermon takes up ideas from the spiritual and intellectual heritage of the Greeks (the Areopagus address); and they indicate both the past and future fortunes of the church (Miletus).

143 This is introduced simply because the author is a man of culture, for only a ·familiarity with such expressions can explain the use of this saying here, where it is not really appropriate. . . . A voice from heaven does not speak in proverbs, and, if it speaks in Aramaic, it is certainly not proper for it to speak Greek proverbs. The proverb does not exist in a Semitic form. Nor does it occur in the other accounts of the same voice from heaven in 9:4 and 22:7. It must therefore have been added by the author in keeping with the style of what is the most literary of the three accounts of the conversion. It is intended to show that Paul is among those who have struggled against God in vain; it is also intended to provide the educated reader with the pleasure found in this sort of literary embellishment.

144 that they do not agree with the narrative part of the text in all parts, but rather add to it, occasionally correcting it.

145 that prophecies of future afflictions had already been given with regard to Paul . . . that he had been three years in Ephesus and had there earned his bread by the labor of his hands — none of which had been mentioned previously.

146 enhancing the significance of the moment by the insertion of a speech.

147 He writes a history which he believes has happened according to God's will.

148 He desired . . . not only to illuminate the situation but also the way of God; he did not wish to testify concerning the capabilities of either the speaker or the author, but rather concerning the gospel.

149 not a historian but rather a preacher.

150 Admittedly, we have seen that speeches consisting of only a few sentences are not without analogy among the historians of antiquity. But even the longer speeches of Acts are still much shorter than their secular counterparts, for they lack at least two elements characteristic of the speeches of the historian: the deliberate element (the debating for and against) and the epideictic element (the rhetorical elaboration of ideas with which the author is concerned).

151 The apostolic speeches in Acts are clearly intended to be summaries of these theological concepts of the author. They are not to be regarded as witnesses to early or still less the earliest primitive Christian theology, but rather of Lucan theology toward the end of the first century.

152 We ascribe this title [*sc.* "historian"] to him only because he did more than compile traditions. He attempted in his own way to unite in a meaningful, continuous narrative both the traditions of the church and what he himself had discerned. Secondly, he attempted to make the meaning of the events clear.

153 where Luke wishes to work as a historian and where we admire his accomplishment on entirely unbroken ground

154 but . . . to present and to illuminate the typical

155 And thus it is possible for him to discharge his other obligation, viz. that of being a preacher, through the literary techniques of the historian.

156 recognition that Acts must be considered much more a work of composition than has hitherto been the case.

157 as even as conservative a scholar as Bauernfeind

158 elements of tradition . . . prove to be products of the Lucan literary composition.

159 abbreviating, supplementing, and modifying . . . part of a greater unity

160 (1) One does not, therefore, make demands of Acts which are greater than the circumstances of its origin will allow it to fulfill. One no longer seeks to find in it a documentary report or self-portrait of the apostolic age; instead, one discovers in it the image which a later Christian epoch construed concerning its own past. Acts does not reproduce Paul's teaching concerning the world and salvation; it is a new model from an age in which things have changed. . . . (2) With this is connected a second point: this new model of Christian teaching from the postapostolic age also found acceptance into the Canon, in spite of the fact that it differs greatly from the theology of Paul. The result of this for us is the following: the idea of the New Testament Canon is not to exclude Christendom from the task of coming to its own understanding of the Christian message in a later day; rather, it accepts this task. This is true for the age in which Acts was written just as much as for the age of the Reformation and for our present age.

161 Perhaps one can express this difference most clearly by means of a short formula: For Paul, the history of salvation is concealed in history (and also only recognizable to faith: *theologia crucis*); for Luke, the history of salvation is already visible in history.

162 a companion of Paul

163 The picture of Paul in Acts, as also the general picture it gives concerning missionary beginnings, shows that here we have no fellow-worker of Paul telling his story, but rather someone of a later generation, at a time when the true perspective is no longer possible, trying to give an account of things in his own way. Occasionally some have praised Luke because they have supposed that he has presented a very faithful picture of the primitive theology of early Christian times. But it is his own simple theology, which he shared in common with his church, which he everywhere assumes and which should be understood as lying behind the sermons, prayers, liturgical expressions, and occasional remarks in Acts.

164 The real Paul, admittedly, did on one occasion claim to possess the "signs of an apostle" . . . these wonders were so little out of the ordinary that his opponents simply denied his ability to perform miracles.

165 However, the real Paul, as he himself admits, was anything but a master of the improvised speech. In dictating his letters, he has found words which have echoed through the centuries; but as a speaker he was feeble and made no impression (2 Cor. 10:10). When Luke paints such a different portrait of him, it is not the result of an illuminating remembrance but rather of the presumption, so tempting to a later generation, that Paul the great missionary must have been also the great orator.

166 His basic design was, it seems to us, the desire to suggest to his readers a connection between his work and the Greek Bible, which was for them the sacred text *par excellence*.

167 It is not impossible in this case that the author *ad Theophilum* had performed this function at certain periods. One could even suggest that he did so during the final period of Paul's life and kept the journal after the death of the apostle, or when he separated from him.

168 Luke places himself in the situation in which the church finds itself because of the absence of the parousia and the rise of an inner-worldly history. He tries to overcome these by writing a history.

169 In the case of these redactional connections, one is not allowed to ask after sources for particular items of information; still less are historicizing reflections concerning the trustworthiness of the form of Luke's work appropriate. Luke has stylized throughout, not on the basis of actual information but rather on the basis of theological reflection.

170 All the mistakes which have been made by New Testament criticism have converged in Acts as in a focal point.

171 has not only historical value but also can show that it is not so simple to demonstrate with certainty the leading ideas of Acts.